Advance Praise for
Behind Closed Doors

"Ken Khachigian has written the most lucid, most important work about the postwar period. For an inside look at how ugly politics can be—and how noble—you cannot miss this book. I still love Ken after fifty years and you will, too, when you read this jewel of a memoir."
— **Ben Stein,** economist, law professor, multi-Emmy
award–winning actor, speech writer for presidents
Nixon and Ford, novelist, and screenwriter

"This is essential reading for anyone wanting to know how Ronald Reagan shaped his crusading message of economic growth through tax cuts and limited government. Khachigian's is a fascinating account by one who takes you into the rooms where the decisions were made."
— **Larry Kudlow,** host of Fox Business Network's *Kudlow*
and former director of the National Economic Council

"To understand Nixon and Reagan, the two crucial presidents and coalition builders of the last third of the twentieth century, the insights of Ken Khachigian, the confidant who advised them both, seem indispensable."
— **Pat Buchanan,** White House aide to presidents Nixon
and Reagan

"Ken Khachigian is a great conservative and patriot, and his book will give you the inside view of a presidency that will go down in history as one of greatness and strength."
— **Ed Rollins,** Ronald Reagan's White House
Political Director

"Ken Khachigian offers a riveting account of his thrilling journey through American history at the sides of two monumental Presidents. If you care about where America has been, and where it's going, this is a must-read!"
— **Monica Crowley, PhD,** former Assistant Secretary of the Treasury,
news analyst, and bestselling author

"Ken Khachigian will draw you inside a generation of White House leadership and details how Reagan revived the American economy and lit a prairie fire of patriotism across America."
— **K. T. McFarland**, American political candidate, former government official, and political commentator

BEHIND CLOSED DOORS

IN THE ROOM WITH **REAGAN & NIXON**

KEN KHACHIGIAN

Post Hill
PRESS

A POST HILL PRESS BOOK
ISBN: 979-8-88845-272-1
ISBN (eBook): 979-8-88845-273-8

Behind Closed Doors:
In the Room with Reagan and Nixon
© 2024 by Ken Khachigian
All Rights Reserved

Cover design by Conroy Accord
Interior photos courtesy of the Ronald Reagan Library and Foundation and
the Richard Nixon Library and Foundation.

This is a work of nonfiction. All people, locations, events, and situations
are portrayed to the best of the author's memory.

Post Hill Press
New York • Nashville
posthillpress.com

Published in the United States of America
3 4 5 6 7 8 9 10

Table of Contents

Chapter 1

THE END AS THE BEGINNING

LeaderShip 80 lifted off for Iowa from Los Angeles International Airport, and instead of the captain's voice, Willie Nelson was wailing "On the Road Again." The passengers laughed as Ronald Reagan rolled an orange down the aisle while rind and juice splattered on cameramen and film crews. Economic adviser Martin Anderson leaned over with a broad smile and said, "Welcome aboard!"

SEPTEMBER 29, 1980

Until now, I had given up hope of being other than an observer of the presidential election. Only six years before, I sadly turned in my White House pass as a casualty of Watergate's melodrama, and now, with only five weeks remaining until election day, I was the newest scriptwriter for Ronald Reagan's biggest starring role.

I didn't begin my adventure on Ronald Reagan's stage as a walk-on. The audition covered many years, with coaching by the president who resigned. I wouldn't have had the opportunity or the preparation for entering Reagan's circle as wordsmith, confidant, and adviser without being tested in the preceding years. My incredible decade at the summit of government and politics arose out of the dust of political collapse.

AUGUST 8, 1974

There was little to do but wait.

I told Pat Buchanan about the memo I had written to the Old Man and taken over to Rose Mary Woods. "It's too late, KK; it's locked in." Yet, it wasn't official, so I went upstairs to see Rose. Was there any way I could help? She was at her typewriter, crying. She tried to be cheerful and told me my memo was good. Then she turned. "I'm sorry; I can't talk anymore." She was typing Richard Nixon's resignation speech.

Steadily, the White House Police began locking the White House doors, and as I reentered the Executive Office Building (EOB) up to room 128, I saw the president's attorney, Fred Buzhardt. He was wan, wasted, sunken. Throughout, he had been stellar, wily, and creative with legal maneuvers for naught. He stopped to talk. "It's all for the best, Ken."

I was dubious and angry: "I hope they will leave him alone."

Fred looked directly and piercingly at me with words I would never forget: "Don't worry; that's part of it. He's not leaving without those understandings being reached." He repeated, "Don't worry about that, Ken." I remembered them a month later when Gerald Ford issued Nixon's pardon.

Buchanan and I sat moping when my secretary reported the *Washington Post's* Carl Bernstein calling. "What's the mood there?" Only a predatory ass would think to call at such a moment. It wasn't enough that Bernstein would cash in on Nixon for the rest of his life; he was gloating over his political corpse. I thought of only one response: "Why don't you go watch 'Deep Throat,'" and slammed down the phone. He called back immediately to complain to my assistant Jo Ellen Walker that I hung up on him.

She replied, "Yes, he did," and hung up on him again.

That night, the president delivered his resignation speech.

AUGUST 9

The weather was overcast—a metaphor. The East Room, quiet and funereal. We waited for Nixon and his family. Marine aide Major Jack Brennan bellowed their arrival: "The president of the United States and the First Lady!" Tears flowed from fellow speechwriter Ben Stein and, nearby, Chris Albert, the rare female military aide. When Nixon finished, the room was silent, except for the piercing voice of United Press International's Helen Thomas, shoving and screaming at the Secret Service, "Get out of my way; let me through!"

The Old Man entered the white-top helicopter for the last time, turned around, and waved. He left, and as the honor guard rolled up the red carpet, we slumped off, wondering what came next. Later, with John and Pat Coyne, my wife Meredith and I fought our way through the drunk and drugged-up mob celebrating in Lafayette Park to ponder our future over drinks at Trader Vic's.

FALL, 1967

I was a second-year Columbia Law student but had loved politics since attending California Boys State in high school. The opportunity was Richard Nixon's improbable comeback to the presidency. I wrote a letter to Nixon at his 20 Broad Street law office to volunteer on his campaign. The first letter was unanswered, so Meredith walked over another from where she worked on 30 Wall Street.

Patrick J. Buchanan responded to say he would "be delighted to get together...to see if something cannot be worked out." Buchanan, an affable, rapid-fire talker, signed on with Nixon in 1965, on leave from an editorial writing job at the *St. Louis Globe-Democrat*. About my interview, Buchanan always joked that my Columbia student credentials made me a suspect as a "Rockefeller spy." It began a lasting professional and personal relationship as Pat became boss, mentor, colleague, and lifelong friend.

Ann Volz supervised me answering correspondence at the cramped 521 Fifth Avenue headquarters that evolved into a full-time summer research position thanks to Martin Anderson. Marty was a brainy economist best known for skewering government overreach in his book, *The Federal Bulldozer*. Next door to my sixth-floor cubicle when the campaign moved to 450 Park Avenue was Nixon's foreign and defense policy adviser, Richard V. Allen. Dick was a self-assured, wise-cracking thinker with prolific writing and briefing skills. The eclectic team included Nixon's law partner and "idea man" Len Garment—a former jazz saxophonist in Woody Herman's band, along with my domestic policy chief boss, Alan Greenspan, a Woody Herman bandmate of Garment's and an acolyte of Ayn Rand.

Among the most important men I met and whose friendship I treasured was Bryce Harlow, whom Nixon knew from their Eisenhower days. Bryce's fascinating work history included clerking for General George C. Marshall. Harlow designated me his headquarters contact for incoming messages while he traveled with Nixon. When South Dakota senator Karl Mundt unfairly took me to the woodshed for a perceived oversight, Bryce salved my wounds in his quiet Oklahoma drawl, saying that "the only thing a senator can't stand is an unattended microphone." His wordsmithing talent made him a favorite of Ike's, who called him his "meat and potatoes" writer. He was a true mentor who shared his extraordinary wisdom throughout the Nixon years.

After completing law school and joining the State Bar of California, Meredith and I returned to the East Coast, and I arrived in the EOB eighteen months after Nixon's victory to join Herbert Klein's communications team. The former editor of the *San Diego Union* and one-time Nixon press secretary, Herb now oversaw a substantial operation to support administration policies. My job was to produce sharp-edged prose with punchy and quotable language destined for local, regional, or national news for delivery by White House surrogates in Congress, cabinet members, and national Republican figures.

It was perfect training for the 1980 campaign years later, where I was expected to produce provocative messaging for daily headlines and sound bites to lead the evening news. My first White House days with Nixon also taught me the art of working under pressure with the focus on writing for limited word counts—the fifty-yard sprint instead of the long-distance run.

Subsequently, I was assigned to work with Pat Buchanan to research likely 1972 Democrat party opponents, and after the primaries documented the leftist views of South Dakota senator George McGovern. We put the information to use at daily 9:15 a.m. meetings in Chuck Colson's office for daily messages sent to Republican communicators throughout Washington. Following a postelection White House reorganization, my efforts earned me a position on the presidential speechwriting staff and a modest promotion.

The Paris Peace Accords ending the Vietnam War were signed on January 27, 1973, and all was going smoothly...until February 7 when the United States Senate created its Select Committee on Presidential Campaign Practices, and the Watergate special prosecutor was appointed three months later. Attorney General Elliot Richardson made the inexplicable decision to appoint a partisan Democrat, Archibald Cox, to head the Watergate Special Prosecution Force. Cox operated Jack Kennedy's 1960 presidential campaign brain trust against Nixon and quickly proceeded to bring on many of his Kennedy-era colleagues to his staff of nearly forty lawyers. The fox was in the henhouse.

On October 20, Cox rejected a White House compromise regarding the verification of White House tape recordings, and that evening, Cox was dismissed by Solicitor General Robert Bork after Nixon fired both Richardson and Deputy Attorney General William Ruckelshaus for refusing to dump Cox. On October 30, the House Judiciary Committee began consideration of possible impeachment procedures, and on February 6,

1974, the House, in a formal resolution, directed the Judiciary Committee to begin the impeachment inquiry.

10:05 A.M.—AUGUST 5, 1974

"The Old Man's not going to resign," Buchanan told me as we sipped coffee upon his return from presidential chief of staff Alexander Haig's strategy meeting.

Buchanan and the president's lead Watergate defense lawyer, Jim St. Clair, did not see Nixon during the previous day's Camp David sessions, advising only through Haig and press secretary Ron Ziegler as intermediaries, but it appeared the message was to stand ground. However, Pat alluded to the new tape recordings of which we had been told a few days earlier, but cautioned, "We're not going public just yet." He confirmed it was specifically the June 23 conversation between Nixon and chief of staff Bob Haldeman.

Pat didn't disclose that he had already read that tape transcript, which, at the time, we mistakenly believed involved Nixon directing the CIA to prod the FBI to deflect the investigation. He also withheld that he was already in the resignation camp and said as much to the president and first family. I would have been sickened to hear that Pat had counseled pulling the plug. I strongly believed the president would be better served by actions that were bolder and more aggressive, elements that were lacking in our anti-impeachment efforts. The failure to keep the staff informed in the face of resignation rumors only weakened internal determination and resolve.

At 4:00 p.m., the June 23 tape was released. The president's statement was interpreted as acknowledgement that he had asked the CIA to request the FBI to back off for national security reasons. My colleague Geoff Shepard dubbed it the "smoking gun" tape, and the wheels began coming off our defense. Just four days earlier in Al Haig's office, our anti-impeachment efforts had been decently structured. With a few words, Nixon blew our plans out of the water.

The end was set in motion on July 24 when the Supreme Court ruled eight to zero that the president must turn over recordings of sixty-four conversations to the presiding judge of the Watergate cover-up trial, and I ended a working vacation to monitor the House Judiciary Committee's final deliberations. I wore three battle hats as a lawyer with writing skills and political judgment. To help manage the "war room," Haig brought on a young West Point graduate and Vietnam veteran, army major George Joulwan—a loyal and committed aide he could trust to get things done. Years later, George earned four stars to become supreme allied commander, Europe.

JULY 31

Joulwan called me into his cubicle office to get my views on organizing for the impending impeachment proceedings. "Everybody I talk to says Khachigian is the key, and everybody wants you working for them." Joulwan bemoaned that even in the midst of crisis, there was attempted empire building, with separate senior staffers looking to create the strongest teams—conflicts between Ron Ziegler and Ken Clawson, and between Ziegler and Haig. That's a natural disease in the White House with individuals who rise to the top, and it later seriously infected Ronald Reagan's staff. When service, vanity, advancement, and public notice are combined, nearly all who pass those portals are driven to excel and gain the president's favor. However, big motors don't always propel vessels in the right direction, leading to outcomes that can have especially acute consequences at 1600 Pennsylvania Avenue.

Ken Clawson, smart, aggressive, and mouthy, was a former *Washington Post* reporter now serving as director of communications. Joulwan thought Ken was looking for more staff and power to do as he saw fit for high-profile combat, but made it clear, "We've got to bring Clawson under control."

I was in no position to make staff assignments or demands regarding my role. "Look, George, put me wherever you want, but wherever I go, we have to be more aggressive, less defensive, and willing to take the fight to the public and to the Democrats on the Judiciary Committee." George Joulwan thanked me and told me to stand by. With our asses on the line, I thought personal aggrandizement shouldn't be a consideration, and I wondered if the president knew his staff was acting in this fashion as his presidency hung by a thread.

AUGUST 1, 6:45 P.M.

Al Haig called us in to discuss the full impeachment defense. Colonel Alexander M. Haig began his service as military assistant to Henry Kissinger and rose quickly to earn his fourth star in January of 1973, when Nixon appointed him Army vice chief of staff. Handsome, charming, self-assured, and a chain smoker, he sat at Bob Haldeman's former seat at the conference table, lit up a cigarette, and called us to order. Jim St. Clair sat adjacent, and on either side were Buchanan and Bill Timmons, the head of congressional relations, along with presidential counselor Dean Burch. Scattered around were Clawson, David Parker, Bill Baroody, Joulwan, David Gergen, Ray Price, John Price, Chuck Wardell, Jerry Jones, and me.

Al began with the timeline. "The House Judiciary Report is going to the full House on August 9, and we have to go full steam ahead if we're going to make the fight." He noted that the House debate would start on August 19, with a Senate trial in late September or early October. He put his papers down, snuffed his cigarette, and peered over half glasses. Haig already knew about the June 23 tape, but only dropped hints: "We've been doing a tape review, and we have to make some shifts in argumentation." He paused, then quietly said: "There are some bad spots." The room grew silent and Al leaned back, sporting a big grin: "When it's quiet like that I can hear the assholes tightening up all over the room."

We all needed that good laugh. He added: "It's just another bucket of shit in a huge cauldron of shit." Assignments were parceled out: to Timmons for the Senate; to Baroody, to deflect support groups away from the sour economy. Joulwan got out the charts breaking down meeting schedules for the "Strategy Group" and the "Work Group." I got assigned to the Work Group to move to Capitol Hill two days before the House debate and be chief writer in a "situation room" along with spokesman Larry Speakes and attorney Mack Howard. Substantive Task Forces were assigned for Articles I, II and III. Clawson would oversee communications, but not day-to-day stuff.

Not knowing what the "bucket of shit" looked or smelled like, I walked out of that meeting thinking that at last, we were on a mission to try to rescue the Old Man's presidency.

AUGUST 2

Our first Work Group meeting was Friday afternoon. We still weren't aware what was on the tapes, but Haig and Fred Buzhardt, the president's other principal lawyer, knew. I asked, "Is the president willing to dump it out now, the good and the bad?" There was general agreement that whatever was on the tapes, we had to get it out and level with the leadership support we had in the House and communicate the president's commitment to fight. At least I got one assignment coming out of the meeting—to prepare deputy press secretary Jerry Warren a one-pager summarizing the talent arrayed against us. Later that morning Jerry went out to the press briefing room stating for the first time the president "faces an uphill struggle" to avoid impeachment.[1]

The president's weekend wasn't quiet. Vice president Ford spoke of significant erosion of support for the man who appointed him, and the Senate's number-two Republican, Robert Griffin from Ford's home state, called on Nixon to resign.[2] At Camp David, Buchanan and other senior staffers, unknown to me, had determined that the June 23 tape would put the Old Man over the side.

MONDAY, AUGUST 5, 10:30 A.M.

The Work Group met in the Roosevelt Room—my favorite conference location. With its polished mahogany table and soft leather chairs, the room—named by Nixon in honor of FDR and Teddy—conveys a sense of warmth and dignity. I made it a point to observe the flags arrayed along the back wall, each representing one of the branches of our military and draped with dozens of ribbons signifying the great battles fought by that branch going back to the Revolutionary War. Looking at those flags, or the portrait of TR confidently astride his horse, it was impossible to believe any political adversary could reach us.

We sent the president three options to review after an internal damage assessment was completed: an Oval Office speech, a press room statement, or a written statement. "There's no sign of resignation," said Joulwan. "The idea now is to be totally forthcoming; to get everything out—the good with the bad." I concluded it was likely to be less good than bad, especially when Joulwan blurted out, "Apparently, there's one single damaging tape, and that's what we are going to have to get out."

After lunch, Buchanan and I saw the president, wearing his favorite old blue sport coat, returning to the West Wing from his EOB office. He was stoop shouldered, looked tired and avoided us when we went over to try to say hello.

3:45 P.M.

Haig began a briefing for our small team. Instead of being mired in boring civilian administration, he could act the role of an Army general again and thrived in this entangled environment. His voice was steady and firm. "The president has been reviewing 64 tape recordings, and most of the review has been completed. With one exception, most of it is consistent with all the previous stuff." The "exception" was the conversation between Nixon and Bob Haldeman on June 23, 1972. He laid his glasses aside, set down the transcript, and reported a statement would be going out at 4:00 p.m.

Leaning forward, Haig forcefully began: "What the country needs is a group of dedicated public officials. The past week has been difficult for the president, but he has put everything out with the bark off. It's time to exercise discipline and loyalty—to the country, if not to the president—until we get through this difficult time." He pleaded, "Please don't talk to reporters." Ha! A couple of those in the room were already continually leaking to favored journalists.

At 7:30 p.m., Joulwan gathered the Work Group to ask each of us to give an assessment. Senator James Eastland's former aide Larry Speakes started. "We have to roll out a defense by tomorrow, or it's too late."

Georgian Powell Moore from Senator Richard Russell's office drawled, "We'll go down badly in the House, and as of now will be convicted in the Senate."

Dave Parker, the quiet representative from scheduling, thought senators Goldwater and Stennis would call for resignation within days and that defense attorney, Jim St. Clair, would leave.

Jerry Jones from presidential personnel spoke dejectedly. "We haven't got anything left, and we've got to get out."

"He should get out with a public speech," said Mack Howard of St. Clair's legal staff. "Nixon's got to be apologetic and repentant. St. Clair's heart's not in it. He may not last a week." Outside the room, Howard took me aside. "Jim was blowing his stack. 'The bastard lied to me! The son of a bitch lied to me!'" It appeared Jim St. Clair was trying to play it both ways.

Buchanan told me that in the privacy of the past weekend's Camp David meetings, Jim was the hardliner counseling against resignation.

The Old Man's forces were folding tents at the first whiffs of gunpowder.

It was David Gergen's turn. He was a moderate without much stomach for protracted combat. He sounded staged and pious: "The only honorable course is to resign and do so in a couple of weeks. He should move rapidly and directly."

I replied, "This is no time to pack it in, and we can't bail on the Boss now without at least taking the case to the public. This is just one tape, and we should make every congressman take a stand and not let any of them off the hook." I was flailing against conventional wisdom, but I wanted something to hang on to and not reflexively head for the high country. My colleagues were understandably exhausted from the day-to-day fight and playing nonstop defense. The so-called "smoking gun" allowed them to put an end to the agony and return to a normal life.

I admired Joulwan. He heard everyone's views, but in the military tradition he had a mission, so he dispassionately proposed a different posture. "We can portray the president as an underdog and a fighter. We should emphasize his overwhelming strength as a peacemaker and argue that he's the best one to govern at this moment." He reported there would be a cabinet meeting at 10:00 a.m. tomorrow and a quadriad meeting to follow, and, pointing to me, "Khachigian's been assigned to write the president's talking points."

Haig walked in and sat down next to me and left me no maneuvering room. "Here's what we want him to say," he said, and I rapidly took notes as he spoke. He suggested the president stake his position by saying: "Stand me up to the Constitution." Haig continued dictating more points: "Why he took this action—what he expects to do. 'I want to talk about all this [impeachment] and then we'll go to Ken Rush [deputy secretary of state].'" Al paused to make sure I was writing it all down, and then added: "Be very careful—don't portray a kamikaze attitude. Don't be stubborn, that we're going to the end." Al knew I could string together arguments that the president was being screwed by a pack of Nixon haters employing a double standard not applied to other presidents. But he didn't want me putting in front of the Old Man any other course than resignation. That was the unmistakable course Al was pushing.

I continued writing plain vanilla, and that's what is recorded in my contemporaneous notes: "Pursuing constitutional course. What's good for the Nation.—Assassinated President—One forced out of office.—Grave mistake to do it. Best interest of America is to pursue constitutional course. No fanaticism—No bunker complex—no public be damned attitude. Tough times. There will be diversions, but let's proceed with our work."

As I reviewed Haig's instructions while writing this book, it's clear that they verify the many assertions that Haig lubricated RN's resignation—at the very least to hasten Nixon's exit from office.

I wandered into Ron Ziegler's office, where he was barking out instructions to his assistant, Diane Sawyer, a brainy, hard-working Wellesley College graduate who arrived from a Louisville television station. Diane quickly gained Ziegler's trust and had worked for weeks to help collect and prepare the White House tape recordings transcripts for release. When I transcribed a recording for a white paper debunking the accusation that Nixon was on the take from the dairy industry, Sawyer and I compared frustrations with the trying process of deciphering the tapes.

Diane Sawyer shown with me and Nixon presidential assistant Ray Price when we prepared briefing books for the Frost/Nixon interviews.

Ron was punchy from fatigue and from bearing much of the brunt of the stress from the Oval Office. Despite knowing the likely outcome, Ron must have decided to feed my determination: "Right now, Ken, I want you and Pat to begin advising me for the fight. You two are the best at it, and you need to start preparing."

I actually believed him and left his office thinking my talking points might make a difference. Though I was originally scheduled to attend the next morning's cabinet meeting, I received word no staff would be allowed other than Haig and Ziegler.

TUESDAY, AUGUST 6

I arrived that morning to see Buchanan grinning with a positive report, "The St. Clair boy gave a helluva stirring stemwinder speech at senior staff supporting the Old Man. Jim was also the hardliner in the privacy of Camp David over the weekend, but when you get him in the public, he softens." That confirmed Mack Howard's comment; with his aides and privately, St. Clair was critical of the president's course and in favor of resignation. Impeachment was never going to be a dignified legal engagement like those in which St. Clair excelled in paneled courtrooms with gentlemen adversaries, and the charming and urbane attorney was naïve about the manner of the fight. The impeachment defense would be conducted in a short alley on a dark night with long knives. If he was ambivalent, he should have quietly resigned long ago, but I think the allure of national attention was too much to pass up.

10:35 A.M.

The Work Group gathered, mainly to go through the motions. Bill Timmons was tasked with measuring congressional sentiment, but we already knew that from the *New York Times*, *Washington Post* and three television networks. Buchanan suggested an assignment for me: that I document past presidential abuses of power and blend it together with a speech that he recently delivered supporting the president. And my notes from that day read: "Go ahead and plan for House debate. Let's start cranking it out again." That was a fool's errand, but Pat was looking to keep me busy.

In 1974, a Japanese army lieutenant, Hiroo Onoda, emerged from the Philippine jungles after twenty-nine years of refusing to believe that

Imperial Japan had surrendered. He remained loyal to a cause that was lost and hopeless and agreed to give up his sword only when ordered by his former commander. Buchanan took up that storyline and dubbed me "Onoda"—a title he reserved for me over the decades of our friendship.

3:30 P.M.

We learned that GOP Minority Leader John Rhodes was going out at 4:00 p.m. to announce that while he would not support resignation, he would vote for Article I of Impeachment. Still, the Work Group continued to strategize in a fog of unreality. "The cabinet meeting was good," Joulwan reported. But what will we do about the accelerated impeachment procedures, someone asked? Dave Gergen, who was leaking our meetings to his friend, Bob Woodward, oddly suggested: "Let's put Jim St. Clair out with a legal defense." We shuffled out after the air of unreality was underscored by a very bizarre question: "Would it be a good idea for the president to address the farmers coming in tomorrow?"

With useless meetings, personal tensions were also high. Mort Allin was a very close friend who prepared the president's daily news summary. With Buchanan and me, Mort rounded out a loyalist troika fighting RN's battles. Mort had robust passion along with a booming voice. He marched across the hall into our suite: "Goddammit, the Old Man has blown it, sold us out, and we have nothing left to stand on." We were unnecessary adversaries, but were now shouting at each other, the result of an atmosphere thickened with inflexibility, anger, and helplessness.

WEDNESDAY, AUGUST 7

There were no meetings or assignments. The president's family was in town—like the gathering when Grandma's on life support. The president's sons-in-law, Ed Cox, and David Eisenhower, came over to meet with Buchanan. I watched and listened. Nixon should go to the Senate, they argued, but not fight tooth and nail; only let "nature take its course." It was a time to grasp at anything that might avert resignation.

Around 11:00 a.m., I poked my head back into Pat's office: "We're not doing any good here or learning anything; let's go to the West Wing." We crossed West Executive Avenue and over to the left, crowds pressed against the fencing on Pennsylvania Avenue, craning for a view: The death watch. We walked into Ziegler's office where—alluding to my new moniker "Onoda"—he teased me about committing *hara-kiri*. That was a rare departure from the tension that gripped Ron throughout the week—with his abrupt interruptions and nervous requests that I not take notes. Pulling on his cigarette, he said the Old Man was making decisions and "knew all the options," as if the senseless made sense.

I left to see Rose Woods at 11:45 a.m. Rose Mary Woods had been with Nixon since coming to the capital in 1951 from a small town in Ohio, never wavering through triumph and tragedy. She was furious at Haig, fully convinced that he was disloyal to the president. She had been through the nightmare of publicity, interrogations, and grand jury appearances regarding allegations that her accidental erasure of a tape recording may have been intentional. She feared her phones were tapped. Rose was nursing a terrible cold to multiply her emotional misery but said we still owed it to the Boss to fight on. She pulled out a telegram from the Washington Redskins' coach, George Allen, urging the president not to resign.

I kept busy by writing a memorandum to Nixon, futilely pleading that he reject resignation. His adversaries had argued for over a year that the country could survive impeachment, so I argued back that the country could therefore also "survive the complete unfolding of that process," and that whatever agony America had been suffering was "preeminently fostered and encouraged" by his opponents. "Resignation is not in your character," I argued, and his instinct "surely must be to fight." I closed, hoping that he could grasp the will expressed in "If"—Kipling's lovely poem—to "Hold on!" I left the memo with Rose. Like George Allen's telegram, I knew he would never see it.

It was like the last day of school, with no homework and no schedule, so I wandered around the West Wing "campus." Bill Gulley, the loud, wisecracking military liaison, saw me and called out: "Ken, meet Pat Nugent." Holy shit; it was LBJ's son-in-law. They were back; now I knew it was over! The barber was in the West Basement, so one way to make the hours pass was to get a haircut. The secretary of interior, Rogers Morton, passed by as I walked out. "Hello, Mr. Secretary," I said, and then blurted awkwardly, "How are things going?"

With a big sigh, he said, "All right, I guess."

I wonder what he told his family that night about the inane, clueless White House staffer asking such a weird question.

There was little to do after Nixon resigned. President Ford settled in with new staff members in key positions. Anything other than routine speech assignments was going to Ford's people. In daily phone calls from San Clemente, Diane Sawyer, and Nixon's personal assistant, Steve Bull, painted glum portraits of life at the old Western White House. Soon, Ron Ziegler invited me out for a few days. The president needed assistance from a loyalist who was discreet and familiar with the issues. I was pleased to be asked and in forty-eight hours joined Ziegler, Sawyer, Bull, and Jack Brennan in California. Few of my other colleagues would have been interested in that assignment; they were too busy salvaging their jobs with Ford.

The San Clemente office complex was composed of two buildings on the site of the Coast Guard's Long Range Navigation station. I passed through the security gate and down the quarter-mile drive to the compound and shocked to see two Coast Guardsmen desultorily volleying a tennis ball across a net strung across the helipad. On previous trips, all I ever saw on that helipad was the gleaming presidential helicopter. It was an apt metaphor for Nixon's fall.

In four and a half years in the White House, I never had an official, one-on-one meeting with the president. Suddenly, I was thrust into visits on critical personal decisions. In the rush of the resignation, there wasn't time to establish a budget for his post presidency, or to determine the available resources for his support. His personal finances were a mess; the California and New York bars continued to pursue disbarment and discipline; and alongside real legal problems, he remained the target of crackpot subpoenas. Resignation had not stunted the chase.

I worked to resolve the issue of his post presidential papers, the status of the Nixon Foundation, a review of the disposition of his Florida properties, and, importantly, to protect his financial viability. He had to pay back taxes due to previous bad advice, and now the government wanted repayment for certain property improvements he reasonably assumed were tied into security arrangements.

While working on very serious issues to bring structure to his shattered life, I was also overwhelmed by a singular impression: In every conversation, Nixon was already looking forward. Each included some form of detailed instruction to extricate himself from the past and move ahead. On August

24, he abruptly looked up from one of our working meetings to say, "Ken, I want you to think about doing extensive work on writing my memoirs."

At the end of the month, the president's DC attorney, Herbert J. "Jack" Miller began spending time with Nixon. Jack headed the Criminal Division in Robert Kennedy's Justice Department but gave strong and zealous representation to Nixon. I worked closely with him and his associate, Stan Mortenson, on several legal matters over the years and Jack, especially, provided a jovial, fun-loving after-hours presence.

As I made plans to end my temporary assignment, I noticed a Washington emissary was meeting with the president, Ziegler, and Miller. Benton Becker had shuffled in and out of Nixon's office more than once. On Labor Day weekend, I departed for home from Marine Corps Air Station El Toro aboard a Lockheed JetStar, one of the military's courtesy shuttle flights to accommodate guests and confidential documents to San Clemente. Becker was seated across from me, and after wheels up, he leaned over and asked, "Do you know why I was out here and what we were doing?" When I responded I was unaware, he nodded and turned back to his open briefcase and a stack of reading materials.

Eight days later, I learned with the rest of America. Becker had been negotiating Gerald Ford's pardon of Richard Nixon. Naturally, I thought back to what Fred Buzhardt had confided to me on August 8 in the EOB, and wondered if that was what Fred had in mind when he said RN wasn't resigning *"without those understandings being reached."*

Soon after my return, I was summoned down the hall where Paul Theis, a longtime Republican Hill staffer, had set up shop as director of President Ford's speechwriting office and my new boss. Paul was mild-mannered, and I knew he did not enjoy the order handed him by his hard-edged supervisor, Bob Hartmann. My service on President Nixon's Watergate defense was reason enough to put me over the side, but my tour of duty in San Clemente sealed the deal. Paul knew I had a young family and said that he and Ford's personnel team would help with efforts to place me elsewhere in the government. But I needed to be out as soon as that could be arranged.

In mid-November I settled in as speechwriting assistant to the secretary of agriculture, Earl Butz. I missed the White House mess, the barbershop, and workout room, but all in all, things weren't so bad. I no longer worked on Saturdays, had more time at home, and I got a little pay raise. Working with Earl Butz, Purdue University's former dean of agriculture, was a treat.

He was one of the truly great old-school orators and dictated the heart of his speeches, requiring only a little fact-checking and cleaning up on our part.

Butz had a wonderful sense of humor, often reflected in biting wit. In January, 1975, I accompanied him to a meeting in my hometown, Visalia. We then drove on to Fresno, thirty-five miles north. Winter skies in the San Joaquin Valley are plagued with blankets of "Tule Fog." On our drive to Fresno, the fog had lifted on the ground, but not above. When they can be seen in the winter months without the fog or overcast, the great Sierra Mountains on the east side of the valley are eye-catching and majestic. So, seated with Butz on the drive up Highway 99, I gestured to the right and said, "Mr. Secretary, the Sierras are over there. Normally, on a clear day, we'd be able to see them snow-capped and beautiful."

Butz didn't miss a beat and leaned over: "Ken, there isn't much to see in Indiana, but you don't need a clear day to see it."

Chapter 2

RETURN OF THE NATIVE

Richard Nixon's post-resignation years in San Clemente deserve a separate book. His repair and recovery over five and a half years and his respite at La Casa Pacifica provided solitude for the writing and planning that prepared him for his eventual return to the "fast track" of the East Coast. It was my opportunity to pack up with Meredith, Merissa (five), Kristy (four), and our dog Daffy to return home to California, family, and more congenial climes. It also opened the door for a close-in education at the side of a political and historical giant of my generation.

JUNE 2, 1975

I reported for work, and Nixon had already started on the book deal he signed with Grosset & Dunlap. Within weeks, Nixon had inked another contract with British celebrity David Frost for a series of ninety-minute television interviews. Telling his story was important, but restoring his financial health was also critical. Each of these deals fulfilled his goals.

Nixon quickly formed his Nixon's post presidential "administration" with Jack Brennan as chief of staff, and an aide from Nixon's Senate days, Loie Gaunt, handling administration. Nixon asked Frank Gannon, a former White House Fellow who worked with Don Rumsfeld and Ron Ziegler to lead his research and writing team with Diane Sawyer and me serving as principal researchers/writers. Judy Johnson came from Ziegler's press office to help with research, and the staff included Bob Dunn, Carl Howell, Nora Kelly, Marnie Pavlick, and Cathy Price. Ray Price arrived later to help with the book and David Frost interviews. When the book's manuscript had a typing crunch, Rose Woods and Marje Acker came to the rescue.

While I enjoyed digging into his 1950 Senate race or his Supreme Court appointments and dozens of other archival records, the gold stars of my San Clemente days were the hundreds of hours of digressions with RN into updates on national politics, personalities, and insider gossip—all of which were central to my portfolio. He had a voracious appetite for current events, and I was his source. Our conversations were enriched by three decades of his vast insight, knowledge, and background into the American and international world of politics and government.

He digressed on other issues with Gannon and Sawyer, and when we added up the hours of these in-office conversations along with managing his new life and his growing interest in golf, I often wondered if we didn't add a few months to the book's publishing date. Nevertheless, these departures from the grind of writing were critical to putting his resignation in the rearview mirror and offering intellectual and mental engagement outside the confines of San Clemente.

I continued as liaison with Nixon's attorneys as we dealt with the nonstop demands for documents, along with intermittent new charges, appeals from cases that were unresolved, and a stream of judgments from cases flowing from actions of former staff members. From time to time, I also juggled press inquiries, not as an official spokesman, but more as an "information-collector."

Working on RN's memoirs and discussing the '76 presidential campaign at the former Western White House in San Clemente.

JANUARY 2, 1976

Nixon buzzed to pick my brain on the unfolding presidential campaign calendar. I sat down in front of his beat-up brown chair and ottoman that was placed so the Pacific Ocean was viewed through the bay window past his shoulder. The blue water glistened while he opined as he puffed slowly on his pipe. "Ken, if Reagan loses New Hampshire and Florida, he's finished." With that prediction regarding the '76 campaign, Nixon kicked off what would become nearly twenty years of our discussing presidential politics in meetings, phone calls, letters, and memos.

Nixon would have been an exceptional campaign manager. Candidates are terrible at managing their own campaigns because of their emotional involvement. But when RN's own outcome wasn't at stake, his analysis was detached and coldly dispassionate—shrewder and more strategic. Nixon's insights into personalities, their strengths and weaknesses, and their flaws and skills allowed for subtle measurement of candidates and the direction of their campaigns. He could spot a phony in an instant and was especially adept at judging politicians' grasps of issues—notably in foreign policy.

My dialogues with Nixon in San Clemente would prove indispensable to the success of my relationship with Ronald Reagan. The breadth of experience he offered gave me the credentials I brought to the Reagan campaign in 1979 and 1980 and, even more importantly, to his presidency. It was through Nixon's lens that I more fully appreciated Reagan's genius as a communicator and why Dick Nixon hovered as an unseen *éminence grise* to Reagan in the '80 campaign.

He liked Reagan, but he also spoke in candor. The portrait that emerged of Reagan through those casual conversations with Nixon opened a window into Reagan's political persona that proved invaluable to my ability to complement Reagan's innate talents for leading and communicating. He had professional respect for Reagan's enormous talents at connecting with people and observed to me more than once, if Reagan combined sophisticated policies with those talents, the results at the ballot box would be explosive.

His deference to Reagan's political skills arose during Reagan's eleventh-hour pursuit of the nomination in 1968; he saw how the California governor captivated the heart of GOP delegates. But Reagan also didn't fit Nixon's classic candidate mold, and he was therefore surprised at the Gipper's rise in New Hampshire. He lectured me more than once, "Reagan's a philosophical stemwinder, Ken, but contrary to opinion, he's not a fighter. He's not a sledgehammer." Those were virtues Nixon admired in former Democrat Texas governor John Connally, who switched parties and served as Nixon's treasury secretary. The Old Man admired candidates who could preach heaven *or* hell in equal doses.

I knew I could get a rise out of Nixon by telling him candidates were making their medical records public. "Especially demeaning," I told him, was Frank Church's. He looked up to listen as I told him that the Idaho senator reported having a cancerous testicle removed as a young man.

Nixon practically came out of his chair. "What the hell are we coming to? My God, putting something out like that!" Then, shaking his head, and without appreciating his own humor, said, "How can a candidate run for president on one ball?"

I stifled laughter. It was generational moment. Nixon couldn't imagine presidential candidates baring their medical records and surely not broadcasting the deletion of one's testicle.

Nixon's interests in Reagan's fortunes became more intense when he won his first primary against Ford on March 23. "I couldn't care less who wins one way or the other. But I'd like to see the press and pollsters who predicted Ford would win easily proved wrong after Reagan wins this damned thing." He loved a competitive race to keep the nation's interest, and he was not unhappy to see Ford's fortunes take a hit. Ford and his staff had been treating Nixon poorly for several weeks, and there was some feeling among those of us on the receiving end they were getting what they politically deserved.

I began to more fully appreciate Reagan's ability to deliver a message after his March 31 televised address in advance of the Wisconsin primary. I knew Nixon would want my views, so I tuned in and was even more impressed because of the strength he showed overcoming poor production quality. Billy Graham called Nixon the next day and offered his own high praise that Reagan's speech was very good.

Our captivating political dialogue continued through the primaries, and one day in May, Nixon read to me his recommended road map for the various strategies Ford and Reagan should be using for the remainder of the primary season.

I knew what he wanted to do, and I said, "Mr. President, as much as you'd like, you can't pick up the phone and call in your advice. It would leak out and come back to bite you." It was a sad moment in his San Clemente exile.

He paused and conceded, "You're right, Ken, we can't be in a position of recommending anything to either Ford or Reagan. Reagan's a good listener, and he would pay attention. But we can't get involved with that."

While Nixon wanted to get his book done, he was far more interested in what was going on with the primaries. Ford won the May 18 Maryland and Michigan primaries, and Nixon asked me to come in late that night. "Reagan has got to win in Kentucky and Tennessee, and he has to win four out of the next six states in order to stay alive. This week is a big one; it will determine whether Reagan wins in California."

I witnessed what every political reporter would have salivated for—eavesdropping on Nixon's game plan for Reagan to win. "He can't make any foolish comments about privatizing the Tennessee Valley Authority. He should kick the environmentalists; that won't be popular in Oregon, but it will in Tennessee and Kentucky." Laughing, he said, "Kick 'em in the ass."

When Reagan lost Tennessee and Kentucky, Nixon changed his mind. "The margin is not much. I don't think losing both states finishes Reagan off." With the boredom of the book and golf, the only thing that kept his mind fresh and alive was politics. He loved watching the sport, the struggle, and the clash—spirits to open each day. He marveled at how well Reagan was doing against an incumbent president. "Good God, he's running even with an incumbent. He's got to do well; it's a question of keeping the party from going to the Left, Ken."

MAY 25

Nixon read that Reagan would be sixty-six on his next birthday, and for the first time raised the subject, "He's the youngest looking sixty-five I've ever seen. He looks very good for that age." As the primary season closed, Nixon couldn't see where Reagan's delegates were, and reviewed each state in detail with multiple variables. He also noted that Ford was doing poorly in precisely the states he would need to win in November. "Jerry won't have a whore's prayer to win in New York, Pennsylvania, or Massachusetts."

JUNE 2

We walked through all the different analyses, and Nixon paused and sighed: "Gosh darn; isn't it frustrating not to be able to help out in the election?" He looked away and his voice trailed off, "Damned silly Watergate."

After Reagan delivered a July television address, Nixon tutored me again on Reagan's communicating ability to move the political needle. "He was effective and persuasive, Ken, and it's this type of thing that shows Reagan could wage the better campaign than Ford. If they're both behind in the polls, Reagan's use of TV could bring him up. I don't care how far behind he is; when someone can use TV that effectively, he can catch up; maybe not to win, but he'll pull up."

Nixon's insights about the strategies and techniques of campaigns were intuitive and penetrating, and I made sure to take careful note. Four years later, I put Nixon's counsel to very good use.

JULY 26

Nixon had less admiration for the Gipper's political instincts. Returning an early morning phone call from Marty Anderson, I instead reached David Keene, another pal from his days as Spiro Agnew's aide. Keene reported that Reagan preannounced his vice presidential running mate: Senator Richard Schweiker of Pennsylvania. I was incredulous. Keene tried to pass off this Hail Mary move to sway convention delegates as a "Nixonian bold move." I ran in to tell Nixon, but Pat Buchanan had already called to inform him, and he was baffled and agitated.

"How does he sell it to the South? How the hell could Reagan say that the vice president has to be compatible with the presidential candidate? He said *he* [Reagan] couldn't be compatible with Ford; how the hell can he be with Schweiker?"

Nixon fumed: "Schweiker voted with every bug-out proposal that came down. The Cooper-Church Amendment, ABM, against our Supreme Court nominees. He always voted with the liberals. It's cynicism. It's all lost now. Reagan doesn't have a chance. It will just be interpreted as opportunism. It reflects more on Reagan than it does on Schweiker. It was lost anyway; maybe this was his only chance to get the nomination." The following morning, Nixon summarized the Schweiker decision with one of his famed political aphorisms: "I've dealt with the Right, and they won't accept this.

Liberals can be ideological, too, but they want power. Conservatives just want to be right."

That campaign gimmick upended a year of RN's strategic thinking for Reagan. "They are boys playing a man's game." Shaking his head and complaining with remorse tinged with bitterness, he said, "Goddammit, I regret not being able to have direct communications with Reagan—that I couldn't pick up the phone and talk to him about something like this. I think I could have talked him out of it in two minutes. Or maybe five minutes. I've always worried about him being a bit thin. That's always been his basic problem: that he's a bit thin."

That was a frustrated outburst by Nixon, and he didn't mean "thin," in the sense of being vapid. What he should have said, and what I later discovered, is that Reagan could be too trusting. Reagan was lured by his staff to go against his instincts, and it not only wasn't enough to overcome Ford's delegate strength, it had the opposite result of infuriating his conservative base. He fell more than one hundred votes shy of the nomination.

Even before Reagan and I became close, I saw problematic relationships with his staff and how he placed too much faith and trust in them and less in his own judgment. The Schweiker debacle was another event in Nixon's "postgraduate" school that proved to be an invaluable laboratory in preparation for the years ahead. Later, I would try to help Reagan work around staff who pressed him into philosophical positions that didn't fit him.

Ford extended a gracious gesture by inviting Reagan to address the GOP convention following his own acceptance speech. Reagan's impromptu remarks kept the hushed crowed spellbound, and Nixon ended the semester of Reagan 101 with two more takeaways. He directed my attention to Reagan's use of the anecdote about riding down the Pacific Coast Highway with the Blue Pacific on one side and the Santa Ynez Mountains on the other. "People will remember the 'blue Pacific and Santa Ynez Mountains.'"

Then he initiated my focus on Nancy Reagan. Gesturing with his pipe, he reiterated praise of Reagan's talk, "Classy. Really classy." He quickly added, "His wife's classy, too, the way Nancy's been conducting herself." Nixon was drawing my attention to Nancy Reagan as playing far more than a supporting role in the drama of her husband's career—his second reference to her in this election season.

Weeks earlier, I asked RN what he thought of Nancy. "She is very frank and very intolerant of Ron's opponents. She has more ambition than he does, even while she's just happy playing the role of housewife. She's the toughest of the bunch."

In case I missed the point, a year and a half later, Nixon told me of Ronald Reagan's phone call to him the day after Hubert Humphrey's funeral. Nancy yanked the phone away to say she was incredulous that Ford didn't ask Nixon to share the military plane provided to take him back to Washington to the funeral. "After all," she snapped, "he got where he was by one vote—yours."

We continued to have brief visits as the fall campaign unfolded. Despite ongoing cool treatments accorded him by Ford's staff, he saw how inept, weak, and unprepared Jimmy Carter was and always concluded by saying, "For the good of the country, Jerry must win."

Reagan was politically adroit by doing campaign spots for Ford, and I studied them carefully because Nixon would ask my opinion of the commercials as well as an ongoing education in stuffing political persuasion into thirty seconds. Reagan called Nixon the Friday before Election Day, chafing that the president's operatives wanted him to readjust his entire schedule to campaign alongside Ford in California. Nixon added another perceptive observation about Reagan: "He doesn't show his anger by talking harshly, but I could tell he was very upset." Nixon and I both knew if that had been done to Nixon, he would have expressed his anger *very* harshly.

Bryce Harlow called on election eve with an update. He reported the tightness of the election with exquisitely descriptive words: "The margin will be thin as restaurant soup."

And it was. Nixon consoled: "Actually Ford did pretty well, Ken, considering all things. You can't lose the whole South, New York, and Pennsylvania and win the presidency."

DECEMBER 10, 1976

I walked in as Nixon set down a newspaper that reported a "summit meeting in the Oval Office of Republican elder statesmen"—excluding him. RN couldn't resist assessing the field that included Reagan, Nelson Rockefeller, and John Connally. "Look at it, Ken. Take Rockefeller. He's finished in the party. He couldn't draw flies. There's nothing he can do. Reagan—I think he wants to run again in 1980, but I don't think he can. He'll be sixty-nine years old. Connally—the trouble with Connally is the party. It's getting the party leadership to accept him. He's getting older, too."

People have never understood—especially based on the "Nixon tapes"—that the Old Man thought out loud, and his political musings in casual conversation were usually on target. But that morning, he was off the mark in the case of Reagan. That's because when it came to Reagan's age, RN's thinking was framed by his own career—winning a Senate seat at age thirty-seven, swearing in as vice president at forty, nearly winning the presidency at forty-seven, and succeeding at fifty-five. By those standards, Reagan at sixty-nine would seem very old for the office.

Chapter 3

THE FROST–NIXON INTERVIEWS

Nixon made it clear he wanted to influence the direction of the David Frost interviews, but he faced two major obstacles to achieving that objective: his own staff and Frost's.

Eight weeks before taping the David Frost interviews, Nixon asked me to split off from the book to take overall responsibility for assisting him to prepare. Diane Sawyer was already immersed in the memoirs' Watergate minutiae, so she was assigned that area of the briefings. We knew Frost wasn't going to play the patsy, so as the interviews neared, we probed harder in each practice session.

David Frost's preliminary visit with Nixon after signing a contract for the Frost/Nixon television series, with Jack Brennan, Nixon's San Clemente chief of staff.

I raised what I believed would be a central issue for Frost: whether a crime was committed.

Nixon replied, "Well if I'm asked, I'll have to say that I didn't. I don't think I can answer that. You have to have intended to commit a crime, and I didn't." Nixon's view was clear: If he admitted to committing a crime, "it would dominate everything, and nothing else would emerge. There is a very fine line to be drawn, Ken. We must avoid a defensive, *mea culpa*, weak attitude. We've got to be strong. The people aren't going to want to see weakness."

Frost was building his own team. The key deputies were Robert Zelnick and James Reston Jr. Young Reston, as Zelnick called him, was the namesake of the iconic *New York Times* columnist. Behind his pleasant demeanor, he had a lustful animus for Nixon. Zelnick was an attorney and former NPR national radio reporter. While not sharing confidences, Bob Zelnick and I began communicating to make sure we understood the dialogue's direction. He was the smartest and best prepared of the team and a tough adversary. We had mutual respect and grew fond of each other as intellectual combatants and would become close personal friends afterward. We engaged in dueling banter, and I enjoyed Bob's deep-throated laughter at the jokes I made at Frost's expense—and muffled mine when he jabbed at Nixon.

The jabs hid his real concerns. As Frost later recounted in his 1978 book about the Nixon interviews, *I Gave Them a Sword*, Zelnick delivered a worried—and respect-filled—lecture regarding Nixon's skills:

> "Don't you know what you're up against? This man is not only one of America's cagiest politicians, he's been a member of the bar for almost forty years. He's tried cases at trial, presided over committee hearings, argued before the Supreme Court of the United States.... You're in against a master, man, a master. Everything he wanted these interviews to accomplish for him will be on the line.... And he's a fighter.[3]

Frost's side also had no knowledge of the growing dissonance in our house with just over three weeks left to prepare. Diane Sawyer had been researching Watergate for almost two years. Just as she later displayed in her storied broadcast journalism career, Diane poured energy, brainpower, stamina, and determination into her work—and a toughness hidden under the looks of a young Lauren Bacall. She felt she was losing her ability to convince Nixon of certain facts and he would try to avoid the subject of his Watergate involvement—or just stonewall.

Nixon contemplated several goals with the British television personality's interviews. To move forward, Watergate had to be addressed in a conspicuously public forum—something written words could never achieve. He could also lift mounting financial pressures off his growing legal expenses. Frost was charming, urbane, witty, and pleasant company, all of which Nixon liked in place of those "dull anchormen." In addition, "Frost will be better, Ken, because he won't be so obsessed with Washington. Better yet, you stick it to the networks." Nixon was especially pleased that Frost was willing to go into broader subjects, including his views on heads of state, both living and dead.

I prepared briefing books on various domestic issues, the Vietnam War, and coordinated with Ray Price on foreign policy Qs and As. Sawyer submitted her Watergate briefing books but continued to be concerned about Nixon's responses. She shared offices with Frank Gannon, who was editorial director for the memoirs and whom Nixon did not want distracted from book preparation. Nevertheless, Diane shared her concerns with Frank and brought him into a meeting with me.

She spoke to me with words that carried wounds as well as demands: "Ken, the president has to confess to lying to the American public and breaking his binds of trust with the nation, and you need to go with Frank and me to convince him of that." I agreed that the goal of the interviews would fall short without acknowledging more than expressions of regret and remorse, but also that Nixon misled. "Look," I responded, "I know Frost will press him to say he lied. He will corner him to admit as much, and how he responds is crucial to where we end up. But the Old Man's been through hell, under bitter partisan attack, and, on the big issues, doesn't believe he knowingly lied. And whatever else you think Frost, or we, will get him to say, he will never admit to committing an impeachable offense."

Sawyer and Gannon wanted me to join them in a meeting with Nixon to help them press their views of confession. RN sat in his corner chair, serenely puffing on his pipe. Diane asked Gannon to take the lead.

Nervously, Frank filibustered, but finally got around to telling Nixon he had to concede two essential points: (1) his breaking a mythical bind of trust, and (2) lying. The Old Man was silent, stoic. He nodded his head. Then Diane spoke, and I followed.

Nixon responded quietly and firmly. "By admitting guilt like you want me to do, I will lose what small support I have without gaining anyone. Let's not deceive ourselves about this. We're not going to win any friends by our candor." Diane and Frank disagreed, but on the point where I thought RN was absolutely right, I believed there was a middle ground between denial and a groveling confession. Nixon remained unflappable throughout an uncomfortable session that lasted over two hours. The result clearly showed that he would resist Frost just as he resisted us.

Nixon saw what he had achieved by giving in—resignation of the office he had fought so hard to gain. So, we had to try looking at this through his eyes. What would concession gain him now, that he had not already lost? Until the day he had resigned, America had witnessed a tough, uncompromising, and thick-skinned veteran of political wars. But what I saw in San Clemente was a man wounded and brittle from the pounding of events that exploded out of control, followed by months and months of ongoing and savage personal attacks with damned little sympathy outside the walls of our compound. In that context maybe the harder line was best

FEBRUARY 28, 1977, 9:53 A.M.

Nixon asked me to come in. "I want to discuss the strategy you, Frank, and Diane came up with yesterday." He had to resolve in his own mind how to render judgment on himself. "Ken, let's not be under any illusions. Frank and Diane aren't being realistic. They are naïve to believe that the public is going to come around to my side if I say the things they want. I know one thing; I'm never going to say I committed an impeachable offense. I'm not going to say I committed a crime. I won't do that."

His voice turned quiet. "The family can't accept my saying that I lied... not without taking in the broad leap of things." By the "broad leap of things" he meant the degree to which he, too, had been misled and by the distortions heaped upon him over two years.

I tried being the devil's advocate, floating that by making admissions he could dispose of the worst charges and then argue everything else from a stronger position.

He shook his head. "That's a bunch of bullshit. If I say that I was a criminal, then Frost is just going to start listing things and saying, 'Was that a crime?' or 'Was this a crime?' Also, I'm going to address the question of whether or not there was an impeachable offense, and on that, I am sure as hell going to say 'no.'"

In subsequent meetings, Sawyer continued to argue that RN should say he lied and was sorry for putting the country through agony, but not in a *mea culpa* or breast-beating tone. She hadn't convinced him—or me—how to achieve one without the other. Still, Diane was a formidable advocate, and like Frost, she was buried under thousands of pages of Watergate records convincing her we had the losing side. So, on March 10, I argued Sawyer's position to Nixon with a different tack—that Frost wanted to box him into a corner, with a television camera doing a close-up on his face and embarrass him to answer whether he lied.

"Sir, that could be more uncomfortable than just saying it out front. At least I think that's what Diane has in mind."

Then, RN confronted me: "Do you agree with Diane, Ken?" I fumbled. I was now facing off against the man who stared down Khrushchev, Mao, and de Gaulle. It might be easy after a couple of Scotches at the office Christmas party to brag about "what I told the president." This wasn't the office Christmas party. "Well, perhaps you could say, 'When I made this or that statement, it's clear that what I said had the effect of misleading the investigators.' Or 'When I said thus and so, it was not the truth.'" To these, RN nodded his head. He was prepared to acknowledge how he had misled, but not to directly say, "I lied."

But trifling screwed us in the White House and would be destructive with Frost. Behind the charm, Frost was a coldly ambitious bastard looking for approbation from his friends on the Left and the entertainment industry, and Zelnick and Reston had signed on for red meat. In the end, Frost would resort to highly savage questioning with a litany of contradictory public statements and tape excerpts leaving Nixon no escape routes. It was uncomfortable, and I didn't approach it with Sawyer's alacrity.

I said: "Mr. President, the only way we can deal with Frost's attacks is to preempt them. However you decide to do it, David must come away hearing you've admitted to not telling the truth at critical points. I believe that's what Diane means when she formulates her draft answers in such a cold, direct fashion."

He looked away and puffed on his pipe. "Maybe that's true. Well, we'll just have to work on that and consider how to do it." Thankfully, the line buzzed; he was interrupted by an incoming call, and I left hoping I said the right thing, and glad to get the hell out of the room.

He continued to sound me out as he wrestled with answers. For over two hours on March 12, he reviewed Sawyer's briefing materials, complaining again that she had gone overboard. I tried again to mediate: "Mr. President, Frost's goal after the broadcast is to permit people to say you've answered all the questions on Watergate." The Old Man shrugged, repeating what I heard him say so many times: "We'll never know the complete story for sure; I don't know it now. There will always be questions remaining. Ken, [John] Mitchell still denies everything. I've asked him questions point blank, and he still denies. What can I do?"

Then, he referred to perjury and the frequency it was mentioned in the Watergate tape transcripts—to which he was always sensitive given his role in the Alger Hiss case. I repeated what was doctrinal in Nixonland: "Hiss would have gotten off scot-free if he hadn't lied about it."

RN answered quickly: "So would we, if we had handled it right."

With the first interview six days out, RN girded for battle. "I can't be contrite, weak or pusillanimous. I am going to be bloody but unbowed. I have to be myself. Diane wants me to be weak. Oh, not necessarily weak. She just wants me to do it differently, and I won't." After we returned from our dress rehearsal to test the set-up and sound with Frost, RN was self-confident and pleased. To ensure I wasn't missing his point, he turned back to me as he left the office that evening: "It's naïve on Diane's part to think my critics are going to change their minds. Well, you've done everything you can. Now it's up to me."

Ray Price and I arrived to settle down next to Frost's producer John Birt at the Monarch Bay home and filming location of Harold and Martha Smith. Frost opened surprisingly, and stupidly, by asking why RN didn't burn the White House tapes. So, RN filibustered for twenty minutes and threw Frost's timing off before moving on to further questioning.

Back at the office, RN mused over Frost's questions, especially one with shades of Reston's effort to psychoanalyze—whether his mother was the stronger of his two parents. Reston had a bizarre dream of turning the interviews into psychoanalysis. As Frost described it in his book, Reston held "theories about Nixon's penchant for self-destruction, his view of death as an ally, 'survivor guilt' growing from the boyhood death of his brothers, the authoritarian mentality that came from stern paternal upbringing...."[4]

The next tapings moved into foreign policy, leading with the war in Vietnam. Nixon hit Congress hard, blaming it for cutting funds to the government of South Vietnam in 1975, causing It to be overrun by the Communist North. "Someone had to say it. It's the truth, and Ford should have said it. It was the Congress. I couldn't make Ford look sappy; I had to get him off the hook." As with most of the tapings, our post mortems provided the best insight as he unloaded to Price, Brennan, and me. They also allowed Nixon to decompress, let off steam, and stake his ground.

After the interview covering the Marxist Chilean Salvador Allende, Frost covered the complex relationship with Kissinger, trying to goad Nixon to unload on his former aide. Nixon handled it deftly and was kinder than he later shared with us privately back in his San Clemente office. There, he described with incredulity how Frank had counseled him: "Gannon's suggested responses on the Kissinger thing included a recommendation that I say of Henry: 'But one thing about Dr. Kissinger, he was never mean or cruel.' My God! Henry was always mean and cruel. He was mean and cruel to Bill Rogers. He was mean and cruel to Al Haig and his staff. Not mean and cruel! That wouldn't be the truth. It would be the opposite of the truth."

I wasn't surprised that Bob Zelnick had concluded with outrage that Nixon had gotten the best of David in the pre-Watergate interviews. He took David to the woodshed. "Don't kid yourself. [Nixon's] set up perfectly for kicking your tail from one end of Monarch Bay to the other."[5] With John Birt adding, "Yes, you can't back down with Richard Nixon, because he takes it as a sign of weakness."[6] Stung, Frost saw his reputation slipping away, so looked to do to the Old Man what no one in Congress, the judiciary, or media had accomplished.

Thus, a prosecutorial Frost put Nixon on the defensive most of the first Watergate session, hammering away from the records and tapes excerpts. They slogged it out on the June 23, 1972 conversation, with Frost charging that Nixon instructed Haldeman to press the CIA to order the FBI to thwart the investigation. David convincingly laid out all the appearances of an obstruction of justice.

Nixon had barely returned to his office when Jack Brennan slipped in before anyone else to tell RN bluntly: the interview was a disaster. My heart couldn't deceive my eyes and ears; I reluctantly agreed, and so did Sawyer. When I met privately with Nixon, he began: "Brennan says it wasn't any good—that I appeared cornered and on the defensive. Well, there are a lot of corners, and we can't avoid them. Watergate is all corners. Don't get down, Ken. We got in our best shots, doing the best we can. Look, we started behind the goal line on Watergate, and it is all we can do just to get the ball up *to* the goal line. We'll just keep trying."

April 15, 1977, was far more memorable than the typical income tax day. It concluded with Nixon's historic personal resolution of his Watergate role and an expression to the nation of remorse and hoped-for reconciliation. From someone who was there at Nixon's side throughout, here for the first time is an account of the deliberations behind his dramatic and emotional statement of anguish aired on national television.

8:50 a.m., RN called for me, and instead of studying and making notes in preparation, he was puffing on his pipe—fatigued, dejected, and concerned. "Sit down, Ken. Let me tell you something." He then recounted how, at 11:00 p.m. the previous night, Frank Gannon had caught up with him walking home, to say he read the transcript from the first Watergate taping. Gannon accused him of being "defensive and niggling" and had to change strategies.

"He says I should come out in the next session and just say that I lied to the American people and that I obstructed justice, even if I thought I had not violated the law. He even suggested that I plead an 'indisposition' and not do today's taping and delay it over to next week to allow time to prepare."

Gannon had written in his midnight memo to RN, "You must be prepared to talk about lying and to use that word," and furthermore to say, "I did, in fact, obstruct justice."

Nixon's face and voice revealed a mixture of disgust and defensiveness. "Ken, when I left last night, I was bone-tired and wanted to get to bed, and then he hits me with this. What the hell do they want me to do? Should I just say I lied? Is that what I should do?"

I had seen him feel sorry for himself, but not quite this deservedly. Frank's obtuse and inconsiderate approach near midnight, while the Old

Man was exhausted and at his lowest, was the least sensible way to achieve a positive result—plus intermeddled in my area of responsibility.

I hadn't earned the nickname "Onoda" lightly and told Nixon he should stick with our earlier formulation. Yes, some of his White House statements turned out to be untrue and had the effect of misleading people, but if Frost was looking for the weighted words, "lying" and "obstructing justice," he wasn't going to get them. RN had had already decided that, not only for his own sense of self-worth, but for Mrs. Nixon's and Tricia's and Julie's sakes, he was going to refuse to give Frost a *National Enquirer* headline. I agreed with standing ground.

Nixon continued bitterly, "I don't want Frank reading any more damn transcripts and bringing me stuff at the last minute like this." He clearly hadn't slept and paced the room, slipping in and out of his kitchen as he gulped coffee. Soon, he left for Monarch Bay, and I was fearful he would enter this final interview wracked with fatigue and distracted by the previous night's tension.

RN asked me to come to his makeup room for final points and wondered aloud: "Ken, do you think I should say I lied and take the Gannon line? Oh, hell, they do it out of their hearts. They think they're doing me a favor; they're just so emotionally involved in this whole thing." As upset as he was, he also respected Sawyer and Gannon for their intellect, insight, wit, and brainpower. But in this fight, they were off the mark regarding RN's character. Neither had been with him in the middle of political battles nor felt any special sting at the raw partisan animus that motivated so much of the opposition to Nixon throughout his career and presidency. For each, the cut and thrust of politics was distasteful and alien.

A few minutes into the taping, there was a loud retort, like a pistol shot. David's face turned ashen. A set light had popped, and with Frost still shaken, I viewed the break with good fortune and asked Brennan to move RN to his room. We needed additional prep on the June 23 conversation, and I grabbed Diane to accompany me. Frost would be pressing the point that Nixon *ordered* the CIA to get the FBI off the case rather than just *suggesting* it. In the previous taping, RN made it sound like it was permissive, not an order, and I told Diane he couldn't leave that impression.

I also recalled a memo by CIA director Richard Helms telling his deputy, Vernon Walters, to warn the FBI not to run afoul of CIA operations, and that may have attached credence to RN's view that the CIA would have relevant concerns. While it wouldn't disprove the effort to stall the investigation, it could at least raise the potential that the CIA had "hopes" of finding some legitimate way to turn the FBI off. Nixon thought this was a good point, and in frustration snapped at Diane: "That's right. Walters told me about that memo, and I had forgotten it. Why the hell didn't you put it in my briefings, Diane? Why the hell did you leave it out?" It was pure oversight, and Sawyer was crestfallen. She was the last person who wanted to let the Old Man down with her research. He immediately softened. "Oh, don't worry; it's not your fault. But dammit; it should have been in there."

I tried to divert him and reminded him he had to master the new information in the little time we had. But Diane was very upset and near tears.

Nixon was unable to use his "preemptive answer," and during another break, said, "I haven't found a way to work it in, yet." When Frost led him to a point where he could actually work into our planned statement, David interrupted, so RN never gained a head of steam. Finally, Frost took a break to change reels and suggested lunch, but Nixon opted to keep going and went back to his room during the pause.

Brennan took Frost aside, and when I tried to approach, Jack motioned me away while mumbling something about talking to Frost alone. Jack didn't bear my substantive responsibility, so I didn't want him making representations for which I would take the heat. I knew Frost was looking for some kind of confession, and it was Jack's belief that by admitting the worst, RN could get everything behind him and move on with his life. But I didn't want to be surprised, and I knew Nixon didn't either.

I walked back to see Nixon and complained that Frost wasn't allowing him to get his points across. "Mr. President, we're at the eleventh hour, and I think you still have to make clearer your own understanding, at least, of how close you came to the boundaries of the law during the March–April period of 1973, because after the break, David is going to come after you with everything he's got on whether you entered the cover-up. You simply have to acknowledge that you went to the edge of the law, and you can see how it could have been misinterpreted."

He nodded and returned to his displeasure with what happened the night before. "You know what Gannon said? He said that I should do this because the honest liberals would give me credit. Oh, hell, Ken, there is no such thing as an honest liberal. You know that. Do you agree?" I responded that "honest liberal" was a contradiction in terms. But right now, being pissed off at liberals was not serving him.

As RN continued pacing, Brennan burst in: "I've cut a deal with Frost. He won't use the material from yesterday's taping if you'll admit to certain things." Taken aback, Nixon naturally asked how that was defined. "If you say you broke faith with the American people," said Jack, "and say you're sorry and admit that you put them through unnecessary anguish—that kind of thing."

Nixon shot back: "Does he want me to say I broke the law?"

"His staff is pushing that; he's fighting them," replied Jack. "There were tears in Frost's eyes, and if you'd only give him that, I think he'll be satisfied."

Nixon scowled: "For Chrissakes, of course I would have said those things anyway. Does he think I'm stupid? I was planning that." It was clear that through the turmoil, he was working on his own framework for the conversation to come. If there was to be a confession, *he* would shape it, not us. I was witnessing the kind of decision-making that had taken place multiple times at critical points in Nixon's political and personal life.

Jack walked out, and RN asked my view of "the deal" and what Brennan meant. Still pacing, he vented once more: "Ken, I don't want any-body talking to Frost. Do you think Frank and Diane have been talking to him? I don't want that. Hell, if anybody can't listen to me around here, they can resign. If they don't like it, they can leave. Now, Ken, I don't want anyone else dealing with Frost; you understand?"

Brennan returned to report that Frost would, in effect, agree on the points we discussed and would not push RN to say he committed a crime or obstructed justice—although David would continue to believe that.

The taping resumed, and Frost wasted no time:

> "Would you do what the American people yearn to hear?
> Not because they yearn to hear it, but just to tell it all, to
> level and so on. Would you go further than the 'mistakes'?
> ...there was wrongdoing. Whether it was a crime or
> not—yes, it may have been a crime, too...and I'm saying

this without questioning the motives, right—I did abuse the power I had as president, or not fulfill the totality, the oath of office…And I put the American people through two years of agony, and I apologize for that."

If ever there was to be a moment of expiation for the chaos left behind on the South Lawn, it was now.

"I would say that the statements that I made afterwards were, on the big issues, true: that I was not involved…in the break-in, that I did not engage in and participate in or approve the payment or the authorization of clemency, which, of course, were the essential elements of the cover-up." Then he described the massive battles we had been conducting in the White House in a poisoned atmosphere with a partisan special prosecutor and Senate committee and hostile press. "Now under all these circumstances, my reactions in some of the statements and press conferences and so forth after that, I want to say here and now, I said things that were not true. Most of them were fundamentally true on the big issues, but without going as far as I should have gone…. And for all those things, I have a very deep regret."

For Frost, Sawyer, Gannon, Brennan and all the rest of us, Nixon put the stake in the heart of the word "lying."

He continued: "I'm simply saying to you that as far as I'm concerned, I not only regret it, I indicated my own beliefs in this matter when I resigned. People didn't think it was enough to admit mistakes. Fine. If they want me to get down and grovel on the floor, no. Never. Because I don't believe I should." Then, in the form of a self-inflicted penalty, he finally gave Frost and his PR people the headline they were looking for. "I gave them a sword. And they stuck it in. And they twisted it with relish. And, I guess, if I'd been in their position, I'd have done the same."

Still, it didn't seem enough for Frost, who wanted him to concede to "some covering up. That there were a series of times…that in fact you were, to put it at its most simple, a part of a cover-up at times?"

RN responded that "I did not, in the first place, commit a—the crime of obstruction of justice. Because I did not have the motive required for the commission of that crime."

Frost retorted, "We disagree on that."

But RN continued: "The lawyers can argue that. I did not commit, in my view, an impeachable offense…. I impeached myself. That speaks for itself. By resigning. That was a voluntary impeachment." Nixon continued with regard to purported actions by Bob Haldeman, John Ehrlichman and John Mitchell: "I will admit that acting as a lawyer for their defense, I was not prosecuting the case.... [T]o the extent that within the law, and in some cases going right to the edge of the law in trying to advise Ehrlichman and Haldeman and all the rest as to how best to present their cases, because I thought they were legally innocent, that I came to the edge."

But even though he didn't regard his actions as a cover-up and reiterated that to Frost, he made clear: "...[U]nder the circumstances, I would have to say a reasonable person could call that a cover-up.... I let down my friends. I let down the country. I let down our system of government and the dreams of all those young people that ought to get into government.... I let the American people down. And I have to carry that burden with me for the rest of my life."[7]

It was over, and Nixon and Frost were mobbed in the living room. Brennan, Price and I took turns shaking Frost's hand, and Diane Sawyer kissed him on the cheek. Birt and Zelnick warmly shook the Old Man's hand. Frost departed for his chilled bottles of Pouilly-Fuissé and bowl of Cuban cigars in his Beverly Hilton suite. We adjourned to the temporary government buildings of the former Western White House, where Nixon would seek our views.

Dick Moore, Diane Sawyer, and I walked in as he sat with his feet propped up on the beat-up ottoman. We barely sat down when he shot a look at Sawyer: "Well, you got your *mea culpa*, Diane."

There was a sting in the good-natured jab, so I tried to turn it aside with a mixture of deserved respect and staff sycophancy: "It wasn't a *mea culpa*, Mr. President, it was done with great integrity."

Then, turning to Diane again, he used some impressive name-dropping to offer up one of his classic aphorisms of political life. "I remember talking once with Willy Brandt [former West German chancellor] about their *Ostpolitik* policy of the time. I said: 'Never try to win people who are against you. You don't win friends you don't have by losing the friends you do have.'"

He ended this day of emotional turmoil by questioning himself as he opened the lobby door to walk home. "Well, I violated my own instincts. I hope it wasn't a mistake. I probably shouldn't have. But I did. It's all passed now."

Nixon was already anticipating criticism when the interviews aired. "Oh, I know they always want to cut me up. But, you know, they should just really ignore me. If they want to see me go away, they should ignore me. They should do what the Russians do and the Chinese do when they want to get rid of someone—they make him a nonperson. The press makes the mistake of not leaving me alone, and they really keep me in the news."

On opening night, Meredith and I hosted a "viewing party," and when RN called the house, Jack teased him and said he was "shitty."

Without laughing, Nixon asked, "What does Ken think?" We both laughed, and reassured him that he did great, and we were proud.

Then he assumed a familiar fatalistic position: "There's nothing we can do about it now. Watergate is there; so be it. It's the reason we're sitting here."

But the Old Man summed up the Frost interviews better than any of us could. "The whole thing turned out about fifty percent better than we thought, and sure a hell of a lot better than we had a right to expect it to be. If we didn't do this thing, I'd be dead as Kelsey's nuts. But at least this gives us life or keeps us alive. I'm not just going to go away like a lot of them would like me to."

Chapter 4

COACH NIXON

It was back to work on the memoirs interspersed with chatter about the 1980 presidential election. John Connally was RN's flavor of the week because "he's tough and smart." We also regularly discussed Reagan. He admired Reagan for having a flexible and far-reaching mind, yet felt his weakness was that he "was just not a student." Those appeared to be contradictory views, but Nixon measured Reagan against his own work habits. While Nixon's idea of a relaxing weekend afternoon would be meeting with the British foreign secretary; Reagan's was cutting brush on the Santa Barbara ranch. He also didn't forget Reagan's support during the rocky years of Vietnam and Watergate turmoil and made a point of telling me, "I intend to treat Reagan generously in the book. He was a stand-up guy in those years." I made special note when he said, "Ford's not like Reagan. Reagan can write his own speeches. Ford can't. Ford told me once he simply can't write."

The manuscript was delivered in March of 1978, and we both understood I needed to look ahead. Nixon had his own ideas about my future, and in September, he laid it out: "Ken, I think you could go to work for Reagan. I don't want you to wait too long and miss the boat in working for some of the campaigns. I don't think you should go in as a writer. [Ha!] Go in as the issues man and oversee the news summary." He laid on some flattery—that I had picked up a substantial education in foreign policy working for him.

Nixon wanted to cement ties with the Reagan operation, and one way was through meetings with his former staff member, Lyn Nofziger. Lyn was a consultant to the Reagan for President campaign and an entertaining visitor full of political gossip. Offering to give "discreet advice to Reagan" through Nofziger was the Old Man's way of getting his foot in that camp.

There was one message he wanted Nofziger to get to Reagan. "Ken, Lyn needs to tell him he would be well-advised to tone down his quips—they make him not appear to be a serious man. Maybe one opening gag; that's enough and goes one hell of a long way." Nixon measured Reagan against himself—like when he said Reagan was "not a student." He grew to appreciate all of Reagan's communicating techniques, and while it wasn't Nixon's style to crack two or three jokes, it was very much Reagan's. RN was great at telling political stories, and Reagan's forte was spinning tales and telling jokes. Two different ways of effective communication.

Nixon's riffs on Reagan sounded just like a campaign manager advising his candidate to avoid mistakes and win over voters. When he was caustic, blunt, and tough in his assessments, I viewed him as "Coach Nixon." Those who weren't close to Nixon were prone to dismiss his candid appraisals as ungracious. That's not the way I looked at it. Instead, I viewed his observations as grooming a star athlete for national competition. As coaches push and prod to bring out the best in their athletes, "Coach Nixon" saw raw talent in Reagan and was frustrated when it wasn't released to its highest level.

With the 1980 presidential election approaching, Nixon began gaming out Reagan's potential running mates. He especially liked Indiana's young senator, Richard Lugar. "He's the smartest of the bunch, Ken. Well-educated and smart. He's a real sleeper. Reagan would be wise to pick him. Of course, the best ticket—the one that won't happen because they won't pick each other—is Reagan and Connally. They would have won in '76." He claimed that Ford would have won with Reagan or Connally on his ticket in '76. Nixon also said, "Dole won't work for Reagan, *and Bush won't*." The latter confirms that not every political prediction is a bullseye.

JUNE 2, 1979

I began a new career as a public affairs consultant with my first two clients: Richard Nixon and the Reagan for President campaign. I worked out of Nixon's office in the mornings and the remainder at home. Martin Anderson arranged my gig with Reagan, and I scheduled meetings with him and Lyn Nofziger and also initiated contact with Jim Lake, who began to play a key role. Lake was a fellow San Joaquin Valley native I knew when he served as Congressman Bob Mathias's chief of staff.

The most important introduction Nixon made for me was Stuart K. Spencer, who had plenty of political and business contacts. In the summer of 1979, Spencer may not have been my best avenue into Reagan's operation. Though he oversaw Reagan's winning campaigns for governor in 1966 and 1970, Stu defected to Ford in 1976 and used hardball tactics against Reagan. His apostasy caused a breach that put him in the doghouse with Ron and Nancy.

My May 1, 1979, desk calendar reads: "Call Stu Spencer." It turned out to be one of my single most important phone calls. When I showed up at Stu's Newport Beach office to get acquainted, I found a rumpled fellow who reminded me of a grown-up Spanky from *Our Gang* comedies—hardly a presidential kingmaker. Stu had his feet up on his desk reading the political newsletter, *CalPeek*. He tossed it in his outbox and said, "So, what the hell does Dick Nixon want me to do?" I wasn't accustomed to local operatives being irreverent about the Old Man, but after a few minutes of political palaver, we found many things in common. Mainly, I had the good sense to listen while he spun political tales with a combination of profanity and laughter. We agreed to stay in touch, and he would be on the lookout for opportunities.

Back at the Reagan for President committee, Marty Anderson gave me my first shot at drafting a speech for Reagan. Marty had a draft for the National Federation of Independent Businessmen that he thought was "a little brittle and lacking presidential tone." Under a tight deadline, I turned out fifteen pages. Reading it forty years later, I think that in place of "brittle," I delivered "florid," and it was probably why I never heard back.

Around the same time, *Esquire Magazine*'s respected national editor Richard Reeves lent acidity to Nixon's warnings about Reagan's age. "His rearview-mirror vision of America is Reagan's great flaw in 1980," Reeves wrote. "He seems to have calcified since 1976 when he did have a lot to say. But that is not the only one of his problems. Others are his age, a divided, divisive staff, laziness, and the minor inconvenience of front running."[8]

Was I on the wrong team?

I got another shot at writing for Reagan when I was asked to send in suggested remarks before the New Hampshire Brotherhood of Christians and Jews. This time, Marty called back. "Hey, it was a beautiful speech, and Reagan liked it." He went on with a litany of politically upbeat information about overflow crowds in South Dakota and Missouri. Moreover, the

Southern Political Report was still showing Reagan ahead of John Connally by margins of three to two in key locations. Take that, Richard Reeves.

JULY 10

Nixon surprised me with the announcement he was moving to New York. He had time on his hands and needed to be more engaged in the intellectual and political life of America. New York would be closer to "the action" and a more convenient geography for receiving visitors.

We reviewed the upcoming election and his focus on Reagan and Connally. While his fondness for Connally was unabated, he saw Reagan more firmly in control of the path to the nomination than at any other time since the season started. "Too bad Connally and Reagan don't get along better. That would be a hell of a ticket. Reagan likes Connally okay, but Connally doesn't think much of Reagan. Wouldn't that be a ticket! You know, Ken, Reagan doesn't like to hit hard in his speeches. People think that because he's a conservative and is strong on national defense that he's aggressive. He's not. Connally is."

Nixon admired Reagan, but he thought he lacked Connally's outward toughness. Connally's grasp of politics was visceral while Reagan's was visual and philosophical. He worried that because of Reagan's perceived reticence, Ted Kennedy could beat him in a general election through a combination of meanness and unrelenting drive—in Nixon's words, "because Reagan can't attack." Nixon's memories of Jack and Bobby Kennedy in 1960 were of how ruthless and conniving they were—not only to him but to Hubert Humphrey as well. He added, "You know, if Teddy runs, they will say he has 'grown' through Chappaquiddick and that he's now ready for the presidency."

Coach Nixon advised that Reagan should use the summer to "do very little, stay well and give three speeches"—on energy, inflation and foreign policy. He again expressed concern about Reagan's age. "If only he was just three years younger—you know, it's that seventy-year-old mark that is the sort of magic number." I reminded him that Reagan was in good condition and life spans were growing. Nixon slapped his knee and laughed: "He's a physical fitness nut, and even rides horses all the time! That's right; it's no big thing to be three score and ten anymore."

Spencer and I met again for breakfast, and he was curious about my progress with his old Reagan pals. I told him about attending briefings led by folks from the Heritage Foundation. "That's good. Keep in contact with the eggheads; they'll need you down the line." He chuckled when I shared some of Nixon's views on the relative strengths of Reagan and Connally. "That sounds like Nixon. He likes guys who can throw a punch, but he should never sell Reagan short. He'll step up when he needs to." Stu noted that from time to time he was asked to give a speech and didn't like to write, so maybe I could help for a modest fee. I agreed instantly.

Nixon asked me about the state of my consulting practice, mainly to nose around about Reagan. He was impatient for the race to be reduced to Reagan and Connally and for the others to drop out—especially George Bush. "He's not even serious. He can't possibly win; he's a nice man. He should just get out before he gets hurt."

To ensure I stayed on the Reagan campaign's radar screen, I sent in memos and advice from time to time. One memo to Marty and John Sears proved my shortcomings as a political economist. I argued, "The tax cut issue is not only unlikely to win converts to the cause, it may also go the other way, scaring off voters in large numbers by sowing confusion over the governor's economic policies." Worse yet, I warned that Reagan's embrace of the Kemp-Roth tax cuts would be a political lapse allowing his opposition to saddle him with a campaign blunder akin to the $90 billion budget cut he offered in his '76 campaign. Within days, Marty called to say, "Here's some advice, Ken. Don't waste your time trying to talk Reagan out of embracing tax cuts."

I still had much to learn about Reagan, and becoming a supply-side convert would arrive only after spending personal time with Reagan.

The day Reagan announced his candidacy for president, November 13, 1979, Marty Anderson called to give me my first real important assignment, a basic paper on agricultural policy to be worded in the first person. That really sounded more like a speech to me, with a first draft needed in early December. Marty also touted Reagan's announcement speech and how much I would admire his "North American Accord."

The next morning, Nixon called and pounced, "You're lucky you didn't have anything to do with that speech last night! I can't believe in a presidential announcement speech he would talk about a 'North American Accord' with Mexico and Canada. There was no fire in it." Nixon was disappointed that Reagan's "handlers" were trying to tone Reagan down, "trying to make him look statesmanlike. On the plus side, he looked good, and that's important. But the speech was a dud, and he needs better material."

Then and later Nixon never failed to make clear to me that Reagan could fall short with his words, but his appearance—looking good—would prevail in his favor.

JANUARY 2, 1980

Reagan's campaign began three days of policy briefings to prepare him for the upcoming primaries. I was invited to join a group of about two dozen policy advisers and staff, and finally achieved face time with the candidate. In those three days of meetings held near Los Angeles International Airport, I absorbed valuable observations about Reagan that informed our future relationship.

He walked in wearing a dark green plaid sport coat and maroon tie. It was a garish-looking outfit only Reagan could pull off. If he lit up a Lucky Strike, you could have dropped him into a 1951 *Life Magazine* ad.[i]

The meeting opened with a briefing on polls by Richard Wirthlin. Dick Wirthlin was a Berkeley PhD with a bent for statistics who worked with Reagan on his previous presidential efforts. Dick's data showed President Carter did not yet have great vulnerability over the Iranian hostage crisis due to public support. Concern over inflation was growing, so the economy would be a serious issue, and foreign affairs would loom larger in 1980 than previously believed.

The room was very hot, and several participants smoked—including campaign manager John Sears, sitting next to Reagan. My first impression was to question Reagan's interest as he yawned frequently while peering over his half glasses at his notes.

Next on the agenda was my briefing on agriculture, followed by Richard Whalen's analysis on the energy outlook. Dick Whalen was a cerebral talent and serious observer of the American scene and international affairs, best known for his bestselling book, *The Founding Father*, about

---

i   Stu Spencer tells the story about a suit Reagan wore in 1965 while campaigning for governor. He had a date in his suits regarding the year he bought them. That suit said "1952." As president, Reagan was wearing another old sport coat when reporters Al Hunt and Judy Woodruff came into the office to show off their new baby. The infant was about to throw up on Reagan, and Nancy said: "I wished she puked on it; I hate that coat!" This comes from a telephone conversation with Stu Spencer, June 15, 2015.

JFK's dad, Joseph P. Kennedy. Between the two of us, we added to Reagan's inclination to yawn the remainder of the day. People who witnessed Reagan in this setting believed he was lazy and bored. But I discovered later that he absorbed information more readily through anecdote, illustration, and example rather than words and charts—a lesson his staff failed to learn in preparing him for debates.

The second day included foreign policy and national security briefings led by Dick Allen, on leave from the Hoover Institution. After Dick's comprehensive *tour d'horizon* of the foreign and defense scene, Reagan spoke for the first time with an eloquent overview of world issues and a concise summary of Allen's presentation. He had conspicuous contempt for Carter's weakness in not pushing back against Soviet hemispheric influence.

"You can take Carter; he accepted the status quo with Cuba, even though he said he wouldn't. He should have said to the Russians, 'No more trade discussions until you pull your combat military brigade out of Cuba.'" Soon, Reagan retreated to Hollywood storytelling and his accounts of leadership of the Screen Actors Guild in the '40s and '50s. He really had our attention, regaling us with how the communists operated in the movie studios and the violence they committed: "If they weren't communists by name, they operated through communist front organizations." Reagan was living up to his reputation as gifted storyteller, but I'm not sure it's the one his policy people were anxious to promote that day. Still, it was a welcome break from the wonkery.

The third day of briefings centered on the economy. Congressman Jack Kemp promoted his tax cut bill, followed by historical analysis from journalist Jude Wanniski, coiner of the term "supply-side economics." It was capped by an animated discussion of supply-side economics by a young USC economics professor, Art Laffer, who punched holes in conventional economic theory, which held that when you expand money supply, inflation goes up, and when you contract it, inflation goes down.

Throughout the discussions, John Sears or Ed Meese sat on Reagan's side and frequently interrupted the presenters as well as Reagan to explain to him what he was hearing and treating him as some untutored schoolboy with limited capacity to learn, like he couldn't be trusted to absorb the information on his own. It was not the first time that I would observe his staff underestimate Reagan. That included me until I learned the difference between inattention and impatience. Each of those three briefing days added to my education and understanding of Reagan—offering first-hand exposure that complemented Nixon's tutoring by proxy.

I completed the draft of Reagan's proposed agricultural policy speech for delivery in Waterloo, Iowa, and passed it along to Marty Anderson. I sent a sycophantic cover note congratulating Reagan's editing on my first draft as "displaying a seasoned and skilled editorial hand that your speechwriters envy!" Since this was my first serious "scripting" experience for the leading man, I was eager for positive feedback. The governor let me down easy in a cover note to Anderson:

> *Marty—I decided just to totally re-write so our friend Khachigian could get an idea of my way of saying it. Here is his draft, & mine. Incidentally I'm grateful to him. It sure is easier for me than starting from scratch.*
>
> *Ron*

Oh well.

Chapter 5

BREAKTHROUGH

With fifty-two American hostages in Iran, mortgage rates at 12 percent, and Soviet troops roaming in Afghanistan, it was hard to imagine bungling a campaign against Jimmy Carter's ineptitude. But when Ronald Reagan launched his White House bid, he appeared to be trying.

His rocky entry fueled accusations he was a shoot-from-the-hip cowboy toying with language and facts. He appeared to favor sending direct aid to Afghan forces by "funneling" weapons through Pakistan[9] and also suggested he might be prepared to blockade Cuba to punish Soviet armed intervention in Afghanistan.[10] With dissension over campaign leadership, Reagan fired John Sears, Jim Lake, and Charles Black on the same day he crushed George Bush in the New Hampshire primary—a shocking change that also removed Lake as my friendly insider.

The *Los Angeles Times* spotlighted Reagan's gubernatorial record as one where "many of the statistics Reagan uses are incorrect, others tell only one side of the story."[11] All these early stutter steps recalled Nixon's warning that "nobody can beat Reagan; he can only defeat himself." Nevertheless, I continued writing memoranda to Ed Meese and stayed in touch with Marty Anderson who encouraged me to keep sending memos.

That didn't put bread on my table or offer a role in the campaign.

Stu Spencer also stayed in touch by asking to see my handiwork on Reagan's Iowa speech and inviting me to his coveted political insiders' Christmas party. For a few hundred bucks, I later helped Stu with a professional touch-up on one of his speeches, and when we met, he offered valuable insight into Reagan's campaign operation: "Reagan's being handled by a bunch of damn amateurs who don't know their ass from first base. They need someone to take charge who knows Ron and Mommy and brings operational control onto the road show. Until that happens, he'll make mistakes."

One confirmation of the operational malfunction and disarray came from Jim Perry's long analysis in the *Wall Street Journal*, which observed, "Critics of the Reagan staff say there isn't much of a campaign yet…More than 100 advisers, working on some 22 task forces, are struggling to come up with positions for Mr. Reagan."[12]

And I didn't see a role for me.

JULY 15, 1980

I worked in my garage, dejected at missing two straight GOP conventions, while listening to Jack Kemp's stunning speech preaching lower taxes, economic growth, hope, and freedom. Two days later, I watched Reagan's acceptance speech—especially drawn by his call to "recapture our destiny, to take it in our own hands." Using Thomas Paine's "We have it in our power to begin the world over again" was an apt metaphor against the Carter era's smallness. Once again, Nixon was right; it was not just Reagan's words, but the way he spoke, his mien, and the reassurance in his voice.

Nixon called immediately after the convention to talk about the con-trived melodrama of a possible Reagan-Ford "dream ticket" combining as a political *force majeure*. Kissinger played a prominent role in negotiations to create what amounted to a "co-presidency," with Kissinger returning in a vastly prominent role. In the aftermath, Ford, his political team, and Kissinger drew heat from the political Right for game-playing.

Nixon reported that "Henry" had sought advice, "and I told him to 'shut up' and drop the issue, because Ford would come out looking the worst. This is a media thing, Ken. It's bullshit. Reagan should forget about it and build up Bush. Reagan looks like he stood up to Ford and Kissinger, and that makes him look strong." The Old Man counseled that Reagan would "damn well be advised to consult people who have experience. Bill Casey's a hell of a good man, but he's not up to the job." He predicted, "Reagan's only problems are big 'boo-boos' on the fact side or if he catches a cold—except for those, he's in." Catching a cold was another sharp refer-ence to Reagan's age.

The media exploited Reagan's verbal slips and pounced when he used the term "depression" regarding President Carter's economy—an overstate-ment that required quick correction.[13] Before the Veterans of Foreign Wars,

Reagan reopened wounds by claiming the Vietnam War "in truth, was a noble cause."[14] He stepped on his successful kickoff speech at the Statue of Liberty by ad-libbing that Carter was "opening his campaign...in the city that gave birth to and is the parent body of the Ku Klux Klan."[15]

Nixon accurately forecasted the "boo-boos," but along with the disjointed campaign, they worked to Stu Spencer's advantage, and, ultimately, to mine. Spencer and Mike Deaver watched the campaign launch from the outside. Though Deaver was like a son to the Reagans since gubernatorial days, he had been shunted aside before the primaries. He was the first to be brought back in to stop the hemorrhaging and restructure the campaign tour operation. Then, Deaver convinced the Reagans they also needed Spencer to end further organizational chaos and summoned him from his Newport Beach office with a simple message: "Ron and Nancy want you back."

Stu was surprised because of remaining rancor from '76 and wanted time to think about it. Then Nancy called and said, "We want you back."[16] Stu asked for a meeting and looked into Ron's eyes to make it clear: "We're going to do this the right way and run the campaign from the plane, and I'm going to bring in my own guys." Spencer had one core management belief: whoever controlled the body controlled the campaign. Stu wanted headquarters' phones cut off so Bill Casey, Dick Wirthlin, and Ed Meese couldn't end-run him. The Reagans had to agree to all of his terms. And they did.[17]

Casey, Meese, and Wirthlin must have missed the message and omitted Spencer from a key off-site senior staff meeting. Mrs. Reagan asked, "Where's Stu?" and discovered he was sitting at Arlington headquarters. Spencer observed that "Mommy" was the true "personnel director" of the campaign and that she'd proved it by ordering his inclusion in the meeting, and when Wirthlin phoned, Stu hung up. After that, Spencer set down stringent rules with Casey: "Everyone has to agree; I hire and fire and run it from the plane." Stu called it "payback time."[18]

Following Labor Day, Spencer struggled with the daily campaign organization and its awkward coordination with the headquarters. Since Stu was empowered to "run the campaign from the plane," he felt he needed certain indispensable bodies on board: one for scheduling, one for policy, one to handle press, and, finally, a speechwriter. He brought in an old friend, Joe Canzeri, to work the schedule and was happy with Marty Anderson overseeing policy. Because James Brady had gained experience as Connally's spokesman, Stu liked Jim for media relations and—also—Brady was "one hell of a bullshit artist with reach into federal departments."

But he didn't have a speechwriter, and long speeches were being faxed from Arlington to the plane each night with no one to hone them into punchy campaign prose. Reagan was forced to do his own editing under time constraints. Moreover, Spencer, Anderson, Brady, Deaver, and Lyn Nofziger had no one with whom to interact on daily messages to drive the daily news cycle.

On September 23, I returned from lunch and quickly returned a phone call from Ed Meese. "We want you to be on the plane to assist the governor with speeches. I'm sorry we haven't been able to bring you on earlier, but there was a logjam on finances, and we just broke through, and we will accommodate you." That wasn't the real reason, but I didn't care.

Ironically, for more than a year, I pitched myself as a research director and was a little gun-shy about writing speeches for Reagan. Meese continued, "Keep in mind regarding your clients that Reagan could call them on your behalf. I mean he'll call them personally to help your transition." I told him that wouldn't be necessary. He talked about writing speech inserts under pressure and asked if I could begin the following Monday with the 3:00 p.m. baggage call at the LAX Airport Hyatt.

I called Nixon to report. "Don't hesitate five seconds. I can furnish you things, stuff that can be used in the campaign." I knew the Old Man viewed me as a source to provide Reagan information, and I was more than happy to count on his input. He reiterated his lessons from the previous five years: "Reagan's speaking style is his great advantage. Don't make it appear he's a packaged candidate; use excerpts, not set speeches." He concluded with personal advice that I followed in the campaign and into the White House: "Don't be an errand boy. Be damned assertive. Be sure you have access to Reagan."

Meese's offer was the result of Nixon's advice to me to touch base with Stu Spencer. Years later, I asked Stu why he chose me to be the campaign's speechwriter. "Well, you came into my office one day when you were working with Nixon. You said you were looking to move on, and that Nixon told you to come to see me. I respected Nixon's judgment on political guys. I didn't think Nixon was sending a guy who was an asshole."[19]

Chapter 6

OCTOBER BLAHS

The day before I met up at LAX with Reagan's campaign charter, I visited my good friend Buck Johns, who handed me a mini-cassette recorder along with a dozen blank tapes. Buck asked me to record what I saw on the campaign trail and return the completed tapes during any swing through California, so he and a half dozen cronies could amuse themselves over beers at a local watering hole.

I tried to make tapes each night, or soon thereafter, while my memory was still fresh. The nearly thirty-five thousand words of resulting journals provide the first-hand source material for the following six chapters. Of all the books that cover Reagan's historic 1980 landslide victory, mine is the only one to benefit from contemporaneous observations and an author with a principal role in shaping winning messages and participating in many key campaign decisions at strategic turning points as a senior member of Reagan's campaign staff. Outside of those barflies who listened to fewer than half of these tapes, the contents of the diaries have never been shared and allow me to share unique detail, color, and authenticity provided by the types of observations as seen only through an insider's eyes. These six chapters are not meant to represent an authoritative account of the 1980 presidential campaign. What they offer, among other things, are a peek into the campaign staff, some of our key decision-making, the pressures under which we operated, and insight into the growth of my personal relationship with the man who, in five weeks, would vanquish an incumbent president.

"[T]he World Series is different. Because the entire nation focuses its attention so intensively, it is the venue where one play in one game, and one play by a player often otherwise uncelebrated, so holds our collective attention that it has its own permanence, and it becomes the defining image of the player."

That was a moment in baseball history as described by journalist David Halberstam. It was the seventh game of the 1946 World Series when Boston Red Sox's Johnny Pesky hesitated on a relay throw from centerfield to allow the St. Louis Cardinals' Enos Slaughter to reach home from first on a single with what turned out to be the winning run and a series victory for the Cards.[20]

Such intense focus perfectly describes the final weeks and days of contested presidential elections. The analogy to our long baseball season is also compelling. Candidates survive a long "spring training" primary season, nominating convention, and "opening day" on Labor Day. Their pursuit comes down to the final weeks, final days, and final hours. America's passion becomes absorbed—our "collective attention" held—upon individuals whose raw hunger to lead the nation and free world has driven them to undergo the scrutiny of a vast telephoto lens that homes in on every slip, error, hesitation, "dropped ball" and, occasionally, a triumph.

With few open slots on Reagan's team, I was a critical-position player. The phone call Spencer exacted out of Meese served up an unexpected and intoxicating opportunity for one who consumed and loved national politics. Just like the major leagues, this was "The Show." A week earlier, I was consigned to watching Reagan's speeches in my den. Now I would be writing them.

Stu Spencer welcomed me aboard *LeaderShip 80* to make sure I understood where I fit into his complement of operatives. With me as his traveling speechwriter, his team was finally complete and totally independent of campaign headquarters—or, as he later said: "For 90 days, we ran the campaign from the plane."[21] Lyn Nofziger was another familiar face on board and came over to say hello. We overlapped for about a year in Nixon's White House where Lyn worked on congressional relations. I sat on the aisle, with Martin Anderson as my seatmate through Election Day. Marty was more than a longtime friend and colleague, but also a gifted issues analyst and economist with sound political instincts. Sitting across from me as onsite researcher to verify data and policy arcana was Kevin Hopkins, who alternated each week with Doug Bandow.

The Falstaffian fellow across the table extended a broad smile and a pledge of working closely. Jim Brady had been with Connally in the primaries and earned his assignment through excellent rapport with the traveling press. Jim loved to talk, eat, and drink expensive wine, and, symbiotically, the press loved to pry campaign tidbits over dinners financed by expense accounts. The *Washington Star*'s Lisa Myers enriched her campaign coverage by whispering to Brady that she had a vintage bottle of wine at her disposal if he would join her for sumptuous dining and background conversation. Jim's wicked wit deflated pompous political overreach and kept us howling through long plane rides. He gave everyone a nickname, and mine was "Menian," a shortened version of my ethnic origins.

I was immediately confronted with the campaign's cumbersome process for preparing speeches that bogged down Reagan's message penetration. While only slightly overstated, a dour analysis in *U.S. News & World Report* claimed: "All evidence indicates that, only a month before the election, 15 to 20 percent of the voters are still undecided.... Some blame flagging voter enthusiasm on boredom with the long road to presidential nomination... By the time formal campaigning begins, voters are limp from months of unceasing political rhetoric."[22]

My initial observations confirmed that the Reagan operation was contributing to the latter.

An even more brutal assessment of the landscape was penned in *The New Republic* by moderate liberal columnist Morton Kondracke:

> [A]n interesting gathering took place at a Chinese restaurant in Washington on September 26. Ten of the country's wiser pollsters, political analysts, and reporters registered their gut feelings about how this election would turn out....Result: eight out of the 10 participants picked Carter to win....Had I been there, I think I would have done the same, based on the lackadaisical way Reagan had been campaigning, on Carter's incumbency advantages, and on the feeling that as late October fades into

November, people around the country will decide they just can't risk entrusting the country's future through the uncertain, complicated perils of the 1980s to a 69-year-old, hip-shooting, lightweight, right-wing, ex-movie actor.[23]

Exhibit A was my first assignment—editing a detailed and ponderous farm speech for delivery outside of Des Moines. I didn't have much time to work on it other than helping with a new paragraph on "parity" to repair a stumble Reagan made back in March. The Iowa remarks contained pages of boring agricultural boilerplate for this dusty three-hour round trip, so Reagan improvised from his storehouse of personal humor: "I was going to address farmers in Las Vegas, and a fellow said to me, 'What are a bunch of farmers doing in Las Vegas?' I said, 'Buster, they're in an occupation that makes a Las Vegas craps game look like guaranteed annual Income.'"[ii]

Reagan knew Iowa from his days as the sports voice of WHO Radio in Des Moines and helped rescue the day through identification with his local audience. Nevertheless, my first impression was of an undisciplined and disorganized campaign.

Our first week's relationship bore little resemblance to the way Reagan and I would bond by Election Day. Despite Nixon's insistence that I have access to Reagan and not be an errand boy, I made no effort to push for face time. He stood adjacent to me when rolling an orange down the aisle during each takeoff, but I didn't initiate conversation because those moments for him were agony as he avoided engagement. He often fended off interaction by using humor or telling stories. I observed in my diary:

> Of course, I've seen the candidate on the plane each day. The procedures are such that there is really no sense working directly with him, and that's not the way it works. We met the first day I came on the plane. I think, very frankly, he was just not sure he knew I was coming. He's genuinely a nice man.

I wouldn't describe his silence as being aloof or unpleasant; it seemed he was merely being inward. With strangers, it wasn't a matter of shyness, either. He didn't care to have unfamiliar faces share his space. For someone

---

ii   This and other quotes taken from Reagan's 1980 speeches, unless otherwise noted, are from campaign transcripts and press releases in the author's personal files.

who chose a life in entertainment and politics, my first impression viewed these as surprising traits. I would change my view as we came to know each other.

The Arlington headquarters command staff had a formula for sending Reagan new, protracted speeches that were long on policy and data, but short on political heft or sex appeal. The hierarchy had set an unwieldly process in place to select speech subjects for each event, approve their texts, transmit them to the plane, thrust them in front of the candidate, and rely on Reagan to organize them. Reagan had little time to make edits and, more importantly, less time to assess the political value or communications impact of his messages.

It violated the training I had working in White House communications and sitting at Nixon's knee, and validated Spencer's desire to control the campaign from the plane. After four days on the road, the *Los Angeles Times*' William Endicott accurately captured the scene in a headline: "Reagan Inspires Yawns as He Tries to Avoid Gaffes."

> For a man whose skill at political speechmaking has moved him within striking distance of the White House, Ronald Reagan has developed a peculiar problem in his campaign for the presidency over the last two weeks: his oratory has gotten humdrum. Crowds that once were moved to thunderous applause at his assaults on big government now sometimes stifle yawns as Reagan threads his way through carefully prepared and often humorless texts...His old stump speech has been replaced with set speeches...ground out by a committee of speechwriters, usually focused on a single theme and often geared for a particular part of the country.[24]

I became aware of the underlying causes of these obstacles when they surfaced in Lou Cannon's account of Reagan's 1980 campaign:

> [t]he Reagan campaign evolved into a vast, multilayered bureaucracy headquartered in Arlington and beset by the myriad conflicts attendant to such enterprises. The

Reagan campaign was particularly susceptible to layering because Casey's title of campaign director was largely a fiction. He knew a great deal about organization but very little about the technical requirements of a political campaign, which meant that he had to rely on others for decisions that could have been quickly made by an experienced political professional.[25]

I cornered Stu Spencer to complain that the current system would kill any creativity from the campaign speechwriting operation—and from me in particular. The current remarks weren't very crowd-pleasing, their drawn-out length was unnecessary, and reform was essential. I pleaded for a standard stump speech, supplemented by campaign inserts that (a) spoke to the local constituency, and (b) keyed off the daily news cycle to cater to the media's need for lead stories and sound bites. He and Mike Deaver instantly agreed and delegated Lyn Nofziger to call a meeting to structure the new system.

But now, thirty days before the election, there was extraordinary confusion over how information involving each event would get to the speechwriters at headquarters. Worse, communications on the plane weren't satisfactory. My colleague from the Nixon White House, Bill Gavin, would help with speeches in Arlington, along with another talented writer, John McClaughry. There were good people and a large support unit in Washington whose skills weren't sufficiently used, and I worked to change that. With four weeks to go, my challenge was to try to structure a semblance of organized messaging that would match the day-to-day intensity and pressures that we would face to win the minds of American voters and overcome the advantages the Carter White House had of a team that had worked seamlessly together for four years with a sophisticated communications systems at its disposal.

LeaderShip 80 was my principal working environment—where an IBM Correcting Selectric Typewriter rested on a table directly behind me. I drafted new material in flight as well as when the plane was plugged into power on the ground. Each overnight hotel had excellent staff offices with good working facilities, but they also lacked privacy since that's where staff gathered to unwind, exchange campaign gossip, and infrequently engage in productive work amid the din from typewriters, phones, copiers and the 1980 version of fax machines. I convinced the advance teams to place a typewriter in my bedroom—the only location I could rely on for the solitude I needed for working on longer speeches.

Reagan's most politically impactful words didn't come from hours of planning and careful creative composition; they were stitched together in the back of the Boeing 727. They were written in between stops, under deadline to sate the insatiable—the media's appetite for sound bites and news leads based on whatever was freshest in the news cycle. As autumn leaves turned, the rhetoric that tortured Jimmy Carter was conceived at the aircraft's worktable—sometimes sprung from roundtable discussions with Marty Anderson, Jim Brady, and our two research aides as products of devilish communal political scheming.

Often, the burden rested on me—the Word Donkey—to come up with provocative language to highlight issues cutting up Carter. My imprimatur was to make national and regional news while turning out Reagan's base and disaffected Democrats. At the same time, we worked to satisfy another rule of political campaigns: if we were having a bad day, it was imperative to change the subject.

Reagan's first week in October wasn't a total disaster because those long boring speeches also included information that magnified the calamity of Carter's reign. Two million people were tossed out of work in 1980, and mortgage interest rates were on a roller coaster, averaging 12 percent, and in some places approaching 16 percent. Carter's mishandling of the economy deflected attention from efforts to paint Reagan as risky in foreign and defense matters.

I worried to my diary "that our strategies in going after the blue-collar ethnic, Catholic, standard Democratic constituency is not necessarily going to work, and Carter will begin a push very shortly to draw them back into his fold, branding Reagan more and more anti-labor and as being a threat to peace. If we lose those voters we spent so much time going after, what do we have left?" Thus, in a late-night rumination, I continued by introducing my early view that Reagan should debate: "My argument would be to go for a higher risk, twenty-nine days out here, and go for the debates, one-on-one with Carter—which I think Reagan would do very well in."

The first day back from Arlington tested our new system of producing material on the road and under time pressure. The previous Friday, the

Bureau of Labor Statistics released the producer price index, and we issued a pretty tough statement that worked well, so we considered using it again as we set out for Cherry Hill, New Jersey. Alan Greenspan phoned Marty and me with cautions about being strident. As it turned out, Alan was overly guarded. Here's my diary description:

> So, with about ten minutes leeway, I had to pump out a new version of that statement and under the quick time pressure, put a different twist on it. Charged Carter with using the imperial incumbency in that he 'sugarcoated' economic news. It was a 'cruel hoax,' and all those lines got picked up—including the lead line, which was Marty Anderson's idea, that the numbers had been 'Jimmied.' The story led CBS on the network and on NBC. I would say we drove Carter nuts today because we totally discredited what he thought was good news and put the focus back on inflation, and Jimmy Carter back on the defense.

The other big news item on October 6 was that Nancy Reagan rejoined the campaign after a week's absence, and she, instead of Governor Reagan, rolled the orange down the aisle. Now, the whole family was back together, and she would become an important observer and participant in my efforts.

Carter's presidency was stumbling with an energy crisis and the economy in collapse. Instead of showing strength, Carter did the opposite by lecturing Americans in the summer of '79 that our country suffered "a crisis of confidence…a crisis that strikes at the very heart and soul and spirit of our national will. We can see this crisis in the growing doubt about the meaning of our own lives and in the loss of a unity of purpose for our nation." While he never mentioned the word "malaise," the speech bespoke that term, and thus it was labeled. His weakness magnified when Iranian mobs devastated our national image by invading the US embassy in Teheran to hold fifty-two Americans hostage for what would turn out to be more than a year. It worsened when the US military failed in a secret rescue attempt that cost the lives of eight American servicemen.

That political terrain offered Reagan ample canvas on which to sketch his portrait of change when he first decided to declare for the presidency and to welcome citizens in his 1980 GOP acceptance speech "into a great national crusade to make America great again." Reagan repeated the phrase in two subsequent national GOP convention speeches, and Donald Trump recognized the penetrating strength of the Gipper's communication and co-opted the words into the very definition of his political persona.

With four weeks left, my hope was to release Reagan from the tightly scripted, policy-wonkish, sleep-inducing messages mandated by Arlington's bureaucracy and unleash a leader to convey messages representing everything that Carter was not. I took direct aim at Carter's economic record with the insert of a small gem into Reagan's Langhorne, Pennsylvania, remarks on October 7: "Look around you—at the price of food, the price of gasoline, the interest rates you have to pay to buy a house, the amount of taxes taken out of your paycheck. Look around, then ask yourself: *are you really better off than you were in 1976?*"

That meme resonated in Langhorne and was initially overlooked in the uproar over Carter's meanness attacks. Reagan repeated it in subsequent speeches, and with even greater effect three weeks later when he debated Carter. When I unleashed that line at the Oxford Mall in Langhorne, PA, I never dreamed it would serve as Reagan's defining message in 1980 and resonate for decades as a gold standard in political rhetoric.

Despite Carter's bumbling, Reagan had to defend against his own potential negatives. He was painted as dangerously hawkish on foreign and defense policy and placing the economy at risk with exotic fiscal and tax plans. After the Langhorne speech, I hoped to switch the pressure back to Carter with a memo to Reagan that we address unemployed steelworkers in Steubenville, Ohio on the double whammy of unemployment and inflation.

Instead, Reagan began rambling off-message with uneven views regarding air pollution that were captured by pool reporters Pat Sloyan and Jack Nelson:

> I have flown twice over Mount St. Helens out on our west coast...but I just have a suspicion that one little mountain out there in these last several months has probably released more sulfur dioxide into the atmosphere than has been released in the last ten years of automobile driving or things of that kind that people are so concerned about.... Growing and decaying vegetation in this land are responsible for 93 percent of the oxides of nitrogen.... That's

where the Great Smoky Mountains get their names; that haze over those mountains are oxides of nitrogen.[26]

"Are you better off than you were in 1976?" was such a great message, but it got lost in the chaos and din of the governor's garbled factoids on air pollution.

The damage multiplied a day and a half later in Birmingham, Alabama, when reporters mobbed him at planeside to probe for changes in positions he had taken before local audiences. They started with labor issues, and Reagan appeared to parry them adequately with recitations of past speeches, but the ground quickly shifted, and his air pollution monologue turned into a teaser. He was asked whether current smog problems in Los Angeles contradicted his day-earlier statement in Youngstown that pollution was under control. Heading to his car, Reagan denied saying it was substantially under control and claimed he established "the strongest air pollution acts" as California Governor.[27]

However, the blood was in the water—a scene brutally captured in Bruce Drake's and Doug Brew's contemporaneous pool report at Reagan's next campaign appearance:

> [T]he earlier grillings of the O&W[iii] were merely a pale shadow of the interrogation to which the candidate was subjected by fellow scribe, Diane Curtis. "'Didn't you say air pollution was substantially under control?" "I don't think I've said anything of the kind," Reagan responded. This drove Curtis to greater interrogatory heights. "Do you not read your statements?" she asked. Reagan said, "I said that the energy sources could be controlled within the terms of the Clean Air Act, that we could use sources of energy they're not using." Question: "But you said it was substantially under control, does that mean you don't read your own statements?" Reagan: "I think that the Clean Air Act has done a great deal for this country. Isn't it substantially under control? I think it is, yes."[28]

---

iii New York Congressman, Jack Kemp, once commenting on Reagan's age said that while Reagan might be the oldest candidate, he is the "oldest and wisest." The media following Reagan adopted that nickname and soon shortened it to the "O&W." Many of us on the staff, led by Jim Brady's irreverence, adopted it as well.

Reagan's excursions into hyperbole and unpreparedness reduced the effect of our attacks on Carter for his mouthy insults and divisive attacks. We veered off the paved path, and both the print and electronic media switched coverage and diverted attention to the environmental haze Reagan offered up. It was the perfect illustration of how in presidential campaigns the awkward courtship between a candidate and the traveling press corps can alternate between symbiotic and adversarial.

In the broad scheme of Reagan's economic message, it was "slippage," but the language and tone of the press pool betrayed the eagerness with which Ms. Curtis, as proxy for her colleagues, was looking to score a razor cut on Reagan and took pleasure in watching him squirm. Grillings, inter-rogations, and interrogatories are the jobs of prosecutors. That day, a nor-mally straight wire service reporter slipped out of the realm of objective inquiry into scoring adversarial points that gained her accolades of col-leagues—as clearly reflected in the tone of the press pool's write-up.

John Osborne was a courtly and sometimes crusty reporter for *The New Republic* who often drove the Nixon White House nuts. While in San Clemente and through this coverage of Reagan, we developed a mutually respectful relationship as we jousted with one another. He captured this campaign episode with the perspective it deserved:

> Some silly remarks about environmental pollution got Reagan in exchanges with reporters that effectively obscured his attempt at serious discussion of his economic aims on those particular days. He begged reporters to stop their 'nitpicking,' but of course they didn't.[29]

As the campaign proceeded, Spencer, Deaver, Nofziger, Brady, and I worked to provide information to the reporters—socializing with them, offering insight, tips, and information to make their jobs easier and to reflect well on the O&W. Their lives on the trail, like mine, weren't walks in the park. *Los Angeles Times* reporter Marlene Cimons observed accurately and sympathetically about life on the "traveling road show":

> In the midst of all this chaos, there are stories to be written. Most of the work takes place in-flight, where the steady clack-clack of portable typewriters is a routine accompa-niment to the roar of the engines. Reporters—fighting the

cold terror of impending daily deadlines—all cramped in their seats, typewriters on the fold-down trays in front of them, with no room to spread out notes and no wastebaskets for rejected first drafts. And, upon landing, they usually have only 10 or 15 minutes to phone in their stories.[30]

Focusing on Social Security and economic issues in Florida and the South, we headed to California while Reagan was faced at each stop with demonstrators supporting abortion rights and an Equal Rights Amendment to the Constitution. The pollution goof continued to dog Reagan, and with bad luck, heavy smog at Burbank Airport forced our flight to be diverted to Los Angeles International Airport. Cheeky young demonstrators piled on when Reagan arrived for a weekend event at Claremont College by nailing a large poster onto a tree: "Chop Me Down Before I Kill Again!" Even I had to chuckle at a smart-ass proposal by our impish reporter friends who suggested that Jimmy Carter could be locked in a room with a tree, and Reagan in a room with a running car—with bets on who would try to escape first.

With just over three weeks to go, the organization was steadier than when I arrived, but certainly couldn't boast of its ability to dominate the news cycle and stay ahead of impending crises. The weakness at this stage of the Reagan crusade was a bigger concern than we let on.

Chapter 7

A WOMAN SHAKES THINGS UP

OCTOBER 10, 1980

Reagan referred to Nancy Reagan as "Mommy," and with only twenty-five days before the vote, he wouldn't be wrong to think Mommy was the only woman who loved him.

Women's rights organizations continued their disruptions, and despite a friendly Orange County Leisure World crowd, rallies over the long weekend were scattered with hecklers. "Are you better off than you were in 1976?" resonated with the older folks, but the *Los Angeles Times* reported he was otherwise greeted by protesters who "shouted their opposing views on equal rights for women, Puerto Rican rights, nuclear war, and the former governor's latest comments on air pollution."[31]

Stu Spencer conceded, "I was going nuts. I couldn't sleep. We were on the defense with all those women groups and Reagan making nutty comments on pollution. I had to come up with something. We had to change what the damn reporters were writing about."[32] I skipped the weekend tour in favor of couple of nights at home and returned Monday night, October 13 before the next day's departure for Idaho. My diary takes it from here:

> I'd say it was around six o'clock p.m., but Stu Spencer dropped sort of a bombshell on me. I was sitting in the staff lounge by myself, reading the papers, when Stu came in and said: "Why don't you get a statement ready saying that one of the priorities of a Reagan government is support of women and the lack of discrimination. And, at the end, sort of add in there that for Supreme Court Justice, he appoints a woman."

Holy shit! *"Sort of add in there."* Stu's offhand tone made it sound as though we were only announcing additions to Idaho's Women for Reagan

Committee. He included instructions regarding Reagan's gubernatorial achievements on behalf of women and to ensure that any woman's appointment met the same qualifications and high standards as a man. Today, a woman on the US Supreme Court is routine, but in October 1980, this represented a dramatic departure for the highest court.

What follows is the only insider's play-by-play account of the process our campaign conducted before Reagan made his statement the following morning—one that eventually resulted in the appointment of Sandra Day O'Connor as the first female Supreme Court justice.

"Stu, wait, did anyone check this out with Meese?"

Spencer snapped at me, "Let somebody else worry about Meese. Look they're always doing things I don't agree with, and we need to do this." Stu operated on instinct and a motivation to win. He didn't give a rat's ass regarding the policy nerds or federal judiciary protocols or Ed Meese's views as Reagan's go-to legal adviser. He was looking for a headline to move numbers. The campaign was stalled in neutral; the polls weren't moving; and Reagan was on the defensive where it came to issues that could determine marginal votes among women. Reagan was greeted by masses of organized women's groups everywhere, and he wanted to neutralize them.

Stu told me his decision was based on a lesson learned from Richard Nixon: "Sometimes, when things aren't moving well, you need to do something totally off the wall." Stu had met with Reagan that morning at his Pacific Palisades home to review options for jump-starting the campaign and advised him this was one of those times for an "off the wall" play.[33] There was a part of me that felt cautious, although I also had a messaging rule that paralleled Stu's: When the news isn't going your way, change the subject. National polls showed Carter's lead among women only as slight, and the Supreme Court announcement may have helped, but Reagan's problems in early October were more pronounced when viewed in state-by-state breakdowns.

In the *New York Times*–CBS News poll, Reagan trailed among women 27 percent to 36 percent with 26 percent undecided. In Texas, he trailed 33 percent to 42 percent with 20 percent undecided. In Pennsylvania, it was 30 percent to 32 percent with 26 percent undecided. Similarly, polling by the *Washington Post* in eight key states showed Reagan leading 39 percent to 34 percent among men but behind 38 percent to 31 percent among women. The differences were starker in Carter's home state, Georgia. Atlanta pollster Claibourne Darden was showing Carter with 47.5 percent support among women to only 35.1 percent among men.[34] Reagan was perceived as riskier on issues of war and peace in addition to less friendly on other issues of consequence to activist women. Adding to our concern was the greater propensity of women to vote.

OCTOBER 13, 7:30 P.M.

I began writing the Supreme Court statement, and Spencer walked in to ask me how I was doing because everyone wanted to get their hands on my language. After completing my draft, I took it into Mike Deaver's room, where Mike was on the phone. Diary entry:

> Spencer was sitting slouched in the chair nursing a bad cold. He started reading it as well as did Lyn Nofziger. Stu thought it was exactly what the governor wanted, and Lyn did, too. Deaver had some reservations about the way it opened up, and with him we made some minor changes in the original copy, and Lyn edited it modestly, and then we took it to get typed up. I also expressed to Lyn my reservations about this. I said to him that the problem with this is that it is going to be treated like the Schweiker ploy in 1976, which was thought to be a gimmick.

With my caveat to Lyn, I crossed a boundary by questioning Spencer's political judgment, and Stu would be pissed. But I figured he hired me to exercise political judgment in addition to writing speeches, and I shouldn't stay silent if I saw potential trouble. Hence, I opened a fresh issue that generated several others on the staff to commit the announcement to more serious scrutiny—adding the following new intriguing details to Reagan's historic decision.

THE "SCHWEIKER PLOY"

Nixon and I discussed the "ploy" in 1976, when due to Reagan's lagging delegate count, he preannounced liberal Pennsylvania Senator Richard Schweiker as his prospective running mate. (See Chapter 2.) That, too, was a "totally off the wall" play, but not in a good way. Nixon's reaction to the "Schweiker Ploy" was that Reagan's decision would be viewed as pure opportunism, and it was. There was conservative outrage across the country with several prominent defections from Reagan: Governor Meldrim Thomson of New Hampshire said he not only would not give Reagan's nominating speech, but he also wouldn't go to the convention. Mississippi state chairman Clarke Reed, an early Reagan supporter, came out for Ford. And John Connally, whose political antennae the Old Man especially respected, flew to Washington the day after the Schweiker announcement to deliver his endorsement of Ford.

Preparing for the next day's presser, these four-year-old memories of the Old Man's disdain for staff folly were very much on my mind—"boys playing a man's game." The announcement's obvious political motivation made me concerned it would make people think of Reagan as unserious, that he wouldn't be fully prepared for his press conference, and in the words of my 1980 diary, "he could get clobbered." On the first point, Spencer had the right instincts because the constituency that craved a female on the Supreme Court (women and the media) overcame the mentality that trashed Reagan for the Schweiker move. On the second point, it turned out I didn't give Reagan enough credit for his agility in handling the press.

Nevertheless, I shared my concerns with Marty Anderson. "Marty, this could mess up the entire week if the governor isn't prepared for questioning on some of the technical materials that we've been putting out." I cautioned Marty about the kind of questioning there might be in connection with a Supreme Court justice and reminded him it could "look like the Schweiker thing." That struck a nerve. After all, it was Marty who left the phone message back on July 26, 1976, boasting what a bold maneuver Reagan made to put Schweiker on the ticket.

Later that evening, Marty reported that he had spoken to Ed Meese in DC, and Ed shared my concerns, but said that this was something "they" wanted to do—meaning the governor and Spencer. Resigned to the decision, I got up early on October 14 to finalize the statement. But based on my prodding of the night before and the specter of another Schweiker blowback, Marty had decided to oppose the decision a bit more strenuously and cited the risks to Ed Meese at Arlington headquarters, who began having similar reservations. I recorded the debate's details in my diary:

By this morning, they had decided to change the thrust of the statement to read, instead of the "first" Supreme Court vacancy would be a woman, that "one of the first" Supreme Court vacancies would be filled by a woman. Everything else would remain the same, and Stu Spencer was a bit upset at that, saying that we've got to take risks; that there is much to be gained, and we shouldn't hold back, in effect, with decisions like this. He thought it reflected timidity on part of a number of people. I was in Deaver's room as Anderson was raising the devil's advocate to points in objection to this problem. One of the big problems was whether or not the Chief Justice's seat would open up as the first one—whether he would appoint a woman to that. So, some of these problems were solved by making it one of the first appointments.

Reagan's press conference was scheduled for 9:15, and he and Mrs. Reagan arrived at the Travelodge where they were escorted to a holding room. Spencer and I were waiting for them, and Stu introduced me to Mrs. Reagan—the first opportunity she had to assess the new speechwriter. Reagan took out a pen to edit his opening statement, even as we began discussing how we would answer certain questions. Mostly, he carved it into segments of paragraphs and sentences, so he knew when to pause or where to make a break. This was my first close contact with the missus, so I took notice and observed in my diary that Nancy "also took a very active part sitting across the table from Stu and me."

I wrote the statement to offer a surprise gift in plain brown wrapping. The first dozen paragraphs focused on Reagan's outrage at being accused of insensitivity to women, offered a summary of his pro-female legislation as governor, his opposition to tokenism, along with his intention to appoint the highest qualified woman to jobs when elected. Buried on the second page was the line eventuating in Justice O'Connor: "One way I intend to live up to that commitment is to appoint a woman to the Supreme Court." It was important enough to be historic, but also politically realistic by limiting it to "one of the first Supreme Court vacancies..."

Spencer got the impact he wanted without triggering my "Schweiker Ploy" worries. He wanted a raw political jolt that lacked nuance, and it was an unlikely occasion for me to question his original judgment, and I never challenged his political instincts again. We anticipated every question regarding the Court, and the rest covered the traveling press corps' pent-up other issues because it was Reagan's first formal press conference in a long while. They especially wanted to know whether Reagan was agreeable to a one-on-one debate with Carter, which he was. Most importantly, we achieved Stu's goal in changing the subject away from pollution and the environment—about which not a single question was asked.

During our California layover, my mail included a letter Nixon sent to Reagan earlier in September with advice on preparing for presidential debates. Nixon believed he had special expertise to share about debates, and the letter remains a part of the history of the 1980 campaign—especially how RN returned to his "coaching" role of ensuring that Reagan understood the importance of image and presence over substance. It's excerpted here, with a full copy in Appendix 1.

> *Dear Ron:*
>
> *I thought it might be useful if I passed on some observations based on my experience in 1960 with Kennedy....*
>
> *You know what I learned the hard way in 1960—that how you look is if anything more important than what you say. Let Carter come over up tight, nitpicking and mean. You should be a contrast—strong but not shrill; in command, poised— the big man versus the little man.*
>
> *A tactic Kennedy used effectively was to virtually ignore a question where he had no good answer and to make points he wanted to make. I would suggest you ask your shrewdest advisers...to list eight or ten points they would like to see you make. Then make them even if the questions do not call directly for that kind of answer...*
>
> *Carter's greatest weakness from the standpoint of the average voter is his economic policy.... Always talk about the number unemployed rather than the percentage.*

But the bigger issue is inflation...

In the final analysis in a close election it comes down to how people look at the two men. You come over on T.V. like gangbusters and despite his glibness with facts and figures he comes over like a little man...

Pat and I will be watching and counting our Chinese good luck beads!

Best regards to Nancy
Sincerely, RN

Jim Brady sauntered over during our Idaho Falls layover to ask for my help to work on briefing materials for Reagan's interview with ABC television's Barbara Walters scheduled at our next stop. I told him I could do more than help. Bob Zelnick, my counterpart from the Frost interviews, and I had since become close friends. Zelnick was now director of news coverage for ABC and worked closely with Walters, helping prepare questions and briefing materials for her as he did for David Frost. I volunteered to track Bob down and see if he could give me insight into Walters's interests.

Zelnick's Washington office said he was actually in Sioux Falls for the interview, and after leaving phone messages at the local Holiday Inn, I heard back within twenty minutes. Bob wasn't aware I was working for Reagan, and I soon discovered he had an immense dislike for Carter and was not inclined to vote for John Anderson. So, after a few minutes of catching up and telephone hugs, I said, "Bob, we want to talk about the interview tonight." Without signaling precise questions, Zelnick covered with Brady and me virtually all the general subject areas he had prepared for Barbara Walters, the same way we collaborated in the Frost interviews. After twenty or thirty minutes, Brady and I had solid preparation to make the Walters interview go smoothly on both ends, and we began doping out questions and possible answers. Nixon would have savored the irony of David Frost being put to such beneficial use!

About forty-five minutes into the flight to Sioux Falls, Reagan called Brady and me to the front cabin. Mrs. Reagan was sitting next to him, and smiled as we sat down. It wasn't quite a "welcome-to-my-house-can-I offer-you-coffee-and-cookies" smile. But more like a "I'm-not-just-a-bystander-I'll-be-paying-close-attention" smile. Brady had been traveling with them much longer than I had, and he made a generous reference to the value of her return to the campaign trail. I got the message clearly.

For once, all the other traveling aides were just onlookers. In the previous two weeks, I had a handful of brief interactions with Reagan, and because Brady and I possessed superior information, the Walters briefing offered the first unfiltered opportunity for both Reagans to have and substantive time with me—a "watershed" moment in my relationship with Ron and Nancy. In the primaries, they had mixed experiences with staff, and I fully understood their wariness of new faces. Later that night, I took the time to record the scene carefully:

> The Governor was having some lunch, and was chewing on his food, the blue napkin was tucked into his shirt. He had his half glasses on, and we began discussing the questions. We told him that I knew Zelnick, and that I got some of the questions in advance, and, therefore, we were able to prepare very well. We went down quickly the list of general question areas and the kinds of questions that would be asked, and then we began the Q&A process. Asking, really, the kinds of answers he would give on a number of questions. This worked out rather well, because there were two or three question areas where Reagan's proposed responses amounted to him meandering a bit, or answering the questions in a way that was fairly negative for us…And so I gave him two or three suggestions on deflecting the issue away, then turning it back to a positive. For example, on the question of whether he would have an arms race, I said: "The right answer now, Governor, is to say, Look, arms race…is Jimmy Carter's language, and that's a political overstatement. Those are scare words, and I'm tired of scare words in this campaign. I'm tired of him trying to scare people into voting for him. Let me tell you where *I* stand on it. And this is a way of turning it around."

When we finished, Mike Deaver gave a nod and gesture of approval, and Stu Spencer added, "You and Brady are a good team; you work well together, and that's good." I felt very positive, but consistent with previous exchanges with Reagan, I received very little reaction or direct feedback. The most animation came from Nancy who, two or three times, interrupted to say: "Ken's answer here is good, Ronnie, and you should listen to it." He did listen, but even after two and half weeks on the campaign, I had the feeling I was still on probation. Though he was adopting and using my speeches, or the information in the Barbara Walters briefing—the professor was handing out passing grades. My reaction in the diary was: "he's not yet confident from [sic] his relationship with me, because he doesn't know me that well."

When the Walters interview was over, we walked in, and Zelnick gave me a big bear hug, said it went very well, and everyone involved said Reagan hit home runs with each answer.

While Mr. Reagan didn't hand out many compliments, Mrs. Reagan appeared to appreciate the contribution I was making, and, most likely, that was far more important than any overt pat on the back I was going to get from her reserved husband. Although a close personal relationship with Reagan didn't bloom in those first two and a half weeks, one very important thing started taking hold: he gained increasing comfort in my political "scriptwriting." My first audition back in 1979 taught me that Reagan had tough standards for a speechwriter, and it was no surprise that the bar was set high in the campaign. I knew I was making progress because Reagan wasn't heavily editing the materials I submitted, and my new system of speech inserts exposing Carter's vulnerabilities played to the media's needs. The ABC interview wasn't a breakthrough in our "bonding," but it was a beginning.

The same evening after the Walters interview, I speculated about the prospects of the campaign:

> Sometimes, I think we are going to win it, but other times I think it's going to be very, very difficult, and we still have a big load ahead of us. I think we're going to need to be a little bolder on the foreign policy and the defense issue. Carter talked about the economic issue today, and I think that's crazy and stupid on his part. It's talking about our issue.

While I was contributing to the team's effort and carrying my load, I was still unsure of my personal relationship with the candidate. On my balance sheet, there were more entries initialed by NR than RR. Nancy was responsive and reactive—a good thing. But the O&W had a cocoon around him, a protective layer that I still hadn't successfully pierced.

Chapter 8

PHRASE-MAKING AND DEBATING DEBATES

OCTOBER 15, 1980

We were greeted by a Gallup Poll in Ohio giving Reagan a forty-five to forty-two lead with likely voters. Carter led by one among all registered voters. A jump ball.[35] However, Carter seemed to embrace a tax increase when he flubbed by claiming that among the factors causing inflation was "the government wasn't taking in sufficient revenues to meet a greatly expanding budget." Latching on to that simple message, Marty Anderson decided my current speech for Lima, Ohio, had to be discarded, and I needed to prepare a new one. I had less than two hours from Sioux Falls to Lima to write a script that Governor Reagan had not yet seen. This was when I got better acquainted with Nancy Reagan and secured a ripened understanding of her relationship with "Ronnie" as well as her expanding role in the campaign.

I immediately began working on the new insert while battling a miserable cold. Only a half hour into the flight, Mrs. Reagan visited me to ask in a flat, icy voice, "Why doesn't Ronnie have his speech for the next stop?" I told her it wouldn't be long, and Marty backed me up that it would be worth the wait. Adding to the normal time pressure to finish new remarks and get them edited and reproduced for press handouts there was a new problem: the boss and his wife were wondering what the hell was taking so long. Mrs. Reagan's charm was extraordinary, but on the rare occasion of her displeasure, the cold stare and edge to her voice were uncomfortable.

Not a little panicked and stressed, I hoped my fingers would find magic words to emerge from the IBM typewriter to exploit Carter's weird connection of inflation and high taxes. Fortunately, I was able to concoct one of the more inspired punch lines of the campaign. I rushed it to the typists, Shirley Moore and Michele Davis; Shirley put it onto Reagan's half sheets for speaking, and Michele into press release format after Reagan made his edits. They used Wite-Out to correct typing errors, dried the pages under the plane's air vents, and typed over them.

Both RR and NR were impatient and irritated with having to wait. But Carter's blaming inflation on too little spending and not enough taxing was the perfect setup for Reagan: "We now know what Mr. Carter plans to do with four more years. *Catch your breath, hold on to your hats, and grab your wallets* because Jimmy Carter's analysis of the economy means that his answer is higher taxes." The "catch your breath" line made all three networks that night, so the last-minute change was successful.

It can be advantageous *not* to have extra time to obsess over language. Every speechwriter will appreciate my airborne episode—with the candidate, candidate's wife, and entire entourage awaiting the end results of one's brain searching to transmit magic words to one's fingers in an atmosphere of chaos at thirty-five thousand feet under time constraints. The classic test for the Word Donkey.

After the Supreme Court announcement, the Barbara Walters briefing, and the Lima melodrama, I concluded that in the '80 campaign Nancy operated as Ronnie's Bob Haldeman—Nixon's chief of staff in the 1968 presidential race and through the first three months of his second term. Reagan had no official chief of staff in '80, and I quickly realized that whenever Nancy spoke up, she did it for Ronnie—playing the "tough guy" role that he avoided—just as Haldeman did for RN. Every political leader needs an SOB, and, when necessary, Mrs. Reagan was prepared to be her husband's.

While I typed Lima's speech, Stu Spencer strolled up and leaned over my shoulder. I thought, "Now what? Why the hell is Stu bothering me when I'm on deadline?" He quietly said, "When you get through, I need to talk to you." When I had a moment to breathe, I asked, "What's up?" Where others couldn't hear us, he said, "Don't say anything to Brady or Anderson, but draft me a statement saying that we will engage in a one-on-one debate with Jimmy Carter. Also, go soft on John Anderson, Timmons, and Bill Casey."

That was a shift; until now, Reagan had been saying he would only engage in a debate that included the independent candidate, Anderson. However, replying to a reporter's question in LA the morning before, Reagan stated that John Anderson's removal as a viable candidate would "remove the only reason why there isn't a debate" between he and Carter.[36] I assumed Spencer was engaged in contingency planning, so when I delivered the draft statement to Stu, I pressed my own views that Reagan needed to debate. But in consultation with Spencer, Reagan already made up his mind the night before in Sioux Falls, believing he could no longer dodge the matter after all the debate-related questions posed at the Supreme Court press conference. Stu wanted to ensure that both Reagan's traveling entourage and the leadership at campaign headquarters would not raise any obstacles to Reagan's decision—explaining why he wanted to "go soft" on Casey and Bill Timmons. Spencer also decided that going public on a debate had to be on our own timing, so started stringing the press along. He put out a little smokescreen on October 15, telling the *Washington Post*, "We don't need a debate."[37]

What hasn't been fully revealed until now is an authoritative, eyewitness narrative of the elaborate orchestration conducted by Stu Spencer between the night of October 14 and Reagan's public announcement on the 17th that he would debate Jimmy Carter.

OCTOBER 15, 10:30 P.M. DEARBORN, MICHIGAN

Mike Deaver called a campaign staff meeting to discuss the possibility of a debate without any resolution—though all present agreed that "tomorrow's issue" would be the presidential debate.

It was a sad commentary on national priorities that "no matter where we were tomorrow, the issue would be the debate." The economy was in collapse and foreign and defense policy issues were also at stake, yet our traveling press obsessed on whether Reagan would agree to a one-on-one debate—a sideshow to grab viewers and make headlines. Robert Strauss, Carter's campaign manager, stirred the pot by sending a debate challenge telegram.

OCTOBER 16—THE DEARBORN HYATT

Gerald Ford joined Reagan for an event to include Bush and Michigan governor Bill Milliken. A key behind-the-scenes event also took place—an 8:30 breakfast to discuss our collective debate recommendation to Reagan.

It was the first major summit in a chronology of internal campaign discussions leading up to Reagan's October 17 public statement accepting the League of Women Voters' debate invitation. Because I knew it would represent a page of 1980's campaign history, I made a contemporaneous record of this conversation and each of our subsequent meetings. The versions I faithfully documented—and details of how Reagan arrived at his decision—differ materially from James A. Baker's.

Spencer presided in Mike Deaver's Penthouse Suite, Room 12. Joining Deaver, were Brady, Nofziger, Joe Canzeri, Anderson, and me—along with two new faces, Robert Teeter, a pollster with whom Spencer had previously worked, and James Baker, Stu's pal from Ford's '76 campaign who also ran Bush's primary campaign against Reagan. I had studied Teeter's polls over the years but didn't know Baker. Jim's coat was slung over my chair, so when I sat and leaned against it, he nudged me to lean forward to rescue his jacket's lapels from wrinkles.

I scowled silently at Spencer, "Who invited this asshole?" After weeks on the road, our rumpled clothes didn't meet fashion standards. I viewed Baker as a the "Bushie" newcomer fretting over a couple of creases in his damn Brooks Brothers suit. Stu smiled, and I realized he invited Baker, so I took a breath and cooled down. Still, it was clear that Jim was as precious about his personal appearance as he was about elevating his new status.

I recorded the meeting in my diary hours after it took place. The emphasis on Baker's comments becomes relevant as my account unfolds:

> *Baker started off and gave all the arguments for and against the debate. Basically, that if he doesn't debate, and loses, then he'll forever wonder why he didn't. If he debates and doesn't do well, and then loses, then he'll forever wonder why he did debate.* Bob Teeter reported on the polls, that we were pretty much, or slightly, ahead, but we're not moving above the 41 percent range. We couldn't break that threshold for several weeks, so Carter is gaining on us substantially. *Baker again summarized by saying that there were advantages to debating when we get the national audience if he does well; it might help us win. The downside was that he might not do well at all, and we'd lose.*
>
> Teeter gave the next set of views. Although he tried not to, he interjected and just said that we were not breaking through that threshold of 41 and that the debate might

be the answer—although he did say, "You know, we can win without a debate." Nofziger came down in favor of the debate, and Stu asked him his views. Marty Anderson thought we should debate, and we should set five days aside to do it. Jim Brady is leaning towards the debate.

I argued that one, if we don't debate, we give Jimmy Carter an issue towards the end of the campaign. I mean Carter would be better off with us not debating because he has an issue instead of the debate, and he would pound us, and that a challenger doesn't have the choice against the incumbent to set the agenda on the debate, and that we must accept. We can't be saying we want his job, and then be afraid to debate him. I said that would hurt very much. I argued also that having a debate would help us stem off the "October Surprise"—that we would have a forum in which to answer. And, number three, it could help us to win: that our guy was better.

Overall, the meeting was thoughtful, and we all agreed on Reagan's ability to handle a debate. A few expressed concerns about John Anderson's diminished support, but my view was that Anderson's support was gone anyway, and it was now a two-man race. Teeter confirmed that Anderson had slipped down to the seven- and eight-point range when you crossed off undecided voters—most of whom were with Ted Kennedy. My view was they fell into the anti-Carter category and, in the end, would fall to Reagan.

After thirty minutes, Stu Spencer closed the meeting. "Well, we've got everybody's views and got to keep it in this room. It is very sensitive. We will try to make the decision as soon as possible." Piecing everything together with the benefit of postelection and postpresidential biographies and oral histories, it's clear that from the time Spencer approached me on the October 14 flight to Lima, to the time of Reagan's announcement on Friday morning, October 17, he was orchestrating support for a decision that he and Reagan already reached.

Stu wanted the debates to jump-start our campaign to counter what he believed was our exposure to a Carter revival, plus inoculating against a desperate October Surprise by Carter. He also knew Reagan would hedge if there was widespread opposition from staff and advisers, so Stu's job over seventy-two hours was to mount support to make his candidate comfortable with a decision at which the two of them had already arrived.

We flew to New York that night for Reagan's attendance at the annual Al Smith Dinner—held annually to honor the four-time New York governor and 1928 Democratic presidential candidate to raise money for Catholic charities in the New York Archdiocese. During the flight, Jim Baker and I discussed the debate statement we would put out. Bill Casey and Spencer had assigned Baker the job of debate negotiator, so he wanted to be involved in the wording of the format. I drafted the statement, and met at the Waldorf with Baker, Spencer, and Brady for further discussions on wording. If Carter pulled a stunt by bringing up the debate at the Al Smith Dinner, Reagan would be prepared for a postdinner press conference.

Prior to the dinner, I cornered Reagan in the Basildon Room and brought along Brady and Baker to raise the potential of a Carter stunt. We read him my draft with Baker's and Brady's edits, and just in case, I already had it typed on half sheets. Bob Gray, a Washington PR consultant, showed up with a separate statement for Reagan to say he wanted the hostages released from Iran, adding "even if it is on election eve." That was idiotic to suggest saying something so blatantly political at a Catholic charity dinner. I convinced Deaver to have that phrase dropped.

From my diary:

> Reagan tonight seemed confident with the idea that he would debate as we read the statement to him. Mrs. Reagan, at one point, was listening very intently as we were surrounded by Secret Service men. In the background, the Bishop, who [sic] was waiting for Reagan to go into the other room. Mrs. Reagan took her shoes off and had a pained look on her face, as if the shoes were awfully tight.

Given that Reagan had seen my draft, the decision was pretty much a *fait accompli*. Nevertheless, the morning after the Al Smith Dinner, Bill Casey and the deputies, Ed Meese, Bill Timmons, Dick Wirthlin, and Pete Dailey came in from Washington for one more discussion. Bill, Dick, and Pete oversaw field operations, polling, and advertising, in that order. Wirthlin and Timmons both felt Reagan had the lead over the incumbent and a debate was risky, but they were in a minority view. Bringing the

DC group to New York was mostly a courtesy gesture that wasn't going to change anything. Stu now had more than enough backup to bolster Reagan's comfort in his announcement on the morning of October 17.

Jim Baker began his assigned task of negotiating the format with Carter's side and overseeing the preparation of the briefing books and debate practice sessions. However, Baker also began falsely portraying himself as having a central role in convincing a reluctant Reagan to debate Carter. The self-ascribed magnification of his responsibilities subsequently morphed into something bigger—that his capacity in the debate drama was so prominent that it carried Reagan to victory.

Despite Spencer's request that participants in the debate meetings not speak with the press, Baker not only indulged the press, but embellished his role. He was all over the following week's issue of *Newsweek* magazine, but of special interest was this claim:

> Jimmy Carter and Ronald Reagan finally agreed in principle last week to a one-on-one television debate…[John] Anderson's fast fade in the polls robbed Reagan of his last, best excuse for holding out, and some ominous signs of slippage in his own becalmed campaign overcame his reluctance to give in. **"We've got to do *something* that grabs their imaginations!" his strategist James Baker told him heatedly across a conference table aboard their campaign jet**—and 48 hours later, Reagan bet his stack and his future against Carter's on a media-age gladiatorial confrontation next week.[38]

Jim Baker did not hold the title of campaign "strategist" in 1980, nor was anything he said to Reagan on the campaign plane a factor in influencing Reagan's debate decision. As recorded above and confirmed in the following chronology, Reagan reached the debate decision before Baker ever got aboard *LeaderShip 80*. On the same flight, Baker claims to have "heatedly" talked to Reagan, Jim and I were also discussing Reagan's statement of a preordained decision to accept the League of Women Voters' invitation. His boast to *Newsweek* concocted an unnecessary melodrama to befriend him as a source for the magazine's reporters.

In his memoir, *Work Hard, Study...and Keep Out of Politics!*, Baker portrays the debate as almost not materializing "because some Reagan advisers still didn't trust our candidate.... Stu Spencer and I were among the few advisers in the pro-debate camp.... A good debate would reassure people that he had the intelligence and judgment to be president, we argued.... Stu and I saw one other advantage. Once debates are announced they tend to freeze the campaign."

He then describes a meeting of the brain trust to go over the pros and cons. "Our colleagues finally agreed with Stu and me that if the timing could be worked out to our advantage, a debate could help our candidate."[39]

As confirmed in my diary, Jim took no position and was far from being in the "pro-debate" camp with the senior staff. My contemporaneous account recorded Baker as only "leading off the meeting giving the pros and cons." And later in the same meeting, he offered his views—on the one hand saying there were "advantages" to debating and, while on the other hand, a "downside" if Reagan did not do well, and "we'd lose." Baker's uncommitted position at the Hyatt in Dearborn also contradicted Baker's biographical assertion regarding his views at the meeting with the "brain trust" that took place the morning after the Al Smith Dinner.

Lyn Nofziger also attended the meeting after the Al Smith Dinner and related that morning's discussion in his oral history with the University of Virginia's Miller Center. "[T]here were only two people who didn't want us to debate. One was Dick Wirthlin, who said the polls showed we were ahead. The other was Bill Timmons.... But Stu and I were saying, 'Look, there's no motion out there. You get an entirely different feel out in the field than you do sitting in headquarters.' *There was one guy sitting on the fence on that thing. That was Jim Baker, which figures.*" [emphasis added][40]

In what is among the most authoritative outside accounts of the 1980 campaign Reagan biographer Lou Cannon never mentions Baker in connection with the debate decision. Indeed, Cannon's account conforms my diary's timeline of when Spencer first approached me to draft a debate statement, as well as indicating Reagan's early decision: "[W]ith the campaign in the doldrums, there was no argument from Reagan when Spencer approached him during a flight from Los Angeles to Idaho Falls and proposed that they take the plunge and agree to debate Carter. 'I think I'm going to have to debate him,' Reagan said without reluctance. By now, he had plenty of confidence in himself."[41]

Lyn Nofziger also confirms the timing in his oral history at the Miller Center when he refers to being in Sioux Falls (which followed the visit to Idaho Falls) and going into Spencer's room to tell him "We're going to have to have a debate." When he walked in, Stu was packing and looked up and told Nofziger, "You know, we're going to have to debate." When they headed to the plane, Deaver asked Lyn to ride with Reagan, and on the way out to the airport in the limousine, Reagan told Nofziger: "Lynwood, I think we're going to have to debate." Nofziger replied: "Damn you, I've talked to Stu about this, and we agree, but we decided we would not say anything until we could talk to you on the airplane."[42] The date was October 14.

Spencer's oral history independently confirms that he, too, had concluded that Reagan had to debate, but hadn't said anything. "Then Nofziger and I were somewhere, and he brought it up. He and I were on the same page...There was a meeting held and Casey was on one side. This guy was on that side. I'd already gone to Nancy and said, 'We've got to do it.' She said, 'Okay.' In that same discussion, Reagan looked at me and said, 'I've got to do it.' I said, 'that's right. You've got to do it, so you've got to get ready and do it right.' When that fed back into the rest of the political group, they all said, 'Yes let's do it.' We were ahead. *That's when I brought in Baker* because Casey and those guys didn't want Jimmy Baker around. [emphasis added][43] Years later, Spencer was more emphatic in confirming Baker's absence in the process: "Baker had nothing to do with the debate decision."[44]

Reagan himself sent very clear signals in his October 14 press conference that he would commit to a debate if John Anderson was not a factor. Reagan was asked: "If Congressman Anderson were to actively support the relative importance of a one-on-one debate between you and the president, would you accept the League's offer?" Reagan responded, "Well, if Congressman Anderson removes himself as a viable candidate, then that would remove the reason why there isn't a debate."[45]

Baker's overstated status as a driving force in Reagan's decision to debate Jimmy Carter has been extravagantly perfumed by his authorized biographers in *The Man Who Ran Washington—The Life and Times of James A. Baker, III.* Their embroidery of Baker's purported talents made it appear that Reagan's ascent to the presidency may never have happened without Jim's putative brilliance.

They settled on October 28 at the Cleveland Convention Center—still late enough in the campaign that it played in Reagan's favor. "We were outfoxed by Jim Baker in agreeing to it so close to the election," Stuart Eisenstadt, a top Carter adviser, later concluded. *More importantly, in Eisenstadt's view, Baker's ability to convince Reagan to debate in the first place proved decisive. "His confidence in his candidate may have assured his election," he said.* [emphasis added][46]

In fact, Eisenstadt had no knowledge of how Reagan came about the decision to debate Carter, and the biographers' inadequate research, and Baker's embrace of it, has created a fabled construct around a critical element of 1980's election campaign. Baker filled an important role while negotiating the timing, ground rules and preparation for Reagan's debate. But it's clear he was not a central player in the decision itself. Based on my diary and meeting notes, Baker took a position neither for or against a one-on-one debate.

Jim Baker served in many important capacities throughout his career in public service. However, his and his biographers' revisionist additions to his résumé, and their misleading recitals of his mythic stature, disparage the efforts of countless individuals in Reagan's campaign organization—especially those who accompanied him on his crusade.

Chapter 9

MAJOR SPEECHES AND NIXON WEIGHS IN

OCTOBER 17, 1980

"Ken, the Boss wants to know if you can talk."[iv]

It was the gravelly voice of Nick Ruwe, a longtime RN advance man and former US assistant chief of protocol, now serving as the Old Man's chief of staff. As we prepared to depart for Chicago, I grabbed a pen in my New York hotel room and began taking notes the moment Nixon came on the line. Nixon had sniffed out the back-and-forth of debate discussions, so I filled him in on the morning's pending announcement.

Nixon didn't waste any time. "Carter is mean and can win the debate, but Reagan can win the audience, and on the press side, it could be a knock-out blow." Even though he thought Reagan's political gain would be "marginal," he could "mute the bomb-thrower business." Switching gears, the Old Man shifted to a political critique—asserting our commercials were terrible and weren't getting better. "Why in the world does Reagan need a new issue every day? Just force the press to write the story. There are only two issues: inflation and unemployment. If that's what they are on Election Day, Reagan wins. If it's foreign policy, we lose." Nixon thought the only new issues we could introduce might be crime and drugs.

In rapid fire, he returned to the debate topic. "Ken, Reagan can handle the meanness of Carter, and he has to run a high-risk campaign. He can use the debate to mitigate the 'rash' image, and if so, he wins." His

---

iv "The Boss" was the name used for Nixon by staffs that served him in the '50s and '60s—Rose Mary Woods, Marjorie Acker, Loie Gaunt, Agnes Waldron and others. That included Nick Ruwe and those who served in the '68 campaign. In the White House, Pat Buchanan began referring to him as the "Old Man." Depending on which staffers were talking, RN could be "The Boss," or "The Old Man." Somewhere along the line, I evolved into adopting the latter. Nevertheless, in Nixonland, we always knew to whom we referred when "The Boss" was named.

mind was restless, and I knew he was reading from copious notes he probably scratched over and over on his yellow pad. Though he bounced from thought to thought, he always returned to "Carter has no issue on inflation and unemployment and Reagan has an answer on the issue of war." He concluded with advice on the schedule. "Ohio and Illinois are important, and don't go back to Michigan or New York or Pennsylvania."

I kept careful notes of all these conversations throughout the campaign, but never mentioned Nixon in my diary, except obliquely because it was only six years after his resignation. Despite my deep personal loyalty to Nixon, I worried that political toxicity would damage Reagan if my pals in Orange County leaked word of these conversations after listening to the diaries. Though I received substantial counsel in phone conversations and memoranda from the former president through the final three weeks of the campaign, I chose not to include those references in my recordings. The Old Man had been burned enough by tapes.

My next big assignment was a major foreign policy address promoted as Reagan's outline for his presidential foreign and defense policies. As we flew to Chicago, Deaver summoned me to the front cabin with instructions on the speech's strategic importance and the imperative to remove Reagan's image as a Dr. Strangelove lurking in disguise. Deaver rarely got involved in policy, but kept the pressure on, "Look, Ken, make sure you focus on this speech."

The headquarters had produced a draft, and I figured they could take the lead, so I hesitated and told Mike, "Well, there are some other speeches in other places to give, and I have to work on them, too."

He cut me off. "Forget about them! Spend all your time on this foreign policy speech." I demurred again, saying, "There are certain things the governor ought to focus on these next few days, and I don't have much time."

Mike turned to go back to see Reagan, looked back and me and smiled, "Don't worry, just get the speech done and write it."

Later recording in my diary:

> Some interplay going on in terms of this. They put great
> pressures on me in a rather good-natured sense, I would
> say. Thinking that there would be no problem for us to

get this kind of work completed, and, as always, there seems to be a feeling that writers can do miracle work with these speeches.

However, the incident surfaced the unlikely role of another campaign policy wonk—revealing the silent hand of "chief of staff" Nancy Reagan in play. She was clearly concerned about Ronnie's Cold War image and wanted to soften it up. Deaver was only a messenger.

My friend Bill Gavin was traveling with us and had worked on the speech, and after a brief review, I expressed surprise to Gavin that the language on the SALT II (Strategic Arms Limitation Talks) treaty was silent on the fact that the treaty's main Senate opposition had come from Democrats like Washington senator Henry Jackson and Ohio Senator John Glenn. I strengthened the speech materially by proving that the SALT II treaty didn't go down to defeat because of Ronald Reagan. Instead, we confirmed that President Carter failed in a critically important national defense matter by producing a fatally flawed treaty. It gave Reagan an opening and produced a quotable line that underscored Carter's ineptness.

As we flew between East Peoria and Chicago, Nancy Reagan listened very carefully as I discussed placing the onus on Carter's own Democrat party for the failure of the SALT II treaty. Further, I outlined my suggestion that we offer up a Reagan plan for a SALT III aimed at arms *reductions*—to actually *reduce* the risks of nuclear weaponry. The idea didn't get much of a response out of Reagan, but I recorded Nancy as being "very pleased with this" and thinking the concept "was very positive." If I wasn't making great progress with the candidate, at least I was making inroads with the "chief of staff" and amends for her being pissed off back at Lima, Ohio.

I finished a clean draft at 2:30 a.m. in time for our ten-hour bus tour through central Illinois. Reagan deferred to Nancy's suggestion that he use the limousine for the day's arduous journey. Just as the bus left Lincoln's Tomb for the Pawnee Coal Mine, Tim Elbourne of the advance team—another old pal from California—came aboard to pull me off. "Khachigian, they want you to ride with the governor to the next stop and work on the speech with him." The limo pulled over, and I hopped in. Mrs. Reagan pulled out the jump seat where I sat until the next stop—the Rehnquist Hog Farm in Butler, Illinois.

It's never easy to determine the precise time and place when a relationship begins coming together—especially one as difficult as my early days trying to measure Reagan's reactions to my conversations or contributions to his speeches. But the thaw progressed during the limousine ride through his home state while working on what became the most important campaign speech since his July acceptance speech.

I was squeezed up against the driver with Mrs. Reagan sitting directly behind me. It was awkward because her legs were outstretched at an angle to avoid the jump seat and my back. I apologized, but she didn't seem to mind and said we should just sit quietly. At one point she whispered advice to me, "It's important to remember that Ronnie's at his best when he's emotional, and you need to reflect that in his speeches—to let him show emotion." I sensed those were instructions from him as well as her, and maybe his other "scriptwriters" hadn't gotten that message. While we rode in that contorted position for a long stretch through Illinois, Nancy was prepared to bear discomforts if it served to benefit Ronnie.

Reagan worked quietly. From time to time, he looked up to see people standing alongside the road, waved, and went back to work. Once, he paused and turned to me. He was annoyed at a reference to John F. Kennedy in the text, saying, "Who put that in?" Someone at headquarters had stuck JFK in there, but trying to cover our asses, I said, "Well, sir, *they* put it in to get blue collar Democratic votes." Reagan replied disdainfully, "You know, he wasn't such a great president." I didn't disagree, and Reagan was annoyed and struck it. He looked up again and said, "We also need to tone down the personal qualities of the speech; I can't be attacking Carter for personalizing the campaign and then doing it myself." But, interestingly, even when he was annoyed, it was reflected without underlying anger.

He returned to the bus to complete his editing. I recorded:

> Then as we rumbled along to Greenville, four or five of us around the table munched on some chocolate covered raisins. Reagan would wave at the people and commenting on how sometimes they could see him and sometimes they couldn't. And when we were talking this way, he said, "Go ahead, I can hear you while I do this." As we neared Greenville, the sun was setting and Reagan said, "Look at that big round, or big red puff ball—or something to that effect—over there." It was just interesting; he's constantly

looking at the little things that happen—those colorful events. As we turned the corner into the Greenville town square, where we could see the people spilled all over the place into different corners, it was a big exuberant crowd, and very heartwarming. He could hear the voices outside saying, "There he is!" And he said, "You know, everywhere I go, this is the thing to watch for in the campaign, as we come anywhere near where the crowds are, you can hear them say, 'There he is; there he is!'" And I said to him. "Well, governor, you know that's the title of your next book. Your last book was 'Where's The Rest of Me'? Your next book is: 'There he is.'" And he chuckled.

The socializing was over; we had to get the speech reproduced. Bill Gavin and I, along with one secretary, left the motorcade and with the help of a State Trooper drove at high speeds to St. Louis and were met by local police who got us to the plane—a zany, crazy process bouncing around the countryside from a bus, to the limo, in police cars and then back on the Boeing 727 to get clean copy that we would have to get into a teleprompter by midmorning the next day. I completed it at 3:30 a.m. in the Virginia hotel presidential suite given to me by the hotel manager when the advance team forgot to provide me a room.

Given the slapdash way we had to produce this speech, it was a wonder it turned out so well—thanks, also, to plenty of help in early drafts from Pete Hannaford and Dick Allen. I was especially pleased that Reagan got in strong paragraphs about the flaws in the SALT II Treaty, and placing responsibility right on the Democrats, and a reference to a SALT III Treaty:

> Mr. Carter could not even muster the necessary votes to pass his SALT Treaty in the United States Senate—yes, controlled by a Democratic majority—even before the Soviet Union invaded Afghanistan. It would appear that members of his own party are trying to tell Mr. Carter something is flawed in his approach to arms limitation...As president, I will make immediate preparation for negotiations on a SALT III Treaty. My goal is to begin arms reductions.

And his ending perfectly captured what we saw as we toured through Illinois that day:

> *Recently, I was on the campaign trail in the state where I was born and raised, Illinois. Nancy and I traveled down through the central and southern part of the state by bus and car in a motorcade, stopping at lovely towns; we visited a coal mine typical of our industrial capacity; saw for the first time the tomb of Abraham Lincoln in Springfield. We toured a productive family farm and saw again the amazing gift for technology that the American farmer has and how much he contributes to eliminating hunger in the world. At the end of the day, we stood on the banks of the Mississippi beneath that great silver arch there in St. Louis, Missouri.*
>
> *It was a beautiful, crisp autumn day. Thousands of families had come out to see us at every stop. It was a moving experience, but I was most moved, as I always am, by the young people, the youngsters—from the little ones perched on their fathers' shoulders to the teenagers. You get a rebirth of optimism about our nation's future when you see their young faces.*
>
> *They are what this campaign is all about. Renewing our spirit, securing their future in a world at peace is the legacy I would like to leave for them.*

I got a good report card as well. Joe Canzeri told me the speech was very well received by the front office. Mrs. Reagan especially liked it, and the governor was very happy with my effort, and given Nancy's emphasis on the importance of "emotion" in Reagan's presentations, the foreign policy address allowed me to break out of the mold of pure stump rhetoric and show creative versatility by submitting prose with color and sentiment.

The day's benefits had a minor downside when Reagan went off script at an airport rally after stung by comments from Carter's camp that he was rash and extremist on foreign policy and defense issues. Reporters caught him saying, "The president is determined to have me start a nuclear war."[47] That played into Carter's hands by reviving images of Reagan as the reckless military cowboy. Flying into Louisville, Jim Brady joined me, Stu Spencer,

Marty Anderson and Lyn Nofziger for a meeting regarding next day's strategy in light of Reagan leading with his jaw.

> We got into a bit of an argument over whether or not we should keep this defense/foreign policy issue going forward. I had decided today that we should just drop the thing; that we should just get back onto the economy and quit talking about defense and foreign policy. But Spencer definitely wants to talk about it, so does Nofziger, and so does Marty Anderson...

The meeting continued, and the focus turned to the polling. Here it was two weeks before the election, and even with all of Carter's baggage, the polls were showing no movement—keeping us at a steady 41 percent. Stu launched into an angry, frustrating soliloquy about Dick Wirthlin. "That damn Wirthlin didn't do any in-depth or daily polling to find out what kind of impact Reagan's speech had last night. How the hell are we going to make important decisions without the polling? Well, Dickie Wirthlin isn't sharing a lot of numbers with me. He doesn't know that I'm getting the same numbers from Bob Teeter." Spencer's frustration with Wirthlin was growing.

Spencer continued to want to elevate foreign and defense policy in the coming speeches, and barked orders on what to put in the next speech and make it aggressive and get off the defensive. Though I shared the instinct to go on the attack, I agreed with the advice from Nixon's phone call, "If it's foreign policy, we lose." Stu and Nofziger wanted a new stump speech, and I stayed up until 2:30 a.m. writing an insert for Louisville focused on inflation and unemployment—not defense and foreign policy. One advantage of being the Word Donkey is deciding what issues to advance! I added support for farmers along with a critique of Carter on Social Security—finessing the arguments we had in last night's hotel room.

Separately, Mike Deaver asked me to prepare a speech to highlight Carter's incompetence. Reagan was scheduled to speak the next day at Centenary College in Shreveport, Louisiana, so on short notice I began working on an entirely new topic on which I had no new additional research. With the constant shifting of speech topics, I wondered if the campaign had headless management in these critical moments.

I had conversations with Stu Spencer and Dick Wirthlin about the kind of things that should be done. Again, the idea is not to talk big about military matters, or to bring them up that much. Rather, to try and make the issue without scaring anybody. It's very difficult, frankly, because every time we mention defense issues, it just reinforces the negatives in Reagan. Carter has been very successful in planting the seed that we're perceived as warmongers. So, I began writing the speech, frantically, trying to go against the 8:00 p.m. deadline that Stu wanted to give it to Reagan.

Maybe they thought I could just pull it out of my ass.

Prior to our Shreveport visit, we stopped in Kansas City where there was a note for me in the staff room from "Mr. Hudson." That was Nick Ruwe's code name, and he was staying at a nearby hotel and asked to meet where we couldn't be seen. It was a scene out of a John le Carré spy novel as I snuck out without being spotted. A couple of blocks away, Nick gave me a bear hug and handed over an unmarked envelope and said the Boss would appreciate my passing the information along to Reagan. We visited for a few moments, and I told Nick I was running behind schedule and had to run because I had to write a new set of remarks on an entirely new subject.

Deaver began asking for the new speech after our travels from Kansas City to Shreveport, then across the Red River into Bossier City. I finished it at 10:40 p.m. and by the time it was taken into Reagan, he was in bed. He could only give the remarks a quick review in the morning because his schedule was crammed with press interviews—and then he misinterpreted them for the major economic speech he would be delivering later in the week. Because Reagan's numbers weren't moving, the "strategists" had to try something new. But the logistics of the previous day made it impossible to produce another high-quality speech in a timely manner. So, as noted in Rachelle Patterson's and Jerry Lubenow's pool report, Reagan delivered the "usual" remarks at Centenary.[48]

There are times when I think it's a miracle Reagan won!

While flying to Florida on the campaign plane, I proved it's not only candidates who let down their guard with fatigue. I spotted a forest fire in Louisiana and, recalling the Gipper's reference to polluting trees, I grabbed Jim Brady's arm and said, "Hey, Bear, let's have some fun. We can prove that the governor's right, and trees really are a source of pollution; just look over on the port side of the plane." Always up for a good laugh, Brady joined me as we hustled back to the press section to instruct our media colleagues that if they looked out their windows, they could see "killer trees." Everyone had the good laugh we needed during these tense days, and Brady and I thought perhaps we even softened up our boss's relationship with the fourth estate. It was wishful thinking.

We ended the week in Arlington where I had my first opportunity in privacy to review the document that Nick Ruwe handed over in Kansas City. On Nixon's personal letterhead, the first five pages were headed: "MEMO FOR: GOVERNOR REAGAN." It reflected RN's thoughts along with those of Ray Price, his former White House chief speechwriter. The full memo is reprinted in Appendix 2

In his "analysis," Nixon summarized Reagan's four principal needs:

1. Reassure possible Reagan voters that he is not an ogre, an imbecile, or one who will blunder us into war
2. Continue erosion of Carter's "good guy," "trustworthy and true" public image
3. Remind voters of what a disaster Carter presidency has been for them personally and for the country
4. Give voters not only negative reason to vote for Carter, but positive reason to vote for Reagan.

Nixon's analysis continued that Reagan "needs a strong finish" and voters need a "glimmering of faith that he can and will provide that sense of direction that the country has lost...." Nixon counseled that part of the opposition is "Carterism," and that he "has exposed himself. On the campaign trail he's opened his overcoat to show us Jimmy, Jimmy the mean-spirited, the small-minded, the vicious....no coherent idea of what he wanted to do with the Presidency; and now...he's getting mean and desperate...."

Nixon defined the Reagan crusade as "one of unlocking the nation's—and the people's—potential, of renewing the upward climb, getting us back on track, enlisting our energies and energizing our hopes, fulfilling our dreams, restoring our strength and ensuring our security." On defense issues, RN argued, "Reagan wouldn't send our armed forces careening to every trouble-spot around the globe, but he would be readier than Carter to use the credible threat of force in situations where our interests were directly threatened."

On tactics: "The practice of having a different speech each day should be discarded for this period. Repeat over and over again the inflation and unemployment themes. Don't give the media a chance to report on other issues. They will desperately try to avoid reporting on the economic issue not because they think it is an old story (which they will contend) but because deep down they know it helps Reagan and hurts Carter.... The time is past for reading important but dull lines prepared by speechwriters. [OUCH!]...Hit hard. Excite people...In the debate let the visual and verbal image be the contrast between a small man in a big job and a big man for a big job."

The Old Man followed with six pages of "possible quotes for surrogates and others for Reagan" and then signed off, "Sincerely, Dick." Then, in his handwriting, he added: *"Pat joins me in sending our best wishes for what we confidently believe will be many happy returns for Nancy & you on November 4. RN."*

Chapter 10

AMY AND HOSTAGES

"Dick" Nixon's advice to "Ron" Reagan was the best-kept secret of the 1980 presidential campaign. Nixon knew he could trust me as intermediary, and I knew Stu Spencer wouldn't leak the Old Man's offer of advice, so I gave him Nixon's memo. He kept it "close hold" to deprive Carter an opening to resurrect Watergate and deflect criticism away from his administration's failures. Nixon's advice was shrewd and especially keen and objective when he wasn't the candidate—giving Reagan comfort that his campaign was on the right track. One thing jumped out from the memo: he agreed that Reagan needed to do everything possible to diminish Carter's competence. Continuing through election eve, I received additional written and telephonic advice from Nixon—secretly passing the counsel to Spencer and Mike Deaver that became even more critical during rumors of a hostage release in the election's last forty-eight hours.

OCTOBER 25, 1980

The interim for debate preparation gave Nixon a couple more opportunities to weigh in with advice. He telephoned me to say the Iranians were "putting on an act" regarding the hostage situation. He raised the possibility they might return some, but not all, of the hostages, and if that happened "things were wide open again, and even if they return them all, it's not lost," advising that Reagan shouldn't say anything. However, if the hostages are released, "Why did it take a year? Blackmail? And what price was paid?" But he was also insistent that we get back to the key issues of inflation and unemployment. "On Election Day, the issue will be breadbasket."

On foreign policy, Nixon said the message should be to "remind the voters of all the millions lost to the free world since Carter took office:

Ethiopia, Yemen, Afghanistan, Iran and Nicaragua." A debate memo was on its way, he said, and before he hung up, "Remember, Ken, Jimmy Carter isn't above hitting below the belt. Don't let Reagan carry the nice guy thing so far. People want strength, and a little moral indignation." In San Clemente, Nixon opined more than once that Reagan was averse to hitting hard when required.

Nixon was restless and nearly as consumed with Reagan's election as he was with those of his—searching for every avenue where he could assist. Though it was unlikely new materials would help the day before the debate, he sent along an eight-page, single-spaced set of recommendations on the critical issues of international politics, arms control, and the hostage situation, including a lengthy, possible closing statement. RN also sent me a handwritten note, the central points of which I passed along to Stu Spencer and Mike Deaver: (Both documents are reproduced in Appendix 3.)

> *Dear Ken,*
>
> *In the critical days after the debate—at least one excerpt should be "The Choice."*
>
> *The "grin & bear it line" sums up Carter's economic program in a subtle and effective way,*
>
> *Now is the time to hit clean—but hard.*
>
> *Above all provide lines which will radiate strength and confidence.*
>
> *Warm regards,*
> RN
>
>
> P.S.
> *Also try a hard hitting Halloween release—on the most shocking campaign of "fear and smear" in our history.*
>
> RN

The day before we left for the Cleveland debate, the *New York Times* upended our morning. Howell Raines clearly had too much time on his hands in the home office and submitted a gossip column with several dispatches. The final item memorialized our previous week's hijinks:

> *"Killer trees! Killer trees!" shouted two Reagan aides, Ken Khachigian and Jim Brady, when the plane passed over a forest fire down in Louisiana last Wednesday. They were joking about Mr. Reagan's much-lampooned comment that trees are a major source of impure air.... In any case pundits and picketers had a good time at Mr. Reagan's expense. Students at conservative Claremont College in California, for example, greeted him by adorning a tree with a sign reading: "Stop me before I kill again."*

The *Times* included much criticism of Reagan's environmental record along with negative comments from the League of Conservation Voters—all gratuitous and a violation of what every other reporter that day considered to be off-the-record fun. The last thing I wanted was any public attention, and the Gipper was not amused. Worse, his "chief of staff" wasn't amused.

If Mrs. Reagan had her way, both Brady and I would have been cashiered, but at that point, I was only slightly more indispensable than Jim, and he took the hit for us. No one wanted Brady off the plane, but hell had no fury that day, and no one was prepared to appeal her decision. Casey and Meese assured Jim his penance wouldn't last more than a few days. I apologized to Brady; he shrugged, shook it off, and told me to let it go. By Halloween, he was back on board getting hugs all around.

Nick Ruwe called again to convey additional advice dictated by Nixon. "The Boss wasn't going to let you go without some last-minute wisdom, so here you go." Nixon was irate that Carter's press secretary, Jody Powell, was reported to have said that even if the hostages didn't come home from Iran, the mere issue helps Carter by keeping the economy off the front page. The answer, RN advised, was for Reagan's straight talk to be in this manner: "Everybody wants the hostages returned as soon as possible, but what we must remember is that long after they return, they and millions of Americans will be paying the bill for the disaster of Carter's economic policies."

"Ken," Nick continued, "the Boss is steamed up on this and wants you to get this message in to Reagan. So please write this down, so I can assure him that I passed this along: 'The hour is late but new leaders and new ideas will restore America's strength and put us on the road to greatness again. Let me add that I have noted that Khomeini and his colleagues favor Jimmy Carter. I believe millions of Americans resent this blatant attempt by those who have held 52 American hostages for a year to tell us how to vote.'"

The line clicked, and the Old Man took over from Nick. "Ken, the flip-flop charge on Reagan could be particularly important, but, mainly, the idea is that while he may change his positions, he doesn't change his principles. On the hostage thing, it's very important to say that that isn't the issue. Get what Jody Powell said on Cable News last night." I told RN that Nick had already filled me in. "Okay, then, well, if this gets tougher, you can use what the *New York Times* recently wrote—that the Kremlin favors Jimmy Carter."

He couldn't resist getting in one last debater's advice. "I just hope that he doesn't think because he's doing well, that he doesn't need to irritate Carter. Reagan can't come through as weak. He must be strong, but not personal. All right, goodbye." I dutifully passed these along to Stu and Deaver, but at this eleventh hour, I was unsure they got to Reagan. Still, Nixon was consumed with political energy and felt better knowing he had a safe and reliable method of getting his messages into the campaign.

Ford wouldn't take his advice in '76, but at least Reagan would listen in '80.

After a rally in the lobby of the Stouffer's Hotel in Cleveland and a VIP reception with Al Haig, Senator John Tower, and others, we settled into a staff viewing room at the convention center to watch the debate. Here's how I recorded it in my diary:

> My first impression of the debate was that Reagan started
> off shakily, nervous, not getting to the point, letting the
> question get away from him. I was a bit discouraged. Then,
> the second question came in, and it was on the economy,
> then Reagan caught his stride; he gave an excellent answer.

Really caught on. I think, for the next 40 minutes, Reagan was in command, and then he slipped probably in the last half hour of the debate. But by that time, he had achieved what he wanted to. We were all elated, generally. We felt that he had done a good job, although he had mangled the last couple of questions, and I felt his closing statement was not very good. Perhaps we hold our own people to higher standards than we hold others.

My last observation was an understatement, especially since I undersold the strength of Reagan's closing statement that contained a key historic line: "Next Tuesday all of you will go to the polls, will stand there in the polling place and make a decision. I think when you make that decision, it might be well if you would ask yourself, *are you better off than you were four years ago?*" Reagan remembered and resurrected the line I provided him three weeks earlier in Langhorne, Pennsylvania, and used again to great success in at least one other rally in California. With just over eighty million viewers seeing the debate live and more hearing and re-watching the sound bites, that single line resonated with an electorate devastated by crippling inflation and unemployment.[49]

Two other moments worked against Carter. First, when Carter tried raising the Social Security bogeyman against Reagan, and in frustration, the practiced communicator cocked his head before saying, "There you go again." Viewers saw Reagan as the scolding mentor, making his errant student look small. In fact, that line had been stored in Reagan's memory from his debate preparations with David Stockman. He was about to retort to Stockman in the role of Carter, "There you go again." Instead, he caught himself and said, "I may save it for the debate."[50]

Carter's other bonehead comment was a preface to his response on strategic arms limitations: *"I think, to close out this discussion, it would be better to put into perspective what we're talking about. I had a discussion with my daughter, Amy, the other day, before I came here, to ask her what the most important issue was. She said she thought nuclear weaponry—and the control of nuclear arms."*

In the viewing room, we looked at each other in disbelief that the US president just cited his thirteen-year-old daughter as a source of nuclear age wisdom. It may well be that Jimmy, Rosalynn, and Amy fretted about nukes over family dinner, but across America, voters' minds sketched a portrait of Daddy seeking advice from a teenager on Armageddon.

The next day, I checked in for Nixon's appraisal. "Both were very well prepared, Ken, and both handled themselves well, but on the overall debate, Reagan won the audience, and he won hands down. The bomb-thrower thing is out." Reagan had clearly met Nixon's key test. All things being equal, an audience would make judgments based on appearance and presentation. Nixon then delivered his punch line, "Carter is a typical humorless prig."

He offered a modest critique of Reagan. "He needs a little bit more emotion on why he's running for president and sharpen up the attack lines. The only disadvantage I saw in the debate is I thought the closing statement could have been better." Interesting, how the two of us believed Reagan's closer fell short when, in fact, it probably sealed the deal. Still, the Old Man concluded, "It's not who won the debate; it's who won the audience, and enthusiasm is the big thing." On that, he thought Reagan clearly won.

He shared a final canny analysis of how to view any last-minute political effect of the return of the hostages. "Look at it this way, Ken; the hostages are not an issue in this campaign because once they are home, they, too would have to face the disaster of four more years of Jimmy Carter if he's re-elected."

The "chief of staff" was pleased along with the rest of us, and stood next to me to roll the orange down the aisle. We talked about the debate, and although happy with the positive results, she pleaded: "But, please, no more of those!" She opposed the debate, and it had placed an enormous strain on her. I recorded a self-evident diary observation, "the whole campaign is an enormous strain."

We were joined on the Texas flight by a Hollywood couple from Reagan's past: Roy Rogers and Dale Evans. The singing cowboy was decked out in full western gear and cream-colored Stetson, and Ms. Evans was ready for the red carpet with teased hair, leather skirt, and embroidered boots—movie legends to charm rally crowds in the Lone Star state. I had my own childhood memories of them from radio, comic books, and Saturday matinees. Calling home, I told an envious Meredith about chatting with her childhood dreamboat and listening to him sing "Happy Trails" as he escorted Dale Evans off the plane.

The networks and capital press leaned toward Carter as the debate winner on points. That influenced my own second thoughts about the results, and I should have taken the longer view. Years later, Reagan biographer Craig Shirley heard from ABC newsman Sam Donaldson that he saw Carter's two top aides, Jody Powell and Hamilton Jordan, "backslapping each other and congratulating themselves on Carter's 'win.' Donaldson knew otherwise and yelled out, 'Your man blew it.'"[51]

As judged by history, Reagan's closer must have rung a bell with the electorate. Wirthlin's polls gave it to Reagan by 45 percent to 34 percent; a poll for CBS favored our side 44 percent to 36 percent; and an independent poll for the Associated Press gave it to Reagan 46 percent to 34 percent. The CBS poll regarding the undecided voters, showed Reagan picking them up by two to one after the debate.[52] *Time Magazine* observed, "Reagan was the challenger, who by credibly debating the incumbent could dispel lingering doubts about whether he was up to the job of president." The magazine also reported that Reagan, when asked if he was nervous sharing a podium with the president, quipped, "No, not at all. I've been on the same stage with John Wayne."[53] *Newsweek* revealed the clincher: "'Reagan did what he had to,' a Carter operative said grudgingly. 'He sounded reassuring, and he held his own with a sitting president. That had to help him.'"[54]

The poll bounce gave us needed buoyancy. The mood in our campaign picked up appreciably: by Reagan's own feeling and by the energy level in the crowds, he had emerged unscathed. Reagan especially enjoyed my new scripts—that Democrats shouldn't feel guilty leaving their party, and they owed no loyalty to Jimmy Carter given how poorly he had conducted his presidency. The argument was easy: They weren't leaving his side; he had left *their* side. I took special pride in another line replayed on radio several times. "Jimmy Carter is fond of quoting presidents like Franklin Roosevelt, Harry Truman and John F. Kennedy, but I've noticed that there is one Democrat that he doesn't speak much about, and that is Jimmy Carter." Reagan warmed to the applause, and the punch lines were getting heard by audiences not at his rallies.

We had great events in Dallas and on the Arkansas side in Texarkana with an emphasis on appealing to disaffected Democrats. Then, on to New Orleans, where Reagan became enamored of one of my favorite pokes at Carter. The crowd-pleaser summed up his failed presidency in three sentences: "Mr. Carter did not give us a government as good as the people. He only gave us a government as good as Jimmy Carter. And we know that that isn't good enough." It referred to Carter's failure to live up to his 1976 campaign promise, "I will give you a government as good as its people."

Reagan repeated the line over the next few days to undermine Carter's competence and reassure Democrats they had no obligation to reward Carter's mismanagement.

OCTOBER 30

Spencer took me aside, saying he had been probing information about a Justice Department report on Carter's brother Billy's alleged representation of Libya's rogue dictator, Muammar Gaddafi. The issue was Billy Carter's possible financial enrichment as intermediary between Libya and the US. Hence, "Billygate." The Justice Department had been prodded into an investigation by Congress and various news stories—including scathing *New York Times*'s columns by William Safire charging White House foot-dragging.

Spencer's inquiries sought the possibility of springing this report out of Justice or Congress, and our operations center in Arlington had just sent over stories that the Justice Department had leaked out the report we wanted. I grabbed it from Stu, finalized a statement scolding Carter for impeding the investigation, then passed it back for approval from him and newcomer Jim Baker. When we finally met with Reagan about issuing the statement, he had doubts that I recorded:

> He resisted and showed reluctance to release it and said, "fellas, this is probably not something that I should do. I just have a feeling that they might say I'm being too strident or something of that nature, and therefore I shouldn't—you know, I don't think...I just don't have a good feeling about it." Stu said, "Well, Governor, you know my position, I think you ought to do it. It is a rare opportunity to gain on him." Jim Baker was pretty much in favor. Nofziger sided with the governor, saying, "I think you're probably right; maybe we should just have Jim Baker release it." They also discussed having Bill Casey release it from Washington, but I said you have to release it from the plane to have any clout because that's where the news is made.

Nofziger's negative view of the hit on Carter appeared to grow out of his wish to take the opposite view of Jim Baker. Lyn wasn't crazy about the former "Bushie" being on board, and maybe letting Baker sign his name to hardball political language would put him to a loyalty test. Baker was eager to make his bones and jumped at the chance to get some visibility in an advisory role aboard *LeaderShip 80*. Despite my first impressions of Jim and his Brooks Brothers suit, my job was to work with whomever I was assigned, and if it was Baker, I wouldn't question it. Stu was clearly unhappy that Reagan wouldn't take a swing at Carter. "Goddammit, if Nancy were here, he would have done it; she would have made him do it." Stu was accustomed to Nancy's leverage to help him convince Ronnie to make hard decisions, but today she wasn't around. The episode was another interesting lesson in Reagan's reluctance to swing hard and added insight into Nancy's perceived value as campaign chief of staff.

Jim Baker joined us after the Cleveland debate, and only Stu Spencer and Mike Deaver were aware that Baker's presence was serving as an audition for his upcoming White House job. When we arrived in Dallas, Stu huddled with the Reagans and broached who might serve him as presidential chief of staff. Ed Meese filled that role for Governor Reagan and had every expectation of doing it for President Reagan, but Spencer and Deaver believed that would be a disaster. They would have never acknowledged it would also have been their personal disaster—Deaver for his working relationship within the White House due to Ed's disorganization, and, for Spencer, because Ed would have created walls to inhibit the free communication he had with the Reagans. When Stu raised Meese's name in their hotel suite, both Ron and Nancy said, "Oh no, oh no," and were open to taking a look at Baker.[55] Stu was impressed by Jim's discipline and organization in Ford's failed '76 reelection bid. Meese was exceptionally bright and also possessed Baker's lawyerlike mind, but—unlike Baker—his jovial, open personality didn't allow him to coldly cut people off or shove minutiae onto staff. Ed's inaction when I pled for a role in the campaign in the spring and summer never originated from malice—only from an impossibly cluttered inbox.

With Halloween's arrival, I felt a definite momentum for Reagan and recorded that "barring any unforeseen mistakes, he's got the presidency won. He seems to be in a good mood on the airplane, and the only thing is, again, he's not happy with getting too much new material." I understood why. Back in New Jersey, we overloaded him with economic data on Carter's economic policies—if the rate of inflation continued, a pound of ground beef costing $2.00 would rise to $4.92 in four years; a gallon of milk at $1.75 would cost $4.31.

So, he skipped remarks I prepared for him in Pittsburgh, and in a hot Des Plaines, Illinois' high school gym, he held forth for forty minutes before a raucous crowd of screaming students. He made up his mind about what he wanted to say, and we didn't have much control. For a day, he liberated himself and returned to the Ronald Reagan of the mashed potatoes circuit—crusading to make America great again.

Jerry Ford joined us in Grand Rapids on Halloween, and my job was to prepare a speech tossing bouquets to Ford and then piggyback on their new comradeship to reinforce attacks on Carter's economic and foreign policy record. It was a no-brainer for Ford to put resentments of Reagan behind him because his sweetest revenge would be a Reagan victory sending Jimmy Carter back to Plains, Georgia. Politics in the fall of 1980 brought Nixon, Ford, and Reagan together, each with some grievance against the other at some point in their careers. Now they were united in the cause of rescuing America from the ramshackle presidency of one who had blown up the American economy and left the US viewed as a hollowed-out power in a fragile world.

NOVEMBER 1

It was a crisp, beautiful, and sunshiny fall day in Grand Rapids. Cheerleaders danced on the top of movie theater marquees, and school bands played the Michigan fight song against a backdrop of extraordinary colors. The crowd went crazy when Ford walked on with the Reagans and ripped Carter's economic failures, savoring political retribution at each lavish Carter promise that had fallen short. I prepared a script for Reagan that laid it on thick: "President Ford gave us a world at peace, with America strong across the world and respected in foreign capitals. He left a sense of warmth and good feelings. Where Gerald Ford left strength, Mr. Carter brought weakness. Does anyone honestly believe that if President Ford were in office, the Soviet Union would have moved into Afghanistan? And if you are suffering, as we all are from this economy, do you really think that Gerald Ford would have permitted the inflation rate to reach the unheard-of levels of eighteen percent as they did last spring?"

The lovefest moved to Battle Creek, Saginaw, and Pontiac, where Ford joyfully pounded at Carter by pulling out the replica of a shrunken dollar bill and shouting, "This is what a Carter dollar bill looks like today after all his inflation." He read from articles reflecting negatively on Jimmy and pounded the podium and roared with each verbal blow. Reporters came up laughing, "When's Ford going to get tough?" The "bad cop, good cop," routine was flawless. By the end of the day, America's fate had changed, and I didn't know it for sure, but looking back, the Carter presidency had come to an end, and Ronald Reagan had created an unstoppable force of energy and purpose.

Jim Brady enjoyed waking me up with the words, "Menian, get your ass out of bed." It was no false alarm on the morning of November 2. "Hey man, the Iranian Parliament issued four conditions for the release of the hostages, and if Carter meets those conditions, there's a chance they could be released." I was told to be at an 8:00 a.m. senior staff meeting to discuss our options. Sitting in were Stu Spencer, Mike Deaver, Lyn Nofziger, Marty Anderson and—aboard these last days of the campaign—Ed Meese and Dick Wirthlin. The only paper I had for taking notes were news summaries of Ayatollah Khomeini's announcement, so that's how the record is recorded in my files. Herewith is the only detailed and contemporary insider's account of what Reagan's senior campaign strategic team discussed regarding the hostage situation at the intense moments forty-eight hours before the presidential polls opened in 1980.

Wirthlin relished his rare moment in the inner circle. Stu was usually impatient when listening to Dick and his polls, but Wirthlin had our attention, because he knew Reagan would be eager to hear the results. More than 50 percent of the electorate believed Reagan shouldn't say anything regarding the hostage situation, and only 25 percent even felt that Carter controlled it. Asked if their release would change their vote, 26 percent said they would be more likely to vote for Carter and 21 percent would be less likely.

On the question, "Are the Iranians using the hostages to influence the elections?" Fifty-four percent agreed, 41 percent disagreed. "Should the American people be willing to pay any price the Iranians want to get our hostages back?" Sixty-five percent disagreed, and 28 percent agreed. "It is impossible to believe that Jimmy Carter is using the hostages for political purposes." Fifty-three percent agreed, and 43 percent disagreed. On the obvious question of whether the hostage situation puts America in a dangerous position in the Middle East, 53 percent said yes and 43 percent said no. It was well and good to offer computer readouts for our message, but Dick wasn't prepared to offer specific wording.

Ed Meese reviewed five possible new anti-Carter spots: The weak president, his flip-flops, taking a year to resolve the hostage crisis, Carter speaking a different language, and scenes of Iranian mobs. There was also $200,000 available for saturation radio. Spencer took over, "We need to get Ford and Henry [Kissinger] to meet with the network guys and find out how they'll report any release of hostages. Poke around and see how they'll spin it."

Stu looked over at me to discuss any potential statement. "America is weakened by any hostage release, and we sure as hell can't do any arms and money deal with them. Maybe not publicly—but another message to move with our reporter pals is that they're trying to use the Ayatollah to influence the election." Privately, that was also Nixon's line. Mike Deaver wondered if Jimmy Carter would deliver a speech at the White House. No one really had an answer to that except Jimmy Carter. Nofziger finally spoke up: "Look, no one says a goddamn thing until the White House acts."

That night I added to my diary more details from that meeting:

> We decided that the best thing to is to say nothing about
> the sensitive matter. Reagan would say only that, and we
> would tone down the rallies today a little bit, tone down
> the political quality on what we do. We've decided that
> the White House has the ball in their court, and they
> are in charge—that they've got some risks as well as we
> do, but that we shouldn't give them any reason to attack
> us for being political. There were very few differences of
> opinion, actually. We discussed that Henry Kissinger and
> Jerry Ford could be our principal spokesmen on this mat-
> ter since Reagan himself would not be talking about it
> directly. There was an air of pessimism about this; we were
> unhappy with what the president might do in this situa-
> tion, and yet it wasn't a matter of feeling that things were
> totally out of our control.

While working on the softer speech, I got a call: "Khachigian was wanted immediately in the governor's suite." The Reagans were having breakfast as Spencer, Nofziger, Deaver, Brady, and Meese sat nearby. I read excerpts of a prospective hostage statement—"the issue is too sensitive; everybody wants the hostages out and expects the president to do the right thing." The intent was to put subtle pressure on Carter not to cave in to a bad deal.

Nofziger piped up, "Well, then, they'll ask him, 'What, Governor, is the right thing?'" Lyn thought that was a little too risky, so we decided to pull that out. The governor himself said, "Well, you know, Ken, it is a little too much pap in here. I think I need to give them something about our plan and everything like that. So why don't you—you know..." His voice drifted off. "Okay, sir, I'll cut some of this out, and add some new things about our various plans."

Nofziger was fine sitting on his ass drinking coffee and offering his counselor's advice, but not providing one damn idea for me to fill the space. It's one thing for the governor to tell me to run off and come up with something, but it had become a typical campaign for all the other "special advisers" to be full of suggestions, but never offering actual words. On the one hand we had decided there's a definite position not to comment, but we also had to look like we were still in control. No one in the room wanted to provide language in front of Ron and Nancy, so it was left up to the Word Donkey.

Reagan put down his toast and looked up at me, "You know, if you're wondering why I've got this sad look on my face, it's not because of the events of the hostages, or that I think it's going to hurt us. I'm really upset about the California poll. Dick Wirthlin's poll showed we're down to a forty-two to thirty-seven lead." That was crazy, so I replied, "Governor, that's five hundred or six hundred thousand votes," and everyone in the room agreed. Wirthlin's numbers weren't believable, and given everything going on with the hostage situation, Reagan shouldn't have been worried about California. Nevertheless, that poll had him fretting, and so he was sending Nancy ahead to California to campaign for him.

Stu tried to ease his mind by reminding him that he only beat Jesse Unruh by a half million votes in 1970. But Reagan quickly came back at him, "Well, yeah, but that's only because we stopped campaigning for ourselves to try to help George Murphy win." I recorded that Mrs. Reagan along with the staff didn't seem nervous that morning because we were in a position of strength, but, nevertheless, Mommy also seemed very intense, and the die was cast regarding her going off to California, and for the moment, the two of them were off to church.[v]

While the Reagans were at church, Spencer asked me to call Nixon to find out what the Old Man's views were. Nixon got right to the point when I told him our strategy was basically to say nothing. "Ken, I'm not sure it's wise that we're ignoring the issue. You can say, 'We hope and pray that the hostages come home, and if they come home, we're gratified; that's what all of us want. We want them home, but Tuesday's decision has to do with the nation's problems that will still be there. Then, let us develop the kind of respect and strength that this kind of humiliation will never happen again.'" Nixon was offering a roundabout way of saying nothing; he wasn't counseling an all-out attack on Carter and didn't disagree with our position of being cautious.

Nixon growled, "Ken, this is like LBJ's bombing halt in '68. It's déjà vu. This is *not* an issue in the campaign. We all want them to come home. It's just a goddamned outrage that they're pulling this crap. The ayatollah has voted for Carter because he thinks he'll be better for Iran. However, let Reagan say what millions of Americans think; and that's if Carter politicizes the issue, he should kick the shit out of him. Anyway, I predict Reagan's going to win 351 electoral votes and by five million popular votes." I immediately passed the information to Stu, which he relayed to Reagan later that morning.

Carter's press secretary, Jody Powell, announced they were moving very cautiously; there was no immediate breakthrough, and "We will just have to see and do the right thing." Carter's campaign didn't know we were speculating that he would take a hard line and go the other way by saying, "This is unacceptable to me, and I will not permit the blackmailing of the United States of America. Therefore, I'll have to reject these demands." Our concern was an appearance on national television would cloak Carter with presidential dignity and have a negative effect against Reagan with undecided voters.

More than four decades after the election, *New York Times* reporter, Peter Baker, relied on less than complete evidence to make headlines that our campaign's leadership connived with former Texas governor John Connally to meet with a series of Middle Eastern leaders to pass the word

---

v   In 1980, Reagan's California margin over Carter was 52.7% to 35.9%.

to Iran to stall the hostage release to get a better deal from Reagan.[56] Baker relied on an eighty-four-year-old former Texas pol, Ben Barnes, who had no direct proof of any conspiracies and floated this preposterous story to gain the public attention that eluded him when his political career collapsed in 1972.

It's clear from the frantic nature of our eleventh-hour meetings that the only concern we had regarding a campaign "sabotage" or "October Surprise" were conspiracies inspired by Carter—not by us. Upending Nixon's campaign almost worked when LBJ called a Vietnam bombing halt to salvage Humphrey's race in 1968, so why wouldn't the Democrats do it again? I cited Peter Baker's inadequate 1980 campaign research in Chapter 8. In this phony "sabotage" story," he failed again by not following up on all possible leads to dispute Barnes' fantasies.

Baker never checked with Stu Spencer, Ed Meese, Dick Allen, or me on the purported Connally escapade.[57] Each of us had direct information of our daily strategic interaction with regard to the campaign's tracking of the Iranian hostage crisis. Provoking delays would have been politically senseless, but, more importantly, is disproved by the records I kept of what our team was thinking. I could have easily offered Baker private access to my diary to disprove his canard, but he refused to check with me—just as he failed to check with me regarding Reagan's debate decision, as I noted in Chapter 8. Every live credible source in the Reagan campaign, combined with my contemporaneous diaries, would have breathed life into one sabotage—Barnes's and Baker's concocted distortions.

The hostage matter dominated news in the final hours, and as Reagan left the Neil House, he resisted reporters' shouts saying, "All I can tell you is I think this is too sensitive to make any comment at all." When Reagan departed the Broad Street Presbyterian Church, a reporter shouted that former Iranian foreign minister Sadegh Ghotbzadeh had said there was no way the hostages could be released before Tuesday's election. Did Reagan "have anything on that?" He responded, "As I said before, this is too delicate a situation. I'm not going to comment; we all want them home." He ignored a question on whether a four-phase release was acceptable.[58]

At our next stop in Marietta, Ohio, we put out the brief three-sentence statement I helped write: "I know that as we meet here today, two days before we go to the polls, that we all have on our minds the matter of the hostage situation in Iran. But this is not the time or place for me to be addressing such a sensitive matter. Obviously, all of us want this tragic situation resolved, and that is my deepest hope." Lee Fremstad, of the McClatchy company's *Bee* capitol bureau, quoted Reagan's statement in entirety and captured our approach colorfully: "Reagan treated it much like a time bomb—gingerly and cautiously…"[59]

Reagan decided to go with a less political speech at Marietta—wise because after another whole day of negotiations, Carter returned to Washington, put out a statement they were still working on it, wanted the support of all the American people, and politics wouldn't influence what he was doing. Reagan gave the speech once, then took me aside between stops and repeated that it had a little too much pap. I recorded in my diary that he "bitched at me" at the other stops in Ohio. I attributed it to (a) his anger at Carter, or (b) at this stage of campaign, he was not going to let events dictate his speaking his mind, and he would assert his independence on the path to victory.

Chapter 11

THE FINAL TURN AND HOME

NOVEMBER 2, 1980

There are times when you can't improve on clichés. The smell of victory was in the air.

We couldn't change the hostage situation, so I turned my attention to Reagan's election eve speech, working with a draft by Tony Dolan, a writer brought in by Bill Casey. Reagan had already made substantial and helpful edits on Dolan's draft, using storytelling and illustrations that gave vivid word pictures to his message. Reagan made two interesting edits that caught my eye. In a reference to "the hard years: riots, assassinations, Vietnam, Watergate, our hostages in Iran," Reagan struck out "Watergate." He also struck out an entire paragraph citing the movie *Deerhunter* and the "wounds of Vietnam." To me that showed he had a gut distaste for the Left's conventions of '60s and '70s guilt.

Just as we lifted off for Peoria, where the election eve speech would be taped, I grabbed Deaver and told him I needed some time with Reagan to review the final draft. I reproduced the half sheets that added a litany of "are you better off" and sat down with him to review those along with my changes to his election eve's remarks:

> I told him that I'd taken out the John F. Kennedy quote, and he said, "Good, good." He had mentioned this when we were driving through Illinois two or three weeks ago, that he was tired of quoting John Kennedy. He seemed to have a very good sense of what he wanted to say and no objections to the changes that I had made. Jack Marsh[vi] was there and telling some stories about the Virginia Military Institute. Then, Reagan immediately broke into

_____

vi   Jack Marsh, former VA Congressman and Reagan Secretary of Army one of his stories about when he was first inducted as a second lieutenant in the Army and having dinner with this colonel who met with all his new officers. The story was about the colonel who called him Reagan. "Reagan, I saw you in 'Brother Rat,' and I want you to know I wasn't too damned pleased about it." Reagan told the story at great length, and with a Southern accent. Again…he's a born storyteller; he loves to regale those around him with old stories, and he remembers them quite well.

We closed the day without any damaging fallout from the hostage situation because Carter predictably didn't handle things well, and Ford and Henry Kissinger were good buffers in discrediting the administration's actions. We were up three or four points in the Gallup poll, a swing of six or seven from the previous one. Momentum was unquestionably in Reagan's direction.

There were two problems while planning for the morning's taping: (1) the Reagan/Dolan draft was eloquent and poetic, but still wasn't giving voters assurances to bring them over to Reagan or *reasons* to turn away from Carter, and (2) we still needed to pad it to fill out the half hour. So, I returned to the campaign meme, *"Are you better off than you were four years ago?"* and stretched it into a series of eleven rhetorical questions raising every conceivable negative economic, defense, foreign policy, cultural and institutional failure of the Carter years. Then, Reagan would close the sale with this final question: "And, most importantly—quite simply—the basic question of our lives: are you happier today than when Mr. Carter became president of the United States? I cannot answer those questions for you. Only you can."

With help from Shirley Moore, we finished putting together a clean copy just past midnight. I had a couple of glasses of wine, made a couple of calls to the West Coast, and relished the thought that this would be the last night of sleeping in a strange bed with one last baggage call. Any hope I had of sleeping in was dashed by Dick Wirthlin waking me up at 7:00 a.m.

He wanted to look at the speech even though he had to know I wouldn't entertain changes after Reagan signed off. He clearly wanted to be able to tell the media and his staff he had "speech approval" as well as to leak out key elements. I didn't know it then, but I later discovered this to be central to Wirthlin's *modus operandi*. His officious intermeddling in the speech-making process created an unnecessary divide between us.

Bob Hope joined us in Peoria, cracking one-liners about Carter—the most hilarious being about Amy Carter's important role in foreign policy. I noted in my diary that "Reagan, frankly, talked much too long, as he has for the last few days." The showman had mixed feelings about leaving the road. He wanted it to be over with…but he didn't. Especially toward the end as things were looking good, he couldn't be blamed for not wanting to miss the "roar of the crowd" and the warmth and feedback he'd been getting.

With hindsight, my diary showed I was reflecting caution on the eve of an historic landside—proof that political judgment is easily distorted by being in the center of the action. Still, I captured the drama of the moment.

> Crowds are good, it's another beautiful day…it's so much fun to see the people out with their children, Republicans, enjoying the campaign season, going through this great tradition. With all the cynicism there is, there's still a lot of wonderful emotion involved in this process with signs and bands and waves of people patiently waiting to see somebody—to get some kind of direction. The press feel upbeat; they think we're going to win. I think it's going to be pretty close, and I'm not ready to pick one way or the other, although it looks pretty good right now.

The overnight clips arrived in Peoria with a surprise in the form of an *Evans and Novak* column datelined Des Plaines, Illinois, that included my name. The headline read: "It Could Have Been a Landslide," and it opened with the lede, "Only six days before the election, Ronald Reagan finally fired at the fat Jimmy Carter targets of economics and incompetence—a delay explaining how a potential Republican landslide became a cliffhanger subject to change by Iran's release of the hostages." The column blamed Reagan's late start on public opinion surveys, and quoted one campaign adviser saying, "The damn pollsters took over." It argued that the attack on Carter's credibility didn't start "until Thursday morning, Oct. 30, in a New

Orleans airport hangar," when Reagan "systematically assaulted Carter's competency."

The column continued,

> Recalling Carter's 1976 campaign promise of a govern-
> ment as good as the American people, Reagan told the
> New Orleans rally: "He only gave us a government as
> good as Jimmy Carter, and that isn't good enough." That
> and other applause-getting lines were brand new. Ken
> Khachigian, a 36-year-old California public relations man
> who once wrote speeches for Richard Nixon, months
> ago applied for a job with the Reagan campaign, which
> turned him down as too expensive. Three weeks ago, with
> Reagan's rhetoric and poll ratings sagging, it was decided
> no price was too high. Thus, Khachigian's prose became
> Reagan's rhetoric in New Orleans and across the country.[60]

A couple of days before the column appeared, Novak strolled up to me on the plane to ask my age and spelling of my name. That accounted for Dick Wirthlin coming up to me later that morning to say, only half kiddingly, "I thought you were my friend." Novak had skewered Wirthlin and ad man Pete Dailey as "two California technicians who have domi-nated strategy" and "insisted on avoiding harsh criticism of Carter and even Carter's record for fear of alienating undecided voters."

I told Dick I didn't even know Novak, and of course wasn't his source. In those final days, I didn't really care what he thought, because he and some of the others spent too much time talking to the press with an eye to their own images, not Reagan's.

During an airborne visit with Deaver and Spencer, I turned to Stu, "Hey, did you see this Evans and Novak piece?"

Stu laughed out loud, "Yeah, Novak asked me who's doing all the work, and I said 'Khachigian and Brady.'" He didn't admit to making the hit on Wirthlin, but more than once he complained about Dick being too timid. And years later, he made it clear that he was the one who used me to rip Wirthlin, who was trained as an academic and viewed his data too strictly. Dick was also more cautious and risk averse—which is why he opposed the debate and why Stu called him "Numbers." Spencer operated on instinct and intuition, seeing the broader canvas on which he worked.

The more time I spent with Reagan, the more I understood the necessity to overcome the mechanics; to do away with the "pap"; to let him be "emotional," as Nancy instructed. In 1980 Reagan resorted to his years of training at the radio station, in front of movie and television cameras, and on the "mashed potatoes" circuit. In front of those hundreds of diverse audiences on behalf of General Electric, he absorbed the precise messages voters sought from a leader in the twentieth century—things polling could never achieve.

At Stu's request, I called the Old Man before we left for the west coast, and as soon as Nick Ruwe patched me in, it was clear that RN was following events closely. He heard a report out of London that three hostages were released. But apart from that, he predicted a Reagan landslide. He reiterated his five-million-vote popular vote margin and upped his electoral vote margin to between 350 and 380. He couldn't have been more cheerful.

NOVEMBER 3, 1980, EN ROUTE FROM PEORIA TO PORTLAND

> Just a few moments ago, sitting across from the gover-
> nor reading—he was reading, and he looked very serene,
> very at ease with himself. Actually, he does not look like
> a man who is going to—36 hours from now—who could
> be President-elect of the United States. He hasn't said…
> chatted with anybody, pretty much kept to himself. Been
> very calm. At some point, although don't think he'll do
> it, he should be calling in members of his staff, thanking
> them for their efforts during the campaign.

San Diego was our final stop because Reagan viewed it as his city of good luck due to finishing his 1966 campaign for governor there, with thirty thousand people sprawled across Mission Hill's Mall being entertained by Donny and Marie Osmond and singer/actress Carol Lawrence. He gave pretty much the same stump speech, using every tested line from the past few weeks while adding some new material I gave him that morning. Some loud-mouthed loon began yelling and shouting repeatedly about nothing discernable, although mentioning Lincoln at one point. Reagan stopped in midsentence, looked over in the fellow's direction, and said, "Aw, shut up!" The crowd broke into a big roar, and Reagan immediately took the edge off by saying, "You know, my mother had told me never to say that to anyone, but it has been such a long campaign, and there's been so many people like that, I thought that just this once I could do it."

> At the rally, one interesting thing was that I was talking to Bill Plante of CBS News, and he was standing next to Dan Blackburn of NBC Radio, and we were cracking jokes about the speech, and how he had memorized all lines, and Blackburn would repeat the lines simultaneously with Reagan. Depending how close he got the words, I would grade him with A- or B+. And when Reagan started talking about reducing taxes, Bill Plante looked at me and said, "You know, if I really believed he would do this, I'd be working for the campaign instead of covering it for CBS."

The flight leg back to Los Angeles was one big celebration with everyone in the aisles talking and laughing and even Reagan himself appeared to be in a very good mood. For the orange roll this time, both Reagans came up, and Nancy had surreptitiously put an entire sack of two dozen oranges at her side, and upon takeoff to Willie Nelson's recording of "On the Road Again," she let loose the entire sack to the roar of the newsies. Even the reporters had a sense Reagan was going to win. They might not have wanted him as president, but they had a good feeling about being with a winner. It also meant that those traveling with Reagan would get the coveted spot of White House correspondent over those who had been covering Carter.

Despite getting home at 3:30 a.m. central time, Ed Meese had given me the assignment to have election night remarks ready by 2:00 p.m. on Election Day. After breakfast, I went into my home office searching for a quote that would fit the occasion. I took out Stephen Oates' Lincoln biography, *With Malice Toward None* and found appropriate words around which to wrap Reagan's victory remarks. After his election in 1860, Lincoln assembled newsman to say, "Well, boys, your troubles are over now; mine

have just begun." I wasn't looking to write the most profound victory statement in history, so in place of laying out a dreamy future, I thought what
worked best for Reagan was something relatively low key.

I arrived at the Century Plaza Hotel where Deaver and Bill Timmons
were waiting impatiently for a look at my draft before it went to Reagan.
Then Ed Meese called from Reagan's house and wanted to know when I was
coming over. Once again, I was trying to polish it in a typical campaignlike
situation: a staff office full of fifteen or twenty people with raucous noise
and phones ringing everywhere. Nance Roberts of the press staff quickly
volunteered to type it final using the orator ball on the IBM Selectric.

I cajoled a driver to messenger the draft over to Reagan and cleared
him through the Secret Service. Meese had since returned to the hotel,
and I had to show the remarks to him and Stu Spencer. Stu thought one
paragraph was self-serving and needed to be dropped. After that, I was on
standby at 4:00 p.m. to talk with Reagan. I wasn't surprised when shortly
before 4:00 Wirthlin walked in and asked to see the remarks and a blank
sheet of paper. I didn't have paper, so gave him a copy of my set of the
remarks, and he began to make a series of notes on the backside of what
should go in—itemized, one through four. With the clock ticking, there
was no way I was going to include any of Dick's ideas, but like all others on
the senior staff, he felt like he had to be able to say he had "input" on the
president-elect's remarks.

In his presidency, Reagan repeatedly bridled at the "committee" that
tried to intercede between the two of us. On Election Night, I was forced
to stomach it.

4:15 P.M., ELECTION DAY

    Reagan: Hello, Ken.

    KK: Hello, sir. Congratulations.

    Reagan: Well, thank you.

    KK: Governor, about those remarks I sent over. Obviously,
    I don't mean to put words in your mouth on an important

occasion like this, but I thought they might provide some guideline.

Reagan: Well, that's fine.

KK: Well, I thought also that the Lincoln quote was apt, and that you might be able to use it.

Reagan: Yes, okay.

He seemed a little anxious to get off the phone.

KK: Then I mumbled vaguely about some points on leadership, none of which sank into Reagan, and I wished I never passed them on.

Reagan: Well, I'll tell you what, I was just ready to sit down and put pen to paper.

KK: Okay, that is just fine. I just wanted you to know if I could help or do anything else, I'm here and prepared to help.

Reagan: Thank you, and goodbye now.

KK: Thank you, sir, goodbye.

That was the last contact I had with him. I had the impression he decided he wanted to write his own remarks and put mine aside. My work on the campaign was done. I had nothing else to write, and it was the last contact I had with "Governor" Reagan. NBC projected him the winner around 5:15 or so.

Meredith and I got dressed and went to several of the parties to witness the massive landslide and watch his victory remarks. We fought our way through various guards and managed to get backstage through a side tunnel—less crowded except for all the arriving movie stars. Around 9:00 p.m., he began his remarks, and I could barely hear because the loudspeakers were pointed in the other direction. But then, wow, it was clear that he was reading the statement I had written word for word, beginning exactly the way I had prepared it. I didn't pretend to act detached. Amid the pushing and shoving of the crowd, I was quiet, humbled to have contributed to the first words of the president-elect of the United States.

With that, it was over, and I had to guard against a letdown.

I summarized the election with an analysis in my diary:

> A massive Reagan victory, I must say, was a surprise to us all. To win the Senate seats was just obviously beyond comprehension. I thought we would win, even though the hostage situation was scary to us Sunday, and yet none of us anticipated this kind of victory.... That means that our strategy Sunday morning worked, that we should say nothing, as I argued in that meeting. They (the White House) were walking on eggshells, and we should see what they did and force them to make a mistake, and I think that was the right advice. But in the end where the hostage thing played out, plus on election morning, it was the first anniversary of the taking of the hostages, so there were stories on television, and the newspapers— one year anniversary stories. It was a reminder to everyone that Carter had failed, and that everything was structured around his failure and underscored the fact that he was not confident. That, combined with the fact that Reagan had shown leadership and presidentiality in the debates, plus the fact that once all this happened, it enabled us to get back to the issue that concerned everybody, which was the economy, the economy, the economy. We and the others tended to underestimate how hard the economic conditions were on the people, and I think it showed that we were absolutely correct from the very beginning in our campaign strategy of hammering on the economy and just simply doing it another way each day.

The next morning, I went to the staff room one last time to make a couple of calls. I rose to leave, gesturing to folks sitting around.

"Goodbye, everyone."

"Where are you going?"

"I'm going home."

"You're leaving?"

"Of course. Get me to the beach."

Everyone there would be clamoring for a White House job or a position in the new administration, and I wasn't looking for a Washington gig. I headed back to San Clemente to put my business back together and restore family life.

Stu Spencer arranged for me to help elect a president. My job was done.

Chapter 12

"WE ARE AMERICANS"

While I worked on dozens of Ronald Reagan's campaign speeches, I mostly wrote one to two-page inserts, sound bites, and campaign statements and didn't write his half hour speeches from scratch. So, when the request came along to work on Reagan's first inaugural address, and with the entire world watching, I had one question in mind.

What the hell do I do now?

I missed the excitement of the campaign. For political junkies, nothing comes close to the intoxication generated from the stakes and sheer energy of a national presidential election—the World Series, Super Bowl, and NBA finals all in one place. Yet, it was a treat to be home, without early baggage calls, bad meals, or speech deadlines and a welcome change from the motorcades, creepy hotels, and shoving at rallies.

The media pushed three postelection stories: Why Reagan achieved his unexpected landslide; a crystal ball into his presidency; and administration staffing. The *Los Angeles Times* suggested there were clues to a Reagan victory in the final weeks, such as reports from the Carter team's admission of losing momentum while contrasting a confident Reagan with his bigger, cheering crowds, versus Carter's "smaller, quieter crowds." The *Times* also noted that networks' news was frozen throughout the final weekend over the American hostages in Iran.[61]

Pollster Louis Harris opined "Jimmy Carter lost the election" more than Reagan won it, citing his postelection survey showing Carter's overall seventy-two to twenty-eight negative job performance with his lowest marks coming on his "handling of the economy," eighty-seven to thirteen.[62] After the election, the *New York Times* and CBS reinterviewed 89 percent of over two thousand voters from the weekend before the election. *Times* reporter Adam Clymer observed the economic issue "got new prominence" at the Cleveland debate when Reagan stressed in his closing question: "Ask yourself, are you better off than you were four years ago?"[63]

Carter collapsed in every respect and salvaged victory in only six states.

I was among the names mentioned for possible White House jobs. The *Washington Star*'s Lisa Myers wrote, "Ken Khachigian, a Californian whose speechwriting talents were much appreciated during the campaign, is the favorite for the top White House speechwriter's job."[64] The *Sacramento Bee*'s Lee Fremstad speculated, "Ken Khachigian, 36, who worked in the Nixon White House for Communications Director Herb Klein and traveled with Reagan as speechwriter in this campaign, could be in line for a return to Washington."[65]

I wasn't surprised at Baker's winning out as chief of staff. Spencer and Deaver had ensured that his campaign "audition" had played well. Ed Meese often appeared a bit rumpled and careened in several directions while Baker displayed precision—with creased pants, starched shirts, ties with perfect half-Windsor knots, and polished tasseled loafers. Importantly, he was well organized.

Baker called me shortly after his appointment, and his energy coursed over the line with an intense, animated pitch. "Ken, I'm making staffing decisions, and if not on a long-term basis, at least on a short-term basis, I'd like you to run the speechwriting shop. I can't discuss salary yet. This position would report directly to the chief of staff."

Mental note: why would I move from California for a job on a "short-term basis?" Even if I were interested, how could I take my existing relationship with Reagan and then premise it on conditional terms with a new boss? It was an odd way to offer a job.

I wasn't looking for another White House stint. It was momentarily tempting to return for the elevated senior staff member status along with shaping history and accompanying Reagan on foreign travel. Meredith wasn't averse, but Merissa was ten and Kristy was nine, and uprooting them was a huge factor. I think I would have adapted the least easily to the unruly environment, long hours, stress and inevitable staff conflicts.

Jim described his choices for key White House positions and made it clear that all policy papers would flow through him. "Ken, I'd also like you to pull the laboring oar on the inaugural address. We have the best communicator since JFK. He has a real opportunity to go direct to the people, rather than have the press interpret what he says." Baker paused, then said something strange and that I didn't believe was dictated by Ronald Reagan. *"Let's not get wrapped up around social issues."*

He continued. "There are two things on which the people will judge this administration: One, inflation. That's critical, *even if Kemp-Roth needs to be adjusted.* Two, Reagan was elected on a pledge to reduce government and get rid of its intrusion on their lives." But the comments on "social issues" and "adjusting Kemp-Roth" didn't sound like Reagan and weren't in our campaign playbook. Baker was clearly signaling his intentions to influence policy.

I decided not to drag out a response. I replied immediately and declined. I think he was surprised that someone wouldn't want to be a part of this adventure, and he quickly countered, "Well, then, I'm going to have the governor call you." He needed to check off the speechwriting box so he could get on to the other staff positions.

Dave Gergen called the next day, but Baker interrupted to reconfirm that I would be "pulling the laboring oar" on the inaugural. After Baker dropped off, Gergen told me he was Baker's transition "deputy." Ha! Another Bushie, and a classic beeline by Gergen into a power slot. He outlined the team I would expect to work with, all of whom were close to Baker. He added, "We've been throwing out names for press secretary and so far, have come up with Jim Brady, Pat Buchanan, Jerry Friedheim, and Bill Beecher." Other than Brady's, those names emerged from Gergen's experience with Nixon and Ford—not Reagan. Brady would end up as press secretary, but even widening the search was an insult to Jim's campaign service.

Baker wasn't kidding about a follow-up appeal from Reagan. A few days later, Reagan called and dispensed with the pleasantries.

RR: Ken, I like to have you join me at the White House. We have a big agenda, and I think we can work well together, so I hope you will consider coming and help with some of my speeches, like you did in the campaign.

KK: Governor, I'm honored that you would consider me for this job, and while I told Jim I'm not inclined to accept, I owe you the courtesy of reconsidering. Let me think it over, and I'll let Jim know as soon as possible. As I told Jim, I have a young family, and right now I'm not comfortable uprooting them, after just moving to California a few years ago. If there's any way I can help, you know I will.

RR: Well, I understand your personal considerations, but please reconsider, and in the meantime, I understand you've agreed to help out with some background on the inaugural address.

KK: Yes, sir, I already have some thoughts to share.

RR: Well, all right, many thanks, and see you soon.

Baker came back with a proposal after I declined Reagan's offer. "Okay, I understand. How about at a minimum, if you come back to set up the speechwriting shop and take responsibility for the first several presidential addresses laying out the administration's economic policies. I need someone with experience and whom Reagan can easily relate with."

I think they hoped I would be seduced by the power and status and decide to stay.

I had an assignment, and it was time to go to work.

Thoughtful advice came from Pete Hannaford, a longtime writer for Reagan, and public affairs partner with Mike Deaver. Pete helped draft Reagan's 1980 Republican nominating convention speech and had several suggestions. The most valuable was, "You can't have twenty-five well-meaning people distracting you." I set a deadline of December 12 for those wishing to submit basic thoughts and themes—but not language. Bob Garrick, the campaign's able administrative leader, was designated my contact point in DC. Bob sent word requesting these memoranda, and within days I had a handful of many helpful suggestions.

The next step was to read every prior inaugural address. A few presidents gave more than one, and in FDR's case, four. Reviewing them is a fascinating *tour d'horizon* through America's memory—more than two centuries of US history lessons in a few hundred pages. My bar was set low by the dreadful prose of a few presidents, but any writer studying Lincoln's Second Inaugural Address—epic, poetic, and lyrical—would cower under the creative challenge.

It is Lincoln's most famous, with its closing words, "With malice towards none, with charity for all…" In reference to "the mighty scourge" of the ongoing Civil War, he admonished: *"…[I]f God wills that it continue until all the wealth piled by the bondsman's two hundred and fifty years of unrequited toil shall be sunk, and until every drop of blood drawn with the lash shall be paid by another drawn with the sword, as was said three thousand years ago, so still it must be said 'the judgments of the Lord are true and righteous altogether.'"*

I convinced myself that Lincoln's extravagant imagery and poetry was so untouchable, no one would expect me to rise to it. It was best to focus on Reagan as Reagan, not Reagan as Lincoln. Of the other presidential addresses, among the most interesting and readable was delivered in 1925 by a much-maligned president, Calvin Coolidge.

President Nixon prepared a postelection memorandum for the president-elect with wide-ranging recommendations focused on policy, personnel, and management. Nixon advised that "action on the inflation front" was by far the number-one economic priority, and Reagan should include no foreign travel in his first six months while unpopular budget cuts were being made. Generally, for the top positions in the administration—the critical positions of secretaries of state and defense—Reagan could not afford individuals with "on-the-job training." Nixon made a vigorous case for Al Haig as secretary of state and ruled him out as defense secretary, where, instead, he touted a favorite, John Connally.

He recommended William Simon at Treasury, William French Smith for attorney general, Bill Casey at CIA, and Caspar Weinberger for OMB. He advised Reagan to limit staff members from attending cabinet meetings to cut back on news leaks, and to broaden the administration's representation with the "New Majority," who can help "erase the image of the Republican Party as white, Anglo Saxon and Protestant (WASP)."

Nixon prescribed Bush as a potential director of congressional relations, liaison with various campaign committees, or as special emissary on foreign assignments. From his personal experience, RN believed Bush could be in a "unique position to promote and defend the Administration's foreign policy." The Old Man abjured any official role for himself but welcomed "the opportunity to provide advice in areas where I have special experience to you and to members of your cabinet and the White House staff where you deem it appropriate." (A full copy of the memorandum is in Appendix 4.)

10:00 A.M., DECEMBER 16, 1980

Mike Deaver and I met Reagan in his Pacific Palisades home, seeking first insights for the speech. He was the most relaxed I'd seen, and, importantly, a curtain had lifted, and I finally felt a comfort of relating in a manner unlike any we had in the campaign. We weren't "pals." I wasn't looking for that kind of relationship, but the wariness and distance I sensed in the campaign's travel and tension was undergoing a transformation. Deaver's familiar face helped and made it easier for me to loosen up with Reagan.

"I agree that it not be a laundry list," he said, "but it should be inspirational and a reassurance that it is because of the people, and not the government, that we can do these things [i.e. implement his goals]. For too long, we've allowed others to do our thinking for us." He referred to his 1967 inaugural as governor of California as a "peaceful passage of authority," and alluded that he wanted the same now. "And then, I want to turn to Carter on the platform and extend my gratitude to President Carter during the transition period." Reagan shifted back to philosophy, and his mind and words moved quickly. "Unless we as individuals are free, we cannot have a nation that is free. In the discharge of my duty, I will be guided by this distinction: the federal government did not create the states; the federal government was created by the states."

He paused briefly to collect his thoughts, then said, "The oath I've taken today is not just for the president; it's an oath of every American to preserve and protect the Constitution of the United States." I scribbled quickly to capture all his instructions, especially underscoring, "Ken, be careful not to take a crack at the previous administration." He didn't want a reprise of my stump speeches!

He shifted gears abruptly and looked past Deaver and me with a thought from his memory bank. "There was an old World War II movie about Bataan, and Frank McHugh was in it. In the movie, his character's battalion was under assault, and he blurted out, 'We're Americans; what's happening to us?'" I was accustomed to his sharing movie scenes as illustrations, but when I researched this one, it came from the movie *Marine Raiders*, depicting combat on Guadalcanal, not Bataan.

I made a mental note: "'We're Americans'" can easily be worked into the speech."

About using a teleprompter, Reagan concluded, "Let's think about it." But, Deaver had a strong opinion. "Governor, I think you lose yourself in a teleprompter—not the ones we use in an office setting, but those outdoors." I had no idea what the hell Mike meant by "losing himself." It sounded like some bullshit notion, but the two of them had worked together for many years, and I assumed it had some meaning.

On Inauguration Day, Reagan didn't use a teleprompter, nor did he have one as backup. He delivered his first speech as US president, just as he did on the campaign trail: from a typed-up text on half sheets.

Reagan continued with a checklist for me. "The spiritual element is important, Ken, so let's not overlook it, and in that connection, we also need to reach out to the disaffected." He continued, "I don't want it to sound like a laundry list, but instead we need to apply grand themes that speak to history." On the economy, he had a set view to "attack conditions, not people." I asked about length, and Reagan requested that I aim for fifteen minutes, and it should last twenty minutes on the outside. (It lasted exactly twenty minutes.)

Reagan then had another request for unifying language. "I would like a paragraph in there which reaches out to Blacks. That would be very valuable. However, Ken, any language should aim at all minorities and should be generalized to a broader group." He mentioned Vernon Jordan, the president of the National Urban League. Over conversation at a dinner hosted by *Washington Post* publisher Katharine Graham, Reagan asked for Jordan's input, and despite being an aggressive supporter of Jimmy Carter, Jordan told Reagan he would gladly offer suggestions.

Our visit ended with Reagan staking out strong foreign policy and international messages he wished to convey. "Where people and nations want to help, we will not buy their sovereignty. Our fundamental message is in two parts: One, here in the Western Hemisphere—in the Americas—

without intervention or imposing on their sovereignty—we look to beneficial arrangements. Two, we intend to stand by our allies. I want to give reassurance that, by damn, we are going to accept the leadership that has been thrust upon us."

Jordan checked in with me on December 23. "I'm sending you three different versions for your consideration, Ken. I have no pride of authorship, and just want to be helpful. This is just between us. Don't feel any pressure." I speculated that the "just between us" signaled that Jordan didn't want the broader civil rights community knowing he "cooperated" with a political figure they bitterly attacked during the campaign.

I also reached to colleagues from the Nixon and Reagan speechwriting community—to go beyond submitting concepts and ideas, and, instead, to give me prose I could submit for Reagan's consideration. I turned to Pete Hannaford, Dick Moore, Tony Dolan, Bill Gavin, Michael Scully, Bruce Herschensohn, Noel Koch, and Ray Price. My pals sent dozens of pages of oratory, and I highlighted the best material and sent it to Reagan on Christmas Eve with a cover memo describing the enclosures as "suggested remarks for the Inaugural." I hoped in our next meeting he would return chunks of material appropriate for his speech.

I was wrong.

DECEMBER 30, 1980

Reagan and I navigated through his home's packing boxes to find a room where we could meet—an important one-on-one connection without the overseers and handlers who were distracted by jockeying for positions in the new administration and relocating to Washington. He gave no feedback from the previous week's "suggested remarks," but he had several ideas, and I began taking notes to prepare a first draft.

"Ken, we start with this thing about a momentous occasion to some of us, but it is commonplace to all of us." He cautioned again on tone. "Don't be too harsh [on Carter]; I don't want people in the audience looking at one another for reaction."

"Here's a theme, Ken. The system in America—we have everything we need here. It's the people—this ceremony itself is evidence that the government belongs to the people. Under that system, our nation went from peace to war on a single morning. [Pearl Harbor] They—the people—have all the power to solve things." He referred to a Polish letter he recently came across, with language that caught his eye, "I would rather die than once again live without such freedom."

He paused, and I saw he wanted to wrap up. "I want optimism and hope, but don't want to sound goody-goody. There's no reason to believe that we don't have the answers to things that are wrong." He stood up, as if to punctuate his optimism as I departed. "Good Lord, we've got people in poverty that are wealthier than some kings of one hundred years ago!"

It was time to put pen to paper. We had a solid collaborative relationship that grew out of the campaign, and he expected me to provide a workable "script" that he didn't have to prepare from scratch. I knew he would complete the job—edit and rearrange, rewrite, polish, and mold the clay I gave him. Still, he needed the clay.

I received valuable contributions from Noel Koch and Ray Price, both of which found their way into my final draft. By January 4, I had been through several rewrites and delivered the final version for Reagan to review during his last preinaugural visit to Washington. There were segments of the speech for which my colleagues had submitted significant input, so I listed the authorship of the draft as Khachigian, et al.

JANUARY 9, 1981

Reagan and I visited for his final verdict, and he greeted me warmly, dressed casually in slacks and slippers. With a sheaf of papers in his hands, he gestured me to follow. He apologized for the clutter of packing boxes as we sidestepped them searching for privacy. We found what appeared to be his study, and he grabbed stacks of large index cards off a chair and threw them in a wastebasket. Looking down, he said, "One nice thing about moving is you can get rid of things you really don't need anymore."

I saw he had discarded several dozen of the four-by-six cards he had used for speeches since the 1960s. Shaped by my White House years and archival research for Nixon's memoirs, I was horrified. "Governor, you can't throw those away. Everything you've ever written or said now takes on magnified historical importance." Even as president-elect, Dutch Reagan lacked any ego regarding his past—or possibly even his future. Those handwritten cards were simply "old speeches" and of no apparent value to him. I hope he retrieved them.

Looking up, he offered compliments and thanks for my effort, but noted that it was "too eloquent," and didn't quite fit his style. Um...faint praise. "On the trip back, I started to edit your copy, but found it easier to put it in my own words. You might have trouble reading my writing, so, how about if I just read it to you?" I thought I'd be the first human being on the planet to hear Ronald Reagan's first inaugural address. Pretty cool.

However, he couldn't help himself; he gave the first reading to his secretary, Kathy Osborne. As the showman, he knew Kathy would give him the very emotional reaction he wanted—and needed.

I recognized snippets of language I provided, themes he had asked for, and a framework around which he reworked his own words, phrases, and presentation. I was pleased my work hadn't been in vain, and Reagan had put to use much of what I provided. Reagan kept the fundamental structure of Noel Koch's moving tribute to the monuments as seen from the West Front of the Capitol Building. More importantly, he retained the phrase provided by Ray Price—the one that stood out in the address and branded Reagan's presidency: *In this present crisis, government is not the solution to our problem; government is the problem.*

Many of my contributions survived his editing pen through parallel prose. For example, the "spirit of cooperation" from Carter was changed by Reagan to "your gracious cooperation." My effort at "eloquence" produced prose that was slightly stuffier and formal—an overdose of rhetorical flourish. Reagan lent his version a more conversational tone while maintaining the political and policy content it required.

Reagan continued reading and when he came to the end, he put aside the legal pad that contained his handwriting, "The plane landed before I could finish. But I'm thinking of using the language from a story I was sent. It's an excerpt from the diary of a soldier killed in World War I, and when I work in the material with the monuments and Arlington Cemetery, I think it fits well."

Reagan continued reading from what appeared to be a letter, "The diary was found on his body and under the heading, 'My Pledge,' he had written these words: 'America must win this war. Therefore I will work, I will save, I will sacrifice, I will endure, I will fight cheerfully and do my utmost, as if the issue of the whole struggle depended on me alone.' What do you think, Ken?"

"Um, governor, that's a great story, but I'll have to check it out to make sure of all the details. Can you please let me know where you got that?" Reagan shoved the letter over to me and gave me a look that combined a scowl with being wounded. I know he was damned tired of being questioned. Patiently he replied, "Pres Hotchkis gave this to me. It's something he's kept at his side and used for inspiration, and he thought I could use it. I think it fits perfectly."

I took a quick look at the letter and the story. The soldier's name was Martin Treptow, and Preston Hotchkis was a Reagan pal and lifelong Republican. "Governor, if you thought you were nitpicked as a candidate, that will be multiplied many times over as president. When you tell that Treptow story, reporters will go to his hometown, search out his gravestone at Arlington, and seek his military records. They'll even want to know if there's a copy of that diary somewhere. So, please don't be offended, but we'll have to do a background check."

Reagan finished his draft, embellishing Noel Koch's lovely word pictures of the capital's monuments and setting the scene for the westward reference to the sloping hills of Arlington Cemetery. That allowed his tribute to the bravery of America's war heroes who lay there, and, especially to tell Martin Treptow's exceptional story of duty and sacrifice. While the Treptow story was a perfect fit and would move his audience, it also raised my "uh-oh" antennae. I was determined to protect Reagan from the kind of campaign situation where we had to retrieve him from a factual stumble, and no one else was around to do it.

We weren't quite done. Reagan's buddy, Senator Paul Laxalt, warned that Reagan's talk of "nonpartisanship and cooperation with the Democrats" sent signals he might be trimming on his conservative values. So, Reagan called me to add new wording and clear it with Laxalt. "Ken, here is what that language must convey, 'We in government will start by bringing government back within its means. We're going to do everything we need to do, and not retreat one damn inch from all the things we said we would do.' Okay?"

After Laxalt gave final approval, I inserted this language in Reagan's text: "Steps will be taken aimed at restoring the balance between the various levels of government. Progress may be slow, measured in inches and feet, not miles, but we will progress. It is time to reawaken this industrial giant, *to get government back within its means, and to lighten the punitive tax burden. And these will be our first priorities, and on these principles, there will be no compromise.*"

President Carter loaned Reagan his Boeing 707, tail number 27000, and the Air Force labeled the mission, "The Inaugural Trip of President-Elect Ronald Reagan from Los Angeles, California to Washington, D.C.

on January 14, 1981." I was among the select party to make this first flight. As Mike Deaver, Ed Meese, Jim Baker, and I crowded into the president's cabin to review the inaugural address, Reagan unveiled his famed humor. Somewhere over the Great Plains, he stood, looked out the window, and spread out his arms, "I told Nancy, 'Honey, now it's all ours!'"

Ed Hickey, who would serve as head of White House military liaison, accompanied me to the Pentagon, where we confirmed that Treptow was killed in action while serving in the Rainbow Division in France. So far, so good. Noel Koch joined me on a tour of the monuments and Arlington Cemetery for a flavor of how the speech's ending played, and to determine from cemetery records if Treptow was actually interred in Arlington, as Reagan claimed. However, Treptow was not buried in Arlington "under one of those white markers." Instead, the World War I hero was laid to rest in Bloomer, Wisconsin.

I also needed to know exactly where Reagan would be standing during his address—the scene he faced. With the ceremony conducted on Capitol Building grounds, the Joint Congressional Committee on Inaugural Ceremonies was in charge under the Oregon senator Mark Hatfield. Don Massey, his chief counsel at Senate Appropriations, was my contact, and walked me through the precise protocols at the site.

I then met with Mark Goode, a media producer assigned to coordinate the television networks' inaugural coverage. I took the risk of giving Mark an advance copy of the speech to explain how Reagan's peroration painted a poetic portrait of the shrines to America's greatest leaders and embraced our nation's fallen on Arlington's slopes. "Mark, only a few thousand will be in the immediate audience, but tens of millions will be watching on television. If you tip off the networks to the speech's end, and if they have cameras pre-positioned to pan over to each monument and then over to Arlington Cemetery as he solemnly mentions each, the emotional impact of his words will be magnified many times over." Mark got the picture instantly.

The final advice to Reagan came over the transom from Richard Nixon, offered via a memo through Mike Deaver:

Dear Mike,

I noted in the press that the Inaugural has been completed and I hesitate even to pass on some random thoughts which might be considered for inclusion. I would suggest, therefore, that you scan the attached memo and if you find a thought that is not already covered in the speech or one that you might think might appeal to the president-Elect, pass them on to him. I am sending a copy of this to Ken Khachigian for his information in view of the fact that he as I understand it was responsible for coordinating the various suggestions that had been sent in....

With Warm regards,

Sincerely,

RN

Richard Nixon

The entire communication is included in Appendix 5. However, of special interest was Nixon's intriguing suggestion regarding an informal "grace note" at the beginning, while extending appreciation to President Carter and the First Lady for their dedicated service. "I would suggest that this should not be put in the advance text which is given to the press but that he ad lib it somewhat as a thought that occurred to him on the platform. This way it will greatly increase press attention." The Old Man clearly had not lost his strong sense of using the presidency as theater.

SUNDAY, JANUARY 18, 1981—11:15 A.M.

I was ushered into Reagan's bedroom in Blair House for any final changes. I peeked in to see the president-elect sitting up in bed, having just returned from church services. "Come on in, Ken. I'm under the covers because I don't have my pants on." He was wearing a shirt and tie and didn't want to get his pants wrinkled. A steward had just brought in a tray with toast, honey, and coffee. "Well, now that I've got nourishment of the soul, it's time to take care of feeding the body."

Reagan had eliminated Martin Treptow's name in a previous draft, but now he decided in this bedside editing to restore it. "Ken, I don't think there is any way to dispute there is a diary, although I'm sure he had one." I still had trepidation and owed him one more last-minute caution flag. "Governor, I just want you to be aware that this is such a dramatic story, the press will track down Treptow's family and other sources for verification." Reagan, looked up from his copy, and said, "Okay, but we're still using his name."

There were no rows of crosses planted in Arlington, so it was easy to make the change to "simple white markers bearing crosses or Stars of David." Now came the tug o' war. "Governor, Treptow isn't buried in Arlington; he's buried back in his hometown in Wisconsin. So, as you have the story laid out now, you refer to him as being buried under one of those white markers in Arlington. It won't take long for them to find out his remains aren't there."

In Blair House, delivering to Reagan the final reading copy of
his first Inaugural Address, January 18, 1981.

Reagan put his hand under his chin as if he was studying the situation. Then he replied. "I can't change that, Ken. It's the whole point of my story, of his heroism and the symbolism of Arlington Cemetery." I knew that Reagan's sense of theatre and the emotion and drama he will have created required his version. But it also wasn't true. "Governor, how about this? What if instead of saying, 'under one of those white markers,' we say, 'under *such a marker*' lies Martin Treptow." Reagan thought for a minute, and I could tell he wasn't wholly comfortable, but he conceded. He would be telling the *literal* truth—that Treptow was buried under *such* a marker. As the audience listened to Reagan, it would sound as if the marker was there in Arlington. Hollywood would be served...and so was veracity!

We got to the section regarding equal opportunities and removing barriers of discrimination, and Reagan had one change. "Because there has been such a rise of anti-Semitism recently, I want to add it to read that there shouldn't be 'barriers born of bigotry' either."

"Ken, I've been thinking about it, and the hostage situation has been so much on my mind, and everyone's—that I would like to mention them in a prayer, just before my speech." I knew how strong his feelings were, but I also knew that it would totally disrupt the rhythm of the ceremony and its drama. "Governor, the inaugural proceedings are very structured, and there is going to be great anticipation for your speech. I think you'll distract from that by not going straight into your remarks. Wouldn't it be more appropriate for you to open up the Joint Congressional Luncheon this afternoon with a brief prayer for the hostages?" While he didn't respond, at least he didn't go through with a prayer at the swearing-in.

He returned his working copy to me and said:

RR: Well, are we done?

KK: Yes sir, we're ready to go into production, and I'll get your reading copy to you later today.

RR: Okay, I want to thank you for all your help throughout this production process.

He put aside his tray and let down the business barrier for a personal exchange.

RR: Ken, did you have a chance to get to that ceremony at the Lincoln Memorial last night?

KK: No sir, I was at the office and wasn't able to get there.

RR: Well, that Lincoln Memorial, and in those columns—it's such a beautiful place. I've never been filled with such a surge of patriotism. It was so hard not to cry during the whole thing. That choir [the Mormon Tabernacle Choir] singing "God Bless America"; well, it was cold, but it was so moving, I was crying frozen tears." His eyes filled up again, and he looked up at me. "It's going to be hard to keep my eyes dry."

This was awkward; I didn't know how to handle the president-elect tearing up and testing my emotions. He captured a moment for both of us. He was a long way from Dixon, and I was a long way from Visalia.

KK: Sir, I'll be back after lunch with your reading copy.

RR: Okay, that's fine.

Mrs. Reagan saved me when she walked in, and I hurried out.

As Reagan prepared to leave for a lunch meeting, Jim Baker, Jim Brady, Dick Allen, Larry Speakes, and I stopped him for a briefing on the hostage situation. We watched Steve Bell of ABC News explain the status of the negotiations, and the money transfers before the hostages were released. Reagan believed that we should have gotten the hostages *before* transferring any money and scowled at the television. He pursed his lips and muttered, "Shitheels!"

I returned later to oversee Shirley Moore's final typing of the reading text, and at 3:02 p.m. met with Reagan, asked him to sign a photocopy, and handed it over as photographer Michael Evans memorialized my moment in history. Despite my efforts in "pulling the laboring oar," no one thought to find me a seat where I could watch him deliver it. But when Don Massey and I met to confirm final podium protocols, he said, "Ken, it's got to be so moving for you to be near Reagan when he gives that historic address." I told Don I didn't have an invitation. "That doesn't make any sense," he replied. "After all your work, you should be in the immediate audience."

Overnight, Massey provided two choice seats for Meredith and me on the president's platform, and the view was splendid.

JANUARY 20, 1981, 11:57 A.M.

It was overcast and chilly as Chief Justice Warren Burger administered the oath of office, but when President Ronald Reagan stood at the podium to the cheers of the audience and began speaking, the sun suddenly broke through the clouds, raising the day to fifty-six degrees—the warmest inaugural ceremony in US history.[66]

He spoke directly to what was on the minds of so many Americans. "These United States are confronted with an economic affliction of great proportions. We suffer from the longest and one of the worst sustained inflations in our national history...Those who do work are denied a fair return for their labor by a tax system which penalizes successful achievement and keeps us from maintaining full productivity.... In this present crisis, government is not the solution to our problem; government is the problem."

Reagan drew a clear contrast to Carter's weak view of America's strengths: "It is time for us to realize that we're too great a nation to limit ourselves to small dreams. We're not, as some would have us believe, doomed to an inevitable decline.... So, with all the creative energy at our command, let us begin an era of national renewal. Let us renew our determination, our courage, and our strength. And let us renew our faith and our hope. We have every right to dream heroic dreams."

He also addressed an uncertain world. "As for the enemies of freedom, those who are potential adversaries, they will be reminded that peace is the highest aspiration of the American people. We will negotiate for it, sacrifice for it; we will not surrender for it, now or ever.... We will maintain sufficient strength to prevail if need be, knowing that if we do so we have the best chance of never having to use that strength..."

Finally, the tribute to America's past of greatness and heroism—Martin Treptow's story as well as the imagery of the line he recalled Frank McHugh using in *Marine Raiders*. Both were embedded in the text of his beautiful peroration. Seated on the president's platform, I heard them in real time.

Standing here, one faces a magnificent vista, opening up on this city's special beauty and history. At the end of this open mall are those shrines to the giants on whose shoulders we stand.

Directly in front of me, the monument to a monumental man, George Washington, father of our country. A man of humility who came to greatness reluctantly. He led America out of revolutionary victory into infant nationhood. Off to one side, the stately memorial to Thomas Jefferson. The Declaration of Independence flames with his eloquence. And then, beyond the Reflecting Pool, the dignified columns of the Lincoln Memorial. Whoever would understand in his heart the meaning of America will find it in the life of Abraham Lincoln.

Beyond those monuments to heroism is the Potomac River, and on the far shore the sloping hills of Arlington National Cemetery, with its row upon row of simple white markers bearing crosses or Stars of David. They add up to only a tiny fraction of the price that has been paid for our freedom.

Each one of those markers is a monument to the kind of hero I spoke of earlier. Their lives ended in places called Belleau Wood, The Argonne, Omaha Beach, Salerno, and halfway around the world on Guadalcanal, Tarawa, Pork Chop Hill, the Chosin Reservoir, and in a hundred rice paddies and jungles of a place called Vietnam.

Under one such marker lies a young man, Martin Treptow, who left his job in a small town barbershop in 1917 to go to France with the famed Rainbow Division. There on the western front, he was killed trying to carry a message between battalions under heavy artillery fire.

We're told that on his body was found a diary. On the flyleaf under the heading, "My Pledge," he had written these words: "America must win this war. Therefore I will work, I will save, I will sacrifice, I will endure, I will fight cheerfully and do my utmost, as if the issue of the whole struggle depended on me alone."

The crisis we are facing today does not require of us the kind of sacrifice that Martin Treptow and so many thousands of others were called upon to make. It does require, however, our best effort and our willingness to believe in ourselves and to believe in our capacity to perform great deeds; to believe that together with God's help we can and will resolve the problems which now confront us.

And after all, why shouldn't we believe that? We are Americans.

Chapter 13

TAKING CHARGE

For the president, each new day was Christmas morning—finally implementing reforms for which he spent two decades proselytizing. With his electoral mandate, he was untethered to prove that each of his memorable campaign phrases had real meaning in the lives of his fellow citizens. Government in the United States was oppressive and crushed the human spirit. Taxes sapped the energy that creativity produced. His energy and enthusiasm were infectious throughout five cabinet meetings crammed into less than two weeks to cut the budget, reduce taxes, and deregulate government. The weight of his presence was greater and more emphatic than history has given him credit, and seated behind him, I took notes to preserve a record of his historic undertaking.

The very first days of his presidency drove the policy decisions that shaped Reagan's Revolution—a struggle to lift the nation from the gloom of his predecessor and unwind the Great Society's failures. In his book *Revolution*, Martin Anderson aptly describes the elaborate and detailed preparation as Reagan presided over his cabinet councils and budget working groups in his opening days.[67] However, it was Reagan's philosophical DNA, spirit, and energy that infused the economic changes.

In Chapter 4, I described John Sears treating Reagan like a schoolboy. Sears viewed Reagan as one "who sits at any gathering of close advisers as an interested participant rather than as a leader who orders the discussion…. He's a borrower and an endorser."[68] Biographer Lou Cannon similarly opined that "Reagan had a sense of the direction in which he wanted his economic program to go, even if he did not have a road map for getting there…"[69]

In those first meetings, Reagan was the exact opposite of a passive and detached leader. His drive to achieve where others had fallen short pushed him to become more intensely involved in the minutiae of his challenge. Reagan's knowledge of economics was honed by life in a system that punished his work ethic through excessive taxation, and he had to be intellectually nimble in a career that repeatedly tested his brainpower. He may have needed the "experts" to flesh out the supply-side theories of his tax cuts and reversal of government growth, but the plans were going nowhere without articulation of gut instincts Reagan had compiled in a lifetime.

JANUARY 22

Reagan made things clear to his assembled cabinet, "We came here to do things differently." Energy secretary James Edwards opened with a focus on Carter's failed energy policies, and a recommendation to deregulate the oil and natural gas industry. "Produce, produce, produce," said Edwards. David Stockman, the young OMB director, interjected and looked to the president, "I recommend you do what you pledged in the campaign."

Stockman, the thirty-four-year-old former Michigan congressman, gave up his seat on the influential House Commerce Committee to use his institutional knowledge and command of information to help Reagan make vast changes in the scope of government. He assumed his duties with the zeal and energy of youth—with an ego to match. His restlessness and jolting movements reminded me of the dust devils on our Visalia farm— the dry soil that whirled in hot summer winds. While each cabinet officer came to these meetings with specific presentations, Stockman's voltage quickly exceeded that of his colleagues.

Reagan listened to the debate on deregulation, then decided, "The only question is whether I do it *today*. Then, maybe we'll tell the oil companies to show constraint. We want to announce the decision as soon as possible. You made my day! I have to tell you this is one of the happiest meetings I've had; it's working just the way I thought it would!" Six days later, he signed Executive Order 12287—"Decontrol of Crude Oil and Refined Petroleum Products."[70]

For decades as conservative spokesman and candidate, he had preached this philosophy. Through the reality of presidential power, he was putting it to use.

JANUARY 23

The meeting opened on saving a billion dollars by imposing the indexing of entitlement programs, especially on newer retirees in the civil service sector—despite potential union problems. Reagan chimed in, "Civil servants are supposed to be paid comparable to the private sector, but they are really paid more than the private sector." Reagan couldn't hide his delight with the savings of a billion dollars and exulted, "Well, as Jeb Stuart said, 'Ride to the sound of the guns!'"

That sounded like a line straight from one of his old movies—*Santa Fe Trail*.

Stockman's next dagger was out for the 1974 anachronism, the Council on Wage and Price Stability (COWPS)—237 positions costing $10 million a year, with only twenty or twenty-five doing constructive work. He proposed to eliminate COWPS—giving folks thirty days to leave and turning the money back to the government after retaining the useful people.

Reagan's sensitivity surfaced—shaking his head with a pained look, "Let's do it fast. Being a child of the Depression, it has always been very hard for me to fire anyone. All right, go ahead." He was ambivalent; yet he had also just been briefed on a make-work project that subsidized sloth—a far cry from what happened in the Depression. He added, "Our goal is to reduce the Federal Register to the size of a pamphlet," and agonized that he "didn't want to create a bureaucracy to get rid of a bureaucracy."

Six days later, he terminated the Wage and Price Stability Program with his signature on Executive Order 12288.[71]

JANUARY 24

Stockman reported on the president's imposition of a two-week deadline for all the work to be done on the budget, and each cabinet officer was expected to hold down their department's outlays in the interim. Stockman let down his guard when he acknowledged to a reporter that he was anxious to win approval for huge budget cuts "before the new cabinet officers were fully familiar with their departments and prepared to defend their bureaucracies."[72]

Secretary of State Al Haig was due for center stage. Before sitting down, Haig embraced me and whispered, "These are much better circumstances than back in '74, right?" I didn't disagree. As Al listened impatiently to

budget talk, I watched from behind, thinking he probably felt more qualified to be in the president's chair than his own.

Haig reported on post stress issues regarding the just-released Iranian-
held hostages and cautioned about congressional pressures regarding agreements Carter made for their release. Reagan quickly shut down any debate
within the cabinet. "I believe in covert diplomacy. We don't cause Iran
to lose face. We should make quiet statements due to the fact that three
people are still there. Let's send our objections and comments quietly and
privately."

With a puckish grin, he added with regard to releasing frozen assets to
Iran: "I was just wondering, since it's legal tender, that we give them that
three and a half billion dollars in pennies. It would sure as hell cure their
unemployment problems."

JANUARY 27

Defense Secretary Cap Weinberger was absent, and Reagan turned to Al
Haig and quipped, "Cap's missing, there must be a war."

Health and Human Services Secretary Richard Schweiker argued for
an executive order to put the burden of proof on government, not citizens,
to comply with the law where regulations usurped powers. Reagan gleefully
agreed. "I can't wait to sign that. I don't understand. If you murder someone, you are considered innocent until proven guilty. But if you are charged
with violating a regulation, you are guilty as charged, and you must prove
you are innocent and take the case before the ones who wrote the regulations…who are judge, jury, and executioners." He had a way of reducing
government talk to everyday life—a lesson he hoped every cabinet member
understood.

Secretary of Agriculture Jack Block made another run at getting Reagan
to lift the Soviet grain embargo. Reagan didn't budge. "Jack, my whole
approach on this is one of mixed emotions. I know it hurts our farmers, but
I don't want to give in to the Soviets. From now on, going forward, I want
the policy to be that anytime we give, we get." He was aware of our farm
belt campaign pledges to drop the embargo that restricted valuable trade
opportunities for agriculture. Still, for the moment, he wasn't prepared to
overcome his deep animosity toward the communists.

He was relieved when Education Secretary Terrel Bell changed the subject with his report on bilingual education's "federal control and direction

of something which should be local and giving educators too many instructions. We have no business being involved in this, and I recommend we move quickly to get this done." Reagan savored another opportunity to abolish federal overreach into American lives and ordered Bell, "Go to it full speed ahead. The job is mainly bilingual education, and that's to find a child who doesn't understand the lesson and help him. Go to it; more power to you."

But it was Treasury Secretary Don Regan's mention of the debt ceiling that provided Reagan a platform to lecture his cabinet to understand clearly his mission:

> I know this is a little unfair; you have gigantic departments and big bureaucracies. But it will take time to learn, and bureaucrats can give you the wrong advice. If we're going to get government back within its revenues, we need greater savings. There will be greater savings when you know more about it and achieve programmatic changes. That will allow you to overcome old ways of doing things. Remember, people create jobs to insure their own longevity. We did a thing in California; where the cabinet brings in a budget they need to have, but also brings in a budget which would be your last word if there was a 20 percent cut. And that was a good exercise. It gets down to absolute necessities.

A week into his presidency, Reagan had convened nearly two dozen daily staff, cabinet, national security, and congressional meetings to set the tone for his "era of renewal." His passion and engagement to upend the sleepy capital didn't quite elevate to a Rockwell portrait or Gershwin tune. But pretty damn close.

Attending Reagan's cabinet and budget meetings helped me capture his voice for America's economic future, but it also served a purpose for my pending assignments. I had two major national speeches to prepare—one for national television and the other before a joint session of Congress. Along with my normal writing workload, I also had to build out a support staff to assist me.

Putting the final touches on the historic joint session speech for the Economic Recovery Plan, February 1981—in the Library of the White House Residence.

Room 100 is one of the most sought-after offices in the Old Executive Office Building. Unlike my obscure office suites in the '70s, my expansive corner office was just steps across West Executive Avenue to the West Wing and looked south to the Washington Monument and Jefferson Memorial while sporting a fireplace and large entry with space for two secretarial desks. Given my prospective workload, the latter was far more valuable than the former.

Jim Baker expressly authorized me to build the speechwriting team. Nevertheless, without seeking my approval, Dave Gergen filled two positions before I arrived—Tony Dolan, who worked in the campaign, and Mari Maseng, a communications aide from Senator Bob Dole's '80 presidential effort. On a late-night bus trip in the '80 campaign, I asked Reagan press aide Dana Rohrabacher what he did in the "real world," and he responded that he wrote editorials for the *Orange County Register*. "That's a good background for speechwriting," I said, and while I was building my staff, he repeatedly reminded me of my comment. I believed loyalty should be rewarded and hired him for his campaign devotion.

Presidential utterances are forever embedded in history and cannot be retrieved, so when hiring our research staff, I set the standard that Reagan must not knowingly misstate a fact or a quotation, or otherwise be caught in an error—any of which would be embarrassing at best or, at worst, cause a policy or diplomatic disaster. I established the same research technique used in the Nixon White House, one created by *Time Magazine*. Their method required that each name, fact, number, assertion, or historical reference received an adjacent stand-alone checkmark as an absolute assurance for accuracy.

I retained Misty Church, a valued campaign research aide, to lead off. We added Daryl Borgquist, and I tracked down another Nixon alum, Maureen Brown, to complete the team. I also had an instant executive secretarial team in place with Nance Roberts and Kathy Reid with additional help for staff writers from Karen South and Denise Wilson. Nance was a 120 words-a-minute typist who helped me Election Night and didn't have to be educated regarding the new team. But Kathy was a career White House employee who previously assisted Carter's top domestic adviser, Stu Eisenstadt.

Gergen recruited Kathy to my staff, and I took her on grudgingly but warned she would be on probation due to her Eisenstadt affiliation. She not only turned out to be loyal, dedicated, discreet, and capable, but Kathy Reid became one of the warmest friends of the entire Khachigian family. Within days, she became indispensable to me and to our entire office, bringing institutional memory, wisdom, and White House "street knowledge" known by only very few.

I relied on Kathy for all my later presidential assignments and when we lost her prematurely to cancer, it was a devastating personal blow as well as to the multitudes of the extended White House family who adored her.

JANUARY 28

Reagan's first pitch on national television was due in eight days, and I needed guidance to assemble all the economic and budget pieces I'd heard over the last week. Reagan presided over an historic Oval Office meeting with logs crackling behind him in the fireplace. Bush sat to Reagan's left, and the brainstormers included Stockman, Regan, Anderson, and newly appointed chair of the Council of Economic Advisers Murray Weidenbaum. They competed to instruct the president on economic problems, and Baker and I observed from the back.

Weidenbaum gave Reagan plenty of statistics and blamed the economy on long-standing maladies. Stockman, Anderson, and Regan alternately offered their views of an economic message. But I needed the president's message, not theirs. What made this meeting stand out was Reagan's disquisition on American economics as seen by real people.

The Eureka College economics major believed if having this new power meant anything, his underlings had to understand the challenge ahead and what was expected of us. Shooting a quick glance at me, he turned back to the others and laid out his convictions. "Basically, our nation is economically illiterate. I want to have in mind the fellow who comes home from the factory, and then say things to him in ways he understands. People want to relate to down-to-earth things."

He was only warming up.

> For example, look at off-budget items. Those are gimmicks used by government to hide the debt. They are government programs and run up the deficit, so you have to pay for that. How much bigger is the national debt, than it was before? You need to explain it in their way and that relates to their paycheck. "You've gotten raises, but those raises aren't 'real.' They just moved you into higher brackets." Many women are working, and they suffer too, not because they want to. "You are being discriminated against by the income tax regulations. Some of you might not want to work; and you shouldn't be *forced* to work."

Without question, he was also dictating potential language for his first televised address.

> Let's talk about business taxes. "Business taxes aren't paid by business; they're paid by you. Now every few years, business must keep up with the times. As an individual, you deduct things, and business is the same way. Business has got to be able to deduct their improvements. We try to do that in a way which gives business enough money

to rebuild new plants, and we have to speed that up, so they can rebuild faster. Maybe some of you watching don't manufacture a product; you provide a service."

Turning to Weidenbaum and Regan, he said, "We need to be able to show where government fits into this." With instructions on how to frame messages about "bracket creep" and "accelerated depreciation," and how to put those into laymen's terms, *he* was the teacher, and *they* were the students—spiels from his radio show, hundreds and hundreds of political campaign speeches, as well as countless presentations on behalf of General Electric. As president, he was now empowered to go beyond preaching the gospel and put it into practice.

> We've been living on borrowed time, and we can't cure it instantly. What we can do is bring the rolling boulder to a stop, and then start pushing it back up the hill. All these things government has been doing—well, some of them we simply can't afford. There's no such thing as federal funds. "It's your money." We need to be so blunt as never before and talk about *their* paychecks and *their* jobs.

Stockman tried to interject, but Reagan pressed on.

> We think spending and cutting taxes go together, and we think what we're suggesting is a new approach. "You can lecture your child forever about extravagance, but the most effective way is by cutting his allowance." We've talked for forty years about cutting the size of the government, but that's never happened. No government in history has voluntarily reduced its size. "What we're aiming at is a little temporary discomfort, but we're going to try to end the increase in the cost of living index so in the future your dollar would mean something." We're not going to cut social programs alone. There are some other things we're going to cut, including business items in the budget. It took us forty years to get here; we can't get out in forty days. I remember one day my daughter said, "What do you mean by capital?" That's what I mean by economic illiteracy. We have to educate the nation.

After I completed the first draft, fellas from Treasury and OMB began hovering in my office to influence wording. Stockman and Weidenbaum made the trip over a couple of times, and a young assistant OMB director, Larry Kudlow, made his way over to ensure that the numbers I used were correct. Thirty-five years later, Kudlow emerged as director of President Donald Trump's National Economic Council.

FEBRUARY 3

I submitted my draft to Reagan at 5:00 p.m. I did so after rejecting an officious attempt by David Gergen to suggest that he could have a draft with a "different slant" three hours before getting it to Reagan. Gergen had no authority and no speechwriting role and tried to bypass normal comment procedures—not his only display of disrespect for a colleague—and one of the mistakes Baker made in dispersing power to favored staff without placing boundaries.

I knew Reagan would wield a heavy editing pen, and he did. His personal secretary, Helene von Damm, called two days later to hand me the president's handwritten rewrite of my effort and asked that our office prepare a clean copy.

With the speech just over twenty-four hours away, Reagan called in his cabinet to reinforce his long-held principles: "We're going to think of government as being 'they' rather than 'we,' and I know those professional bureaucrats are frozen in their views. I don't want executive orders disappearing in the sand and never being heard from again."

Were it not for the passion and philosophical commitment he expressed, I don't believe Reagan's early achievements and victories would have ever crossed the goal line. They were logged over the recalcitrance of the pragmatists within his own operation who believed that the only way to make things work was to bend, not shove.

With mere hours to review his final edits, the president and I were joined in the residence by Baker, Anderson, Weidenbaum, and Brady. The Gipper was in an expansive mood, looking up to make a word adjustment or accepting a factual correction. He complained that "our guys [in Congress] are holding up things. They're not used to being in the majority, and they're not used to making decisions." He laughed and said, "Now we have to woo the bastards. If I were campaigning, I'd kick the balls of the party in power—saying they caused it. But not when I'm in office."

It was a fun side of Reagan I didn't often see—like "one of the boys." He set down his reading glasses to tell a story that offered a critical insight into his strong feelings about reducing taxes. "From time to time, I was asked to emcee some event, and one of them was the Pillsbury Bake-Off. These ladies could win big awards for creating new recipes, and just when they were handed their checks, the IRS were waiting offstage to ensure the government would collect its share. It was crazy that these women would work so hard, and then punished for their exceptional creativity. That was just plain wrong."

The others left, and I lingered to raise a potential "stage performance issue." Reagan wanted to remove from his pocket and display a dollar bill, a quarter, a dime, and a penny to illustrate the effects of inflation by the dollar's shrinkage in value to 36 cents since 1960. "Mr. President, won't that be awkward to speak on live television to fumble in your pocket while placing those items in front of the camera?" Reagan gave me a wounded look. "No problem, Ken. You'll see how I do it." I managed a skeptical grin, but he gave a quick demonstration by sliding his hand into his coat pocket and holding out the currency.

In his February 5 speech, Reagan treated America to the same economic lesson he gave in the Oval Office and didn't pull any punches regarding the hand he was dealt.

> I regret to say that we're in the worst economic mess since the Great Depression....[The] deficit is larger than the entire Federal budget in 1957.... Now, we've just had two years of back-to-back double-digit inflation—13.3 percent in 1979, 12.4 percent last year.... In 1960 mortgage interest rates averaged about 6 percent. They're two and a half times as high now, 15.4 percent....
>
> And finally there are seven million Americans caught up in the personal indignity and human tragedy of unemployment. If they stood in a line, allowing three feet for each person, the line would reach from the coast of Maine to California....

Let me try to put this in personal terms. Here is a dollar such as you earned, spent, or saved in 1960. And here is a quarter, a dime, and a penny—thirty-six cents. That's what this 1960 dollar is worth today. And if the present world inflation rate should continue three more years, that dollar of 1960 will be worth a quarter.... We're threatened with an economic calamity of tremendous proportions, and the old business-as-usual treatment can't save us. Together, we must chart a different course.

He summarized his key proposals. Reduce federal tax rates—10 percent across the board for each of next three years; impose a freeze on federal hiring and pending federal regulations; and cut spending, but with compassion for those who through no fault of their own need our help. After appealing to the nation's "common sense," he concluded, "Together we can forge a new beginning for America."

Public support for his measures meant little if he couldn't get Congress to go along, and we had no time to rest between the two addresses. President Kennedy's decision to deliver a State of the Union address ten days after his inauguration was a rare exception to early presidential addresses to Congress. Hence, Reagan's decision to speak to a Joint Session on February 18 was clearly intended to grasp the initiative in that high profile forum. In advance of going to Congress, he wanted to continue the momentum with no let-up on the pressure within his cabinet and his staff.

FEBRUARY 9

Dave Stockman led a working lunch in the Cabinet Room for the economic advisory team. Stockman boasted of job production from a personal tax rate reduction from the top rate of 70 percent to 50 percent. Reagan told the cabinet to put it in the form of a message, "We should be trying to do this on the basis, not of relieving the individual tax burden, but to get the economy moving again." He paused, smiled, and couldn't resist a story. "James Burnham has said that when operating on a Democrat, even the most skillful surgeon cannot separate demagogic tissue from solid tissue without jeopardizing the life of the patient."

Reagan worried that we violated supply-side economics when removing some tax benefits—like the oil depletion allowance—while keeping others. Stockman argued that some of these were just "tax subsidies," Reagan pushed back: "I'm very reluctant to cut these incentive-inducing points. I went through a few dry holes myself; but I went into them dreaming of the income that would have come back tax-free from success."

Throughout Stockman's budget and tax presentation, the president interjected with similar points. While the budget and numbers guy was on a policy track, Reagan wanted him not to wander far from the philosophical one. Making sure everyone in the room got his message, "Don't be too timid. As long as we're taking this dive, it's going to be cold water when we hit it, and nothing can be done about it."

Unfortunately, in the weeks ahead, his team looked for more warm water.

FEBRUARY 10

Each cabinet secretary raised their final concerns over substantial cuts in their departments. NBC News had Reagan "mic'd-up" all day while filming "A Day in the Life of the president." So, the meeting's first few minutes were for the cameras. As the members made their appeals, the president signaled his expectations, either declaratively or through anecdote. He was proud—almost smug—in reporting of his response to a House member who told him while he realized cutting back was important, he pleaded "impact aid" was helpful in his district. "I looked him in the eye and smiled, and said I'd look in to it." Meaning, he wouldn't budge.

Reagan pushed back his chair to leave, then stopped to give another lecture—this one about tax loopholes, and his voice was angry:

> We're not going to talk like the previous administration. These so-called "loopholes"—well, some of them are holding the entire tax system together. I'm hearing some of our folks beginning to say, "put a tax cut here, but put it back on something else over here." Let me just say, the middle class have paid the freight all these years. They could confiscate all the money of the rich, and it wouldn't run the government for a week.

He got up to leave and said, "See, I'm still talking about government as 'they.'" Point made.

Later that afternoon, a small group of us met with Reagan specifically to discuss what should go into the Joint Session speech. Lyn Nofziger joined, and referring to NBC's film crew, popped off, "How's it feel to be an actor again?" With perfect timing, he replied, "I don't mind being an actor again...except, it's a lousy part."

On the issue of his economic recovery plan, Reagan knew what he wanted to say and how he wanted to say it. Despite the landslide victory that endorsed his reforms, Reagan was sensitive to emerging portrayals of him as insensitive. Hence, he wanted me to make sure his speech explained the "why" of what he was proposing. "I want to point out what we're *not* doing. We are *saving* the poor. I know that there are those who think reducing the top tax bracket from 70 percent to 50 percent, like all the tax cuts, benefit the wealthy; but they will stimulate productivity and produce jobs for the more than seven million people out of work."

Nofziger didn't think the seventy-fifty cut could be sold and would jeopardize the tax package and added, "All the editorials will be in an uproar out there." Jim Baker, the pragmatist, was concerned about public opinion, and that a cut in the top rate for high level taxpayers would "jeopardize the chances" of the spending cuts. But Meese knew Reagan's resentment of the high tax bracket and countered Nofziger and Baker.

Reagan bridled, "Well, it would be very hard for me to retreat because I think it's a very important part of what we're trying to do. This tax program is not designed to simply reduce the burden of tax on the people; it's designed to get the damned country moving again. And, frankly, that probably has a better effect on that than some of the other things we're doing." He acknowledged that "some congressmen and some editorial writers are going to make damned sure and paint it as a tax benefiting the rich. Now, what is the best? For me to slide over it, or for me to face it head-on and soften it by saying it first."

Reagan was very clear about what he believed in, getting the wealthy to put revenue into the economy. "This will actually accomplish our goal by taking many of these same people who are not paying taxes, because they have chosen tax shelters and so forth—rather than investing in the open market—and we could say we're convinced it would result in an increase in revenue and create one hundred fifty thousand jobs."

Others argued back and forth on shaping his message, but Reagan continued as the single true believer in the room. He argued that he'd seen auto workers "out there" showing they're ready to take a cut. "There's something different out there; people among the unemployed want something done." Reagan was thinking and acting just as bold in office as he said on the campaign trail. He looked at us around the room and said with the kind of conviction I think he wished we shared: "I've never thought anything about this job was going to be easy." Stockman finally got the message, and offered, "Well, they're going to make the same arguments against the ten-ten-ten cuts anyway."

I regret that I held back my own personal views. There was no reason for me not to have asserted myself as an equal, senior member of the White House staff along with Marty Anderson and Lyn Nofziger. This was one occasion where I should have taken the kind of position I would have taken on the campaign plane and encouraged the president that he was right to embrace the integrity of his position. Nofziger, Baker and the others were exercising precisely the timidity that frustrated the president, and it was left to Reagan to show the kind of conviction and principles that the rest of us should have supported without hesitation.

FEBRUARY 13

Reagan wanted a working draft before heading for Camp David the following day so he could work on it over the weekend. We had a working lunch with Reagan, and his economic advisers continued to bridle at the seventy-fifty tax reduction. Norman Ture, undersecretary of the treasury and primary author of the tax cuts, interrupted: "There is no more effective way to slow down tax shelters than to lower the top tax rate from seventy to fifty percent. It will create a strong shift out of tax shelters because people at seventy percent are most sensitive to changes at the margin." It was music to Reagan's ears.

During a break, Reagan took us all away from the drudgery of the numbers and regaled us with his Hollywood prank on Errol Flynn while filming *Santa Fe Trail*.

> I was playing George Custer; he was Jeb Stuart. We were
> doing a scene where a lady was telling our fortunes. We
> were all in the same uniform, and I was standing behind

Flynn on a Downhill slope. He was very insecure and had covered me up so I couldn't be seen. So during rehearsals, I quietly shuffled dirt with my boots to create a mound. And then when the director said, "action," I stepped up on the mound so I could be seen. I was the tallest man in the Calvary!

The entire cabinet gathered that afternoon for a briefing on Reagan's full economic package. Meese summarized the key elements, and when he admonished the cabinet to make sure "the bureaucracy can't end-run us," the president quipped, "Or else we'll booby trap their swivel chairs!" Stockman previewed the fiscal issues that eventually emerged as dark clouds for Reagan. "In order to achieve our goals by 1982, we still need to find $9 billion to make a total of $51 billion in cuts. We hope by FY 1982 the deficit will be below $40 billion."

Knowing the constituencies of each department would be hearing pleas, Stockman warned, "We have to hang together on the cuts and keep the pressures back." Reagan thanked Stockman, "I'm proud of you," and smiled, "We won't leave you out there alone, Dave. We'll all come to the hanging."

Don Regan and Stockman came to my office to ensure that the tax matters and budget cuts were properly written in my draft. After a late night and finishing touches early in the morning, we faxed it to the president at noon on Saturday. Sunday morning, his military aide called to put me on alert to await Reagan's edits, and soon his handwritten rewrite was arriving back over the Signal Corps' secure line.

One of Reagan's distinctive word pictures caught my eye. In February of 1981, America's national debt approached the shocking amount of $1 trillion! (In 2024, it is $34 trillion.) Reagan wrote: "A few weeks ago I called such a figure, a trillion dollars, incomprehensible, and I've been trying ever since to think of a way to illustrate how big a trillion really is. And the best I could come up with is that if you had a stack of thousand-dollar bills in your hand only four inches high, you'd be a millionaire. *A trillion dollars would be a stack of thousand dollars bills over eighty miles high.*"

Then, the White House operator called. "Mr. Khachigian, please hold for the president."

RR: Hi Ken, just wanted to make sure you got my edits and that you're able to read all of them.

KK: Of course. But, if you'll excuse the question, Mr. President, where on earth did you come up with the number for the thousand-dollar bills reaching up to the sky?

RR: Well, by long division.

I chuckled quietly while picturing him with a yellow pad dividing mysterious numbers into 1,000,000,000,000.

Now we had to determine the true height of greenbacks stacked up to a trillion dollars. Our research team reached out to the Bureau of Engraving and Mint and popped the question. The answer came back coolly: "It all depends on whether you stack them loosely, or they're bound together. Loosely stacked, it would be sixty-seven miles high, and bound together, sixty-three miles." Well, the president was close. Somewhere over the years, he clipped an article—most likely in *Human Events*—regarding outrageous government waste and remembered this number.

The president entered the House Chamber to a standing ovation, but when he handed Democrat House Speaker Thomas "Tip" O'Neill a printed copy, O'Neill scoffed, "Mr. President, good luck." *The Boston Globe* reported he said it the way "one heavyweight says it to another before the championship fight."[73] For all the lore about the camaraderie between the two Irishmen, O'Neill also thought of Reagan as a political naif. He looked forward to teaching the rookie a lesson in Boston-style politics.

After Reagan repeated his familiar depiction of a grim economic landscape, he went on a positive offensive that reflected a vision a world apart from Jimmy Carter's "American malaise."

> It is within our power to change this picture, and we can act with hope. There's nothing wrong with our internal strengths. There has been no breakdown of the human, technological, and natural resources upon which the economy is built. Based on this confidence in a system which has never failed us, but which we have failed through a

lack of confidence and sometimes through a belief that we could fine tune the economy and get it tuned to our liking, I am proposing a comprehensive four-point program.

He outlined the details of his policies to cut spending, reduce taxes, cut regulations, and gain control of national monetary policy:

America's new beginning: a program for economic recovery.... There's nothing wrong with America that together we can't fix.... The people are watching and waiting. They don't demand miracles. They do expect us to act. Let us act together.

He wrote in his diary that night:

This was the big night—the speech to Cong. on our ec. plan. I've seen Presidents over the years enter the House chamber without ever thinking I would one day be doing it. The reception was more that I'd anticipated—most of it of course from one side of the aisle. Still it was a thrill and something I'll long remember.

Hardly back at the W.H. when "Signal" handed me a stack of wires all in support of the program.[74]

He was elated and reportedly reluctant to return to the family quarters, instead loitering around the elevator laughing and talking and having photos taken with some of his Secret Service agents.[75] In a senior staff meeting the next morning, we received the same reports of positive feedback—out of 961 calls, 95 percent were favorable, and it was reported to be three times the volume for a first presidential speech before Congress. Four weeks after being sworn in, Reagan stood on the broadest national stage to seek the culmination of his generation-long advocacy of limited government and lower taxes along with his message of an America availing hope and opportunity.

O'Neill's top aide, Chris Matthews, wrote that seeing the "effect" on his fellow Democrats from the vantage of sitting behind Reagan, the Speaker "must have glimpsed the shape of his future." The reaction Reagan drew "was like nothing he'd ever witnessed...When asked later about the seemingly mesmerized response to Reagan's appearance that night, O'Neill was candid...[H]e told the press that the public reaction to the president's performance was 'tremendously strong...I don't know how many telegrams we've received.'"[76]

Perhaps Speaker O'Neill briefly wondered whether it was he, not Reagan, who needed luck in the bout between the two heavyweights.

Chapter 14

"THE PRESIDENT'S BEEN SHOT!"

MARCH 30, 1981—2:30 P.M.

I was in Marty Anderson's office after enjoying a leisurely lunch in the Mess. I passed up on accompanying the president to the Washington Hilton for his speech at the AFL-CIO's conference and sent Mari Maseng in my place so she could get a feel for how Reagan delivered her first effort as a staff speechwriter. Suddenly, sirens blared from the direction of Pennsylvania Avenue—a symphony of chaos. It had been a drippy morning, and I turned to Marty, "Sounds like there might have been a bad accident near 17th Street." We returned to our discussion when Barbara Honegger burst in with words I last heard in 1963 while leaving my UCSB dormitory for an English 1B class.

"The president's been shot!"

Ronald Reagan loved touting his union credentials as the only Republican candidate holding a union card. As president of the Screen Actors Guild, he was an aggressive representative of his craft and worked to purge its ranks of communist party members. While the AFL-CIO wasn't a natural constituency, it remained a blue-collar group sensible to court, and labor secretary Ray Donovan gained credibility by producing the president at a big union meeting.

I needed a break from the grind of producing every speech, and it was time to test the new team. I asked Mari for a draft I could polish and then pass on to the president. While our combined draft was okay, Reagan rewrote major portions and included a quotation from the legendary founder of the American Federation of Labor, Samuel Gompers, that appeared to repudiate the welfare state. However, our research staff made a correction on the Gompers quote—worded differently from Reagan's.

The president called me Saturday morning. "Ken, the quote I had from Samuel Gompers came back differently than the way I worded it in my draft. Just wanted to check to see what's going on?" I had to explain our archival search and replied, "I'm sorry, sir, we just had to tweak it a bit to make those changes for accuracy." Reagan's version came from his vast personal stack of notecards kept from years of writing his own speeches. I never enjoyed correcting him.

MARCH 30, 8:00 A.M.

Jim Baker was unhappy in the senior staff meeting about a leak of the federalism paper, and Jim Brady referred to the signing of the Dairy Support program. I gave a heads up for a Tuskegee University speech. Otherwise, crickets. I returned to the office where Nance Roberts had finalized the president's Washington Hilton half sheets and grabbed Maseng, who didn't know where I was taking her.

As a newcomer to the team, she had never met the president close up in the Oval Office, and I thought it would be a nice reward for her to accompany me when I delivered his reading copy. I hurried because I knew he was impatiently waiting, and Maseng, tall and long-legged, complained, "Some of us don't have the best knees, you know." Into the West Basement and striding up the steps and down the hall, she finally got the picture. Helene von Damm waved us in, and the president stood and gave an especially broad smile when I introduced Mari as the "rookie" who helped with his speech.

11:46 A.M.

The president called to verify one more statistic. "Sorry, sir, I don't have that at hand, and I'll have to get back to you." Misty Church tracked down the information.

12:06 P.M.

The White House operator reached Reagan, and I closed the circle to confirm the number he wanted. I called Maseng back in to my office. "I've been with Reagan on dozens of these events, and you need to get familiarized with his speaking style. Plus you'll enjoy riding in the motorcade, so why don't you go out to the Hilton with him?

2:27 P.M. MARCH 30, 1981

John Hinckley, Jr. shot the president, Jim Brady, Secret Service Agent Tim McCarthy, and DC police officer Thomas Delahanty.

The term "dodging a bullet" took on new meaning for me. If I had gone to the event with Reagan, and as we headed for our cars in the motorcade, I would have exited the Hilton alongside Mike Deaver and Jim Brady—most likely adjacent to Brady. Thus, the bullets that whizzed by Deaver's head and the one that caught Brady could also have had my name on them—and an unknown fate may have been in store for me if I decided to accompany the president that afternoon.

Marty and I scoured the television news for scattered information. Our meeting was now meaningless, and we wondered what the hell to do. On the first floor we saw Ed Meese, Lyn Nofziger, Dick Allen, and others gathering in Jim Baker's corner office. Baker, Meese and Nofziger left for the hospital where Reagan's lead Secret Service agent Jerry Parr had directed the president's limo driver after seeing what appeared to be oxygenated blood coming from Reagan's lungs.[77]

ABOUT 3:00 P.M.

The Secret Service reported to treasury secretary Don Regan, and he also arrived to Baker's office. An agent came in to announce that the president took a wound entering in the back, and that McCarthy was shot in the chest. Soon, Al Haig walked in and assumed command in the absence of Baker and other senior White House staff.

3:06 P.M.

Haig asked the White House operator to reach Vice President Bush, who had been at speaking engagements in Texas. Bush was in flight, so the Signal

Corps patched Haig through to an insecure line, and he began talking cryptically as I began scribbling on my yellow pad:

> *We had a serious incident. I'm sending a message by secure lines.*
> *I recommend that you return to Washington as soon as possible.*
> *Do you read that? Over. This is Al Haig. Over. It is Secretary*
> *Haig. Over. I'll have a message over to you shortly. All right?*

Haig quickly dictated a message and cleared it with Dick Allen, who could run it through the secure national security apparatus. I then followed Haig downstairs to the Situation Room. Al jousted heatedly with defense secretary Caspar Weinberger and others during those tense Situation Room moments. As the afternoon wore on, the tumult in the press briefing room was no less chaotic, and Haig became enraged when Larry Speakes's responses to rapid-fire questioning turned increasingly defensive. Haig jumped out of his chair, dragging Dick Allen with him to clarify communications and lines of authority.

I followed behind as they rushed up the stairs to the briefing room. I stood to their right and watched while a flushed and unsettled Haig insisted he was "in control, here at the White House" and confused the constitutional rules of succession. Al Haig's clumsily chosen words—in a matter of a few seconds in anxiety and chaos—blew up much of his distinguished career of national service.

My shaken staff was gathered around my television when I returned at 4:15. Earlier, I had called to reassure Meredith that I didn't go to the Hilton with the president, but called again when the girls were home from school. Nine-year-old Kristy was crying, "Daddy, you come home right now. Stay away from the president!" Her plea was another reminder of why I was wise to reject a full-time assignment in Washington.

6:40 P.M.

Though Reagan left the operating room out of danger, Bush had to return quickly to establish reassurance of stable leadership. While the quickest route from Andrews to the White House would have been a Marine helicopter, Bush told military aide John Matheny, "Only the president lands on the South Lawn," so they choppered to the veep's residence and motored to the White House.[78]

CBS and ABC did not distinguish themselves earlier in the evening when Frank Reynolds and Dan Rather shocked us without solid verification that Jim Brady had died.[79] Repeatedly, we viewed Brady lying on the sidewalk after taking one of Hinckley's rounds to his head. We were relieved to hear he survived, but the damage to his brain was severe, and with the dumb luck of the trajectory of the .22 caliber slug, Brady's dreams collided with an angry destiny.

Brady and I bonded on *LeaderShip 80*, and it was impossible not to be captivated by his irreverence, whether scarfing down jelly beans in the Cabinet Room or launching into his thirty-second Indian war dance on the fringe of a campaign rally. He had puckish and specific instructions in dealing with campaign media: "Menian, rule number one is to lure them to buy us dinner every night so at least we eat good, and then, if we work it right, they won't get much out of us."

Brady desperately wanted the White House press secretary's job and confided to me, "I don't know which of these is the worst. Number two is getting it; but number one is not getting it." Because Baker wasn't a Reaganite, he strung Brady along while weighing other candidates. No one else should have been considered given Jim's familiarity with Reagan and the relationships he built up during the campaign.

I returned to the West Wing to see if I could help. Bush was in his office after a security briefing and meetings with cabinet members, and I walked in as he and his press aide, Pete Teeley, were discussing the issuance of a brief statement. Bush was somber, and his clipped words crowded small talk. Teeley had begun preparing comments for a world starving for official news.

Teeley felt the intensity and fatigue of a long day, and along with the office's jangling phones and commotion, he found it difficult to find the precise words. "Ken, it's just not working for me. Can you lend a hand?" After, a few words of guidance from Bush, I slipped a piece of paper into one of typewriters and batted out a short draft. Pete and I watched as Bush did a quick read-through, and then made a few changes to fit his style.

8:20 P.M.

Even the media seemed worn by the time Bush stepped up to the podium. "I am deeply heartened by Dr. O'Leary's report on the president's condition, that he has emerged from his experience with flying colors and with the most optimistic prospects for a complete recovery. I can reassure this nation and a watching world that the American government is functioning fully and effectively." He concluded with concern for the two law enforcement officers who were struck and for "a friend of everybody here, dedicated public servant Jim Brady."

Bush sat as an observer at next morning's senior staff meeting. Deaver reported on seeing Reagan who looked up and said, "I knew I couldn't get away from a staff meeting." The White House doc, Dr. Daniel Ruge, reported that he was cracking jokes all the time—writing them down only when he couldn't talk because of the tracheal tube. Brady, unfortunately, had serious damage to his left frontal lobe. Then, Bush spoke, "I came away with the impression that things worked out very well. My posture will be to sit in for the president, but to give no impression that anyone but the president is running things. It's like the president's on vacation; he's just not here. If you want me to stand in for the president, I will. I want to reassure people that we'll go about our business."

Later, a handwritten letter from Nixon arrived:

March 31, 1981, N.Y.C.

Dear Nancy,

We read the reports today with a great sense of relief as we learned that the president had made such a remarkable recovery.

I realize however that even this good news cannot completely lift from you the great burden you have borne so bravely and admirably. Through the mountain of news reports, one beautiful fact shines through—your total selfless dedication to the well being of your husband.

I cannot go along with the old saw that everything is for the best. But out of this tragic episode a clear national consensus has developed—that the president is a great man and that you are a great first lady.

Sincerely,

RN

◆◆◆

With the president laid up, our schedules came to a crawl. I caught up with friends, got a weekend in California and filled in a few reporters who were looking for backgrounders on March 30's events. Once the president returned on April 11 for home rehab, planning began for a dramatic return and major address to a joint session of Congress. Within the walls, it was no secret; we were going to exploit all his heroic national goodwill to sell his economic plan.

APRIL 14

I returned a call from Nixon, and he offered wide-ranging advice. "Ken, on the economy, don't go to the well too often, and don't worry about minor GOP defections." As for Reagan's health, "I'll be quite direct. It's hard to come back from an operation. Don't waste the asset [public sympathy]. On the first time out, don't give a dull, major speech." Nixon's value was always bringing in historical perspective—in this case, going back to the days after President Eisenhower's stroke in 1957. "They counted all his slips of tongue. So, Reagan might say, 'I hear a lot of questions these days: Regarding the state of my health; the state of my health is excellent. The state of the union is good. The state of the economy is bad. So now is the time for cutting back on taxes.'"

A classic work setting in the Oval Office in preparation for a major presidential address.

171

APRIL 16

Nixon called again, after Reagan issued unconditional pardons to former FBI officials Mark Felt and Edward Miller. The presidential statement was gracious, saying the two served with "great distinction" and further criminal proceedings after three years "would not serve the ends of justice."[80] Felt and Miller had been found guilty of authorizing FBI agents to break into the homes of friends and relatives of fugitive members of the Weather Underground organization in 1972 and 1973—seeking clues to the bombings at the US Capitol, Pentagon, and other public buildings.[81]

"That verdict on Felt and Miller was outrageous," said Nixon, "Judge [William] Bryant's jury instructions were terrible. The president's statement was very good, and I'm so pleased." He paused, then added, "Only one more point, even the *Wall Street Journal* said the Weathermen were an 'antiwar' group. They were far worse than that. Our writing in the memoirs on what they did was some of the best stuff in the book."

Nixon had testified for the defense and even contributed money for Felt's defense. His sentiments may have been different had he known that Felt was "Deep Throat," the *Washington Post*'s serial FBI Watergate leaker.

APRIL 17—9:18 A.M.

With a beaming smile, Reagan waved me into the residence's Yellow Oval Room to join with Baker and Meese regarding the speech to Congress. Wearing slacks, slippers, and a red sweater, he appeared to have gained back much of his strength. Despite a raspy voice, he looked terrific and was in a jovial mood and boasted of a four-pound weight gain to 176 pounds.

I came prepared and started sharing my notes. He stopped me halfway through and said, "Well, I don't know. Maybe while I'm up there, I want to know what you think of my doing this?" He grabbed his chest, began coughing, and pushed his head down on the table. "I just thought about perhaps I could do the death scene from *Camille*." For a just a second, the three of us almost took the leader of the free world seriously. We finally joined in laughter at his perfect mimicking of Greta Garbo's famous 1936 film performance.

He had already prepared a one-page opening to address the assassination attempt and read it aloud. Our aim was to use the speech as leverage to get his tax and economic package through Congress, but Reagan knew it would be insulting without first citing the bravery of March 30's law enforcement officers, along with a renunciation of any notion that it was a sick society that defined the moments of that fateful day.

"But listen, Ken. Once I've finished that discussion, I'm going to want to talk directly to Congress, and go over their heads to the American people about cutting their taxes, cutting inflation, and curing the economy. I want this speech to cover both aspects—taxes and spending. I want to talk about both aspects...taxes and spending. And let them know that I'm not going to talk long."

"Somewhere in there, I would like my words directed straight to the American people: 'I believe you want this program, and I believe you want Congress to work with me to bring it about.'" Looking up to ensure we clearly understood, he added, "I want them to say at the end that I didn't exploit the shootings, so let's keep it a pretty straight message." That would be a neat trick. The entire premise of going to Congress was to take advantage of national amity to boost his policy goals.

APRIL 24

I sat in on his first postshooting cabinet meeting. Reagan demurred after they stood up to greet him with applause, "I should be applauding you; I'm just so darned proud of all of you and how things were carried on." He chuckled, "There were some days when I didn't think I was needed."

Moments later, he announced he was bringing an end to the Soviet grain embargo. "I've been concerned about our credibility, and after meeting with Jack Block and Al Haig, I think we've sent enough signals to the Soviet Union. I'm sending a personal letter to Brezhnev, which is a reply to his letter, which was harsh and intemperate. I replied saying, 'If we're to negotiate, let's do it on the basis of what's good for our people, and not as part of a chess game and maneuvers between governments.'"

Nodding at UN Ambassador Jeane Kirkpatrick, he pursed his lips and said, "It's time to get down to what the hell we can do to improve the lot of people all over the world. I think we're justified in lifting the embargo." Something changed in Reagan's heart as he laid in bed healing, and the cold mechanics of policy gave way to common sense.

APRIL 25

The prez headed for Camp David but called me to check on economic data. We continued working best one-on-one though senior staff wanted to hover over this speech. I was open to factual changes or legislative policy considerations only. I then turned to my good friend Anne Higgins in the Correspondence Unit and asked her to search for children's letters sent during Reagan's recuperation. I wanted to find a nugget to insert that would lighten up the evening and loosen up the glum Democrats who would otherwise sit on their butts and coldly receive his economic message.

Anne produced several letters, but one topped them all. It was handwritten by Peter Sweeney, a second-grader from the Riverside School in Rockville Centre, New York:

> *I hope you get well quick or you might have to make a speech in your pajamas.*

> *P.S. If you have to make a speech in your pajamas, I warned you.*

It was perfect. Now, I only had to find a way to convince the president to use it. Reagan edited heavily, ensuring an ending that was his own, and because of his personal imprint, I would only accept policy corrections and no style changes by speechwriter wannabes. The only exception I made was for legislative aide Max Friederdorf's request for language to praise Congress for coming a "long distance." Max's job was to get votes, and he deserved slack.

APRIL 28

Today's Oval Office visit offered my last shot to get Reagan to put Peter Sweeney's letter in the final reading copy. With only a few private moments before leaving, I said, "Mr. President, you might want to think about using this tonight." Reagan gave it a quick read, chuckled, and handed it back.

Damn, he won't use it! I did some quick thinking about a "court of appeal" and handed it back. "Why don't you show it to Mrs. Reagan; I think she'd like to see it." He looked it over again, and said, "I have an idea," and put the letter in his coat pocket. I successfully sowed a seed for the showman.

Seated in the House gallery, I saw no reference in the advance text to the kid from Rockville Centre. Reagan got to the part of the speech about hearing from "millions of compassionate Americans and their children, from college age to kindergarten," and saw his opening. "As a matter of fact, as evidence of that, I have a letter with me." He reached into his breast pocket and smoothly pulled it out. With perfect timing after the first howls of laughter and applause, he read young Sweeney's postscript. He had all but the most jaded of partisans in the palm of his hand.

After a review of the dismal economy facing America, the president continued:

> Our government is too big and it spends too much.... The answer to a government that's too big is to stop feeding its growth. Government spending has been growing faster than the economy itself. The massive national debt which we accumulated is the result of the government's high spending diet. Well, it's time to change the diet and to change it in the right way...The old and comfortable way is to shave a little here and add a little there. Well, that's not acceptable anymore. I think this great and historic Congress knows that way is no longer acceptable.

At that last line, the forty-plus "blue dog" conservative Democrats started leading the applause and then got up along with the Republicans, cheering and whistling at Reagan's attack on big government. Tip O'Neill saw the rebellion in his ranks, and turned to Bush sitting next to him, "Here's your forty votes."[82]

Reagan himself was surprised at the enormous reaction to his words and wrote in his diary that night: "Maybe we are going to make it. It took a lot of courage for them to do that and it sent a shiver down my spine."[83]

There were no doubts about the president's health and his energy to get back into the fight for his economic program. In three days, I would be leaving the White House on a high note. A jubilant Nixon checked in. "It was quite a hit, Ken, and they [Reagan and team] need to take a moment and capture it. The opposition is on the run." He laughed, "I could see some of my old sidekicks on the Democrats' side sickeningly rushing to the cameras to praise Reagan."

Then, as a former presidential negotiator, Nixon described how *he* would view it from the Oval Office. "I have mixed emotions. I would rather have the Democrats screw it up just a little and suffer political damage. They're in a spot; if they modify Reagan's plan, they should take the blame." Knowing I was about to leave, he switched over to giving me career advice, pleased that I was "leaving on top because when things change, the first ones they jump on are the poor speechwriters." He urged me to take two weeks off and then we would talk again.

Newsweek reported that Reagan was successful "at clothing his Presidency—and smothering his opposition—in a blanket of personal goodwill unmatched since Dwight Eisenhower...." The magazine continued on to report panic among the Democrats and criticism of Speaker Tip O'Neill. "Some pressed him to go on TV and answer the president. ('What kind of fool do they think I am?' spake the Speaker.)"[84]

William Greider's description captured the evening in his subsequent *Atlantic* magazine profile of David Stockman:

> The president's televised address, in April, was masterly and effective: The nation responded with a deluge of mail and telephone calls, and the House of Representatives accepted Reagan's version of the budget reconciliation over the Democratic alternative. The final roll call...was not even close, with sixty-three Democrats joining all House Republicans in support of the president.... The 1980 election results may not have been "ideological," but the members of Congress seemed to be interpreting them that way.[85]

The week concluded with thanking my secretaries, Kathy, Nance, Deni, and Karen with lunch in the Mess as well as a thank-you breakfast with Teresa Rosenberger, who I added to our research staff, and Maureen, and Misty. I finalized staff hires with Ben Elliott and Landon Parvin and lunched with our old Oxon Hill friends and neighbors from the '70s, the Renjilians and deGraffenreids. My last two media backgrounders were with Doug Brew of *Time Magazine* and Diane Curtis, the UPI correspondent whom I had since forgiven for hectoring Reagan in the campaign.

Jim Baker and Mike Deaver described a plan where I could continue helping the president on a private basis from California, and Gergen went along with it for the short run knowing that there would be a speechwriting gap. Reagan agreed to a system where I would take on assignments long distance and send them back and forth via facsimile. He would review my work, and we could collaborate by phone and fax. Baker or Deaver would find a way for the Republican Party to finance it. I actually thought it might work, and probably wasn't quite prepared to give up the prestige of playing at the top.

MAY 1, 1981, 9:45 A.M.

The first thing the president said was, "Do you think it's possible I might be able to go out there with you? They always fight me when I want to go to California, and I miss it so much." I said all the right things about the honor of helping out, etc., and he was very kind, "Well, you know the offer still stands; I wish you could stay, but I know you want to be back with your family. But Jim tells me that you've agreed to continue helping out while you're out there, and that's the good thing about those machines—that we can send things back and forth. And you can still work on speeches, and we can communicate back and forth." I told him I was willing to give it a try.

He was eager to show me the special shorthand from the days he wrote out his own reading copy and used the same shorthand to edit the half sheets we prepared. He tore off a piece of five-by-eight White House notepad paper and wrote a couple of sentences as a sample. I saved the notepaper and gave a copy to Nance Roberts, who briefly tried typing his half sheets with the shorthand, but it never worked out.

My fifteen minutes were up, and the White House photographer was due for my farewell pic. I was anxious to get home, and Prince Charles was waiting to visit. The photo arrived a few days later and was inscribed:

> *Dear Ken—*
>
> *This comes with a heartfelt thanks for all you've done and just between us—for all you'll do.*
>
> *Warmest regard*
> *Ronald Reagan*

Chapter 15

THE FIREMAN

I was home for only a few weeks when Mike Deaver checked in. "I'm calling to follow up on the president's conversation with you about continuing to help with speeches. The president has asked every day this week about you and the status of the relationship, and he's been very concerned about the void since you left. He asked me to set up a consulting contract. Dave Gergen will get back to you." Gergen was especially pleased to capture oversight of the speechwriting process when I left, even telling me, "I want you to know your replacement and the speechwriting staff are not going to have the same independence you had."

After the first economic speeches and the assassination attempt, the communication standards were set very high. A Louis Harris poll showed by a 62–34 percent majority that Americans felt "He is the first president in a long time who makes interesting speeches that give you an 'up' feeling."[86] But after I left, two commencement addresses, at Notre Dame and West Point, required substantial rewrites, and now Gergen called wanting assistance with two upcoming events.

Reagan was to appear at the annual conventions of the National Jaycees and the National Association for the Advancement of Colored People (NAACP). "Ken, we especially need to make the NAACP speech a winner. I'll get two packages put together for you, and I can tell you, the president is relieved that you're working on them." Faxing the speeches back and forth wasn't working, and what the president needed was personal contact. So Deaver called again and asked me to join Reagan at Camp David.

On June 20, the president greeted me in Aspen Lodge with a broad smile. He was still dressed in jodhpur riding pants and boots after horse riding on nearby trails. We went over my suggested changes on the Jaycees speech as well as his thoughts pitching his economic program. He remarked that one of the phrases in an early draft was too harsh: "Ken, don't tackle Congress so hard. It makes no sense when we are talking about bi-partisanship."

My first call as "Fireman," working in Aspen Lodge on three speeches in June 1981 after Reagan comes in with riding boots and jodhpurs after a horse ride.

The next morning, we convened poolside, and Mrs. Reagan came by offering clipped pleasantries; in fact, she was abrupt. I flew cross country on Father's Day weekend to help her husband, and it was strange to get a cool reception. She had a mission. "Ken, why did you leave? Ronnie needs you back here to help. You should be coming back and working with him; he really needs you. Why can't you do that?" Nancy Reagan had several voices. This wasn't her angry, rip-your-eyes-out voice. It was her annoyed, impatient, scolding-den-mother voice. I tried defending. "Ma'am, I really can't move the family again, and I'm sorry, but I told Jim and Mike I wouldn't be staying."

"But Ronnie really is having trouble with the staff." The president interrupted. "Now, Nancy—he has a family, and young children. Let us get back to work." She began to leave, turned back, but wasn't going to let it go, "Well, you should reconsider, Ken." This was a usual routine—with Nancy voicing out loud the frustrations that Ronnie held within. It was clear that my absence and the disruption in speechwriting process had been a conversation item in the residence. Nevertheless, Reagan didn't like conflict and wanted a place to hide.

Returning to the Jaycees speech, Reagan thought his staff wasn't sufficiently spreading word of his economic mission. He put down his pen to get my attention, "Ken, we've gotten away from the effective things we talked about in the campaign. We need to get back to being crusaders—to show how hard we're working to get government out of our lives and to help blue collar workers not be taxed to death. It's hard to bring this about, but we have to make an emotional appeal to counter the other side."

He should have been addressing the responsible parties—Baker, Deaver and Gergen. Regrettably, I was passive. I should have told Reagan that his problem was his own staff that looked upon his revolutionary tax changes as "voodoo economics." I should have revealed that Baker was not a true believer and had confessed to me as far back as the transition he was open to "adjusting Kemp-Roth."

Reagan continued.

> This is going to be my first speech out of Washington
> (on the economy), and I need to explain what it's like in
> Washington, and that they (the Jaycees) need to be put in
> the position of being crusaders. Let's get them to go out
> in the public and put out our program on pure emotion;
> that's what they appeal to and what they do so well. People
> understand the broad picture rather than facts and figures.
> Ken, I'm trying to do this uphill battle, and this gives me
> a chance in front of that group to explain what I'm trying
> to do. Everyone out in that audience ought to go out and
> help—doing the same thing on the president's behalf.

I was at Camp David because Reagan appeared to need the sympathetic ear of a campaign crusader. I didn't fit in to a "family" role like Deaver, but I was a familiar face with whom he could comfortably communicate.

It was the same with Nixon. When he worked in his office, I frequently sat quietly nearby, and Nixon would pause every few minutes to share thoughts—political or otherwise—and then go back to work while I watched silently. David Frost referred to me as the Old Man's "amanuensis"—a hundred-dollar word to describe a literary assistant. It was an apt description for my role with Reagan.

Returning to Camp David to film commercials for the '84 campaign
while Mrs. Reagan and Advertising Aide Jim Lake look on

We moved on to the NAACP speech. One section, dealing with allegations of voting rights violations in African American communities, stirred Reagan's outrage. His lips pursed, and his voice rose, "It's my belief that the federal government is obligated to come to the aid of any individual whose constitutional right is violated, and to defend those rights at the point of a bayonet if necessary. You know, Ken, I wonder if I should put this in—it's a line I've used before—'After all, it was a Republican president who first used those bayonets.'" He referred to Dwight Eisenhower's sending in the 101st Airborne Division to maintain order and protect African American students during the desegregation of Little Rock, Arkansas's Central High School in 1957.

He also wanted to make sure his opposition remained to school busing for the purpose of desegregating public schools. "I just think it's demeaning and insulting to suggest that a Black child can only learn if he's seated between two white kids." He was pleased about a section on Marva Collins, the inner city schoolteacher who, when dismayed with the performance of children in Chicago's public schools, transformed a decrepit building into a private school with disciplinary standards resulting in enormous educational achievements for previously failing children. "There ought to be a few specifics about why I believe that economic opportunity can make a difference in the lives of Black people"—Reagan's familiar refrain of the magic tonic of "opportunity" that would be released in his economic program.

Back at home, the "remote arrangement" of speechwriting wasn't meant to be. The White House management system is complex—requiring oversight and circulation of speech drafts, and it was awkward to obtain long-distance research information. My nascent consulting business got in the way as well, so our effort just drifted away by inertia. My former staff members called to complain about working with Gergen and his staff, and they reported that Dick Darman was also meddling in the speechwriting department—both eagerly tried to fill the vacuum left from my departure.

However, my role as "the Fireman" had been defined. The formal consultancy didn't work, but the stage was set for me to be called either to complement the presidential staff's efforts or engage directly in rescue missions on short notice. Whether it was a call from Baker, Deaver, or Gergen, it was always assumed I would be available. I was honored to be asked and eager to stay engaged, but it was a measure of executive arrogance that, by whim, I should always be available. It was mostly a symbiotic relationship.... until the very end.

I wanted Reagan's economic program to succeed because I had invested political and emotional energy in his crusade, and the congressional vote was set for July 29, 1981. Speaker Tip O'Neill was prepared to stiffly resist any encroachment upon the Democratic Left's tax and spend policies, so the White House was counting on its biggest salesman to pressure House Democrats with a televised presidential address two days before the vote. Even though I, Meredith, and the children would be on vacation in Sun Valley, Idaho at the condo of our friends Hersh and Bobbi Hoopengarner, I was going to try to tune to Reagan's speech.

On Friday morning, July 24, my answering service reported a message from David Gergen that it was critically important for me to call and have the White House operator track him down. Without cell phones in 1981, I called the White House collect and convinced the White House switchboard to remain on until Dave could be pulled out of a meeting.

"What the hell's so important that I have to interrupt my first vacation in over a year? I'm in Sun Valley, Idaho."

Someone must have been all over Gergen's ass because he was all business. "Had no idea you were out of the office, but the president's going on the air Monday to gin up support for his tax package, which looks to be going to the floor next week. We have a draft that's good, but Baker wants you to take a look because he and Deaver don't think it quite closes the sale."

> **KK:** Dave, I'm in the middle of the country in a condo below Dollar Mountain without any office facilities. I don't have my typewriter with me [no laptops in 1981] and don't even have a notepad, so I really don't know how I can help. How can I even look at the speech? There's no way for you to get it to me.

There was a long pause on the line, and he asked if he could call me back. Within a half hour, the phone rang.

> **DG:** Ken, there's a Forest Ranger station in Ketchum. I don't think it's very far from you, and we've called and arranged for the draft of the speech to be sent by fax, but you have to be there to pick it up. We don't want them to see it.

My morning was shot, so I sent the family off and drove to pick up the speech, awaiting in a sealed envelope at the Ketchum Forest Ranger Station. Given time and logistical constraints, there was no way to edit the entire speech. Instead, I sat alongside the second fairway of Elkhorn's golf course and tried to think like Reagan did at Camp David a few weeks earlier—to get back in the campaign mode as a crusader.

I began scribbling on the back of the faxed copy, striking out lines that didn't work, and finally came up with a possible closer:

> In a few days, the Congress will stand at the fork of two roads. One road is all too familiar to us. It leads, ultimately, to higher taxes. It merely brings us back to the source of our economic problems—where the government decides that it knows better than you what should be done with your earnings, and, in fact, how you should conduct your life. The other road promises to renew the American

KEN KHACHIGIAN

spirit. It's the road of hope and opportunity. It places
the direction of your life back in your hands—where it
belongs. One road is timid and fearful. The other is bold
and hopeful...It has been the power of millions of people
like you who have determined that we will make America
great again. You have made the difference up to now. You
will make the difference again. Let us not stop now.

The only way I could transmit my second fairway peroration was to
call the White House and dictate the insert, including the various emphases
and punctuations. The president took it to Camp David for the weekend. He removed only four words from my golf course composition, and
on July 27, 1981, it became his closing plea to the American people to
press Congress to pass his economic recovery program. *Newsweek* reported
Reagan's "national television appeal...lit up the Capitol's switchboards as
brightly as a Wurlitzer jukebox" as he again and again "urged his listeners
to drown the Hill in phone calls and telegrams in his support." Excerpting
one of my lines, *Newsweek* added, "'We have done so much and have come
so far,'" he said, "'Let us not stop now.'"

Two days later, Reagan's dream of tax cuts and slowing down the federal
government passed the US Senate eighty-nine to eleven. Next, a stunned
Tip O'Neill lost many votes in his Democratic caucus and the House of
Representatives handed the president a 238–195 upset victory. O'Neill's
humiliating setback left him fuming: "Listen, it's *Reagan's* unemployment,
Reagan's inflation rate. It's *Reagan's* dollar. It's Reagan's interest rates. It isn't
Jimmy Carter's or the Democratic Party's anymore."[87]

I don't know if Gergen ever told Reagan I drafted his closing words;
he only saw drafts with the names of Ben Elliott and Tony Dolan. I never
heard back from Dave, although in a background briefing with Sara Fritz of
U.S. News & World Report, she wrote that Gergen "credits Reagan's televised
speech with turning the tide on the tax bill."[88] The president wrote in his
diary that night:

> Now, I've just finished my broadcast. The D's are already
> screaming. Calls in the 1st hour were 629 pro—148 against.[89]

The West Wing's ingratitude was literally par for the course, but it was
worth interrupting my vacation to help Reagan translate his "crusade" into

an actual victory with the support of a remote US Forest Ranger station in Ketchum, Idaho.

Gergen called after Christmas asking if I would talk with Reagan about his first State of the Union address. "Tony Dolan has been assigned to write the draft and has the lead, so we're not asking you to do the writing. We don't want to take anything away from Tony—just want you to consult. Can you read the outline and draft and meet the president tomorrow?" This was typical—a last-minute request, assuming I was available, and giving me less than twenty-four hours to prepare. In addition—look, but don't touch, so I'm not sure what they really expected.

DECEMBER 30, 1981

The drapes were closed in Century Plaza's Penthouse Suite, Room 1915, as they would be on all stays following the assassination attempt. Reagan spoke before I could share my notes. He thought I was there to help him with writing and wanted to make sure I understood his direction. Craig Fuller—a pleasant Californian serving as cabinet affairs secretary—sat in. I viewed him as an interloper inserted by Baker, Darman, or Gergen to "report back" if I infected the president by crossing any policy or ideological lines. So I took careful notes and later typed up a more detailed set from a fresh memory.

Given speculation he might back away from pledges not to increase taxes, he barged right in. "Ken, regarding tax increases, I'm not weakening one damned bit. Here today, I read again that those 'unnamed sources' in the White House say I will raise taxes." (In a background interview with Sara Fritz of *U.S. & World Report* the day before our meeting, Baker aide, Rich Williamson said, "Reagan's aides are proposing tax increases of as much as $50 billion, but the president is not expected to buy it...Even if Reagan refuses to go along with all of these, his aides hope they will be thrust upon the president by Congress.")[90]

"I'm not going to do it. That's precisely the mistake Maggie Thatcher made in England—raising taxes at the same time she was trying to accomplish other things, and it cut back on the British recovery [referring to

Prime Minister Thatcher's raising the Valued Added Tax and excise taxes after cutting the personal income tax in Great Britain]."

> Early in my days as governor, I explained the state budget back when conditions were about the same in California as they are here now—there was a very large deficit. It was the very first time the governor came to the people and explained it all in simple terms they could understand. So, let's do the same thing here—that's the general framework I want. Number one, what has been the economic picture facing the country, where we are and where we're going. Number two, what are we doing, and how are we planning to change it?

Even if I wasn't going to be on site to write his speech, I could see that my mission was to reinforce the elements of his crusade before he sat down to edit his draft when he returned to Washington.

"Ken, just look at the ten years between 1971 and 1981. The peoples' earnings increased one hundred twenty-four percent. But there was a total inflation of fifty-five percent." I made a note that we'd have to check those figures. "And look what happened, taxes tripled in that period, so that the typical American was $427 poorer through that period." I thought wow... he's going right back to the 1980 campaign—maybe even back to the 1976 campaign and getting fired up. I thought, maybe it *was* a good idea for Fuller to be in the meeting so he could report back to Baker how emotional Reagan gets about taxes.

Reagan's passions were stirred up by recent Democratic attacks, and he was also annoyed by negative leaks and outright betrayal emerging from his own ranks. Only days before our meeting, the *New York Times* wrote, "Mr. Reagan got Congress to approve his plan to lower income taxes by 25 percent over three years. But now the Baker-Stockman axis in the White House and the Office of Management and Budget wants to mitigate these cuts in the income tax by imposing new taxes in other areas."[91]

"The problem with the old economics," said Reagan, "is that you have to have inflation in order to have prosperity, and that's not right." He illustrated with an apt anecdote from his personal career. "We had insurance when I started in the movie business, and when I first started having some good years, I got a retirement policy. At that time, it would have maintained me in the same kind of lifestyle for retirement. But by the time it came due, with all the inflation piled on, it wouldn't even pay any of the property taxes on my house."

He wanted his State of the Union speech to highlight all the things he'd accomplished, but not defensively. "Let folks know how inflation was eating away at the value of their dollar, and it's coming down—that we're pleased with progress on that, and unemployment, but it's still not good enough. I want them to know that it's my determination to get that fifteen percent interest rate down, even though it's not like the twenty percent plus of the earlier period."

Regarding national defense and foreign policy, he wanted Congress to know: "Never send me to the negotiating table in anything but the strongest possible position. I don't want to see any cuts in defense spending. When I'm out in the public, I can really see an upbeat American spirit since I've been in office, and there's been a greater patriotism." Looking over to ensure I was writing down his words, he said, "People are hopeful now." Then, returning to home base and his crusader theme, "On unemployment, we need to be as angry today as I was on the campaign."

I reminded Reagan of his soft support from women, and he thought we might refer to our arms reduction goals. "Ken, you know what [Deputy National Security Adviser] Bud Nance told me? If we had ratified the former SALT treaty that Carter had signed, the Soviets could have continued to add as much destructive power in megatonnage to their nuclear arsenal every eleven minutes equal to the amount which was dumped on Hiroshima! Any civilized nation which pretends to be civilized must join us to *reduce* arms." He put an emphasis on the word "reduce," and then he laughed and said, "If I say that, you know it will send the Russians to their typewriters!"

He wanted me to know that he and Tip O'Neill were "getting along just fine. Tip says to his friends that he thinks that I'm a beautiful person." Still, he wanted to make clear, he wasn't bending to the Speaker's agenda.

> I'm not buying into the ways of the past—the idea that government could buy off unemployment with make-work. Instead, the only way to do that is to increase productivity and broaden the base of the economy. You can't share scarcity and can't just rearrange prosperity. Let's make a bigger pie and expand prosperity. I want to state

our position authoritatively—as facts and not leave room for other interpretations. I can bluntly make the case for changing the imponderables in our economy. We can change our future because our program is aimed at changing the pessimistic projections of the future and to say: "Let us Americans—I ask you—believe in yourselves, and not in someone else's pessimism."

I reported to Deaver and Gergen and then reviewed Dolan's draft and marked it up with my thoughts. I accomplished my central mission to stimulate his vision and reinforce the virtue of his cause. I don't think Deaver really cared if I worked on the SOTU. Mike's responsibility to the president and Nancy was to create a comfort zone—with a supply of friendly faces and all the resources he needed. I think our exchange at the Century Plaza had its intended effect to strengthen his resolve as he stood before Congress on January 26, 1981:

> The doubters would have us turn back the clock with tax increases that would offset the personal tax-rate reductions already passed by this Congress. Raise present taxes to cut future deficits, they tell us. Well, I don't believe we should buy their argument...Higher taxes would not mean lower deficits...Raising taxes won't balance the budget. It will encourage more government spending....
>
> I will seek no tax increases this year, and I have no intention of retreating from our basic program of tax relief.....
>
> Don't let anyone tell you that America's best days are behind her....

Reagan was set to headline a California Republican Party fundraiser on May 25, and I thought I could help by sending White House political director Ed Rollins nine pages of speech material. It was a hard-hitting defense of his tax and budget cuts and reflected Reagan's strong convictions conveyed from our meetings over the past months.

Rollins loved it as just the kind of boost his GOP troops needed, so sent it to Gergen to be considered in the president's speech. Dave took Rollins aside after the next morning's senior staff and was steamed, "Look, Ken is not the head of speechwriting, and I don't want you backdooring any of this shit into the system." Rollins wasn't intimidated, and shot back, "Remember, Gergen, you were running against Reagan in '76 with Ford, and when you were running against him with Bush in '80, Ken was the speechwriter who the president wanted and was most comfortable with. These remarks are great, and they would go perfectly in California."

When Rollins got back to his office, the phone buzzed, and Jim Baker came on the line. Gergen had gotten to him. "Rollins, you don't pass anything on from Khachigian, and from now on Darman will monitor your paper flow."[92] Something more significant was at play. Baker, Stockman, and Darman were working hard to negotiate with the Senate for passage of what was eventually called the Tax Equity and Fiscal Responsibility Act of 1982 (TEFRA)—a set of tax increases they were pitching to Reagan as nothing more than "closing loopholes" to lower the budget deficit. They didn't want Reagan taking jabs at congressional Democrats or attacking tax increases.

A light-hearted moment after the gripper shared one of his stories.

In addition, the midterm elections approached with the economy mired in recession. Reagan's economic recovery plan offered no quick fix, and the Carter hangover lingered. In August 1982, the unemployment rate approached 10 percent; the inflation rate hovered around 6 percent and interest rates were down, but still about 11 percent. A Republican rout appeared probable, and the White House damage control plan was to put Reagan on the campaign trail to raise money and assist candidates in tough races. I was summoned by Margaret Tutwiler to an offsite strategy session in Washington on August 4 at Blair House with the idea that "the Fireman" could help with the president's remarks.

Jim Baker presided and wasn't looking for my opinion as he instructed in his overplayed Texas drawl. "Khachigian, here's what we need from you—a speech the president could use throughout the fall. One where he acknowledges how bad the situation is, and that he's aware of it. Nevertheless, we have a program that will work, but it won't get done overnight." Pollster Bob Teeter offered, "The most fundamental issue is, do we stay on course or do we return to the failed policies of the past. Democrats are willing to accept this issue." Dick Wirthlin's polling showed the "gender gap" to be unacceptably large, with female voters sensitive that Reagan "hadn't done anything on inflation."

Baker, Deaver and the team preached nonpartisanship, while making sure I understood there was "no alternative that the Democrats have." My notes from the meeting made clear that they wanted it to be known that "the Democrats promise the moon, but they can't deliver, and the bottom line of Jimmy Carter was 21-and-a-half percent interest rates. Moreover, the Democrats are negative, while we need a message of hope with Reagan being the 'president of all the people.'"

Bob Teeter took the core message public to the *New York Times*, revealing that Baker's strategy group had determined that the "patience" theme had to be central. "It's a pretty simple theme. We've made some big changes. The question is, do we want to stay the course and see them through or go back to the policies of the past."[93]

AUGUST 24

I was initially surprised to find Baker and Ed Meese sitting in on my meeting to present the draft speech to Reagan. When the subject turned to taxes, I figured out why they were there. Five days earlier, Congress passed

TEFRA, and the president was poised to sign the legislation. On August 16, he delivered a televised apologia explaining why the nearly $100 billion in TEFRA's tax increases weren't *really* tax increases.

Reagan was relaxed and energized after time on his ranch. He was also well briefed on his mission to convince me that TEFRA was good policy, and I needed to be "on the team." Three weeks earlier, Reagan persuaded Lyn Nofziger he was wrong in joining Jack Kemp to denounce the new tax package—after which Lyn claimed to have a "change in heart." Marty Anderson had also attacked the tax hike and was expected to have a "change of heart" after talking to Reagan.[94] Reagan's current assignment was to ensure that I, too, was on the reservation and wouldn't challenge his policy while working on the year's political speeches.

"Ken, we had stressed the belief that our tax system had to be changed in order to reduce the percentage of the GNP that government was taking in, and to create new incentives. So, we passed the greatest tax cut in the nation's history—$335 billion in tax cuts. Each taxpayer will average $450 in tax cuts this year and $788 next year."

Baker interrupted with apple-polishing. "Look, this tax battle strengthened the president's leadership image. He did the right thing for the country. He pulled off a tax increase ten weeks before the election, and he brought it off. That's huge." I hadn't forgotten what Baker said to me back in December 1980 about his willingness to "adjust Kemp-Roth" if necessary. He was reselling his agenda in front of Reagan.

Ed Meese also surprised me when he, too, took up the cause. Everyone had accepted the party line, so I was expected to as well. Meese added, "This is a comprehensive plan to get deficits down, and increased revenues were a price we had to pay. It's not a compromise in principle; it's a compromise to achieve a goal—a bipartisan compromise to reduce the deficit."

Reagan continued on with his pitch that the taxes in TEFRA weren't really taxes. "Our opponents wanted to increase personal taxes, but ours was tax reform, not increases. One half was eliminating advantages to a few, and seventeen percent of the taxes were new." This was a reference to the new excise taxes. I sat next to Reagan, while Baker and Meese watched me faithfully record his position. "Only my program offers any hope. Look—interest rates are down; inflation is down; durable goods orders are up three percent, and Republicans are the only ones offering hope. I have all the figures back in Washington from the Council of Economic Advisers."

Meese told me to make sure to use percentages to show inflation rate reductions, while Reagan pressed the case again, "Inflation is now less than half of what it was when I took office. This tax increase really answered the fairness charge because the new taxes fall on big corporations, and not the middle class."

Bristling, he gestured toward the window. "See those demonstrators outside? There's one fact I enjoy bragging about, and you can use the figure that we are dedicating the highest percentages ever to helping the poor and needy—fifty-two percent goes toward the needy and twenty-nine percent on defense versus the reverse figures when you look at Kennedy's budgets. But we still need to say this isn't good, because we need to create jobs, hope, new production, and opportunity. We took a sick economy and made it well. By going back to our principles, in only one and a half years, we made progress." With the passage of TEFRA, he had retreated from the enthusiasm of the '80 campaign to slash away at taxes. Today, he was selling additional revenue increases. Somehow, he had become convinced to retreat from the language he pressed me to use in June of '81 when speaking to the Jaycees—language he used when hammering Maggie Thatcher for "the mistake she made in England."

Baker spoke up again. "We want to make sure to have as our bottom line that our opponents have no alternatives. We had some tight votes—came close to defeat on major elements of the legislation and need more help in Congress. For example two votes could make the difference on the nuclear freeze [a resolution introduced in the Senate by Senators Ted Kennedy and Mark Hatfield for a joint US/Soviet nuclear arms freeze]. So we need to end the speech with strength—for the president to have support for a unified image across the world."

SUNDAY, SEPTEMBER 12

While in middle of helping George Deukmejian wage his campaign for California governor, I carved out a weekend trip to meet Reagan in the residence to review the draft he had taken to Camp David over the weekend. He began outlining his view of why he would be on the stump: "I'm not running for president, but a lot of candidates in my party as well as others are running on issues that are critical to the job I'm doing. The facts are that unemployment started about fifteen years ago and got higher each time we came out of the recession. I'd like to refer to myself in this speech as a New

Deal Democrat. But in the New Deal, after all their programs, it was still only World War II that ended unemployment, and I want to say, 'That is a price I will not pay.'"

Reagan is very competitive and got his dander up. "With all the criticism I get, have they suggested an alternative? Without an alternative, I assume they'll return to the same old programs that got us into trouble in the first place." After a few private minutes with Reagan, Baker and Deaver walked in—interrupting their Sunday afternoon to be wordsmithing guardians against Reagan's passions.

"Ken, the ideas are in there, but there's too much on the pure economic problem; in the middle it's too long," said Baker.

"It's a pretty good speech," offered Deaver, "but it needs a grabber at the end." This was typical of the "non-speechwriters." Baker and Deaver never had to write anything on their own, but always enjoy offering critiques—especially in front of the president.

Reagan concluded by plowing the same ground we had in Los Angeles—"What are the Democrats' alternatives? Do you want to go back to twenty-one-and-a-half-percent interest rates?"

And so on. Baker finally offered, "You need more on the hope factor." He didn't define what he meant by the "hope" factor. No one ever does. I would have loved to leave the speech with Baker and Deaver after walking out and telling them to try their hand at putting lipstick on 1982's recessionary pig.

I copied Ed Rollins because he had been excluded from all our meetings, and I knew that he would be responsible for managing the success or failure of the midterm elections, so I thought he should know what Reagan would be saying. I also knew that Ed would fight to make sure the president had an opportunity to see my final draft and, if necessary, would walk it into Reagan himself to make sure it wasn't blocked by Gergen or Darman. Tutwiler asked if I could also prepare a television address for Reagan to give later in October. So, while still in the middle of Deukmejian's hotly contested gubernatorial campaign, I worked on the TV speech, added additional comments submitted by Dick Wirthlin ("'Stay the course' is good; more on peace") and wrapped up 1982's year as "the Fireman."

While Baker opted for a less partisan television address, my efforts weren't for naught as most of my language survived in Reagan's drafts he used in his stump speeches—like the one at a Virginia rally on September 29, 1982:

The choice the American voters have this year is just as important as the one they had two years ago....

America went backwards during those four Democratic years...Government had spun out of control like a washing machine out of balance, and the programs grew automatically. Regulations became more complex and added untold billions in new costs....

Families were driven in the evening to the kitchen table to try and figure out...how to cope with the inflation that robbed their buying power at the same time it reduced their spendable earnings. Young couples didn't dream of new homes; they dreamed of just surviving. Small businesses were hit especially hard. The only sure thing was the unstoppable fattening of the United States Government....

[I]t seems to me that the people who have created the mess we're in—the same ones who took us down the path of guaranteed economic disaster, are the last ones who should be delivering sermonettes on the cause of unemployment....

To my liberal friends I say: You can't create a desert and then hand someone in that middle of that desert a cup of water and call that compassion. You can't pour billions of dollars into dead-end, make-work jobs and call that opportunity. You cannot build up years and years of degrading dependence by our citizens on the government and then dare call that hope. And believe me, you can't drive our people to despair with crises that wipe them out or taxes which sap their energies and then boast that you've given them fairness....

We Americans have been sorely tested by these past few years of discouragement. But we've never been quitters, and we're not about to quit now...To those who are fainthearted and unsure, I have this message. If you're afraid of the future, then get out of the way stand aside. The people of this country are ready to move again."[5]

The speech had the effect Reagan wanted. The *Washington Times* headline was "Reagan Pins Fiscal Woes on Liberals," and the lede from Richmond was: "President Reagan said yesterday the dramatic economic reverses suffered in the Carter administration were the culmination of decades of overindulgence by the liberal Washington establishment."[96] The *New York Times* echoed with "President Scorns Democrats' Rule."[97]

But the critics were also out, and his speech was toned down in later iterations. The president's own team undercut Reagan with harmful leaks. A *Wall Street Journal* article observed "Presidential advisers are deeply concerned that President Reagan's campaign on behalf of Republican candidates is faltering. As at least some of them see it, Mr. Reagan hasn't been able to drive home the central message of the GOP appeal…and is coming across as far more partisan than either he or Republican advisers want him to…. *They want him to appear more 'presidential' and less overtly partisan.*" [emphasis added][98] The leak sounded very much like Baker's faction not wanting to take any heat from their media friends or Congress.

Ed Rollins argued that the tougher themes and rhetoric the president used from my speech was the only way the Republicans would hold seats, and by later clinging to the mushier, "stay the course" message, our base would feel the president had abandoned them. Rollins confirmed to me that Baker believed that if Reagan was too partisan, the Democrats wouldn't support his legislative program like they had in his first two years. By losing twenty-six House seats and barely holding the Senate, Reagan gained no strength in the Congress. Only when his supply-side tax cuts took hold in 1984 did he regain political strength.[99]

Of all the commentary, I was most concerned by the biting critique from an *Evans and Novak* column. "Failing all year long to devise a campaign strategy, the president's men did not even focus the Great Communicator…. Instead, speechwriters patched bits and pieces of old Reagan oratory into a pastiche of warmed-over sloganeering…. there is no hint of the 1980 campaign poetry confronting great challenges at home and abroad…. Reagan is not free of guilt, personally insisting on the dreary 'stay the course' slogan against contrary advice."[100]

At home, I also had to focus on the closely contested California governor's race. Three weeks before the vote, George Deukmejian released his campaign manager. We rebuilt our entire campaign, adding Sal Russo and Doug Watts for media. I took effective strategic control of the campaign, Steve Merksamer oversaw administrative details, and Lance Tarrance provided solid survey research. Karl Samuelian raised last-minute funds paying for two new campaign commercials I scripted in the last ten days. Each homed in on Los Angeles mayor Tom Bradley's geographic weaknesses—one for northern California's market asserting that we needed a governor for all of California, not just one city; the other for southern and central California exposing Bradley as an ineffective crime fighter opposed to the death penalty. Along with an absentee ballot campaign masterminded by state GOP chairman Tirso del Junco, we pulled off an upset victory by less than 2 percent.

Supply-siders forcefully argue that the delayed implementation of Reagan's tax cuts stalled their intended stimulating effect on the economy. Unfortunately, his top White House staff members shared little or none of Reagan's fervor regarding cutting taxes or paring the size of the government. Years later, when Reagan and I collaborated on his 1988 GOP Convention speech, he complained that TEFRA was among the worst decisions of his presidency. "The fellas promised I would get three dollars of spending cuts for every dollar of taxes I agreed to. Instead, for every dollar in new taxes, we got a dollar seventy in *new* spending—the complete reverse of what I was promised. Dammit, that was wrong, and I shouldn't have agreed to it."

Maybe Reagan wouldn't have agreed to TEFRA if he had known that a month before his swearing-in, his new chief of staff, Baker, embraced a readiness to "adjust Kemp-Roth." Baker's protégé, Dick Darman, wrote Baker a memo two weeks *prior* to the inaugural arguing, "For those particularly interested in budget balancing, the easiest way to balance the budget within the next few years is to fail to get a major tax cut…" (Though Darman covered his ass by claiming not to advocate that position.)[101] Reagan biographies and his library's archives are full of examples of his staff maneuvering him into accepting TEFRA's "tax increases" to save his economic recovery—defined as mere "revenue" enhancements, not tax increases.

The cynicism behind Baker's efforts to get Reagan to the TEFRA goal line was demonstrated when Craig Fuller offered a long background interview to *U.S. News & World Report*:

The White House "legislative strategy group" chaired by
Jim Baker has played a major role in shaping key eco-

nomic decisions…that economic policy is determined more by political thinkers such as Baker than by economic experts such as Regan, Weidenbaum, et al, …

The president does not regard his push for the $100 billion tax package as a flip-flop from his supply-side program. Quite the contrary. Reagan went along with the big tax increase, Fuller notes, "to preserve the essential elements of his economic program"—to prevent Congress from tampering with the third year of the income-tax cut.…

Legislative strategy group. Who persuaded Reagan that he had to accept higher taxes to get deeper budget cuts? Primarily it was the "legislative strategy group" under Baker who always believed Reagan should do more to cut the deficit. How did the legislative strategy group persuade the president to accept higher taxes? By driving home this argument: The budget resolution that Reagan ultimately supported and won congressional approval for included "deficit reductions" of $380 billion over three years—$280 billion in spending cuts and $100 billion in higher taxes. Thus, for each dollar in higher taxes, Reagan was getting almost three dollars in spending cuts—*at least this is how the resolution was sold to him*.… [emphasis added]

Fuller explains: "Jim [Baker] has a good deal of influence [on economic decisions] and that influence is vested in his ability to read the political winds on Capitol Hill and advise the president on what's do-able.…"

Thus, as is so often the case, the cabinet council on economic policy, which includes the Treasury Secretary and the chairman of the Council of Economic Advisers, was effectively circumvented in both Reagan's initial decision to support the budget resolution and in his decision to support the Dole tax package…[102]

In his memoir, Jim Baker expressed great concern about deficits and writes about his extraordinary efforts to convince Reagan to raise taxes even though Reagan would rather be criticized for a deficit than backing away from his economic program. Baker acknowledges getting Meese, Deaver, Stu Spencer, and even Nancy Reagan to press Reagan to accept the Dole tax package and quotes Reagan as saying "All right, goddammit, I'm gonna do it, but it's wrong." Then Baker lamely added, "The president later said he regretted capitulating."[103]

In Baker's presidential oral history with the University of Virginia's Miller Center of Public Affairs, he mirrored what Reagan said to me about TEFRA as "one of the worst decisions of his presidency." Moreover, Baker conceded, "The president, of course, with his aversion to tax increases, really didn't like it. I'm not so sure today that he wasn't right..." Baker added that TEFRA was "accommodating to the political exigencies that were extant at that time. That's what he was doing. His heart wasn't in it. And I'm not so sure that we wouldn't have still been all right, even if we hadn't done that—in retrospect."[104]

Once Reagan made a decision, even a bad one, he became defensive in owning it and stubbornly claimed he hadn't been manipulated or misled by his staff—and, more importantly, that he did not break his pledge against raising taxes. In a January 5, 1983, press conference he was confronted by a reporter that "we did have two different sorts of tax increases last year." Reagan bristled and replied that there was a difference between a "users fee" and a "tax for general revenues." He portrayed TEFRA revenues as "a tax to do this particular task" [rebuilding roads and highways].[105]

His staff, including me, should have been straightforward with him—that he was breaking his vow against not raising taxes, that TEFRA was not a matter of "revenue enhancements..." and that he had the political option of taking the fight to Congress. But I was not a policy maker, only there to help Reagan fulfill his dream to heal the cankers eating away at America's economic soul. He laid it out hundreds of times in speeches on the General Electric circuit, in radio speeches and in debates with the political Left. His words resounded in what became to be known as "The Speech," aired on behalf of Republican nominee for president Barry Goldwater in 1964, when he said:

> No nation in history has ever survived a tax burden that reached a third of its national income. Today, thirty-seven cents out of every dollar earned in this country is the tax col-

lector's share, and yet our government continues to spend $17 million a day more than the government takes in....

This is the issue of this election: Whether we believe in our capacity for self-government or whether we abandon the American revolution and confess that a little intellectual elite in a far-distant capitol can plan our lives for us better than we can plan them for ourselves....

No government ever voluntarily reduces itself in size. So governments' programs, once launched, never disappear. Actually, a government bureau is the nearest thing to eternal life we'll ever see on this earth....

Our natural, unalienable rights are now considered to be a dispensation of government, and freedom has never been so fragile, so close to slipping from our grasp as it is at this moment.[106]

What happened with TEFRA was a concession to everything he campaigned against and fought to change. That is what he should have been told by Jim Baker, Mike Deaver, Dave Stockman, and...also by me. He wasn't allowed to be the crusader that he asked me to reflect in his speeches when we met at Camp David on Father's Day weekend in 1981. He was surrounded by accommodationists who convinced themselves that at his core, Reagan was also a pragmatist. So, he only achieved some of what he wished—a reduction in tax rates—but the price of which, at that time, was the largest single tax increase in history and, as he warned in 1964, the government never voluntarily reduced itself in size.

Chapter 16

THE POWER SEEKERS

White House insiders are unmatched in their ability to claim credit, deflect blame, destroy potential rivals, hide information from the president, and leak their preferred narrative to the media with such skill that they build their own mini-administration. They can become their own powerful internal Washington establishments that shape policy even if they might be in philosophical conflict with the goals of the individual whose election brought them there. I witnessed that phenomenon working with President Reagan in his White House, reelection campaign and over debates on major policy issues.

James A. Baker, III, writes of politics as a "blood sport, featuring raw emotion and gutfighting," and, while he views intellectuals "often at a disadvantage in politics," he believes one of his role models and mentors, Elliot Richardson, was successful at it. Hence, he relates approvingly an observation from Richardson: "Washington was a city of cocker spaniels, meaning people who would rather be petted and admired than wield power. *Maybe we hit it off because he knew I would rather wield power.*" [emphasis added][107] In the law, that would be considered an "admission against interest" or just an honest self-appraisal on Baker's part. His overweening ambition and grasp for power was evident from the day he showed up on *LeaderShip 80*.

If I trod his desired path, Jim and I got along. During the early months of Reagan's term, he respected the collaborative relationship I had with Reagan and didn't intrude in the speechwriting realm. I didn't try to influence policy, and Baker didn't edit speeches. The bad news was he left all the meddling to his proxies. He gave his team a long leash to butt into my department as well as others—keeping his hands clean while his consiglieres operated freely. More than once, my colleagues attempted to use me as a useful tool to exercise their power or viewed me as a direct target if they saw me as an obstacle.

Except for first impressions in the '80 campaign, I began my personal relationship with Baker on a positive note. But as I worked with those that he brought with him and explored deeper into Jim's expansive and extravagant use of his White House post during research for this memoir, a grayer portrayal surfaced of his tenure in Washington. It began with the accretion of evidence of how Baker and his team leveraged Reagan to raise taxes in 1982 in a direction he did not wish. Then, as additional research surfaced, and as more obsequious versions of biographies fell short of a complete portrait, I realized a larger story had to be told about Baker and his fellow White House "power seekers."

Baker's appetite to wield power required a team of players experienced in the ways of Washington's politics, policy, and media. He surrounded himself with a group that had knowledge of the mechanics of government and, most importantly, owed complete loyalty to him. They included David Gergen, Richard Darman and Margaret Tutwiler. Gergen and Tutwiler were Jim's deputies in Bush's primary challenge to Reagan. Darman was an Elliot Richardson aide who followed Richardson through a half dozen different stints in and out of government—including resigning with him during what became known as the Saturday night massacre in October 1973.

Dick Darman had worked briefly with Baker at the Commerce Department and writes in his autobiography that "hooked on public policy making" and professing genuine disillusionment with Jimmy Carter, "I had approached Baker the moment his appointment was announced." Baker is widely known for his attention to detail, but he doesn't like to *execute* details; he prefers others to dirty their fingers. Hence, he promptly named Darman executive director of the White House transition.[108] I met Darman when Baker instructed him to arrange my White House consultancy, and Dick efficiently arranged my per diem allowance, expense reimbursement rates and preparation for my FBI clearance. He came from New England wealth, studied at Harvard and Oxford, and also served stints at McKinsey & Company.

Darman writes in his book that 1980's voters had "not actually affirmed any particular 'Reagan Revolution'—something that had meaning only for "a small group of hard-core conservatives and long-time Reagan activists, known as 'Reaganauts.'" Instead, he asserts "the use of the phrase 'Reagan Revolution' was taken to be largely sloganeering or media hype. They had voted for a change of direction, but not really a hard-right revolution.... More than an affirmation of a specific program, the vote for Ronald Reagan was a vote for a nostalgic hero and a rejection of the frustrations of the years before."[109]

He repeatedly derided the "Reaganauts." He writes, "The use of the word 'revolution' seemed way overblown." He adds with his classic condescension, "Further, I had some doubts whether the incoming Reaganauts would even be able to get effective hold of government. They did not control the Congress. And it was unclear to me whether they had had a working understanding of the governing culture for which their rhetoric had shown contempt. I suspected they did not."[110]

Reagan had spent a generation speaking to America, including presidential campaign tours over more than a decade, and hundreds of public appearances and radio talks—many of which included precise details. He served two terms as governor of the largest state in the US. There was no misunderstanding of Reagan's intentions to reduce taxes, diminish the role of government, and rebuild the US military—far exceeding the realms of "sloganeering and media hype." Darman entered the White House as the offspring of bureaucratic America and (a) did not believe in Reagan's mission, and (b) from the beginning had nothing but scorn for the skillset and intellect of those with whom he would work.

He was accurately described in a lengthy *Washington Post* magazine profile: "[O]thers, of all ideological stripes, see him as a deep-dyed cynic who is addicted to the action and power of being at the center of government, and who masks his expediency with grandiose speeches about long term ambitions for the country. 'I think he would do anything to advance himself,' says one former colleague."[111]

On January 20, 1981, I had no reason to butt heads with Darman. I viewed him just as his title described: staff secretary. From my prior White House experience, the staff secretary's job was coordinating presidential paper flow, a critically important position to ensure that before anything reaches the president's desk, and before he signs a document, all have been properly vetted. He was very helpful in ensuring the staffing of the initial economic speeches was smoothly accomplished.

I was unaware of his prior experience with Elliot Richardson, but he knew all about me. As I found out later, he made it a point of knowing everything about everyone else around him—his would-be competitors. A business school classmate of his summed it up, "You know how some people are aware of the net worth of everyone around them?... Well, Darman used to have that for IQ. Any kind of information that might tell him how smart people were—where they went to school, what their parents were like, how they talked—he paid attention to."[112]

I was taken aback in the senior staff meeting during a discussion on public outreach, when a colleague suggested we ask Julie Eisenhower to speak out in support of the president's economic package. Darman smirked at me and said, "That's a contact that would be in your department, not mine." It was his way of saying: "Nixon belongs in Khachigian's province." I wasn't aware of his connection with Elliot Richardson, so I didn't appreciate the underlying rancor remaining from those years.

That was a mere prelude to an unintentional confrontation when meeting with Marty Anderson and Murray Weidenbaum on the cusp of a pending economic policy announcement. Marty oversaw domestic policy development and Murray was chairman of the Council of Economic Advisers. Darman sat in, and I assumed he came as an observer since his job description didn't include economic policy. I took notes as Marty and Murray discussed upcoming decisions, and suddenly Darman began interrupting to assert his opinion on these issues.

I was honestly baffled why Dick, the staff secretary, was overriding Marty and Murray while they spoke. Darman continued to interject and announced he would prepare "this paper and that paper." So, I turned to Marty and said, "I thought this was your job." Wow! Bryce Harlow once shared one of his many great capital anecdotes, and this gem was about President Eisenhower's temper. "When you stirred up Ike's anger, it was akin to looking directly into a Bessemer furnace." Now, I knew what he meant. This was the first of many times I witnessed the eruptive temper for which Darman was infamous.

Dick managed to restrain it till the end of our meeting, but then he followed me out the door and down two flights of stairs and halfway across West Exec. The entire time, he spouted off about his background and education…his Harvard Business School training…his experience in different cabinet departments…and his extensive background in management consulting and advising corporations. "Look, Dick, I'm not questioning your credentials; I was only asking why you're reaching into Marty's jurisdiction." Darman continued ranting, "I'm not restricted to being staff secretary, and I bring job skills here that no else has, and I intend to use them!"

"Okay, Dick, let it go."

I didn't have time to debate Dick's *vitae*, but this confirmed the rumors about the boasts of his perfect SAT scores and unbounded ego. Baker brought him in without a leash, and Darman had one overwhelming trait: He felt he was qualified to do not only *his* job, but qualified for *everyone else's*. Shortly before my departure, he asked if there was a book on speechwriting—so he could learn how to write speeches. "Dick, you can't learn speechwriting from a book. There's no book like that." I later found out why he asked; at the first opportunity, he wanted jurisdiction over the speechwriting staff—just another avenue into power.

Darman portrayed himself as an honest information broker, counted on to present the president "the relevant facts and competing considerations, the pluses and the minuses, in a relatively neutral and direct manner" even if failing to "meet the ideological purity test."[113] That was a crock of bullshit. Darman and Baker were twins—nudging Reagan to go in directions they wanted—making him feel he arrived at decisions of his own doing and not by their pressing him or through outside leaks. Dick was mostly cautious when talking to reporters, but on occasion, let his colors show—he slipped after Reagan caved in on his pledge against raising new taxes.

Darman viewed TEFRA positively, as a sign that Reagan was "abandoning an 'ill-conceived' economic policy." He made this concession on deep background to *U.S. News & World Report*'s Sara Fritz that the "White House Staff is being torn apart by a serious power struggle.... On one side are Baker, Darman, Fuller, Stockman and other 'moderates.' On the other side are Meese and the right wingers. Deaver tends to side with Baker... Darman thinks that the attack by outside right-wing groups on Baker and his people is being orchestrated inside the White House by the Meese crowd.... After denying that the struggle within the White House is an ideological one, *Darman then admits that he is trying to change the president's economic program.... The tax bill represents a breakthrough to Darman.* Reagan can no longer claim to be a supply-sider, he says. 'It's like being a little bit pregnant. You can't do it.'"[114]

Darman let down his guard even further in the same interview:

> The Baker-Darman crowd is threatening to leave at the end of the year unless President Reagan gives them more authority....
>
> Ever since the 'Big Three' system fell apart, says Darman, the White House has operated very inefficiently. Instead of having a Big Two, Three or Four, he says there are

now at least six or eight independent players—*including himself*....

[A] spirit of teamwork...has been lost at the White House. "We have devoted an excessive amount of attention to supposed power struggles—who's up and who's down," he admits. He says the struggles get even more bitter further down the ladder among the 54 Special Assistants to the president. Darman adds that *this group includes "many incompetent conservatives."*[115]

Darman's power grip included an October, 1983 incident where he ordered information withheld from press spokesman Larry Speakes regarding the invasion of Grenada, placing Speakes in an untenable position with little preparation when thrown in front of the media. Larry never forgave Darman and started telling people that Jim Baker would give him two lines, and "Darman would take one of them away." Two years later, Speakes told a *National Journal* writer that Darman was "the ultimate second-guesser."

Speakes records in his memoir, "I added that although Darman was an all-pro Monday morning quarterback, his response had always been 'No way' whenever I asked him to brief the press on subjects he knew about."[116] By refusing to go on the record, Darman maintained his flexibility as a cynic and critic without ever bearing responsibility or having the president or First Lady see his name attached to the baggage of his sentiments.

Speakes describes another Darman power trait—threatening retribution:

Before long I received Darman's handwritten response— complete with a threat addressed to me as "PERSONAL AND CONFIDENTIAL," on the stationery of "The Deputy Secretary of the Treasury." It read:

"I was disappointed to read your comments about me in the latest *National Journal*. You may feel I 'second-guessed' a lot. I guess you do not much appreciate that I helped and defended you a very great deal—at times when your position was at great risk.

"It has been my experience that the wheel turns 'round and 'round in this town. Please be assured that the next time I am in a position to influence the prospects of your success, failure or capacity to serve, I shall remember your thoughts."[117]

An aggrieved Darman issued another threat in October 1984 when he felt he received unnecessary blame for Reagan's performance in the first debate with Walter Mondale (more to come in Chapter 19). After a tongue-lashing by Senator Paul Laxalt in front of a handful of us in Baker's office, Darman describes threatening Laxalt:

"[I]t's beginning to look as if some people may want me to take all the blame, and then some. You need to know," I said slowly and clearly, "there is a limit to how much I'll take. I will take a reasonable amount. But it's got to be at least halfway reasonable."

I didn't say what I would do if it were halfway reasonable. *I just looked Laxalt coldly in the eyes, without blinking, and let him imagine.*[118]

Darman was indispensable to Baker as his "on board computer." He provided Baker the numbers he needed, organized agendas for his legislative strategy meetings, and was on hand to prepare him for whatever detailed information he required—in the kind of concise formats that made Baker always appear prepared and informed. Darman's indefatigable energy and drive to be recognized with insider's access lent him the willingness to fill that role, and he knew his control of the information flow gave him enormous leverage. Nevertheless, his ego created *some* boundaries.

As recorded in that *Washington Post* profile:

During the Reagan years, Darman's staff was instructed to keep a bibliography, with separate sections for mentions of Darman in books, in periodicals and in newspapers.... As for the morning newspapers, secretaries were told to clip headlines and only the portions of the stories that dealt with Darman...

The stories that described Darman as an "aide" to Baker would not be saved at all.[119]

David Gergen didn't share Reagan's political philosophy, began his voting years as a Hubert Humphrey Democrat, and was most comfortable working for Bush's more moderate policies. So, Jim Baker had to clear a path to bring him into the White House and his inner circle. One of the traits Gergen shared with Darman was a mild contempt for the conservatives around Reagan, claiming in his memoir that Reagan "realized that most of his inner circle was inexperienced in national government and didn't run with the Washington crowd."[120]

That wasn't true—Dick Allen, Marty Anderson, Lyn Nofziger, Cap Weinberger, Bill Casey, Jim Brady, Ed Rollins, and I, just to name a few, had a great deal of experience and didn't need counsel from "insiders" like Darman and Gergen. But Dave claimed that Reagan needed the "realists," as he referred to the Baker team, to help guide Reagan. It was natural for him to try to usurp my role as Reagan's chief speechwriter on Reagan's first economic speech and to not want to give up any turf he presumed was his.

To Dave's credit, his repeated efforts to acquire power in Reagan's White House didn't equal Darman's level of connivance and brutal aggressiveness. His personal qualities were more refined and gentlemanly. Nevertheless, he sought both internally with Baker, and externally by exhaustive exposure with the White House media, to expand his role and raise his profile to exert influence. Dave's method to ensure that every major news organization was aware of his position as a major player was his nonstop availability to offer "backgrounders" (a fancy Washington term for leaking).

His initial amorphous title of assistant to the president and staff director gave him putative authority over communications and speechwriting. Yet, after I rebuffed his effort to override my draft on the first economic speech, his frustration led him to write Baker a memorandum requesting a "Clearer Definition of Duties:"

> I would very much like to move now to obtain a clearer definition of my responsibilities and authorities within the organization.... [O]thers on the staff sometimes feel I am butting into their territory and the whole process is much more confusing than it ought to be.... It is increasingly clear, I believe, that the area where I can make per-

haps the greatest contribution to the president and to you
is in communications.[121]

Gergen's memo pushed for a sweeping takeover of communications—
specifically "clear responsibility to coordinate the ground activities of the
communications department, the press office and speechwriting/research."
He asked to have authority to clear all press releases and preside over meetings prior to press briefings and release White House statements. In a little jab, he noted that Jim Brady had a "fairly expansive view of his own
responsibilities" and would resist unless there were "clear directives" from
Baker, and he invited Baker's protection to "step in first." If Jim Brady had
uncovered this covert attempt to oversee and pull a power play on him, he
would have intensely fought it. He also asked for roles to work with Deaver
on scheduling, have responsibility for all presidential briefing books, and,
most importantly, sought "access to the president...on a regular basis in
order to make the communications operation work."[122]

It's hard to fault Gergen given (a) his restless and competitive personality, (b) watching Dick Darman's increasing domination of meetings and
insertion into policy, (c) his lack of profile to tout with the media that
clamored for leaks, and (d) resistance by Brady, me, and others to have
Dave intruding in relationships we had built with the president on the
campaign trail. I don't think he wanted to control the process so much as
to influence it—to "edit" policies and decisions rather than be responsible
for their creation.

His wish was fulfilled when the president formally announced his
appointment on June 18, 1981, as assistant to the president for communications. Lou Cannon led his story in the *Washington Post* with "The White
House reshuffled its communications arm yesterday to strengthen a section
weakened by the wounding of press secretary James S. Brady and the departure of chief speech writer, Kenneth Khachigian.... In his new role, Gergen
will be in charge of the press office, the Office of Communications...and
the speech-writing office. Speech-writing has been a trouble spot since
Khachigian departed May 1...."

Baker made the announcement while also announcing the arrival of
fellow Texan and Bush alum Peter Roussel as a deputy press secretary. After
announcing that Gergen and Speakes would "share daily briefing duties,"
Baker "fled the room" when asked how a "dual spokesman system would
work."[123] Larry Speakes conceded to reporters that things "have not devel-

oped as he envisioned."[124] But Larry was masking his unhappiness with Gergen's muscling in on his territory.

Speakes later wrote, "I considered it my initial job to keep Gergen out of Brady's job, to keep Brady's seat warm in case he came back. Guerilla warfare broke out almost at once between Gergen and his staff and me and mine. He was always trying to stab me in the back, telling Baker that 'Speakes didn't get this quite right.' But Baker would pass that on to me, so I was aware of what Gergen was up to, and I had my guard up." When Gergen briefed, Speakes had an aide reduce the podium to its lowest height so the very tall Gergen would "tower over it like Ichabod Crane."[125]

Darman's visions of a White House power struggle orchestrated by Meese and his right-wingers on one side against the Baker/Darman/Fuller/Stockman wing confirmed the ongoing effort by Baker's team to diminish Ed Meese's role as a serious player. It didn't take place in the first few weeks because Jim Baker was careful to study his prey before bringing him down. But if Jim Baker came to Washington to "wield power," he would have to ascend where no one else other than the president or First Lady was able to challenge its exercise. That required Baker to blunt Meese's standing with the president, and, perhaps even more importantly, with the media and capital chattering class.

He and his staff set out to do so with surgical gloves and scalpels.

Darman's ego was worn on his sleeve; Jim Baker's was embroidered inside his Brooks Brothers suits and displayed with discernment. Knowing of Meese's long ties with Reagan, he circled him warily. Key Reaganauts remained skeptical of Baker and still viewed Meese as directing much of the incoming policy changes. If Baker was going to establish his bona fides as a meaningful quarterback, he couldn't let Meese be seen as numero uno at 1600 Penn.

One of the first signs was an article in *U.S. News & World Report* that rankled Baker, but he dealt with it by using Dave Gergen as a proxy. With Darman, Tutwiler, and John Rogers running administration, Baker had insulation his biographers labeled as the "Baker Republicans, a powerful and fiercely loyal cadre for him in the internal fights to come. 'Baker had all these lieutenants and we all swore by him and thought the world of him, Gergen said.'"[126] Hence, finishing up a backgrounder with two White

House reporters from *U.S. News*, Sara Fritz and John Mashek, Gergen took Mashek aside, as recorded March 20, 1981:[vii]

As a loyal *caporegime* to Baker, it was expected that Gergen would take Mashek aside to make clear that Baker wasn't just on site to make the trains run on time while Meese was Reagan's top man. Any uncertainty I had regarding Baker's obsession for his portrayal in the national media was erased over a lunch with Robert Novak, the legendary syndicated columnist and television commentator.

Novak always rang me up on his California visits to catch up on West Coast politics, and in turn, I would mine him for similar whispers from DC. Bob had become a committed supply-sider and conservative, and on one of his stopovers our conversation turned to Jim Baker's role in the White House. Over pasta at Orange County's acclaimed Antonello Ristorante, Novak leaned into me with his takeaway on the chief of staff, *"Baker was consumed by his ego—once telling me: 'Remember, Bob, it's important what you write about the president; but it's even more important what you write about me.'"*

I was never fully shocked about Baker's massaging the media or having his staff do so on his behalf, but that was over the top. A comment like that to a reporter, even if offered in jest (which I don't think it was), is felony stupid. Jim Baker knew then, and must appreciate even more now, that absent the opportunity that Reagan gave him after the 1980 election, he would likely have spent the remainder of his career advising Texas oilmen on their drilling rights over steaks at Houston's Petroleum Club.

That vignette from Novak also explained why Baker and his team worked to cruelly demean and degrade Ed Meese. Dave Gergen was only one of the team that carried Baker's water. Several weeks after that *U.S. News* interview in March, Dave responded to a reporter's query as to why Baker was so much in charge in June of '81 on the tax issue:

> Gergen says (self-servingly) that reporters have always been mistaken when they regarded Meese as the first among equals at the White House. Baker's stock is rising—and the tax issue is the prime reason.[127]

---

vii In a private chat with John Mashek after the interview, Gergen expressed the view that our nine-to-five cover story portrayed Jim Baker as little more than a "paper-shuffler." He showed John several portions of the article he had circled. It's unclear whether Gergen was speaking for Baker or himself. The story probably does portray Meese more favorably than Baker. Could this be a first sign of jealousy between them?

Rich Williamson, who was close to Baker, added insight to how power's allure easily infected those in the White House. Rich was especially unhappy with *U.S. News & World Report* for being excluded in its photo layout on top presidential aides and "spent the better part of an hour supplying...his opinion of most other top people at the White House. His obvious purpose was to demonstrate to me [Sara Fritz] how close he is to the center of power. He was critical of Lyn Nofziger and Ed Meese. But *he had high praise for Jim Baker, his immediate boss.*"

On the one hand, Williamson told Ms. Fritz that the "Big Three were working well together because they were determined "to avoid conflict." However, the interview also recorded that "Baker gets high marks from Williamson for good political sense and administrative skills. 'Ed Meese spreads himself too thin and he's not decisive enough—he can't make a firm decision,' says Williamson."[128]

Sadly, many of Meese's wounds were self-inflicted. Based on my own experience in the 1980 campaign, I knew he tended to juggle too many balls, and though he was a prodigious worker with large brainpower, his distractions didn't allow the focus or follow-through that Baker worked hard to showcase in front of Reagan and the First Lady. Ed's staff was not as driven and skilled in the capital's culture, and Meese viewed reporters warily and, for the most part, as adversaries. The advantages for Baker and disadvantages for Meese were fairly summarized in Peter Baker's and Susan Glasser's hagiography of Jim Baker:

> As important as any factor in Baker's rise was his assiduous courtship of journalists. Baker recognized, as Meese and others did not, that power in Washington was driven in part by the *perception* of power and that no one did more to create or preserve that perception than the media—especially the national television broadcasters, who still dominated an era where millions of Americans stopped everything to watch one of the three nightly newscasts. Like other Republicans, Baker assumed most reporters skewed liberal, but unlike many of the Reaganites, he did not view them as the enemy. He understood that what they really wanted more than anything was a good story. If he kept them supplied, they would be happy—and less likely to come after him.[129]

Meese was also unaware of an asp in his immediate circle—one who apparently sniffed out that promotional advancement might arrive more quickly if chiming in on his boss's weaknesses. Craig Fuller, the cheerful young man whose career was advanced as Meese's cabinet deputy, joined in on undercutting Meese. Fuller's knife came out after Ed took a severe pounding for not awakening Reagan when US fighter planes shot down two Libyan MiG-23 jets after an unprovoked attack in the Gulf of Sidra on August 19, 1981.

While staffing Reagan in Santa Barbara, Fuller gave reporter Sara Fritz of US News the fodder:

> Craig Fuller, a Meese lieutenant…says that Meese has a "serious public-relations problem…." The problem began when Meese failed to rouse the president during the Libyan shoot-out last week…. But Fuller volunteers that it was a serious public-relations mistake. He adds that Meese got his back up when reporters pointed out this flaw…. Fuller says the wake-up flap would never had occurred had Mike Deaver or Jim Baker been here in Santa Barbara with the president. Not only would they have awakened the president to tell him, says Fuller, they also would have readily admitted the mistake if they had failed to do so.[130]

Fuller's self-assurance in building up Deaver and Baker at the expense of his own boss was polished the previous month when he had no problem telling the same reporter how he lied to Meese about a story in her magazine:

> Fuller says Meese was furious about our cabinet-rating story. "He wanted to find out who you talked to," Fuller laughed. (Fuller was one of our sources.) "I told him you just have to get used to these things. Stories like that are traditional."[131]

Baker didn't always leave soiling of hands to others. In the aftermath of the Libyan "shoot-out" incident, he saw his opportunity. So, when he sat down with various reporters, he didn't hold back. In one background interview available in the National Archives, Baker was unusually candid:

Baker offered some harsh criticism of Ed Meese. Not only did Meese fail to awaken the president after the Libyan attack, but Baker also faults him for failing to press Reagan to decide on his defense-budget cuts in mid-August...

According to Baker, Meese's problem is simple: "He can't see the forest for the trees."

This criticism of Meese is not surprising. Others have described him as disorganized and indecisive. But it is the first time that Baker has expressed such a view of Meese.

According to Baker, there's no doubt that Meese erred when he did not wake up the president last week. "Everybody recognizes it was a mistake," says Baker. "He recognizes it, too. It's never a mistake to wake up the boss...."

Baker also criticized Meese's efforts to cut off questioning by reporters during photo opportunities. He notes that this questioning is traditional and adds that Reagan does a good job of answering the questions. He says that he and Meese have discussed their differences about press relations, but refuses to talk about it....

Caution: Baker asks that we protect him on the stuff in this memo about Meese. Not only should he not be quoted by name, but everyone should be careful not to discuss this information outside the office. It would jeopardize our relationship with him.[132]

Two weeks later, Baker, Meese and Deaver decided to combine interviews with magazine reporters, acknowledging that "their relationship was strained" during Reagan's Santa Barbara vacation. "Baker is trying to undo the damage caused by his indiscreet remarks about Meese out in California," they wrote. One of the scribes noted that "after sowing the seeds of discord while he was in California with Reagan in August, Baker seems to have persuaded a lot of people in the White House that the published reports of strain among the Big Three were caused by reporters who had too much time on their hands."[133]

In the same interview, Baker added to his list of career embellishments. In his effort to patch over any differences among the "Big Three," Baker still managed to find an example where he and Meese disagreed—by taking "credit for being the one member of the triumvirate who pushed Reagan into naming a woman to the Supreme Court."[134]

Was this ignorance, or was Baker flat not telling the truth? The benign explanation is that for lack of traveling with Reagan in the campaign, Jim simply didn't know that the candidate, at an October Los Angeles press conference, made a commitment to appoint a woman to the first vacant seat on the Supreme Court. The less generous version would be that this is just one more example of Baker taking personal credit for an achievement owed to the president and Stu Spencer.[viii]

Warning reporters that the slip of tongue regarding his indiscreet comments on Meese could jeopardize their "relationship with him" was another of Baker's methods of establishing fealty. When Ed Rollins made politically rash public comments about Maureen Reagan's California US Senate candidacy, Maureen lit up the White House switchboard, and Deaver and Baker demanded that Rollins offer an abject apology to the president to save his job.

But Baker wanted to position himself properly, "You've got to go to the woodshed, and he'll [the president] kick your ass good, but I saved your ass." Reagan was gracious, gave Rollins a pass, and told him just to be "real careful" going forward. When Ed reported back to Baker, Jim couldn't leave it alone and hammered Rollins, telling him he was "a mighty lucky man. *And just remember who your friend was.*" [emphasis added]

Baker was very practiced in that art form from the time many in the White House wanted Dave Stockman fired for stupidly commenting in the media about manipulating the budget. It was unlikely Reagan would fire Stockman because of his key budget role. Still, Baker believed he had to orchestrate a "public woodshedding," and in a George Patton profani-

---

viii Baker gave a different version in his oral history interview at the University of Virginia's Miller Center when he was asked about his involvement with "the nomination of Sandra Day O'Connor to be the first female justice of the Supreme Court." He replied: "There had been some talk during the campaign about the fact that he might be the first President to nominate a woman to the Supreme Court...I really didn't have much to do with that, except to take charge of the arrangements for announcing it, briefing her." Interview with James A. Baker, III, Miller Center, University of Virginia, Final Edited Transcript, p. 33, June 15–16, 2004

ty-laced performance secured Stockman's understanding that lunch with the president would be "humble pie." He made sure that Stockman knew, "All of the rest of them want you shit-canned right now...*If it weren't for me, you'd be a goner already.*" [emphasis added]

Stockman's and Rollins's thanks should have been directed to Reagan only. He was never going to fire either of them. Baker's collection of markers matched the subtlety of Don Corleone when, on his daughter's wedding day, he told the groveling Bonasera, "Someday, and that day may never come, I will call upon you to do a service for me."

The White House had a way of fomenting dreams of imperial status in even its most lowly inhabitants.

My interoffice phone (I-O) rang late one afternoon in February 1981. The I-O is a separate phone line where senior staff members can reach one another without going through their secretaries. An earnest young man—who shall remain anonymous—came on to relay a message from another senior member of the White House staff. "Hi there, Ken, this is Earnest Young Man *calling from the West Wing....*" I immediately shouted to Kathy Reid: "There's some self-anointed little asshole on the line; would you please take a message?"

"Calling from the West Wing!"

In that little twerp's mind, the Old Executive Office Building, adjacent to the West Wing, might as well have been located at my 1970s rental in Oxon Hill, Maryland. After all, there were two sets of Secret Service passes—one was imprinted "EOB" and the other was earmarked for the "WH." In Earnest Young Man's view, even if he was sitting in some five-by-seven cubicle in what was known as the West Basement, he was still sixty or seventy steps away from the Oval Office and therefore closer to the center of power.

Power—even reflected power—is an extraordinary elixir in Washington. It's a heady experience to pass through the massive gates where the US president resides. Like any intoxicant, power in the nation's capital can have a destructive effect—turning good men and women against each other; fostering distrust and betrayal as well as feeding the intense need for identity, attention, and recognition. Of the seven deadly sins, all but sloth emerge from the seduction that beckons.

The seduction begins by sweeping away the inconveniences that trouble lesser mortals. At the White House, we had coveted parking spaces just steps away from our office; the White House Mess in which to dine; and the Executive Mess set aside for the thirty-five of us who were most senior of Reagan's staff. When we needed haircuts, Milton Pitts was available at a makeshift salon for fifteen dollars just across the Situation Room. A tiny elite enjoyed portal-to-portal car service, and sixty-five of us had access to a car and driver for official business.

In the Reagan White House, those perks were the mere cotton candy of power—nothing compared to real power. Real power was influencing policy, outmaneuvering rivals, gathering domains of authority and, often above all, ensuring that outside opinion makers and the media were aware that a particular staff member was first among equals. That required a display of skill in the connivances of politics and execution of the machinery of administering a vast array of complex decision-making in a system that relied on deal-making, deal-breaking and achievement of goals, whether good or ill. Or, in Jim Baker's favorite term, succeeding in what's "do-able."

Ironically, the title of Dave Gergen's memoir is *Eyewitness to Power*, and yet when he left the White House, the *New York Times* reported that "an associate said Mr. Gergen had spoken of the need for 'rejuvenation' after nearly three years of labor and *'infighting' with the administration*." It is possible that the "associate" was actually Dave Gergen speaking to the *Times* "on background," airing his own grievances. A significant example of one was Gergen's unpleasant relationship with Darman, illustrated briefly in the chapter that follows. Dave's magnetic attraction to power continued when he joined Bill Clinton's White House after voting for Clinton over his friend and previous political benefactor, George Bush. I was not surprised.

Baker, Darman, Gergen, and Stockman were all strong personalities sharing a common lack of enthusiasm for Reagan's "crusade." Baker and Darman signaled it on paper before entering the administration. Gergen had no philosophical connection with Reagan and joined because it was a ticket to the summit. Stockman attempted to implement Reagan's revolution but allied with Baker in pressing Reagan to do the opposite of the greatest goals he had dreamed to achieve in Washington. They saw themselves as realists and pragmatists. I saw them as accommodationists who, on the shoulders of the president, pressed their views and their places in history.

Like me, they witnessed Reagan's excitement in his first week of office when hearing reports and budget reviews at cabinet meetings of cutbacks in bloated government. His thirty-year-long dreams of chopping waste and bureaucracy—finally fulfilled. He literally exulted at hearing plans for tax cuts to stimulate investment and trimming stupid and overbearing regulations. However, those who rode into office on the back of Reagan's victory didn't embrace his crusade—not with the same zeal as their desire to "wield power." The enticement of all the force and authority of the White House and the reach of the executive branch was so tempting that it often overrode the central purpose that should have drawn them there: the call to service.

The White House commands the attraction of men and women with great intellect, skill, and self-confidence. The demands to perform in the service of the presidency are extraordinary, and so it necessarily draws individuals of enormous energy, stamina, and mastery of the interconnection of policy, politics, history, and American government. But entry into the White House also emerges from the successful execution of arduous political campaigning and should meld the formation of the executive branch with ideas forged in the heat of politics, along with loyalty, patronage, and philosophical commitments.

Wielding power and mining the force of the institution for self-aggrandizement weren't unique to the Reagan White House. While ambition can give rise to excellence, it shouldn't be promoted at the expense of colleagues or to diminish their integrity undeservedly. In the Reagan White House, it worked to undermine the president and all he wished for in seeking the heights of leadership. As a young aide in the Nixon White House, I witnessed matters at a lower level, but in working for Chuck Colson—in the years before his redemption—the bullying, the pressure, and intensity with which he brought to his position appeared to have little purpose other than to lay claim to being a "go-to" power center in the executive office.

Chuck looked for forgiveness after serving in prison for his obstruction of justice. And even Bob Haldeman, who ran an intimidating and controlling staff operation for President Nixon, reached out to me when I visited his home in connection with research for RN's memoirs: "Ken, don't do things the way I did them." Bob's use of White House power was different than Colson's or Jim Baker's or Dick Darman's, but the creation of that atmosphere is a toxic cocktail unnecessary for the successful practice of democracy, and my anticipation of its ongoing presence in the Reagan

White House was among the principal reasons for my decision to reject the president's offer to be his assistant to the president for speechwriting.

Reagan had a celebrated aversion to conflict, and his countenance for the leaks, entanglements, and conflicts can be explained by his shielding himself from such behavior. Mike Deaver didn't intervene because he was immersed in scheduling and first family issues, so the comfort zone in allying with Baker made life less complicated. In the early months of his administration, Reagan appeared to achieve the baby steps of his crusade. But as his term moved forward, the management process and his staff operation worked against his "time for choosing"—the revolution in changing the economic, domestic, and cultural direction of America.

Nancy Reagan had sensitive and unsentimental antennae to all those around Ronnie, and she wrote of Jim Baker in her memoir that she believed he did a "fine job" because he knew "a lot about politics and had many good contacts in Congress...*more inclined than Ronnie to compromise and make deals.*" She did laud Baker's loyalty and effectiveness in getting Reagan's programs through Congress. But tellingly, she added:

> He also cultivated the press assiduously—perhaps too
> much, because he leaked constantly. Although he did a lot
> for Ronnie, *I always felt that his main interest was Jim Baker.*
> He was an ambitious man...I wouldn't be surprised to see
> him run for higher office in the future. [emphasis added]

His main interest *was* Jim Baker—to wield power, raise his profile, and enhance his reputation. To be sure, he helped get the Reagan Revolution underway, but without question even more of what the president wanted achieved could have been done had Baker and his team embraced Reagan's dreams as assiduously as they did their own.

> *"Remember, Bob, it's important what you write about the
> president; but it's even more important what you write
> about me."*

Chapter 17

SUITING UP AGAIN

Reagan wore a fluffy Century Plaza Hotel bathrobe when Room 1915's door opened at 10:00 a.m. on December 28, 1983. He sported the same smile that must have wowed Jack Warner in Dutch Reagan's screen test. "You can see I dressed for the occasion." Mike Deaver followed, and we began discussing the timing and wording of Reagan's reelection announcement.

Though claiming only he and Nancy knew for certain, his intentions were an open secret. In June, Stu Spencer checked in with me to make sure I was available for a central role in the reelection campaign, and just before Christmas, asked me to come by to talk about the president's speeches. Though the president kept talking like he hadn't made up his mind, Stu chuckled, "That's a lot of bullshit. He's too much of a competitor, and we've got to start planning. He'll announce right after the new year, and they'll ask you to write his speech."

The meeting with Reagan was kept off his calendar, and without the usual photographer, there was no public record of my presence.

"You know, Ken, I haven't come to any direction at all, yet. Just not sure what I want to say in the five minutes I'll have." But just when I thought I'd have to start suggesting language, it was like the umpire shouted, "Play ball," and Reagan was back on air for a Cubs game at WHO. He began spinning out ideas.

"It's an unfinished job. Progress has been made; still what's out there must be done." He paused, and I heard the familiar Reagan—the one that the "power seekers" never truly understood. "Our economic problems have stemmed from the government taking too much money from the private sector, and the answer is for the government to do less spending." After a brief pause, he said, "let's do the announcement at the end."

"Now, I know it's tempting, but don't be partisan—with Congress coming back, and I'll have just done the State of the Union speech, it won't help to be partisan. We can start out with what we started to do in 1980. We reduced the size of the bureaucracy. We made it more effective. We reduced the size of the growth of government."

Deaver interjected, "Let's give credit to bipartisanship, because that's how we resolved the Social Security issue."

Reagan picked up momentum, "But with all of that progress, it's only a start. The deficit is still too big because of overspending by government. There is much to be done, and the job is far from finished. Therefore I will ask the people to return me to office to finish the job we started. I'm going to be a candidate for president."

Ten days before his announcement, the president would be delivering a speech on US–Soviet relations, and both Deaver and Reagan thought it deserved a reference. Deaver suggested adding reminders of our disappointments in not achieving things *we* wanted to do, so Reagan picked up the theme.

"Yes, there have been frustrations, but there are broad goals ahead—an America where there is autonomy of local governments…an America at peace…. we still must, as we reduce deficits, to require balanced budgets in the future of government." Then something sprung from one of Reagan's twenty-year-old notecards: "Thomas Jefferson said there should be a clause in the Constitution that said you couldn't borrow money."[ix]

He wanted to make sure I included one phrase…"Act worthy of yourselves. One thing the people have told us. They want a government beholden to them—one that's fiscally responsible. It's not that they want me, but they want the policies, and we've strived to be on this course."

---

ix   This was one of those historical "facts" I could never be sure of until I had the research folks check it out. Reagan had a collection of facts and figures mined from the conservative newsweekly, Human Events. The vast majority were on the mark, but every now and then, a slightly exaggerated fact or apocryphal story would appear. While running Reagan's first campaign in 1965, Stu Spencer took away Reagan's subscription to Human Events to limit his meandering into areas that stirred up problems with less conservative constituencies. After he was elected Governor, Reagan said to Stu: "Can I have my Human Events back?" (telecon with Stu Spencer, November 5, 2013)

Deaver added two themes he believed were important…that the country yearned for a two-term president, and Reagan restored pride and dignity to the office. Reagan concluded with favorite themes.

"You do not become president; you are given temporary custody of the office of the president. I ask again for four years of custody and hope to leave it stronger than when we found it. Then, there are the social things, and we need to allude to these: school prayer, abortion and others."

I submitted a final draft to Reagan two weeks ahead of the announcement. It was intercepted by Jim Baker and Dick Darman, both of whom made edits before the president ever saw it. Most were substantive regarding Reagan's record, but Baker made a conspicuous change. In California, Reagan instructed me to allude to school prayer and abortion. Thus, in my draft, in a litany under unfinished business, I included the following wording "…keeping America at peace in a more settled world, *protecting the lives of the unborn*, and seeing if we can't find room for God in our classrooms." [emphasis added] Jim Baker struck out the reference to "*protecting the lives of the unborn*." His initials were adjacent to the edit.

Reagan specifically asked me to "allude to abortion and school prayer," and I did. Baker's removal regarding the "unborn" was a unilateral exercise of power that wasn't assigned to him, but consistent with his caution to me when working on the inaugural address "not to get wrapped up around social issues." While researching this book, I discovered Baker reinforcing his beliefs to an inquiring reporter: "The president is very pro-life, very anti-abortion. His commitment is very clear. *But he can't get out front.* It's too divisive." [emphasis added][135] Later in the campaign, Jim would admonish me one more time against raising "social issues."

"In Hollywood, I wasn't known as a good script-writer, but I was known as a pretty good 'script-doctor.'" That's how Reagan softened the blow when he was about to make substantial edits to one of my assignments. In private life, Reagan wrote his own speeches, but as California governor, and later for his syndicated radio shows, he didn't have time to write all his speeches and scripts, so though he still loved writing, Reagan grew to rely on the aid of "ghosts" like Pete Hannaford.

Reagan heavily marked up my draft, reworked it at Camp David the weekend of January 21, then asked to meet two days ahead of the announcement to review his revisions. For our brief twenty-five-minute visit, the main annoyance was Dick Darman's unnecessary presence. With no ear for political rhetoric or any sense of how to connect with voters, Darman never belonged in any communication meeting or electoral strategy session. But Baker couldn't control him, and also appreciated his presence in such meetings to guard against the false dread that Reagan's mind might be polluted with deviations from the "party line" they concocted.

On January 29, I joined Reagan and the First Lady in the Oval Office to watch him deliver his nationwide remarks. I was pleased Reagan retained language I had inserted with mischievous intent—to be spoken just fifteen seconds after his brief introduction: "I've come to a difficult personal decision as to whether or not I should seek reelection." Maureen Reagan was also in the room, and her head swiveled with a deer in the headlights look—a nanosecond of disbelief that Dad might not be running again. I smiled, and she sighed in relief, realizing the Hollywood actor staged a classic move to capture the attention of his audience to keep them tuned to the end.

> When I first addressed you from here, our national defenses were dangerously weak...and at home we were adrift....

> ...(W)e were on the brink of economic collapse....

> Inflation had risen to over thirteen percent in 1979 and to nineteen percent in March of 1980....

> Interest rates over twenty-one percent—the highest in 120 years....

> Well, things have changed.... our work is not finished. We have more to do in creating jobs, achieving control over government spending, returning more autonomy to the States, keeping peace in a more settled world, and seeing if we can't find room in our schools for God....

> We have made a new beginning. Vice President Bush and I would like to have your continued support and cooperation in completing what we began three years ago. I am therefore, announcing that I am a candidate and will seek re-election to the office that I presently hold.

That evening, his diary entry was understated:

> *Tonight I went on Nat. T.V. for 4 min. & 41 seconds to announce I was a candidate & would seek re-election. The response has been terrific—calls, wires etc. running 10 to 1 in our favor.*[136]

Days earlier, Nixon checked in to send me ten copies of his new book and offer advice. Even with Reagan's poll approval at 56 percent, his close trial heats against Democrats were of concern to Nixon. "Look, Ken, you have the possibility that Reagan could win the popular vote and lose the electoral vote. He can win California and Florida, but I've been talking to [former Texas governors] John Connally and Bill Clements. They say Texas is 'tough titty.'"

Oval Office sit-down and Dutch outlines his 1984 GOP Convention speech.

The Old Man had done his political homework. "Ohio and Pennsylvania are going to be hard because you know as well as I do that the recovery has not been as quick as it could." Referring to civil rights activist Jesse Jackson running in the Democratic primaries, he said, "Jackson won't win, but he'll make a deal with Mondale to get the Black vote out. Remember, Reagan won Mississippi, Alabama, South Carolina, Tennessee, and Kentucky by less than thirty thousand votes each. The West will be a complete win, but the South could be close."

He offered anecdotal perspective by referring to his former House colleague, Minnesota's George MacKinnon. "Old George MacKinnon told me many years ago when I ran against Gahagan [Nixon's Senate race opponent in 1950, Helen Gahagan Douglas]. Run like you're a million votes behind, and then you might win by one vote." He instructed me to pass along guidance. "Back in '72, we had hard hitters like Agnew and Connally, so you need to set up a 'Truth Squad' from the Senate and House, those in safe seats or who aren't running for re-election and can go on the stump and attack the Democrats' ticket."

With that, we were off and running.

I faulted myself for remaining passive in 1982 while Reagan was lured into backsliding on opposing tax increases. So, in 1984 I sent him two memoranda pleading for steadfastness against new taxes during internal budget reviews. Treasury's Don Regan publicly hinted that the president might be considering a "contingency tax," and Reagan maneuvered uncomfortably in press briefings.

I fired off my first memo on December 16, 1983 (reprinted in Appendix 6) pleading that the tax issue:

> ...be put to bed—period.... Talk of taxes—contingency or otherwise—merely allows your opposition to build a national debate around an agenda they create instead of one determined by you. This is not unlike what we went through with TEFRA some 16 months ago. But in that instance, the Congress completely deceived the American public. They have not given—and they probably never intended to give—the three dollars in spending cuts for every dollar of tax increase....

This issue truly defines the legacy of your presidency…
the only chance we'll have in this century to turn back the
juggernaut of government gone crazily out of control….
(Y)ou can, I believe, recapture the fervor and excitement
of the crusade you led in 1980…

I sent it to Dick Darman with a cover asking him to put it in Reagan's
evening reading while expressing my concern that the "contingency tax"
debate would "cripple our ability to carve out an aggressive position in
the campaign." Sending the memo to Darman—a TEFRA godfather—was
handing the hen over to the fox, and it never got to Reagan. Darman knew
Baker would cover for him.

From Reagan's diaries, we've learned that he had to struggle with his
own staff's pressures to raise taxes. January 5, he wrote, *"Tomorrow Don
Regan & I do battle with our team members who want to raise taxes because
of the deficit. He and I want to reduce spending instead."*[137] Four days later:
*"Budget luncheon meeting. We're really divided. Don R. & I want to battle
down to the wire for more spending cuts as an answer to the deficit. Stockman
& Feldstein plus others want a tax increase. I think they are wrong as h—l."*[138]

Reagan seemed resolute in holding firm, but his own team ganged up
on him again, and he relented:

> *Earlier Ed, Jim, & Don Regan came in with a budget plan
> which does involve some loophole closing in taxes—mainly
> some Xmas tree items the special interests hung on our 1981
> tax reduction. With this is an ongoing plan for budget reduc-
> tions. Together they are a down payment on an ongoing pro-
> gram to reduce the deficits leading toward a balanced budget.
> It may work. I've said okay.*[139]

This was the pattern of compromise that resulted in TEFRA. He
gained no concessions from Tip O'Neill and the congressional leadership,
just more partisanship. Reagan made a January 25 diary entry about prop-
ositioning the leaders *"about naming some reps. to meet with on [sic] people
about a bi-partisan approach to the deficit. Tip ranted on that all we had to
do was tax the rich more & cut the fat out of the mil. budget. He knows that is
crap but it again is a tip on what their campaign will be."*[140]

Reagan appeared increasingly defensive, and I thought it was senseless to negotiate with O'Neill and Democrats whose political agenda was to cripple him in advance of the fall campaign. I shared my concerns with Jim Baker and Don Regan, and Baker asked me to summarize my thoughts in a note to the president. Looking for an ally, I copied Regan, because I knew Darman had no option with those two on my side. My memorandum of February 27, 1984, was received and sent to the president on the 29th. It's excerpted below, with full text in Appendix 7:

MEMORANDUM FOR THE PRESIDENT

I believe the time has come for you cut off the deficit talks with the Congress and go on the offensive with a plan that not only recaptures the policy ground for you, but also happens to be good politics as well...

First, make a public announcement that you are disappointed with the Democratic congressional leadership's refusal to be realistic or fair...then say [you] will prepare a detailed down payment on the deficit, and...present these ideas to the Congress and the Nation within 10 days. Remind the public of the fast one pulled by Congress in connection with TEFRA...

I believe, reluctantly, that the president must be visibly in front regarding defense cuts...because of my understanding that Congress not only has in mind deeper and more dangerous cuts, but that the Administration would likely have to swallow some of these cuts whether it wants to or not...

[T]hese cuts now can be combined with domestic spending cuts and loophole closures to start the effort to control the deficit....America cannot tax itself to prosperity and balanced budgets....[T]his entire package ...should be presented in a televised Oval Office speech—an educational speech like the president gave in February 1981... The goal: ...use the bully pulpit to put the president back in the preeminent leadership role, and to stimulate public confidence which will preserve all that we have achieved.

Darman reported Reagan received my memo, was receptive to my idea of a television address, and a following day's meeting would discuss the matter.

MARCH 7, 1984

It appeared Reagan was swayed.

> *We had a meeting with our Deficit Downpayment Negotiating group. I'm afraid I blew my top at one point. It seemed to me they are willing to let the Dems. run with the ball because they don't think we can stop them. I told them before we do that, it's time for us to agree on our position & then let me take it to the people (T.V.) and smoke them out. The way we're going we're not exercising any leadership. Besides—our position is on the side of the Angels & leaves the Dems on the wrong side of the debate.*[141]

Don Regan followed with a positive message—"Ken, the memo convinced the president he should be taking the lead and getting out front to protect against further defense cuts and hold the line on personal tax cuts." I was pleased that I stiffened Reagan's backbone against gutting defense appropriations, but I was sheepish about backsliding on so-called revenue measures. The good news was that Reagan never budged on his original personal tax cuts, made incremental progress against entitlements, and preserved the critical defense spending ending the Cold War. The bad news was that even he couldn't prevail against the leviathan government.

There are two versions of the 1984 presidential campaign, the one that is conventional and the other that has been overlooked. The second version is about too many of Reagan's "fellas" thinking they knew better than Ronald Reagan or Stu Spencer how to run the show—clamoring to substitute their power and influence over its direction in general, and its messaging in particular.

If the 1980 campaign was a box office hit, the 1984 sequel—with a strong and popular incumbent—was sure to attract massive egos of strategic wannabes both in and outside the White House who believed their titles endowed them with monumental political messaging skills. After the votes were counted, the historic results underscored the axiom that victory has a thousand fathers. The record shows otherwise.

Reagan acknowledged in two separate diary entries—November 1, 1983 and January 18, 1984—that Stu Spencer was the singular strategist in his reelection campaign. "Stu Spencer came to the house for dinner—we talked politics—what else? *I'm glad he's with the campaign.*" [emphasis added][142] Reagan never spoke that way about anyone else. Stu never labored over long campaign plans, so he dictated specific ideas and thoughts to an aide, John Roberts, who wrote them out for Stu's approval and signature. The thinking, planning, and strategy in Reagan's 1984 reelection campaign was derived from Stu's political genius—and later in meetings outside of Baker's command structure.

Ed Rollins had his hands full as operational campaign director and didn't mess in Stu's territory or mine. Lee Atwater fancied himself a strategic mastermind and produced prolific memoranda, none of which he wrote. He handed off the task to his bright young consigliere, Jim Pinkerton. But with Lee's name on the memos, *Newsweek* magazine's postelection book credited Atwater with "eloquent" thinking. While the Atwater/Pinkerton memos didn't influence Spencer, there were two that Rollins commissioned after the 1982 midterm elections that were channeled to Jim Baker and touched on Baker's sensitive nerves. One claimed that social issues from the 1980 election—like abortion—"may have peaked," and the other argued that the "opinion-making elite is virtually unanimously pro-choice."[143]

Two other strategic *poseurs* in the '84 campaign were Richard Darman and Richard Wirthlin. Dick Darman was a process-oriented, policy analyst, budget expert with a management consulting background. Baker allowed Darman to oversee the speechwriting operation, and Dick believed his raw intellect germinated political wizardry. Dick Wirthlin was a PhD economics professor turned pollster and was useful when providing raw data, but meddlesome when he believed that analyzing digits and graphs translated seamlessly into word combinations that resonated in voters' judgments.

They each wrote prolific strategy memos that Spencer largely ignored, but—again—were offered to *Newsweek's* campaign book as if the real decision-makers actually paid attention. I had to work around Darman on speeches, and he eventually failed in trying to intercede between me and Reagan. That didn't prevent him from leaking negative commentary to undercut the president's campaign messaging. Wirthlin was less careful in hiding his tracks, and his frustration and unhappiness at being over-ruled by the president led him inexplicably to undermine his own patron, Ronald Reagan.

APRIL 2, 1984

Nixon asked to meet at the LAX Marriott to share advice focused on for-eign policy.

> Right now, the president shouldn't take cracks at Mondale or Hart; keep him above the battle, like Eisenhower did. As for the campaign, I'd like to see Reagan take on the new isolationists. As far as summitry goes, we need to agree on the rules of engagement and resolve things before war. There's a profound difference between the Soviet govern-ment and the Russian people. The Russian people are a great people. They may not like their government, but they love their country.
>
> Reagan is portrayed as merely an anti-communist. The thing is not to see things merely in military terms but should ring out that our interest in these people [the Russians] is for themselves, not just as an anti-commu-nist. No question after World War II there was a Soviet threat, but you can leapfrog the differences—these two great nations must talk.

We concluded with RN seething over media prejudgment of ongo-ing special counsel inquiries into Ed Meese—that they were convicting Ed prior to his confirmation as Attorney General. "It's just not fair, Ken, he's getting kicked in public by the media and not being defended. George Bush ought to be out defending Meese on behalf of Reagan."

Mike Deaver tracked me down on April 3 for a brief meeting with the pres-ident. I wasn't on Reagan's preset schedule, (see Appendix 8) but Deaver and I were penciled in as additions. "Well, Ken, Mike says they've roped you into the campaign again. I just want to thank you for signing up, but I also have another favor to ask. Mike wants to keep a thin campaign crew travelling with us, and Stu will be one of them. But I would feel better if you would also agree to go on the trail with us—like you did four years ago. I know it's not easy, but Nancy and I—and Mike and Stu—feel it's important that you be there."

That was a no-brainer. "Of course, Mr. President. I was hoping you would ask. It will be an honor, and I'll put on my running shoes, so let's get out there." Deaver ushered me out, and the brief meeting confirmed a private discussion I had with Stu over my campaign role when he said he had expectations of my being on his winning road organization in the fall.

APRIL 6

Baker called an all-hands summit meeting to establish lines of authority and make formal assignments. I was there with Mike Deaver, Stu Spencer, Ed Rollins, Lee Atwater, Margaret Tutwiler, and Dick Darman. Jim reasserted Stu's mandate as the campaign's strategic overseer, with Rollins and Atwater tasked to set up the headquarters, state, and regional political operations, monitor budgets, and to coordinate with Deaver to prepare for the media team. He officially confirmed my role heading up the issues and research team. Wirthlin's polling would report to Baker, Spencer, and Rollins.

Finally, Baker announced the campaign's traveling team. The standard White House press and advance support operations would accompany the president, and Tutwiler would travel as the White House political liaison to the campaign. Baker looked sheepishly to his right at Darman and said, "The president wants only two people from Reagan-Bush travelling with him, and that will be Stu and Ken."

Baker failed to tip off Darman, and when he heard my name, Dick looked coldly at Baker and suddenly, and loudly, erupted, "That would be a big mistake! You can't have Ken travel with the president. That's a serious mistake. Why would you do that? I'm in charge of speechwriting!" Darman was accustomed to imposing his will, but he clearly overstepped with the raw insult. The entire room fell in astonished silence at his brute animosity and ugliness.

With Darman's hammerlock on the speechwriting staff, Baker lacked the balls to inform Dick it was a preordained decision that offered comfort to Reagan and the First Lady for the campaign's writing needs. Baker back-pedaled. "Now, Dick, that's not my decision, and it's not yours; it's what the president wants." Darman wouldn't hear of it and continued ranting.

I had enough of his infantile rage.

> Dick, you really don't know what you're talking about. You don't know a goddamn thing about politics or speech-writing. I don't know why you're even in this meeting or why anyone asks your advice, and I'm not going to listen to any more of your bullshit. If you don't want me on the plane, why don't you walk next door and tell the president of the United States he's making a mistake. You can go straight to hell...I've taken enough of your crap over the years, and I'm not going to spend the rest of the campaign taking any more shit from you.

Because his bullying manner, ego, and breadth of power bred fear in the White House, no one spoke to Darman like that. His outbursts and tantrums encouraged peers and subordinates to steer clear, so it was a shock when someone pushed back. Rather than brook further humiliation, he stormed out. When I returned to headquarters, my first visitor was Lee Atwater. "Damn! I've never seen anyone talk to Darman that way. Wow, that was amazing. I loved it!" Word must have gotten around because Dave Gergen sought me out a week later at the White House Correspondents' Dinner. Dave had a couple of pops to embolden him, "I heard about your match-up with Darman. That was great! Darman used to get to me...he just got to me!" Smiling broadly, he added, "I was so pleased when I heard what you said to him."

Ed Rollins wanted to take opposition research away from Dick Wirthlin and took me aside. "I've got to put you in charge and get enough time out of you to handle it all, and if Gary Hart wins the Democratic nomination, it's 10 times more important because he's got some good people working for him." Rollins also had another reason: in addition to Dick Wirthlin's deficiency in gut politics, Dick had submitted a monstrous budget for sur-vey research, and Ed feared he would pad it higher if he could add opposi-tion research.

I brought Kevin Hopkins from the White House as my deputy because of his institutional knowledge of Reagan and hired Gary Holmes, Hopkins's colleague. I added Sheila Dixon—a brainy and talented writer from the White House communications shop. With bare walls, a few chairs, a couple of desks and no equipment, I had the beginnings of a staff at our headquarters adjacent to Capitol Hill.

Between travels to California, I filled out the research team with Arnold Tompkins, a Vietnam vet out of DHS, Spencer Warren, an eccentric New Yorker who added spirit, and grew the organization with Jim Strock, Bill Harada, and Leni Liftin. Burdened with organizing and paperwork two more aides were critical—the principal one being Sally Campbell, a South Carolina college graduate whose drawl increased depending on circumstances. She became indispensable for her tireless work ethic. Jan Grazer joined our team from California and brought relentless cheeriness.

MAY 14, 1984—THE SOVIET AMBASSADOR TRIES TO INTERFERE IN THE ELECTION

Dick Darman was an unwitting intermediary in Soviet ambassador Anatoly Dobrynin's crude effort to influence the outcome of the '84 election. The day after attending dinner at *Washington Post* publisher Katharine Graham's home, Dick made a detailed record of his conversation with fellow guest Dobrynin, and addressed it to Reagan's national security adviser, Bud McFarlane.

Dobrynin took Darman aside privately for "what he said was the purpose of trying to get a message through to us," and lamented that the state of US–Soviet relations "was at a very low point." Further, "the lack of effective channels of communications could prove dangerous." Despite the Soviet decision on the Olympics (its boycott of the '84 games), "He said that the Soviets would be perfectly happy to see a substantial improvement in the relationship prior to the U.S. election...and used the possibility of negotiations as a case in point..."

Then in item (4) of Darman's memo, Dobrynin crossed the line:

> Possibilities of negotiation. Dobrynin asserted that they were anxious to get talks going on such subjects as the nuclear test ban treaty and space. *He said that these would be helpful to the president politically in the election year.* He

said that we didn't have to have full-fledged negotiations, but could have discussions. [emphasis added][144]

In the tendentious atmosphere of the Trump era, Dobrynin's suggestion to connect elevated diplomatic dialogue with the potential of a political treat would have carried the stench of "collusion." Dobrynin's crude offer went nowhere, as confirmed by Reagan's response when a reporter asked him, a month later, what he was going to do "with this arms race?"

> I think the very fact that we're stronger—yes, the Soviet Union is unhappy because, for the first time in a couple of decades, we are preserving our security ability. We're building up our military, and we're not unilaterally disarming while they continue their massive arms buildup.... But when they're ready to come back to the table, it probably—or might not be till after the election, I don't know. But I think that the world maybe is a little safer that it has been in the past.[145]

The Democrats held their national convention at San Francisco's Cow Palace and it was a predictable partisan slugfest. Stu Spencer called me on the first day of the convention to let me know he had submitted an issue framework to Baker proposing that Reagan make a five-minute national television speech following the Dems' convention tying Mondale to the congressional leadership and call it a Mondale/Ferraro/O'Neill ticket— arguing that Reagan tried to get things done, but Congress was "do-nothing" while sitting on several sets of issues. "I want the damn hook to be, 'the "president comes out swinging.'" He gave me a two-and a half page outline plus attachments that were more suited for a State of the Union address!

I drafted what Stu wanted, but it was wasted effort since his idea was nixed in the hierarchy. Instead, Reagan went on the road delivering political speeches responding to the Democrats' attacks. I had no hand in those speeches that came out of the White House speechwriting shop. I like tough rhetoric, but one of their lines was dopey and over the top: "The National Democratic leadership is going so far Left, they've left America." Spencer winced and made sure it was removed from subsequent speeches.

I turned my attention to Reagan's GOP Acceptance Speech, and Baker wanted me to submit an outline, something I didn't ordinarily do. Baker, Darman, and Wirthlin were process oriented, and even though the final product would end up flowing from my typewriter and Reagan's pen, they wanted a "treatment" for the script. So, I prepared a three-page summary for each audience—the one in the convention hall and the one watching on television.

Baker was extremely risk-averse and especially so in the 1984 campaign. In one of our strategy meetings, we all had a good laugh when Jim acted hesitant and cautious, and Tutwiler said out loud what we were all thinking, "Baker, you're a total wimp!" The only purpose of my submitting a summary memo for group review was to ensure I wouldn't take advantage of my personal relationship with Reagan and slip him any wicked ideas.

Baker chaired the meeting with me, Deaver, Darman, and Rollins, so they could comment on my outline before it went to the president. Baker liked that it focused on the future and was not too boastful. Darman bizarrely worried about references to families. "We need to do a lot of polling before we do that; do we alienate Yuppies?" I ignored him, and Rollins rolled his eyes. Darman still hadn't figured out that you don't learn speechwriting by reading books.

Rollins had a similar experience in a political meeting when Darman asked, "Do you have any books on how to run a campaign?" Rollins laughed, "There are no books, because guys like you would read them and think you could run a campaign."[146] Dick Wirthlin submitted his views via a memorandum, and his numbers made him obsessed by even the most indirect wording that could raise the "age issue." So he cautioned against the president taking a "nostalgic look" back at America's greatness.[147] Dick enjoyed presenting positive polling data to the president, but I doubt he ever said to him, "Mr. President, I need to caution you about making your age an issue."

Spencer, Baker, Deaver and Rollins all had experience in the cut and thrust of politics, so I gave weight to their views. But Wirthlin's compulsive embrace of data resulted in a tin ear for communications. Polling can offer guidance and trends, but imprisonment to polls is wrong and potentially fatal. When combined with Darman's misguided belief that he had political skills, the two of them added burdens to my job.

Jim Baker erred in infusing Darman with power and authority in areas that weren't native to Dick's strengths. The brainpower Darman brought to analyze policies, budgets and manage paper flow were apposite to the subtlety, creativity and poetry involved in reading political movements and translating those talents into content, tenor and spirit that move individuals to act or refrain from acting. Baker's great loyalty to Darman translated into a lack of will to resist Dick's intense ambition and drive. The result was to vest Darman with authority far beyond his skill range—a combination that damaged Reagan in October.

JULY 13

I had my first speech meeting with Reagan, and Baker, Deaver, and Darman again insisted on joining. The president had skimmed my memo and had his own ideas:

> Rather than just going back to Carter and Mondale, let's go back a quarter century of control by the Democrats of both Houses of Congress. In 1932 there began a great Democratic domination that existed for 50 years with only occasionally a Republican majority. The Democratic platform that began this whole thing pledged autonomy to local and state government and reduce unnecessary costs. So, why do we draw up a platform? Why don't we just adopt theirs? It's never been used!

> They've criticized our plan in their ads, but looking at our economic plan from 1980—by early fall of 1980, the possibility of a balanced budget was already gone because of a worsening economy. Remember, we operated on their budget in 1981, and none of our programs passed until late 1981—and even then, not fully implemented until 1983, and that's when the recovery began.

I could tell he was pissed off from watching the Democrats pound him at their convention. I wasn't sure how I would fit all his familiar lines into the speech, but they represented his philosophy.

> Remember, Ken, one does not become the president; one is given temporary custody over the institution called the presidency. Some people have become the president and seem to think that it's all theirs. Regarding my 1976 convention speech, they were writing about people they (our opponents) knew nothing about. What did they know about us? Well, they should know that we preserve their freedom.

> Was it compassionate to create programs that then found families that lived three or more generations as wards of the government? Or is it more compassionate to create a government of more opportunity so they won't need government? If welfare is doing its job, then we should be able to boast at the end of each year how many aren't needing it.

No surprise—these were the "crusading" themes going back to our June, 1981 Camp David meeting, and he was looking for a repeat of messages from the General Electric tour and as governor of California. Baker cut in, "Mr. President, you have restored pride and confidence in America." Stu Spencer stressed they polled strongly as themes we discussed in several of our strategy meetings. Reagan moved on to foreign and defense policy.

> I had the German Defense Minister in today, and he gave us credit for providing leadership to NATO and for bringing it together. You know, in World War I, Wilson had his 'Watchful Waiting' policy that he says kept us out of war. And the Kaiser just kept knocking off our ships because he knew we wouldn't fight back. Before World War II, Congress by one vote almost did away with the draft.

The meeting ended, and I escaped the "committee" for California and my last opportunity for uninterrupted working time. Moreover, I had to prepare Reagan's Labor Day campaign kickoff slated for delivery in Fountain Valley, California.

Reagan recorded mixed feelings about our visit in his diary:

> *Ken Khachigian came by—he's working on my acceptance speech—Repub. convention. I remember when I did all such things myself. No way now—no time.*[148]

I tried to satisfy the senior staff's need for input as well as that of other well-intended wannabe scriptwriters. Dick Wirthlin continued to press his views with long memoranda and comments—mostly annoying me with "data" promoting his obsession about the "age issue." He worried extensively about "alienating non-Republicans," and needlessly repeated mentions of focusing on themes that "point toward the future."[149]

Before drafting a single word, I kept notes on scraps of paper, parking receipts, hotel memo pads, torn pieces from newspapers. I scoured polls, past Reagan speeches, and solicited research from Gary Holmes, Sheila Dixon, Jim Strock, and Spencer Warren. They called themselves the "Fritzbusters," and loaded me with a library of liberal overreach by Mondale and his running mate, Geraldine Ferraro, along with damning economic data of Democratic regimes of bygone years. I also looked to resources from Kim White at the White House—materials for an important theme I would shamelessly exploit—US pride and patriotism surrounding America's hosting of the summer Olympics in '84 and the Statue of Liberty's renovation.

JULY 31

After five drafts, I turned in the completed product to Reagan, where he was staying at his ranch. Darman forced the draft to filter unnecessarily through him and others, and Wirthlin again fretted that there should be "more emphasis on the future and less on the past." He added, "I am very concerned about directing our attacks against the 'Democrats.' We risk alienating Reagan Democrats which are a key to victory…. I have an overall feeling that the tone of the speech is too partisan and too tough sounding."[150]

It was Reagan's speech, not mine, and he would be the final arbiter on its tone, and as always, he was gracious about my assistance. "I'll want to take my own hand to it, Ken, but it seems to cover all the points. The fellas have loaded me up with homework, conference calls and the like. But thank you very much."

Reagan didn't do a complete rewrite, and he retained nearly all the peroration I hoped would rouse the audience's emotions. Still, his "script-doctoring" was substantial, and he ignored the kibitzing from the "committee" by toughening up my rhetoric significantly. He struck themes about Democrats' control of government and its growth over his lifetime and added attacks on the totalitarian nature of communism and its threat to the world—language that I had not provided.

On the flight to Dallas, Baker insisted on adding last-minute language. I conceded to his leadership, and his contribution was actually solid and appropriate. Dick Darman was again unnecessarily present when I arrived in the presidential suite to deliver Reagan's final draft though there was no creative contribution he could possibly offer. He horned in to reinforce his status or sat in at Baker's request to shield Reagan from my poisonous thoughts. In a rare gesture of praise and display of sentiment, Dick reported choking up with emotion at the moving poetry at the speech's conclusion. If it worked for Dick, it should work for those listening and watching. I was in for a surprise.

On convention night, Reagan took America "down memory lane"—reminders of the mess he inherited and the extraordinary economic progress since then. It included Democratic mismanagement, excessive taxation, out-of-control spending, and upholding family and religious freedom. He set the stage for a showdown between two very different visions of policy, politics, and culture in November.

Then, as I hoped, the "actor's" manner changed, and voice modulated as he opened a scene and recited a classic American narrative:

> *We came together in a national crusade to make America great again, and to make a new beginning. Well, now it's all coming together. With our beloved nation at peace, we're in the midst of a springtime of hope for America. Greatness lies ahead of us.*

> *Holding the Olympic games here in the United States began defining the promise of this season.*

> *All through the spring and summer, we marveled at the journey of the Olympic torch as it made its passage east to west.*

Over nine thousand miles, by some four thousand runners, that flame crossed a portrait of our nation.

From our Gotham City, New York, to the Cradle of Liberty, Boston, across the Appalachian springtime, to the City of the Big Shoulders, Chicago. Moving south toward Atlanta, over to St. Louis, past its Gateway Arch, across wheat fields into the stark beauty of the Southwest and then up into the still, snowcapped Rockies. And, after circling the greening Northwest, it came down to California, across the Golden Gate and finally into Los Angeles. And all along the way, that torch became a celebration of America. And we all became participants in the celebration.

Each new story was typical of this land of ours. There was Ansel Stubbs, a youngster of 99, who passed the torch in Kansas to 4-year-old Katie Johnson. In Pineville, Kentucky, it came at 1 a.m., so hundreds of people lined the streets with candles. At Tupelo, Mississippi, at 7 a.m. on a Sunday morning, a robed church choir sang "God Bless America" as the torch went by.

That torch went through the Cumberland Gap, past the Martin Luther King, Jr., Memorial, down the Santa Fe Trail, and alongside Billy the Kid's grave.

In Richardson, Texas, it was carried by a 14-year-old boy in a special wheelchair. In West Virginia the runner came across a line of deaf children and let each one pass the torch for a few feet, and at the end these youngsters' hands talked excitedly in their sign language. Crowds spontaneously began singing "America the Beautiful" or "The Battle Hymn of the Republic."

And then, in San Francisco a Vietnamese immigrant, his little son held on his shoulders, dodged photographers and policemen to cheer a 19-year-old Black man pushing an 88-year-old white woman in a wheelchair as she carried the torch. My friends, that's America.

However, I had made a rookie mistake. I didn't anticipate a crowd that was so hyper that there was no way Reagan's poetry worked in the convention hall as it did on paper. At the patriotic references, they interrupted with chants of USA! USA! Then, at each mention of a state, or city, the delegates from that state or city jumped up, cheering and hooting.

Washington Post columnist Richard Cohen wrote of how moved he was reading the speech, but hearing it, "the tone changed…Walt Whitman wrote that he could hear America singing. In Reagan's text you could both hear it and see it…But in the hall, every mention of a city, region or state got a cheer that stopped the president in his tracks…Somewhere along the line, a poem to America got turned into the Johnny Carson show, where the mention of a town always evokes a cheer from someone."[151]

My heart sank as I watched and listened in disbelief as something I strived to leave as a combination of art and politics was buried in the chaos of conventioneers' madness.

The second story out of Dallas was one of shattered egos and betrayal. Reagan rejected the counsel of those who pressed me with their memoranda, and Dick Wirthlin took special offense that his boss, the president, chose his *own* message to deliver, not Dick's, so he wasted no time in making his bitterness known. He fed his coterie of media followers what they wanted: that Reagan was too partisan, didn't look to the future, and blew his opportunity to appeal to a Democratic base.

Whether it was to *Time* or *Newsweek* or others who rang him up, Dick was only too happy to confirm that Reagan didn't do as "urged" by "some aides" to "explore a vision." He was eager to confirm that the "tone of the convention" and "the Fritz-bashing" by Reagan had squandered his prime-time platform." Wirthlin and Darman were savvy in Washington's ways and knew their dissents would get optimum attention if expressed to the dean of the capital's political commentators—the *Washington Post*'s David Broder.

Direct from Wirthlin's playbook, Broder wrote that Reagan "muted what some of his political strategists had hoped would be a mostly positive appeal to the likely swing groups in the campaign against Democratic presidential nominee Walter F. Mondale…. [S]ome of Reagan's aides hoped for a speech tonight that would be at least as high-ground, forward-looking and positive. But Reagan had other ideas." Broder went on to quote "some of (Reagan's) own top advisers were telling reporters earlier today that 'it is foolish to bash Mondale as much as we have done...'"

"These advisers noted that, generally speaking, the more partisan a national election becomes, the better the Democrats do.... Making the election a highly partisan contest is essentially Mondale's strategy, not Reagan's..."[152] When *Newsweek* magazine published its postelection book, it reinforced the same complaint from Wirthlin: "The Republican convention...became a festival of Mondale-bashing and Reagan himself did not affect that posture above the battle usually favored by incumbent presidents. That had been a matter of some debate within the campaign command; a minority, Dick Wirthlin prominent among them, argued for less grapeshot and more future."[153]

In a *Washington Post* column that featured Dick Wirthlin telling reporter Martin Schram that Reagan's lead over Mondale grew by only one point after a "successful convention," it was not coincidental that Schram's next sentence blamed the lack of movement on "wooing already-committed Republicans rather than such crucial swing groups in the electorate as blue-collar Democrats and independents..." Schram continued, "One senior Republican strategist said afterward: 'This was an opportunity lost. We'll never again have...people sitting in from of their television sets for a week and watching whatever we want to give them." Schram discovered his culprit in a wily Svengali: me.

"But in the end, the Republican National Convention was very much a Kenneth L. Khachigian production. This little-known speech-writer who served in Reagan's 1980 campaign reviewed and reshaped virtually all of the speeches delivered at the convention. Khachigian's role as speech 'coordinator' was planned. But some Reagan advisers were surprised to discover that he felt the first goal of the convention should be to stimulate Reagan loyalists, guard against apathy and inspire the already committed—and that was how he crafted the speeches."[154] That must have surprised Roger Bolton, a congressional aide hired by the campaign as the coordinator of all the campaign's surrogate speakers. Roger had oversight of assisting in the research and preparation of their convention remarks.[155] Schram's sources lied to him; I had no role in any convention speech other than the president's.

Before I arrived on the campaign in 1980, Reagan's message was also mired in Wirthlin's surveys and accounted for Stu Spencer's complaint in an *Evans and Novak* column that "The damn pollsters took over." Spencer wasn't a fan of Wirthlin's poll-clinging and timidity and needed my more aggressive speeches to challenge Jimmy Carter. When Dick didn't get his way in the 1984 campaign, the larger betrayal was to his patron, Ronald Reagan, without whom the former economics professor would have been stuck lecturing undergrads at BYU. Along with Darman and Baker, he was just another power seeker.

Reagan's inner-circle whiners and media critics completely misread the Gipper. They resented that he knew best how to shape the message of the 1984 campaign and that he knew better than they how best to relate to the American electorate. Reagan edited my speech draft and added extensive new material to deliver the message he wanted—to defend his record and lift the spirits of his party. That is exactly how he played it in Dallas, and it received rave reviews where it really counted.

Baker and his team were needlessly spooked by establishment criticism of the convention speech, so Jim asked me to be less partisan at California's Labor Day rally and added specific forward instructions: "Let's keep Mondale's name out of the speeches. When it's time to take a shot, it will sound more presidential if Reagan talks about his 'opponent' and doesn't directly attack Mondale. That reduces the dignity of the office." So, I folded in high-toned rhetoric about a nation of uncharted frontiers, and that America wasn't about "promises,"—as the Democrats pledged in San Francisco—but about "possibility." I never mentioned Mondale's name.

In my library of anecdotes, I unearthed one with language that became a fixture of Reagan's reelection. Dwight Eisenhower had once recounted the story of a government worker arriving in Washington for the first time and spotting the words carved into pedestals at the National Archives: "What is past is prologue." The fellow asked a DC cabbie what the words meant, and he replied, "Oh, that, well that's just bureaucrat talk. What it means is, 'You ain't seen nothin' yet.'"

Eisenhower's tale was the perfect setup for Reagan to define his reelection as not only one of contrasts with the other party but also offering a future signaling great potential—for the economy, for peace, for values and creating opportunity.

"That's our message this year. We will carry it across America. You ain't seen nothing yet."

Chapter 18

MORNING AGAIN IN AMERICA

I was in California for a rare weekend off when Jim Lake interrupted me with an early morning phone call, "We have a new project for you." Lake was a longtime pal from Bakersfield and formerly top aide to Olympic star and congressman Bob Mathias, who represented my hometown. Though sacked with John Sears in 1980, he was back in good graces and assisting Mike Deaver with the '84 advertising team. He quickly made the ask. "I want you to talk to Phil Dusenberry. I told him you'd be perfect to help him film Reagan for the convention documentary, and Phil will call to pick your brain and let you know what he has in mind."

I had a brief acquaintance with Dusenberry in one of the campaign's first meetings where he was a leading member of "The Tuesday Team," a conglomerate of advertising all-stars recruited to form the Reagan–Bush in-house ad agency. I sat in at Rollins' request to track issues with Doug Watts the media director from California with whom I worked in Deukmejian's campaign. Until Lake's phone call, I didn't anticipate the substantial role I would assume in '84's advertising.

Dusenberry had a storied reputation as creative director at BBDO—overseeing marquee clients like Pepsi, whose ad with Michael Jackson made news when Jackson's hair caught fire too close to the filming's pyrotechnics. Dusenberry also cowrote the screenplay for *The Natural*, so I knew when we talked on June 27, I had to be prepared with my own ideas to offer him guidance. He was looking for help in scripting Reagan for the GOP convention documentary—words the president could use while being filmed. When I gave Dusenberry a wonky run-through of Reagan's positions on administration issues, he indicated he needed more than that. The real reason Lake directed me to Dusenberry was to provide a "co-star" with whom Reagan shared a comfort level.

Filming acclaimed "Morning Again in America" 1984 campaign documentary at Camp David with Phil Dusenberry, famed producer of Michael Jackson's Pepsi commercials.

"The whole idea, Ken, is to create a very personal, almost intimate visit with Reagan—his thoughts, ideas, hopes and achievements over three and a half years. We'll take him into the Oval Office, at home, at Camp David and reminisce and look to what the next four years brings. As he talks to you, the film will capture the actual actions he took in office...for example, if he talks about foreign policy, we'll cut to film of China and Japan, etc. Raise his trip to Normandy and let him talk about it while we show parts of his speech and dissolve to him in the Oval Office."

I felt a huge burden because this was all new to me. But then, Dusenberry wasn't looking for David Frost's skills; he wanted Reagan to have a familiar, relaxed companion sitting across from the president. "Ask Reagan questions; script it; give him talking points; or show him photographs of great moments and ask him what memories are triggered. We need to make it natural, believable and accurate. You can throw him questions, but I would love for you to have dialogue that would be natural and believable regarding things he said or used in the past."

As our meeting ended, I tested Dusenberry with my favorite idea for a commercial that promoted peace while maintaining a strong national defense. I described the flags hanging in the Roosevelt Room, and the separate streamers from the battle campaigns that were draped from the service flags of each military branch. I gave Phil a word picture of the president gesturing to the Roosevelt Room across the hall from the Oval Office and reciting how the weight and responsibility of the presidency meant never adding another ribbon to any of those flags. Dusenberry's focus was elsewhere and replied, "That's something we should think about, Ken, and I'll take a look next time we're there."

JULY 8, 1984—CAMP DAVID

Dusenberry greeted me upon my arrival, and was uncertain about presidential protocols, so I teased him for being the only one wearing a tie. The Reagans strolled over; Dutch in jeans and a casual western shirt, while Nancy was wearing a bright red sweater, blue jeans, and tennis shoes. Her laid-back and cheery mood was important in creating a relaxed environment for Ronnie and everyone else. The First Lady was also an accomplished flirt, so she made her way around the crew and staff ensuring their comfort and issuing warm smiles all around.

"Mr. President, I'm not sure I know what the hell I'm doing, but Phil says between the two of us, we should be able to work this out. I'll guide you through familiar issues, and we'll just have a conversation." Dusenberry took the role of director, describing his expectations, and then said the magic word Reagan heard thousands of times. "Action!" I opened with the 1980 economy and the changes he made. As Phil instructed, there would be a pause, and Reagan had the option of looking directly at a camera or looking at me (while the camera ignored me). Then, he would begin talking—in a smooth, confident, and practiced manner that was so native to his craft.

We covered the economy, foreign policy, his visit to Normandy and the American cemetery where World War II's heroes were honored. I asked Reagan about the assassination attempt, and the entire Camp David set became quiet and turned somber. The actor performed spectacularly as he described New York's archbishop, Terence Cardinal Cooke visiting him in the Oval Office and advising that in sparing Reagan's life, God "must have been sitting on his shoulder." "He must have been," Reagan replied to Cooke. "I told him whatever time I've got left, [pause] it now belongs to someone else" (as he gestured with a finger skyward).

Phil knew he had singular talent, but I don't think he conceived the filming would go so amazingly well. My tag team with Reagan worked because I served up softballs, and he hit them over the fence. I was over my opening day jitters and well prepared for follow-up shoots on Monday and Tuesday. Jim Lake and Mike Deaver probably had more faith in me than I did. Their concept was right about combining Reagan with a familiar face who had knowledge of his presidency.

As *Newsweek* magazine described it:

> The taping simply recorded a series of conversations between Reagan and his speechwriter Kenneth Khachigian, who has an easy rapport with his chief. Khachigian triggered the president's recollections by reminding him of something he had once said... By all accounts Reagan gave a masterful performance requiring very few retakes.[156]

We repeated our routine in the Oval Office, the Rose Garden, and on the South Portico. When we brought George Bush in the Oval, I stimulated conversation between the two as Dusenberry and his team put together new footage. On the South Portico, they brought in Baker, Meese, and Secretary of State George Shultz. I briefed each on the expected dialogue and helped initiate the conversations for additional presidential recitations of his record and second term hopes.

Reagan enjoyed being under the lights and especially enjoyed engaging with the set's crew members—displaying his knowledge of camera placement and lighting. On the South Portico, he tested the crew arranging the large lights, "Say, do you fellas know what gobos are?" While gobos are still in use, Reagan's reference was to studio lighting dating back to the '30s and '40s, where he explained the gobos were used to cut back on reflections or flares. Even the older crew members were impressed, but mainly enjoyed the camaraderie with Reagan as he relaxed while recording footage that would dazzle the GOP conventioneers and American voters.

There were several other critical members of the Tuesday Team, led by its "president," Jim Travis, on leave from Della Femina Travisano & Partners, who was the glue that held the team together with his affable demeanor. Jim Weller, whom Travis perfectly described as "a manic depressive who never had a manic day in his life," also came from Della Femina.

New Yorker Tom Messner came from Ally & Gargano and created spots for Pan Am airlines and MCI Communications. I teased Messner about working for a Turk (Carl Ally, who was actually Turkish and Italian). He produced what he called a "cheapo" ad comparing "Reaganomics with Mondalenomics," slashing Mondale's lust for soaking Americans with more taxes.

Roger Ailes was an irregular attendee at Tuesday team meetings and later helped with Reagan's second debate, where our paths crossed briefly. Roger was also producing media for Mitch McConnell, a relatively unknown Kentucky county judge seeking to unseat incumbent US Senator Dee Huddleston. McConnell and I coincidentally shared membership on the obscure, nonpaying National Institute of Justice Advisory Board. I was so impressed by one of Ailes's ads against Huddleston that I recommended him to oversee media for Deukmejian's gubernatorial reelection a year later.

Travis added Sig Rogich, who ran a Las Vegas PR firm with strong political ties to Laxalt. He was good social company, so we shared time as two westerners away from home. His principal contribution was arranging to buy the rights to use Lee Greenwood's "God Bless the USA," which served as an inspirational theme for the GOP Convention and every Reagan rally. Years later, it pained me to reprimand Sig for falsely taking credit for one of the most significant commercials I created for the campaign—and into which he had zero creative input. It was a sad denouement to the camaraderie we once enjoyed. Sig was a great bullshit artist with a fine talent for the camera's eye and knowing where to stand when the White House photographer took photos of Reagan at work with the Tuesday Team—giving the appearance he was involved in film production, when he was not.

On the way to meet Dusenberry for another day of White House filming for the convention documentary, I casually repeated to Jim Travis my idea about an ad revolving around Reagan and the Roosevelt Room flags. Travis eagerly jumped at the concept as potentially powerful and asked that I write a script, which I quickly produced and sent to the White House. Reagan added a few edits to fit his language and cadence, and we shot it in the Oval Office with Reagan sitting behind the Resolute Desk.

Four times in my life America has been at war.

It's a tragic waste of lives and it makes you realize how desperately the world needs a lasting peace.

Just across the hall here in the White House is the Roosevelt Room, named after the two Roosevelts who served here, one a Republican, one a Democrat. Many decisions are made in that room.

And often as I meet with my staff, I gaze up at the five service flags, each representing one of the five military services.

And draped from each flag are battle streamers signifying every battle campaign fought since the Revolutionary War. Each ribbon, a remembrance of a time when American men and women spilled their blood into the soil of distant lands.

My fondest hope for this presidency is that the people of America give us the continued opportunity to pursue a peace so strong and so lasting that we'd never again have to add another streamer to those flags.

(Music under)

When editing the convention's "Morning in America" documentary, Dusenberry put "Roosevelt Room" at the very end with cutaway footage of a raging river, stirring patriotic photos of Americana and concluded with a still shot of Reagan on Air Force One's steps beaming in a victory pose—all with Lee Greenwood's voiceover singing "God Bless the USA."

How could we possibly lose?

The principal reason for me to travel with Reagan in '84 was to be available to provide new messaging if contingencies arose on the road. Otherwise, Ben Elliott's speechwriting staff took over the principal burden of his stump speeches. My "Fritzbusters" ensured that Ben's pros had plenty of ammunition to expose the bad taste left behind by Carter and Mondale. When I wasn't on the road or overseeing my staff, my role in the fall expanded as a certified member of the Tuesday Team while also adding responsibilities of a parallel messaging operation to circumvent the president's favorite pollster.

Dick Wirthlin's coveted position with Reagan was set in stone, and his repeated calls and visits to offer Reagan data gave Jim Baker no option to work around him. Out of earshot, Jim coronated the pollster with a special name: "Numbers." Spencer also called him "Numbers," and out of frustration in communicating with Wirthlin, preferred working with Bob Teeter, with whom he worked closely in Jerry Ford's campaign. Stu invited Teeter in for rump meetings where the three of us could influence campaign messaging with Bob's help. Teeter was less dogmatic as well as more facile than Wirthlin when converting data into political communications. He also didn't wear his ego on his sleeve.

In a September 28 meeting, Teeter joined Spencer to tell me we needed something new despite Reagan's high poll numbers. "We've been running a string of softball commercials, but now we need more bite, and the only way is to put our strongest weapon on the air…the president. Your Roosevelt Room commercial was the most believable commercial of any they've ever tested."

Flattery is nice, but I knew I was only as good as my last gig. Teeter continued, "We need 25-second bites for two waves of commercials to offset the gauzy, warm feel-good ads of the summer and introduce a sharp contrast; two men and two ideas." He thought "Morning in America" and convention cheers could make Reagan seem out of touch with America and vulnerable to attack. The three of us agreed on a need to change the tone, and with Stu's and Bob's support, Jim Baker was unlikely to disagree.

These "rump" strategy meetings are critically important to the history of the '84 campaign's strategic direction—and testimony to Stu Spencer's instincts to introduce new thinking. Unlike Wirthlin, Teeter didn't obsess about Reagan's age or worry that pissing on Mondale would hurt the president with Democrats. Just the opposite. Now I had a free hand to draw a sharp contrast and to work directly with Reagan to script commercials for filming in early October at different White House locations—and without interference from Wirthlin or Darman.

It can be more difficult to write a thirty- or sixty-second commercial than a twenty-five-minute speech. Telling a story in 110 or 115 words is agonizing, and advertising copywriters will attest to spending hours and hours in achieving the precise syntax and word sequences to win over viewers and listeners. For those commercials, my deadline was to review scripts with Reagan on the return leg of our campaign visit to Houston on October 3.

Mrs. Reagan intervened in our airborne editing (described in the next chapter), so the president polished the wording back at the residence. Based on the messaging plan we put together in September, I prepared more than ten scripts for an ambitious day of production following Reagan's first debate with Mondale. It was the busiest weeks of the campaign—monitoring Stockman's and Darman's debate preparation sessions…scripting new spots and coordinating their production…all while writing Reagan's speech for his October 12 whistle-stop tour of Ohio.

OCTOBER 11

Jan Mahan Duval from the office of media relations had organized camera placement exactly as the script envisioned and was there to greet me, Tom Messner, Jim Weller, and art director George Euringer on the South Lawn. We were fortunate to film on the South Grounds given how spooked the Secret Service was since the 1981 assassination attempt. However, no other location would work for this concept.

Reagan agreed that Mondale could not match the weight and credibility of the presidential office; any reference to Reagan's residing in the executive mansion underscored that view. For this particular sixty-second spot, the president retained my exact wording, and we titled it "FUTURE FOR YOUNG PEOPLE:"

> *This place* [gestures back toward White House] *has a way of making us think about the kind of future our young people will have. Everything we do here—we weigh on tomorrow's scales.*
>
> *Keeping our economy strong and free from the terrible inflation of a few years ago will bring stability and economic freedom. These will expand new employment opportunities so important to those just leaving school for their first jobs.*
>
> *And keeping America strong and always searching for peace— well, nothing is more important than that.*
>
> *This magnificent house is 192 years old now. It stands watch on our stewardship—a guardian for future generations. What we do here may be important, but what we leave behind is even more important. I take no obligation more seriously.*

Reagan didn't require much direction and was flawless, so we followed up with thirty-second versions. We moved to the Oval Office to delineate the candidates' differences—something Spencer and Teeter believed was very important, especially after Reagan's flat first debate performance. I drafted a sixty-second version citing Reagan's achievements in clear distinction over Carter's failures, while leaving room for future progress. Reagan liked the script, but doctored it to make the contrasts clearer and his successes more pronounced. It had a simple title, "PRIORITIES":

> *Campaigning in 1980 we said we'd reduce inflation, and we have. We said we would lower interest rates, and we have. We said we would reduce crime, and we have. We said we would lower taxes, rebuild our defenses and get America working again.*
>
> *Today, taxes are down—our defenses are strong and more than 6 million new jobs have been created.*
>
> *Working with you we got those jobs done. We've got to do more.*
>
> *We must build a lasting peace while protecting our freedoms.*
>
> *We must help those who haven't shared fully in the recovery. We must create new jobs, improve education, and further protect you from crime. We must provide more security for the elderly and opportunity for our young.*
>
> *We pledge cities of promise. A countrywide of renewed vigor and a nation strong with opportunity and pride.*
>
> *I don't think America ever stops wanting to be better— because Americans are only satisfied with doing our best.*

Jim Travis chose Jim Weller to direct production for camera placement and proper lighting. After shooting a couple of the shorter versions and then the sixty-second spot, Reagan was getting impatient with additional takes. He always took special pride in successfully filming commercials with one reading. Weller was accustomed to shooting commercials with mega budgets, professional actors, and unlimited schedules. After three takes of "PRIORITIES," Weller said, "I'd like to do just one more, Mr. President."

I'd only seen Reagan's visible anger a couple of times, but his face flushed, and he gave the unsuspecting Weller a look reserved for cowboy villains in the movies. I rushed over and grabbed Jim to pull him away while Reagan said, "I'm through for the day, fellas." He pulled the microphone off, thanked us, and walked out. A dazed Weller looked around, wondering what happened. Returning to headquarters, Messner and I couldn't stop laughing as we ribbed Weller—adding to the lore of the Tuesday Team. Those lovable hucksters probably shared those Reagan–Bush whoppers for many years at Madison Avenue cocktail hours.

Media watchers in *Public Opinion* magazine's postelection analysis strongly endorsed Spencer's and Teeter's concept that "Reagan on-the-air" was the campaign's strongest weapon:

> [T]he most important Reagan spots were not the acclaimed good-feelings and waving-flags lifestyle productions, but the straight stuff used after the debate. The idea was simple: Let Reagan be Reagan. As one Republican campaign insider, admittedly no admirer of the Tuesday Team, said: "Following the first debate, we had to show that Reagan was upright, in charge, with all his abilities intact. Reagan on camera, for as many appearances as possible was the ticket."[157]

Better yet was the grudging praise by the liberal writer Sidney Blumenthal in *The New Republic*:

> His talking head spots are marvels of nuance. He has total confidence in the camera and the microphone; they are his old friends. In one ad he establishes eye contact with us and talks about a "clear choice." Then he looks away, dipping his head for a second, projecting the appearance of natural thoughtfulness and intimacy, although he's reading a script. With this small gesture the distance between the viewer and the performer is closed. "And it's a very simple choice." The camera is slowly, almost imperceptibly, moving toward him. We are physically getting closer to Reagan; we are being taken in. "It makes you wonder if they remember how things used to be." This line, deliv-

ered with conviction, has no meaning, but it's evocative and affecting. "There's a better life ahead. But only if we look ahead…" We see only Reagan. His triumph is one of manner over matter.[158]

Baker's, Darman's, and Wirthlin's distractions in the first two weeks of October—with debate preparations and then with debate damage control after Reagan's stumbles on October 7—freed me from their meddling to write scripts based on my own instincts and Spencer's and Teeter's issue clusters. Moreover, Nixon sent me a memo on October 2 that was intended to provide advice for the debate but also raised an extremely overall point: "…all that matters is to leave the impression that people are better-off now than they were under Carter-Mondale and that they will be better off in the future under a Reagan Administration than under a Mondale Administration."[159]

Reagan was dynamite on camera, yet it was the iconic "Bear-In-The-Woods" commercial that produced the most buzz for 1984's advertising campaign cycle—and the most focus-group tested ad. The bear ad was produced and narrated by Hal Riney from San Francisco's Ogilvy & Mather agency. Riney was a legend for creating and adding the voiceover for Gallo Wine ads. His soothing, velvety voice was also perfect for narrating the convention's "Morning in America" commercials and others in the campaign's early days.

A grizzly bear appeared onscreen, lumbering through the woods while a thumping drum gave an ominous warning sound. Riney's voice unwound the story:

> *There's a bear in the woods. For some people, the bear is easy to see. Others don't see it at all. Some people say the bear is tame. Others say it is vicious and dangerous. Since no one can really be sure who's right, isn't it smart to be as strong as the bear? If there is a bear?*

The commercial concluded with the bear silhouetted, stepping backward while the camera pulled out showing a man facing the bear with a gun slung over his shoulder. We joked that if you looked hard enough, there was a reddish hew to the film (though there wasn't). It was quirky enough that viewers had different interpretations, but the underlying point was clear: that a tough Reagan would face down the Russian bear—something Mondale wouldn't do.

KK finalizing the script and Reagan prepping for the camera to capture film for the campaign documentary.

We showed it early in the campaign without a lot of weight, but it wasn't aired in earnest until around the third week of October, just before the second debate. After the election, much was written about the bear. While brilliant and provocative, it has also been surrounded by a mythology that it triggered a momentum that either rescued Reagan after his first debate's stumbles or boosted him from mediocre victory to a landslide. Both observations are wrong.

Peter Baker's and Susan Glasser's biography of James Baker portrayed "Baker and the campaign team" deciding to get off the defensive after Reagan's poor performance in the first debate by shifting "to something a little closer to a policy argument…" The biographers' conclusion was "invoking Reagan's peace-through-strength approach to national security…" as represented in the Bear ad.[160] That portrayal misrepresents the history of the '84 campaign. Spencer, Teeter, and I shifted the campaign into policy arguments far before the first debate and before the Bear ad was aired. By relying on Baker for their guidance, his biographers were deflected from the campaign's true postdebate "rescue plan" that was shaped by Nancy Reagan and Paul Laxalt as described in the next chapter.

The idea that the bear ad sparked a landslide is also a campaign legend promoted by Dick Wirthlin. In addition to focus-group testing the ad, he touted testing it "on air in at least four different markets" and represented to *Advertising Age* magazine, "We knew we had a winner, but didn't run the ad until the Friday before the second presidential debate on Sunday which focused on foreign policy. We ran it heavily through the week and after the debate, and I give that ad a lot of credit for boosting what could have been a closer race to a landslide victory."[161]

The election was never close after Reagan's quick recovery from the first debate, and a convincing victory was well-established prior to running the bear ad. The Gallup organization showed the president with a comfortable fifty-eight to thirty-eight lead in mid-October (before the October 21 debate). Ed Rollins presided over daily political meetings in October where he opened by reviewing Wirthlin's overnight polling results—a "rolling average" of the previous four nights. My contemporaneous notes record that Rollins reported on October 17 that Wirthlin's own four-day tracking showed Reagan "holding steady" with a seventeen-point lead over Mondale—almost exactly the margin of victory on election day. The vaunted impact of the bear ad is a fabulist canard.

Still, Edwin Diamond and Stephen Bates may have produced the most realistic postelection analysis in *Public Opinion* magazine.

> In all, we found, presidential campaign advertising was a sideshow to the election and not the main event...The voters loved Reagan in November as much as they had in January, and $50 million in TV advertising was just so much background music to the affair.[162]

Chapter 19

NANCY STRIKES BACK

Reagan began the fall campaign with a relatively light schedule—official presidential activities bookended by a handful of political events. The stump speeches produced by Ben Elliott's speechwriting team referred to Mondale as "my opponent" or "the other side"—the result of Jim Baker's directive not to mention Mondale by name. Reagan was always great with his own spontaneous repartee on the trail, but it was very helpful for us to engage Doug Gamble, a Bob Hope joke writer, to complement Reagan's personal storehouse of humor. Gamble provided great lines, and the self-effacing gags about senior citizenship eased any stigma about Reagan's age—the issue that Wirthlin repeatedly overstated. Quips also helped Reagan make strong political points without appearing mean or contemptuous.

We visited Nashville for a *de rigueur* visit to the Grand Ole Opry to celebrate country legend Roy Acuff's eighty-first birthday, where Reagan achieved both goals. "Roy, the other day I met with some senior citizens in the White House, and I told them the only way I could sum up my feelings about older folks is to greet them by saying, 'Hi, kids.'" Then, a nice poke at the opposition, "I think we all better remember that the other side's promises are a little like Minnie Pearl's hat—they both have big price tags hanging from them."[163]

The Gipper enjoyed campaigning, especially repeating a litany of Mondale's embarrassing past positions and statements, and the attacks made on Mondale by his own Democratic primary opponents. My staff had done a wonderful job of assembling a long list of Fritz's vulnerabilities. But candidates don't run unopposed, and with Mondale down twenty points, his deficit led him to desperation. He found an opportunity to savage Reagan with a September 25 speech at George Washington University, and "reposition" his campaign by bashing Reagan over the "moral imperatives of the future."[164]

"The new Reagan proposed regular consultations with Soviet experts," bellowed Fighting Fritz. "The old Reagan is the first American president since Hoover not to meet with his Soviet counterpart. The new Reagan criticizes South Africa, while the old Reagan cozied up to apartheid...I won't permit this crowd to steal the future from our children without a fight. I won't let them put ice in our soul without a struggle. They have a right to ask for your vote. But I'll be damned if I'll let them take away our conscience."[165] It was less new Reagan and more new Mondale.

Juiced up by a small bump in the polls and pressed by his staff, Mondale upped the ante the following week. In front of a partisan New Jersey crowd, he crossed the line of rhetorical excess, and it caught Reagan's eye while reading the White House news summary over breakfast on October 2.

The president was greeted with the headline from David Hoffman's article in the *Washington Post*: "Mondale Challenges Reagan's Competence." "Walter Mondale, attempting to raise doubts about President Reagan's competence on war-and-peace issues, charged that Reagan's arms control efforts are 'doomed' because 'he has not mastered what he must know to command his own government and to lead' on foreign policy." The news summary also included Alan McConagha's *Washington Times* blurb of Mondale charging the president of "taking refuge in a 'parade of alibis' for the terrorist bombing in Lebanon."[166]

ABC News's Brit Hume reported Mondale's charge that "Harry Truman had that sign on his desk that says The Buck Stops Here. Mr. Reagan should put a sign on his desk that says The Buck Stops Everywhere—But Here.'" The ugliest may have been Mondale's cheap shot reported by Tom Brokaw of NBC News, "You can dream all you want, but if you believe that nuclear missiles can be recalled after they've launched, as Mr. Reagan did, you won't lead toward a safer world. If you don't learn that most Soviet missiles are on land-base, as Mr. Reagan didn't bother to learn, then your efforts at arms control are doomed."[167]

While Mondale was in New Jersey, Reagan gave a hard-hitting address at The Detroit Economic Club on the history of liberal economic failures and the growing success of his recovery program. He was so pleased that he recorded in his diary, *"Without naming him I laid into Mondale—1st time I've done that. Was very well received.*[168] The takeaways from the diary entry signaled (a) Reagan's growing frustration with Mondale's attacks on his economic policies, and (b) drawing attention to not "naming" his opponent. I would soon discover in spades why not "naming" Mondale was on Reagan's mind.

Mrs. Reagan wasn't with us in Michigan, but she arrived Tuesday night, October 2, for a large fundraising dinner in Houston, Texas. In his Houston remarks, Reagan once again referred to Mondale as "our opponent." That day, Mondale tried to step away from the harshness of his remarks in New Jersey, but in politics, no air freshener works for bad odors, and Reagan had his fill.

Air Force One lifted off from Houston's Ellington Field at 9:35 CDT for the brief flight to Andrews Air Force Base. Somewhere over Mississippi or Alabama, a steward asked me to step forward to the president's cabin. I wanted time to work with the president on final edits for the new television commercials, and I brought them along to review. Reagan was sipping a soft drink and gave me the kind of grudging smile that meant I represented work after his long forty-eight hours on the trail. Mrs. Reagan sat across leafing through a magazine and nodded at me—half warmth and half caution as I sat to review the scripts.

These were ads to film a week later, and with the president tied up with debate preparation, it was my only opportunity to get his input. I explained the strategy behind the messages that Spencer and Teeter wanted to emphasize and that we would be filming on the South Lawn as well as the Oval Office. He looked down and made a couple of changes on one script while I tried to elicit more thoughts on wording, timing, tone, and content.

Throughout, the First Lady looked at me in a way that made me feel like I'd forgotten to walk the dog. She clearly had very little interest in these commercials, and I found out why when she interrupted me in midsentence. "Ken, why isn't Ronnie using Mondale's name in his speeches? Why are you keeping Mondale's name out of his speeches?"

Um…This wasn't "Nancy with the Laughing Face"—the Camp David charmer from our July film outing. This was Momma Bear watching over her cub, like she did when my speeches weren't quite on time in the 1980 campaign, and she wandered back to crack the whip. Anyone who's ever been on the receiving end of these kind of messages would recognize the icy edge in her voice when it was delivered for effect.

Filming '84 campaign commercials on the South Lawn of
the White House—my "Secret Service Look."

It didn't matter to her that it wasn't I who wrote the speeches to which
she referred. The Labor Day kickoff was the last major speech I had written,
and in the interim, I had been focused on working with the Tuesday Team
on commercials and cracking the whip on my Fritzbusters. Infrequently, I
offered timely updates to speeches by Ben Elliott's staff if a local or national
issue arose while we were on the road. Beginning on Labor Day, I would
have loved attacking Mondale by name; Nixon's one-time reference to me
as his "nutcutter" was not wholly inaccurate. But Jim Baker's postconven-
tion instruction to lay off Mondale by name was also advocated by Dick
Darman, who pressed his subordinates to play along.

Despite my differences with Baker, I didn't rebel against the staff system, so my first instinct was to defend Jim's decision and try to mollify the
First Lady. "Ma'am, the thinking here is that the president might be better
off staying above the battle."

That didn't work.

"Ken, Mondale is kicking Ronnie in the teeth. He's just beating him
constantly. Why should Ronnie give him a free ride?"

Reagan didn't look up; his head was faced down over his paperwork with his pen appearing to dangle over one word. He wanted to stay out of this fight.

"All I can say, Mrs. Reagan, is that the feeling is that the president looks more dignified by not getting down to Mondale's level—more presidential."

Nancy scowled, "Do you think Mondale cares about being presidential? Did you see what he said about Ronnie yesterday? That Ronnie's not competent? Are you okay with leaving him alone to do that to my husband?"

The president never lifted his head, never made a sound. He looked like he wanted to be in another airplane—anywhere but having to listen to this beating. I understood what was going on. Just like when she acted as chief of staff in '80, she was doing the same now: she was saying everything Reagan could not bring himself to say. She was mouthing his words. He was tired of being hammered by that pipsqueak Mondale, and "Mommy" was delivering the message he couldn't bring himself to say.

But after taking a few minutes of these beatings, I decided I wasn't going to eat any more of Baker's shit. I was one of the few around that did *not* owe their loyalty to him, and I refused to get my ass kicked by the president and First Lady for a decision he made.

"Ken, this can't go on, and you aren't giving me a real answer."

I took a breath. Here goes! "Mrs. Reagan, I'm sorry, but Jim Baker instructed me to leave Mondale's name out of the president's speeches. He made that very clear." I barely got the words out, when Mrs. Reagan reached to her left and pressed a button. Seconds later, the steward walked in.

"Yes, ma'am."

Tersely, "Get me Jim Baker."

Unsuspecting wouldn't do justice to Baker's expectations as he jauntily walked in. Within seconds, he saw Reagan disengaged, staring at scripts trying to ignore us, and then looked over at me. He knew Nancy had one of those javelins he complained of catching.

"Jim," Mrs. Reagan paused to glance at me, "Ken, here, says that you told him not to mention Mondale by name in Ronnie's speeches. [Glance turned to a glare.] Now, why would you do that? Yesterday Mondale said Ronnie was a warmonger and made alibis about the Beirut bombing. And you don't want to attack back and use his name?"

"Now, Nancy." Baker used her first name when he had to push back with the First Lady; he had to show he could be on her level. "He's the president, and it's not right for him to get down to Mondale's level." Baker tried the same arguments I used, and reflected Wirthlin's beliefs that harsh rhetoric would "turn off" undecided Democrats. When trying to bring home a point and go on the offensive, Baker's Texas drawl thickened.

"Well, I just think we can win this race without bashing Mondale—and without making the president look mean or intemperate." Baker was stung by media criticism of Reagan's Dallas acceptance speech—especially the tough rhetoric the president himself inserted to hit back at critics. As a staff man, Baker didn't understand that the "javelins" he purportedly caught were nowhere near as piercing as the ones directed to Reagan by Mondale, Tip O'Neill, Jim Wright, and the national media throughout his first term and in this election. It was only after Reagan's diary was published that we discovered how rankled he was by the "demagoguery" of his political opponents.

Nancy cut Baker off.

"That's enough, Jim. Now get this straight. Going forward, Ronnie will refer to Mondale by name—not just as 'my opponent.' I don't want any more 'Huckleberry Finn' speeches. There will be no more white picket fences. Is that clear? No more white picket fences."

Where the hell did those descriptions come from? "Huckleberry Finn and white picket fences" were perfect metaphors. Obviously, outside the circle, Ronnie and Mommy had pillow talk conversations. "White picket fences," sparked warm and fuzzy imagery from the children's show, *Mr. Rogers' Neighborhood*, and the First Family was having no more of it.

Baker got up, nodded curtly, and spun back to his cabin—but not before shooting a look at me as if I'd called a foot fault in the determining set of tennis. I stayed for a few more minutes to see if Reagan added any changes to the scripts. During the duration of this explosion, he never lifted his head—as though he never witnessed the crime. Passing Baker's and Darman's glowers, I took my seat, and following a routine smooth landing at Andrews, Baker stalked toward the presidential helicopter as I headed to my ride.

Mike Deaver passed by, "You must have really pissed off Baker. What did you say?"

I gave him the only honest answer, "Mrs. Reagan was chewing my ass, and I decided I didn't have to eat her shit for something I didn't do, so I told the truth, and Jim didn't like it." It's not the first time Mike heard this kind of story; he shrugged, caught up with Baker, and flew off with the others on Marine One. I went back to headquarters to work at my job returning Walter Mondale to Minnesota.

Two days later, I attended Baker's standard political meeting, and to his credit, he acted as if nothing had changed in our relationship. But the First Lady's message was clearly received. "Here's the thematic stuff for next week. We're going to Charlotte, Baltimore, Michigan, and Ohio. There's going to be a more explicit, sharp contrast between Reagan's proven leadership and Mondale's failed past. We need a sharper, more confrontational posture; that helps with the soft Democrats." His presentation may have been for my benefit, and even though the next couple of speeches didn't mention Mondale by name, the contrasts were stepped up. Still, it wouldn't be until after the debate that the Gipper got the kind of language he wanted.

Baker replayed his 1980 role and focused on overseeing the upcoming debates with Mondale. After the Dallas convention, Baker called a political meeting where he assigned Darman to head up debate preparation, with domestic issues handled by White House public affairs director Mike Baroody, and foreign and defense policy by Bob Sims, deputy press secretary for foreign affairs. In the same meeting I was assigned preparation of the Labor Day kickoff speech, and lost focus on what would have been an opportunity to protest Darman's lack of rapport with Reagan for the critical debate role.

Nixon sent me a handwritten letter and three-page, single-spaced memorandum in anticipation of the October 7 debate—recommending to put the debate in "proper context" by passing on "general observations." (Full memo and cover included in Appendix 9.) RN asked that I caution Reagan, "Always remember, he is not talking to the media—but to millions who have not heard the lines before."

He advised that media and staff are "wildly exaggerating the importance and impact of the debates," and that "debates can affect the result, but only by two to three points—not massively." It turns out the Old Man was prescient in noting that Reagan "could 'lose' the debate decisively and still win going away. Consequently, Reagan should be encouraged to take the whole event in stride, adopt his very relaxed, confident manner, and, above all, not worry about every miniscule debating point on the types of questions you suggest he might be asked."

Nixon had high praise for Reagan's "excellent lines" on gut pocketbook issues in the Detroit Economic Club speech and urged that he use them again because "the great majority of the television audience will not have heard Reagan use these lines...". He emphasized: "Don't let Reagan get bogged down in detail with regard to the nitpicking questions the media will be asking. Don't let him or his overeager staffers worry about slips that may occur. Remember that what matters most is overall tone, which solidifies the impression people already have of a confident leader they can trust."

Historians looking into Reagan's underperformance in the Mondale debates should look no further than the structure of his debate preparation. Everything about it had the effect of undermining Nixon's concept to allow Reagan to adopt a "relaxed, confident manner" without bogging him down in detail.

His first practice debate was scheduled for October 4. But the day before, just after we arrived from Houston and the tense airborne confrontation with Baker, they scheduled Reagan into what he called *"a long afternoon at the Oval O."*[69] The "long afternoon" included over forty minutes of debate preparation with nine people stuffed into his office pressing him with facts, messages, and counsel.

This bombardment of faces, information, and procedures after two and a half days on the campaign trail was a classic misjudgment of Reagan's need for downtime, or at least be briefed quietly by a familiar face without hard edges. Stu Spencer wasn't involved, nor was Mike Deaver. And though I would be invited to observe the practice sessions, Baker and Darman kept me away from personally briefing or relating with Reagan. I had been in several meetings with Reagan where there were seven or eight or nine people in the room, not all of whom he knew, and in those circumstances, he mentally shut down.

The next day, Darman scheduled him in the theatre setting of Room 450 in the Old Executive Office Building, creating a format that mimicked Louisville's first debate. David Stockman played Mondale's role while a panel threw out questions. For ninety minutes, Stockman flailed at Reagan with ear-piercing intensity, contradicting him and interrupting—taking almost too much pleasure in role-playing the opponent's part.

His attacks startled Reagan with their ferocity and antagonism—charges of purported presidential failures...cruel cuts to the poor...the worst record on the environment...out of touch and not in charge...currying favor with religious groups. The Stockman battering ram continued without pause to talk through how Reagan might respond. Any opportunities I had to assist with messaging was cut off by the preset procedures dictated by Baker and Darman.

When the savaging ended, a flustered Reagan frowned and scolded Stockman, "You better send me some flowers, because you've been nasty to me."

Chastened and wondering if he'd crossed a line, Dave lamely replied, "Baker made me do it." Perhaps Baker's notion was to shake Reagan from complacency, but there were better ways than unleashing Darman and Stockman to undermine Reagan's self-confidence. The afternoon session went a little better, because Reagan was prepared for an intemperate Stockman, but the premise continued.

The die was cast; they had gone about this the wrong way. Baker's fundamental concept was sound: to shield Reagan from the vulnerabilities of his first-term policies, and how Mondale might exploit them. But it should have been done through a process of less heat and confrontation. Reagan spent decades preparing for debates and resonating with audiences by learning lines and studying in quiet. Instead, his staff exposed Reagan to humiliation in a roomful of onlookers by the rat-a-tat-tat attack they concocted.

For the Barbara Walters interview in the 1980 campaign, Jim Brady and I had a relaxed give and take with Reagan—with Nancy, Spencer, and Mike Deaver sitting in. That was far more effective in prepping the candidate for hardballs coming his way. The same thinking went into choosing me as the intermediary for filming Reagan for the convention documentary. Stu Spencer opined that Reagan always needed to wake up in the morning to a familiar and friendly face. With Baker and Darman's debate prep, he got neither. Instead of putting Reagan in a comfort zone, they shredded him in the sessions I witnessed.

It was easy to conclude that the comprehensive briefing book given to Reagan violated Nixon's wise advice "not to get bogged down in detail." This is the single instance where I disagree with Stu Spencer in analyzing Reagan's campaign. Stu concluded that Reagan fell short in his first debate with Mondale because he was lazy and didn't study his briefing books. The night after we had the final debate prep at Camp David, Spencer stayed the night and watched movies with the Reagans and then observed that Reagan "was supposed to do his homework at Camp David. He didn't do his homework...You're going to hear all these excuses. He was over-organized...hell, he didn't even read the briefing books."[170] However, Reagan faithfully recorded his activities in his diaries, and on the weekend prior to the Louisville debate, he referred to a debate rehearsal at Camp David and, after an afternoon ride, "lots of cramming."[171]

The president clearly underperformed in Louisville, and Mondale came on just as strong as Stockman. The mock debates that were supposed to prep Reagan for that eventuality didn't work. Reagan stumbled when trying to recall too many of his talking points and lost track of the bigger picture. More than once, Mondale caught him off balance, and consequently, our attempts to give him an uplifting closing statement failed when Reagan rambled with a baffling discussion of economic numbers, the defense budget, and a reference to spare parts and hammers.

In his oral history, Jim Baker attributed part of Reagan's problem to not memorizing his close about "driving along the Pacific Coast Highway."[172] But that problem occurred in the second debate, not the first, and Baker's memory lapse in his oral history wasn't unusual—I had my own, as well. But the "Pacific Coast Highway" statement didn't lose the first debate. Nancy Reagan was determined to find a way to help her husband recover two weeks later.

Her distress left her looking for answers, and she turned to Paul Laxalt, who joined her on a separate flight back to DC while the president flew off to other commitments. The Nevada senator had attended the mock debate sessions in the OEOB and witnessed what I saw. Laxalt told Nancy that Reagan had "been 'brutalized' by those who'd prepared him for the debate."[173]

She set out to exercise more influence in the campaign and had two immediate ideas. The first was ordering Stu Spencer and Mike Deaver to fire Dick Darman, whom she felt bore the responsibility for "brutalizing" Ronnie. Next, she saw that Reagan was scheduled for a whistle-stop campaign tour of Ohio aboard the Ferdinand Magellan—the same car Harry Truman used in 1948 for his "Give 'Em Hell" campaign against Tom Dewey—offering an opportunity to revive his confidence by going on the attack.

As for Darman, Spencer couldn't find him to convey the message, and Jim Baker's defense of his protégé was confined to passing the decision off to the president after telling Darman, "The First Lady wants you out." As Darman writes in his memoir, he quickly discovered that with Jimmy Baker, loyalty was a one-way street:

He was a friend, and was ultimately to become a much closer friend. But he had a tendency to be careful when it came to putting his interests at risk.... He reminded me that I had always said that if I ever became an undesirable burden for him, I would go—grateful for having had the opportunity to serve.[174] x

Deaver's report paralleled Baker's, "The First Lady does want you out of the White House...Laxalt gave her an earful after the first debate. She was angry and upset. You became the main target."[175] Neither Spencer nor Deaver had much stomach to pull the trigger and figured she would cool off, so Darman dodged a bullet by just laying low and staying out of sight. While Baker and Darman evaded responsibility, Laxalt didn't miss his chance to take a shot—telling waiting reporters that Reagan had been "smothered" and "brutalized" by his debate preparation.

He arrived at Baker's regular political meeting and took command at Jim's conference table, brushing off the chief of staff like an errant school-boy. "You all brutalized Ron in the debate preparation, and he lost his confidence. It wasn't fatal, and we'll recover. But he's not happy, and Nancy is very, very upset. And they're both tired of the weakness in his speeches, so for tomorrow's Ohio trip, here's what's going to happen: Khachigian's going to write the speech, and none of you will see it. It's going to come straight to me, and from me, it will go directly to the president."

I hustled to my office and called in Kevin Hopkins, Sheila Dixon, and Gary Holmes to start digging up quotes I needed because I only had a few hours to prepare a draft. I found a message that President Nixon was looking to talk, and I knew he wasn't going to be happy. "Goddammit, Ken, Reagan should not be concerned about facts and figures. The most important thing is demeanor; that's the thing Mondale did. I have an idea for a spot—take two of his excellent answers, the one on Social Security and the

---

x   Darman's patron was equally prepared to put him over the side in 1992 when President Bush's beleaguered re-election campaign faltered, and blame was directed at the economic team deemed responsible for the 1990 tax increase. The campaign's management proposed that Bush call in the resignation of Darman and others on the economic team effective at the end of the first term. "Baker liked the first part of the strategy; he had been Darman's friend and protector for years but was perfectly willing to make a human sacrifice of him if that was what it took to win the election."

one on taxes and replay them on cable; they will show he wasn't befuddled." The Old Man was frustrated, but full of ideas as usual.

"Your best commodity is Reagan and keeping the whole thing on the basis of the economy—even bringing economic policy into the foreign policy debate that's coming up." He talked about the live studio audience being against Reagan and then got to the politics. "Don't worry, this is going to tighten up some, but don't schedule him too heavy. Keep him upbeat so he's buoyant and strong. Mondale is still a plodding, dull man. The challenger always has the advantage, and the debate is the first good day Mondale's had. It still will be landslide margins, and it ain't over until it's over."

I closed my office door and started pounding away on my IBM Selectric. With no one looking over my shoulder, it was the most fun I'd had in recent weeks. I knew I had the imprimatur to kick Mondale's ass from one end of Ohio to the other—in Nancy's words: "No more white picket fences." It was everything Reagan wanted and everything Baker, Darman, and Wirthlin had argued against. At every opportunity, I threw in Mondale's name and made it sound like a profanity.

It was a gorgeous, crisp autumn day and the crowds packed around Reagan at every stop as he stood on the back of Truman's car and tore into Mondale. The train left Dayton, and he delivered the first of five whistle-stop remarks at 2:00 p.m. in Sidney and concluded the last in the dark at Perrysburg. After the third stop, Baker called me in to cut down the speech because we were behind schedule, so I began working with Reagan on editing out lines. Each time, Reagan resisted by saying, "I can't do that; you should see the look on their faces when I say that." He could turn a crowd of thousands into an intimate theatre, and he didn't want to withhold any of the adoration that was soothing the wounds of the beating he felt after Louisville.

It was described vividly in Rowland Evans and Robert Novak's *Washington Post* column, datelined Lima, Ohio:

> Gone was the Reagan mush that dulled voters' senses in the earlier campaign forays since the staging of the Dallas convention. The president's rhetoric—and more than rhetoric, his true intent—was clearly tailored to bloody

up Fritz Mondale and bloody him badly. Crossing the western salient of Ohio, one of the Republicans' greatest strongholds, was an angry Ronald Reagan who wanted his emotion to hang out in full public view…

The president's departure from the strategy of protecting his immense lead by ignoring his opponent and avoiding controversial second-term proposals was ordained in the White House on Thursday morning. James A. Baker, III, the president's chief of staff and the high priest of the strategy of caution, made no effort to override the unanimous insistence of Reagan's political managers that the president take the offensive.…

That meant substituting Reaganesque verbalisms of favorite speech-writer Ken Khachigian for the bland pronouncements preferred by Baker…Khachigian performed well and Reagan even better in his talks to large, enthusiastic Ohio trainside rallies here and in half a dozen other quiet, restful towns.[176]

I had greater satisfaction when *Newsweek's* crew of writers published its postelection book describing Reagan's "retooling" effort on his whistle-stop through Ohio. "Khachigian touched up a three-year-old attack speech. *Baker and Darman didn't much like it or him*, but they deferred, and Reagan, for a day, was Reagan again, riding an adrenaline high and giving 'em hell on wheels." [emphasis added][177]

Next was the foreign policy debate in Kansas City, Missouri. Baker got the message to moderate the methodology in debate prep, but more importantly, the need to pump the president's morale and composure. Stu Spencer asked me to check in quietly with Nixon for advice and memos he could pass to Reagan that would both offer policy assistance as well as bolster his self-confidence. The recognition of Nixon's decades of political intuition had prompted many within our senior circle to refer to him—per his New Jersey residence—as the Sage of Saddle River. And my call with the "Sage" prompted the first (Appendix 10) of three letters and memoranda— two addressed to me and one to "Ron." (The other two are reprinted in Appendices 11 and 12.)

In his first letter to me, Nixon shrewdly advised it was easy to counter Mondale's charge that Reagan hadn't made any agreements with the Russians by noting Mondale's Senate vote against the ABM treaty. "The Russian leaders are not philanthropists, and they're not fools. You can't get something from them in a negotiation unless you have something to give." Regarding arms control, "we must remember that the only kind of arms control that contributes to peace is one that is based on equality...That is why verification is absolutely indispensable." As for Reagan's intervention in Grenada, Nixon urged Reagan to say that without doing so, "the Caribbean would become a Red Sea."

However, he continued to believe the issue of the campaign was the economy. Though Kansas City was a "foreign policy" debate, Reagan "should, if at all possible, work in a statement on his economic policy.... either in expanding an answer to a question or in his closing statement." RN believed the winning argument was "a strong economy is an indispensable foundation for a strong foreign policy." More than anything else, "he must show the difference between himself and Mondale, who is a peace-at-any-price man." (See Appendix 10.)

Nixon's next letter was more prolific—defending against Reagan's aversion to an arms control agreement, why he hasn't met with the Soviets, and supporting the tough language used against the Russians by saying, "Let us understand at the outset that the <u>Soviets are the world's champions when it comes to using harsh rhetoric</u>." He ticked off possible responses to charges that Reagan would send forces into Central America, how "Star Wars" was important to prevent nuclear destruction, the need for united action against terrorism, and "<u>by retaining the option of first use of nuclear weapons, the U.S. and our NATO allies are in fact reducing the danger of nuclear war</u>."

The Old Man added thoughts on Reagan's possible closing statement and sharpening up his lines. Two of them stood out that I believed would appeal to Reagan: "The president should again make the point that during his watch not one inch of territory has come under communist domination or been lost to the West." And, "During [Mondale's] ten years in the Senate no Senator voted against our defense programs more often than he did." (See Appendix 11.)

RN checked in by phone to get a reading on the debate prep and to let me know he prepared a letter for Reagan. "Ken, I'm going to the Bahamas for a little sun, so I sent a letter to Reagan today, and you'll get a copy. I called him two days after the Louisville debate and told him a standoff is all that we need in this next one. He's got a safe lead." (Appendix 12)

Nixon's analysis was generous but guarded. "Reagan wasn't the best, but it was close, and it was the media a week later that tried to shape opinion." Then, the most insightful of all observations, "Just remember, Ken, a week after the debate, no one will remember anything anyone said."

The two-page letter from Nixon to Reagan was intended to generate confidence in the "upcoming bout with Mondale." "You have every reason to be confident as to the outcome.... Only because he did better than expected and you did not knock him out of the ring did the media seize on the opportunity to make it appear as if he had won.... This, however, is now an advantage to you. You go into the debate Sunday as underdog."

Spencer had a point in wanting Nixon to write—to infuse renewed poise in Reagan—and the Old Man delivered with his close:

> (Y)our almost unanimous support among Republicans, overwhelming support among independents and young voters, and a solid base among conservative Democrats who left their party permanently as you did thirty years ago can mean only one thing: You will win an overwhelming victory in the popular vote on Election Day and a decisive victory in the electoral vote approaching the one you achieved in 1980.
>
> Pat joins me in sending our warmest regards to Nancy and to you,
>
> Sincerely,
> *Dick*

The president was more at ease, better prepared, and less off-balance in the foreign policy debate prep sessions. At one pause after several questions, Reagan turned to Stockman and said, "Once a bastard, always a bastard." I wasn't sure if he was referring to Stockman as Mondale or Stockman as Stockman. Then later in the first session, a question was raised on the bombings in Beirut and in Reagan's "rebuttal," he looked up at Stockman with a big grin on his face, "I've gone over my time, so all I will say is, 'Damn you, you're a liar.'"

We returned the second morning, and before any questions, Reagan offered, "I feel so good that everything from here is downhill." The president knew Stockman would ask why he hadn't met with Russians, and he responded, "As for my not meeting with my Soviet counterparts, they keep dying on me." Then chuckling, he added, "I won't say that on Sunday night." It was clear that knocking down the "white picket fences" and taking back his crusading role had a positive effect. Reagan was back on his game.

Ben Elliott and I were tasked to produce a closing statement to prevent Reagan from falling into the meandering goof-up from Louisville. This was "speech by committee" with Teeter, Baker, Wirthlin, and Darman all having ideas in a group meeting in the Ward Room of the White House Mess. Darman's included quoting JFK—which Reagan, in 1980, admonished me never to do. I argued that by the end of the debate, the president's mind would be distracted, and trying to recall precise language of a closing statement would be impossible. Instead, I suggested that the statement should be wrapped around a story with which he had great familiarity—one he had related at the '76 Republican Convention about writing a letter for a time capsule to be opened on America's tricentennial in 2076. He had told that story dozens of times and could recite it with precision, filled with all the lovely word pictures of the "blue Pacific and Santa Ynez Mountains." It would relieve Reagan of memorizing a new script. We had a consensus, and the president agreed.

A new personality in the foreign policy debate preparations was Roger Ailes, who was given leeway to interject his views, and he brought volumes more experience to the process than Darman's group. Ailes saw that Reagan needed positive feedback against the negative hits by Stockman and he took that philosophy into the holding room just before Reagan took the stage. Ailes also had a hunch that one of the panelists might want to try to "stand out" on national television by making a dig at Reagan's age and warned Reagan to be on the lookout.

When the *Baltimore Sun*'s Henry Trewhitt asked, "You already are the oldest president in history, and some of your staff say you were tired after your most recent encounter with Mr. Mondale. I recall, yes, that President Kennedy had to go for days on end with very little sleep during the Cuban missile crisis. Is there any doubt in your mind that you would be able to function in such circumstances?" Reagan was ready with perhaps the most quotable comeback of his presidency: "Not at all, Mr. Trewhitt, and I want you to know that also I will not make age an issue of this campaign. I am not going to exploit, for political purposes, my opponent's youth and inexperience."[178] Everyone, including Mondale, burst out laughing, and though the debate lasted another hour, that single sound bite ended any question of whom the winner would be.

As for my "strategic genius" in giving the president his "familiar" wording for a closing statement, it turned out that the four-minute time limitation didn't allow him to shape it precisely the way he wanted, and he was cut off before he could put it in context. What's in the time capsule? That became a standing joke by inquiring reporters, and I had to laugh along with them. It didn't matter; we were off and running to finish the drubbing of Mondale. Ben Elliott and I worked on a stump speech to close out the remaining two weeks of the campaign, some of which Reagan mixed in with the standard stump speech that Peggy Noonan wrote. And in the last two weeks, I took a more active role in writing inserts for various rallies—never more than three or four hundred words, much like the ones I did in 1980.

Noonan's basic speech was enlivened by research material provided by my "Fritzbusters." But writing in her memoir, Peggy swallowed one of her colleague's assertions that the "campaign guys" were telling political reporters that they, the "campaign guys," not she, had written "the speech." Since I was the only "campaign guy" helping with Reagan's road speeches, her assertion is (without naming me) that I claimed credit for her work. She writes that she learned this was "normal behavior in the Reagan White House" and in that milieu "people lied with gay abandon."[179]

Not only was I falsely accused of attaching my name to Noonan's creative work product, but worse, that it was common for folks like me to lie about doing so. I never sought attention or accolades for something I didn't produce. The White House crawled with shit disturbers, and it's possible that someone made a deliberate effort to stir dissension. It's also quite possible that reporters could have reached wrong conclusions regarding the president's campaign speeches since I was the only speechwriter they saw on Air Force One. They also knew I had a heavy hand in several of his speeches, including the Ohio whistle-stop, and contributed language in inserts during the final two weeks.

But the only person in the Reagan White House who took credit for one of Peggy's speeches was her friend, mentor, and boss, Dick Darman. Noonan writes in her memoir that she reviewed with Darman a proposed speech line where Reagan would say of the Democratic Party, "They've gone so far Left, they left America behind." Darman instructed her to drop the word, "behind."[180] Then in *Newsweek*'s postelection book, for which Darman was a source, the authors write of Reagan going to Texas after Mondale's nomination and saying of the Democrats, they had "'moved so far Left they've left America.' <u>Dick Darman had written that line, straight out of his June strategy paper</u>; he didn't *believe* it, but it was something Reagan could plausibly say, and it seemed to Darman important to get it out early—to put this guy in a coffin as soon as possible." [underscored emphasis added][181]

After Ohio's whistle stop, Reagan's decision was to go full bore on Mondale, a decision derogated by the political amateur Darman, who was sharing with reporters privately that it wasn't allowing for an "historic" victory, but only a "partisan" one.[182] Darman and Baker never truly identified with the political culture of Reagan—and were unable to grasp how his last campaign was a crusade against the economic and social disaster he had fought against for three decades. They were overly sensitive to criticism, and especially to media critics who didn't align with Reagan's view of America. Everything Reagan stood for had been maligned by Mondale, Tip O'Neill and the Far Left, and the president was determined to win by rebelling against those who preferred political pabulum over political encounters.

We poked Mondale in the eye one final time by scheduling Reagan for an airport rally on the steps of Air Force One on a stopover in Fritz's backyard. The night before, I drafted a brief statement, and with a minor edit by Reagan, he read it to a hastily assembled crowd gathered at the Rochester Municipal Airport. When one of the traveling reporters asked him, "Will the Gipper run up the score in the closing minutes?" Reagan laughed, "I don't think of it as running up the score. The Gipper would never quit before the final whistle."[183]

From there it was off to the West Coast and to finish in his "lucky city," San Diego. Meredith picked me up, and after a night at home, we left for the Century Plaza in Los Angeles to celebrate, and where I needed to put together Reagan's victory remarks. In the same suite, 1915, where we met 313 days earlier to prepare remarks to declare for reelection, Reagan and I sat down at 3:00 p.m. to approve my final draft.

KK: Congratulations, sir. It looks like a massive land-slide—even bigger than yours in 1980.

Reagan: Well, I've crossed my fingers on both hands. It's hard to believe with all the bickering and fighting that some of those numbers would be right.

KK: It's clear that they are, so are you okay with the remarks?

Reagan: They look fine; leave them, and I'll take a look. Maybe [he chuckled] I'll ad lib "just one more time, you ain't seen nothing, yet."

With that, I was out the door, exhausted with the rest of the campaign crew and in need of rest. Like every other campaign, it was time to prepare for the letdown. Spencer and I had the benefit of dropping off in California and taking back our private lives. Everyone else would be heading back to the capital, maneuvering for jobs and power and touting their singular contributions to the landslide delivered by the leading man, with Nancy in the supporting role.

Chapter 20

CRISIS AT HOME

R eagan had little time to savor his landmark victory. His impending visit to Germany to participate in ceremonies marking forty years following the end of World War II was engulfed in controversy when his staff scheduled him to speak at a German military cemetery where dozens of members of the despised Waffen-SS combat divisions were interred.

Reagan wasn't just hearing it from the media, he was hearing it from Nancy, who writes in her memoir: "Many Americans, and especially war veterans and members of the Jewish community, were especially outraged. So was I. I pleaded with Ronnie to cancel the trip.... I was furious at [Chancellor] Helmut Kohl for not getting us out of it, and again I urged Ronnie to cancel the visit."[184]

Mike Deaver had arranged the trip, and Nancy was working him over as he described it:

> But now she was convinced that I had ruined her husband's presidency, and perhaps the rest of his life. We had a very painful, emotional confrontation. I let her finish and said, "Nancy, it's done...Let me get on with it, please...."
> I made a mistake. Now I was trying to fix it. Nancy nodded her head and, without a word, walked out.... Almost to the last minute, she insisted the trip should be canceled... She said so to her husband. I have never, not in the years I have known them, seen the Reagans engage in a no-holds-barred argument...I doubt that they have ever exchanged the really ugly words not uncommon to most marriages.... In this case it ended when the president said: "Nancy, I simply don't believe you're right and I'm not going to change my mind." She pressed him no further.[185]

APRIL 22, 1985

Deaver called me and didn't waste time with small talk. His voice was terse and edgy with less than a request and more of a command with the First Lady's voice wrapped in his. Reagan had his ass in a crack; Deaver had helped plunge the president into a political and cultural quagmire, and the priorities of my private life were secondary to Nancy's wish that I pack my bags.

"It's vital that you get back here within 48 hours because we need historical rhetoric for the president's trip to Germany. We've arranged for a visit to the former Bergen-Belsen concentration camp and another to our Air Force Base at Bitburg, and he wants your thoughts for his remarks." Mike was jumping all over the place, and I could tell he was taking lots of heat because his words were meandering. Deaver and I were not especially close. When working with him, I was just another member of his production company. But he was always supportive of my relationship with Reagan and Nancy, and, unlike so many others on the staff, he didn't constantly second guess my work.

Bill Henkel, the head of advance, would convene a meeting to brief me as soon as I arrived, but I knew I had to scramble to prepare for my eventual sit-down with Reagan. My notes of the conversation with Deaver reflect I was already thinking ahead—scribbling down bursts of ideas: "Eisenhower's memoirs." "Talmud." "Check Adenauer." "Rise and Fall of 3rd Reich." I made a note to engage Kim White, a bright staff researcher, to begin gathering information.

In the decade of our collaborations, the eulogy Reagan delivered on May 5, 1985, at the Bergen-Belsen concentration camp stands alone as the most significant and consequential. Along with his remarks at the Bitburg Air Base, for which I was also given oversight, I never bore a heavier personal weight, nor a more serious portent regarding the outcome. Reagan's authorized biographer, Edmund Morris, judged the presentation at Bergen-Belsen "the best speech of his career."[186] Lou Cannon writes in his masterful Reagan biography that the "moving address at Bergen-Belsen would prove the last great commemorative speech of his presidency."[187]

The volcanic eruption over his proposed visit, and the discordance it created, produced the first intensely personal crisis of Reagan's presidency.

Without resolution, it would have scarred him personally, blemished his legacy, and stalled the momentum of critical policy initiatives in his second term. In the intense ninety-six hours I had to prepare this speech I had to find the right creative tools, search for contrivances to enrich the narrative, and find just the right emotional pitch without seeming phony.

The timing of 1985's economic summit of Western Allies in West Germany coincided with the fortieth anniversary of World War II's cessation of hostilities. Helmut Kohl saw Reagan's German military cemetery wreath-laying as salving the war's wounds. Cementing Kohl's friendship was important for the US to protect its continued deployment of Pershing II Intermediate-Range Ballistic Missiles at West Germany's US bases—all aimed at Soviet Union targets.

The event was Deaver's last great "production" as the president's stage-setter before leaving for the private sector. When Deaver scouted the cemetery sites in February, winter snows obscured a critical detail at the Bitburg cemetery: more than forty of the headstones belonged to members of Hitler's murderous Waffen-SS. Once April's snowmelt exposed the markers, the story broke with an ensuing international uproar.

It was quiet in San Clemente, and like the president I was still savoring the forty-nine-state landslide. Despite the internecine staff warfare, I still had a prominent role in the reelection and played a more central role in media strategy and production, including writing those key closing commercials. The beginning of Reagan's second term looked promising with the economy rocking along at a solid 4 percent growth rate along with his approval rating comfortably over 60 percent.

With a new house purchase as a distraction, I only casually followed the stories about the Nazi gravesites in local papers and on the evening news. I thought a small change in White House planning might avert any problems. As the president noted in his diary, that was wishful thinking with the controversy worsening each day through Easter week:

> *During much of the week—the press had a field day assailing me because I'd accepted Helmut Kohl's invitation to visit a German mil. Cemetery during our visit to Bonn. I had turned down a <u>not</u> official invite from a W. German politi-*

cian to visit Dachau in his district. All of this was portrayed
as being willing to honor former Nazis but trying to forget the
Holocaust…I have repeatedly said we must never forget the
Holocaust & remember it so it will never happen again. But
some of our Jewish friends are now on the warpath. There is
no way I'll back down & run for cover.[188]

In subsequent communications with Kohl, Reagan agreed to visit a
different military cemetery at Bitburg and add a visit to a former concentration camp, planned originally for Dachau.[189]

The president fueled the controversy during a session with regional
editors and broadcasters on April 18, when the questioner informed him
that fifty-three senators signed a letter requesting he drop the cemetery trip,
and then asked: "In light of this and the wave of other opposition, would
it damage German-American relations to seek some other gesture of reconciliation and drop that visit?" In his lengthy response, Reagan declared
that the "young men" buried in the cemetery and "carrying out the hateful
wishes of the Nazis…were victims, just as surely as the victims in the concentration camps."[190]

The comparison was viewed by many as insensitive, and the reaction
reflected as much. The president wrote in his diary that night:

Another back breaker. The press continues to chew away on
the German trip & my supposed insensitivity in visiting a
W.W. II German mil. Cemetery in spite of the fact I'm going
to visit a Concentration camp. They are…really finding
every person of Jewish faith they can who will denounce
me…. The evening T.V. news was again filled with my sin-
ning against humanity by going thru (In May) with the visit
to the German Mil. Cemetery.[191]

The matters turned for the worse on April 19 in a Roosevelt Room
ceremony for Jewish Heritage Week, after which he presented the
Congressional Gold Medal to Elie Wiesel, a survivor of Auschwitz and
Buchenwald. After hearing Reagan movingly relate the searing tragedy of
the Holocaust and rendering a touching personal tribute to him, Wiesel
rose and began addressing—and then lecturing—the president.

Wiesel implored the president to cancel his Bitburg visit. "That place, Mr. President, is not your place. Your place is with the victims of the SS. Oh, we know there are political and strategic reasons, but this issue, as all issues related to that awesome event, transcend politics and diplomacy. The issue here is not politics, but good and evil. And we must never confuse them."[192] Camera lenses homed in on Reagan, capturing his anguished face as the words slashed at his honor and integrity while he endured the public scolding. The tightness around his mouth mirrored the one I saw at Blair House on the eve of his first inaugural when word came that Iran was dragging out the hostages' release. Wiesel's symbolical identification of Reagan as insensitive to the horrors of the Holocaust would only stiffen the Gipper's resolve. Nevertheless, the film, photos, and Wiesel's words flashed a message over the world: Reagan's tone deafness to Hitler's victims.

Typical was *Newsweek*'s overheated cover: *"The Wounds of War: Furor Over the Reagan Trip."* The lede captured the Roosevelt Room event in its agony: "His tone was respectful and gentle, but Elie Wiesel's words were devastating—and Ronald Reagan, sitting just a few feet from the sad-eyed chronicler of the Holocaust, had little choice but to listen.... [His] impassioned plea was surely one of the more remarkable moments in the annals of the White House—and just as surely epitomized one of Ronald Reagan's most painful political blunders."[193]

Reagan made it clear he wouldn't budge, writing in his diary later that night:

> I told our people, Don (Regan) et al there was no way I could back away in the face of criticism which grows more shrill as the press continues to clamor. Mike D. is back & said Kohl was going to phone me.... The call came while we were meeting. Helmut told me the Camp would be Bergen-Belsen not Dachau. Then he told me my remarks about the dead soldiers being the victims of Nazism as the Jews in the Holocaust were had been well received in Germany. He was emphatic that to cancel the cemetery now would be a disaster in his country & an insult to the German people. I told him I would not cancel.[194]

The abrupt change in sentiment toward the president was a dramatic reversal of the smooth press relations Reagan had been enjoying. From the time of his Ohio whistle-stop, his "age" put-down of Mondale, and final landslide victory, the national political media were at least partly collaborative in a Reagan lovefest. Now, it appeared they were releasing months of built-up resentment for being "taken in," and not wanting to appear they were playing for the Gipper's home team. Writing in his Reagan biography, *Dutch*, Edmund Morris captured the moment perfectly: "When a bushfire like Bitburg flares after a long news drought, the American press becomes pyromaniacal."[195]

Earlier that year, Pat Buchanan was elated to have been invited by Don Regan for a second tour in the White House, but within weeks found himself in the center of this storm as Regan's ally.[196] As a White House veteran, he agreed with the president that it would be a horrible mistake to cave in to media pressure. When Deaver discovered that SS troopers were buried in the cemetery, he told Buchanan, "This thing will really get great now." Pat confirmed that was the reason the First Lady gave Deaver the message to request that I "come back to DC to work on the speeches to help the Old Man."[197]

Parachuting in for a rescue mission on these remarks could easily serve as a classic case study in crisis communications on the one hand, and the craft of "remote" speechwriting on the other. I was on the other side of the continent as this wildfire spread and needed to assimilate ten days' worth of staff interactions, decisions, and conflicts. Moreover, the international venue was unfamiliar, as well as the precise protocols and emotional atmosphere the president would face—all of which the two speeches had to take into consideration. Finally, whatever comments emerged would have to be politically palatable in two societies—the Germans' and ours.

I'd played the "Fireman" role several times before, but on every other occasion Reagan's integrity wasn't questioned. Bitburg was a towering personal crisis—where he was battered in the national and international press, by allies in the Congress, and second-guessed within his own team. Compounding the wounds was the absence of sympathy from his customarily reliable source of support—Nancy. Each day of the crisis, Reagan was alternately bewildered and enraged by the anti-Semitic trope encircling him. By exercising his duties as commander in chief and buttressing US foreign and defense policy with a valued American ally, he still found himself undercut, attacked, maligned, and even ridiculed as having a politically and religiously insensitive tin ear.

Only later would I find he had unstinting support from one friendly corner: Richard Nixon's. Don Regan and Pat Buchanan realized the president could use a boost from a voice who understood the stakes, so Regan asked if Pat would reach out to the Sage of Saddle River.[198] Nixon replied with a six-page, single-spaced memorandum labeled "Eyes Only/Strictly Confidential." (See Appendix 13.) He left off his name for fear it would be leaked to discredit Reagan's decision. Because Reagan was concurrently losing congressional battles on his support for the anticommunist Contras in Nicaragua, Nixon's memorandum also served as a foreign and defense policy *tour d'horizon*.

Nixon's message was direct:

> (H)aving accepted Kohl's invitation to go, it would have been a major mistake for him to have changed his mind and refused to go because of domestic political pressure. The image of being a weak leader would have encouraged opponents at home and abroad to apply pressure on him in the future whenever he made a decision they didn't like ....

> By the same token, by going through the fire of criticism, the president has immeasurably strengthened his image as a strong leader who will do what he thinks is right regardless of political pressure. This will help him in the balance of the second term as he deals with the Soviets, other foreign governments, and his political opposition at home.[199]

That was welcome counsel, and Nixon added to Reagan's resolve. A subsequent diary entry showed he received similar support from former president Gerald Ford.[200]

After Monday's call with Deaver, I had forty-eight hours to tidy my affairs, caught the red-eye flight to Washington, DC, and was ready for my first meeting late Thursday morning with my former Nixon colleague, Bill Timmons, a lobbyist in the private sector who confirmed Reagan's dismal standing with Congress. I checked into the White House and was shown to my guest office in the OEOB, room 179 that was already set up with an

IBM Correcting Selectric typewriter identical to mine, and conveniently adjacent to the speechwriters' research office—whose help would be critically important. Bill Henkel already had my first briefing scheduled with professionals from NSC and State. The meeting included Marshall Breger, Reagan's Jewish community liaison, researcher Kim White and Joanne Hildebrand, senior trip coordinator for the advance office.

In normal circumstances, I would have direct familiarity with the speech venue to tune into Reagan's emotions as he toured the camp. On this occasion, I had to rely completely on Henkel's description of Reagan's moment-by-moment itinerary and step-by-step surroundings for his appearance at Bergen-Belsen—as he entered through wooded pines, viewing lifeless mounds and a lone obelisk. Henkel described the heather, not yet in bloom, all around the countryside.

As the meeting opened, one phrase hung in the air. Someone, perhaps Henkel, opined it was important "to try to redeem this day from the ashes." I made a note of that language, and from that offhand comment emerged what would be one of the president's most important lines and themes. With that memorable phrase standing out, this was one occasion when my disparagement of the wannabe writers wasn't entirely warranted, and I owed an apology for protesting their intrusion into my scribbler's domain.

For these remarks, I didn't have the luxury of time, and there was no aid from the president's personal wordsmithing. With the time squeeze, the president would be looking for language that could serve as a final version. So, that night I began scrawling ideas for my next day's meeting with Reagan. I wrestled with language that would fit an ill-defined occasion about which I knew only one thing for certain: it was a massive personal, institutional, and, potentially, diplomatic crisis.

From my notes:

- *"Glistening hope..."*
- *"Unspeakable cruelty..."*
- *"People whose death was inflicted for no other cause than their very existence."*
- *what a waste; what an inglorious waste."*

Somewhere out of my past, I remembered William Faulkner's words, "man will not merely endure; he will prevail." Was there a nugget there for the speech?

- *Earlier, sitting with speechwriters Mona Charen and Ben Elliott, Mona slipped me some of her notes and pointed to her favorite that I might find helpful.... "as hell yawned forth its contents." I underlined it.*

FRIDAY, APRIL 26

When I entered the Oval at 4:30, the president extended none of his customary gestures about California, my family, or work. The room with cheerful colors had no cheer. I sat at his left, with Deaver on his right and Henkel nearby. The attacks had taken their toll, and for the first time in my experience, he didn't smile. In place of the normally ruddy mien was a drawn, worn appearance, and the president got directly to the point, his voice tired and more formal and intense than any of our conversations.

"Ken, there are themes that must come out of these remarks:

"Number one, no one of the rest of us can completely understand the true feelings of the victims of the camp and the prisoners. They will have a memory beyond anything we can recognize or imagine. We recognize this.

"Number two. But it is important that we remember the Holocaust for the purposes of reassuring it never happens again."

There! I had the beginning and end of the speech. Moments later, he looked around at each of us to punctuate his observation that the "whole world were victims of the evil that started with Hitler." And: "Out of these ashes came something good." There was that phrase again, and his mention assured it would be a theme that would work its way into my draft.

He brought up his conversations with Kohl and his host's request not to celebrate an end to the hate, evil, and obscenities that the war ended but, instead, "to look now to celebrate forty years of peace and the confidence it brought to our [German] people...Here we had a reconciliation."

From the notes I prepared, I passed along a few of the thoughts to see if they would stimulate usable language, but Reagan didn't bite. Looking down at his notepad, the president began to meander, talking about the strength of our postwar alliances with Japan and Germany. He searched for words to reprimand his critics: "I find myself thinking—but we killed these people. Are we holding a grudge? Should we say: all these people have met the supreme judge, and they will be judged by Him who has the only right to do so."

The president had another appointment and stood to end our brief meeting that was never recorded in "The Daily Diary of President Reagan," the official minute-by-minute log of every presidential event, meeting and phone call with precise times and durations—including where and with whom. Either by oversight or intention, our meeting was omitted and also absent from his personal calendar, nor recorded by the White House photographer. The only documentation that exists is the one in my hand-written notes.

The president was doubtlessly wounded by the volcanic events upending his life and scavenging for greater meaning. Upon returning to my little office and rereading my notes, it was obvious, except for his tone, a policy reference and a couple of key phrases, Reagan had not given serious thought to his speeches at Bergen-Belsen or Bitburg. It was not unusual for him to offer scant guidance in our collaborations, but these were the most critical personal appearances since he assumed office, and I yearned for more substantial direction.

Nope, this time the leading man was looking for scripts, and Mrs. Reagan requested my help because he was relying on me for providing them. Just as important, she knew what else he needed, and that was a familiar face. When the media, the Congress, many old friends, and the missus herself were wondering if he had lost his senses, Ronnie needed the comfort of a nonjudgmental coworker whose loyalty he wouldn't need to question. So, on my end, stumbling was not an option. In addition to a lifeline, he needed a pal.

Desperately needing background material to make the remarks special, I turned to the speechwriting research staff which had the resources of the entire government and dozens of major libraries at their command. Teresa Rosenberger was an alumna of the Nixon White House and had returned to help train the other young women in the fact-checking method used by the Nixon research staff. Kim Timmons began devouring Anne Frank's *The Diary of a Young Girl*, looking for the single most appropriate quotation I could use. Kim White and Rosenberger were on hand for added background and to assist a very skilled speechwriter, Josh Gilder, as he drafted Reagan's Bitburg Air Base speech. While Bergen-Belsen was my principal responsibility, Deaver made clear I was to oversee both speeches. I was expected to put a polish on Gilder's eloquent prose.

My special research needs required long-distance help. Henkel referred to the heather that was just about to bloom all over the countryside. From his first mention of the "blooms," I was consumed by using springtime as a metaphor. That would portray the perfect image of new life rising out of the cold and darkness of winter, just as redemption and hope emerged from the tragedy of the Holocaust. But to make this theme work, and seem real and not contrived, I needed to have a "real time" view of what the president would witness as he approached Bergen-Belsen—whether he would visually "see" the heather as Henkel had.

I asked Joanne Hildebrand to contact the lead advance man in Germany, Jim Hooley, for a description of the president's view from the window of his helicopter as he flew from Hanover to Bergen Belsen. Joanne left her DC apartment at 3:30 a.m. for a call to Hooley in Germany, who had trouble appreciating this bizarre request from Khachigian. He complied with vague accounts of farmland and trees along the route. "That's not going to work," Joanne pressed. "I need very precise descriptions. What do the farms look like? Do they have growth or color? Is the heather in bloom?" Hooley griped that he was busy with more important duties, but he knew my work had priority, so on his next advance trip from Hanover he made a precise record of what he saw and relayed it through Hildebrand.

The meeting with Reagan was emotionally draining, so I headed to Clyde's in Georgetown for a drink. My 1984 campaign assistant, Sally Campbell, was going to meet me with an update on her new job in the White House political affairs office but was stuck in traffic. To kill time, I began jotting ideas on my only available notepad: a Clyde's cocktail napkin.

> *Somewhere here—at Bergen-Belsen—lies Anne Frank. Everywhere here is a memory—pulling at us, touching us— making us realize that such memories never wear down— never flag. They take us where God intended us to go— towards learning towards healing—towards redemption.*
>
> *Show the endless stretch of our heart—unfailing capacity for change and the knowing commitment that each one of us can make the world better.*

Like all "scratchings," the precise words never survived the final cut, but when I returned to the office that night, those notes helped refine my thoughts. Reagan would never be aware that some of the elegant and poetic language in his eulogy originated on a Clyde's cocktail napkin.

SATURDAY, APRIL 27

As I watched Reagan at the White House Correspondents' Dinner, I wondered, if he really wanted to be there. His diary entry that day validated my observation: "*The press is still chewing on the Bitberg (sic) visit. I'll just keep on praying.*"[201] The mood was tense and the laughter strained. Several of the president's jokes received only polite response, and the normal warmth of previous occasions was missing. The disquiet of Bitburg could not be dismissed. Did he see the evening as *de rigueur*—just an official box to check? Still, Reagan ended the evening as a class act, reminding his tormentors that "we all believe in the same ideas; we just disagree sometimes on how best to preserve and protect our beloved country and our beloved freedoms. It's good to remember tonight what we have in common."

Even after spending a couple of weeks as his audience's punching bag, his bedtime diary entry reflected the sunny side Reagan always seemed able to summon:

> *The White House Press Corps dinner—Mort Sahl entertains.*
> *He's funny as always. He also pledged his allout* [sic] *support*
> *for what I'm doing. I had some good material & was well*
> *received.*[202]

One important diversion remained before I started writing. My close friend from our years as neighbors in Oxon Hill, Jim Renjilian, pressed me to accompany him to Arlington Cemetery for Genocide Remembrance Day—the seventieth-year commemoration of the Ottoman Turks' systematic deportation and extermination of our Armenian forebears. I tried to beg off, pleading my deadline thirty-six hours away. Jim convinced me, without much arm-twisting, that my heritage commanded I join him with the small group of Armenian Americans living in metropolitan Washington.

As I listened to the choir and service conducted by local Armenian clergy, I began hearing other voices—ones I heard as a young boy. Many of my parents' social friends were, like Dad, Armenian immigrants, and genocide survivors from his ancestral village, Chomaklou, in Turkey's Cappadocia region. When they gathered to visit, they sometimes softly referred to the *Caghtagahnatoun*—the coerced exile from their homes when the Turks murdered the population of Anatolia by arms, starvation, pestilence, and forced march. My grandfather emigrated before 1915, but my grandmother, father, aunt, and uncle were compelled along with their fellow villagers into the Syrian and Jordanian deserts, initially by foot, then later stuffed into cattle cars.

Chomaklou's schoolteacher, Aris Kalfaian survived and later chronicled these horrors in a book. I read his descriptions of the deprivation and cruelty suffered in the first forty days of their journey walking through the Syrian desert. Kalfaian described how their situation worsened when they were "packed like cotton into crowded, dirty and lice-infested cars, exposed to scorching sun during the day and to freezing cold at night... When seven persons were about to die on the train, we were ordered to dump them off the wagon cars in the desert of Wadi Sirhan, to make room for the surviving."[203]

Kalfaian described in detail the squalor of their camps, the condition of which was "impossible for the human mind to grasp, or for intelligence to adequately portray." Typhus pervaded throughout the camps, hideous lice clinging to the deportees' bodies and pores. Starvation prevailed to the extent that those "refugees still clinging to life often resorted to devouring the remains of decomposing animals or even sifting through horse manure for stray grains of barley gone undigested."[204]

Dad rarely spoke of these deprivations, though when he did, it was the memory of overwhelming hunger that haunted him and his family, and at age sixteen, he lost his mother, his brother, and sister. The reason he avoided liquor was to prevent the slightest intoxication that might trigger melancholy and echoes from those horrible years.

The music and prayers in Arlington jolted me with reminders of my heritage and brought back those plaintive memories from my childhood. In 1915, there was a Bergen-Belsen in the Syrian desert that history had forgotten, and the pain and suffering endured by the victims and the survivors of the Armenian Genocide suddenly made my mission very real during our quiet ride back to the White House.

I went immediately to my office and began writing. All the notes I made, the scraps of paper on hotel stationery, the napkin at Clyde's and the meeting with the president—were spread about my desk. The clattering of the keys on the IBM typewriter began shouting through me the story I absorbed that morning and the one the president—and I—needed to tell.

Chancellor Kohl and Honored Guests:

This painful walk into time has done much more than remind us of the destructive war that consumed the European continent more than four decades ago.....

I had a beginning and then worked through the day to finish my first draft. Editing was different in 1985—pen on paper—not through computer-assisted backspacing or movements of mouse and keyboard clicks. I printed it out to have a document on which I could make written changes. Monday morning, I began rewriting with a new opening that sounded better: *"This painful walk into the past..."* With that, and after multiple other edits and rewrites, I was comfortable with a draft to send around for review by senior staff and for final fact-checking—giving me less than twenty-four hours before my submission to the president and our final meeting.

I still had to finish up the Bitburg Air Base speech with Gilder, and his version was very good and needed only minor edits. Reagan had previously cautioned me that he wasn't President Kennedy's fondest admirer, so I struck out "Ich bin ein Berliner." Instead, I translated the phrase into English. Other than taking out a reference to Germany as "one of the staunchest champions of freedom and vigilant protectors of human life" as hyperbole, we had a working product.

While shepherding the Bergen-Belsen draft through staff bureaucracy, I kept thinking Gilder's draft still needed something to match Reagan's theme of post–World War II reconciliation. With Reagan, anecdotes and stories often worked better than oratory, so with only twenty-four hours left, the research team had to find an appropriate one.

Teresa Rosenberger located a 1973 *Reader's Digest* article written from the memories of a twelve-year-old German boy. As the fierce fighting of the Battle of the Bulge surrounded his mother's cabin in the woods on Christmas Eve, 1944, three American soldiers lost behind enemy lines showed up at their door, and she allowed them in. Then, four German Wehrmacht arrived with weapons in hand. The boy's mother demanded all to lay down their arms, and they sat down to supper. One of the young Germans had studied medicine at Heidelberg and helped a wounded American, and on Christmas morning all headed back toward their respective lines.

If those combatants could reconcile as enemies on that night of Christian devotion, why couldn't allies find ways to do the same in peacetime? The perfect story. Nevertheless, I had to resolve my concern that the story might be apocryphal and would hold Reagan up to ridicule for promoting a Hollywood fantasy. Teresa ran it down and triple-checked it for accuracy. I polished it into the Bitburg draft, where it took up nearly a quarter of the president's remarks.

The next hurdle was Marshall Breger, the special assistant to the president who was catching hourly hell in his role as liaison to the Jewish community. Pat Buchanan pulled me aside: "Ken, I showed the Breger fellow this story about the soldiers and Christmas Eve dinner, and he went nuts. 'Khachigian's got the president praising Nazis. What the hell is he thinking? I'm getting enough heat from the Jews without Hitler's troops being portrayed as warm and fuzzy. He's got to take it out.'"

I reassured Pat: "That's not the goal, Pat. It's a story about humanity. Hell, even the rabbis would approve of the humanity behind it. Go back and tell Marshall, it's staying in." I understood Breger's concern, but the *Reader's Digest* story was precisely the tone Reagan wanted, and Reagan even embellished the final version. As Nixon repeatedly reminded me: "What works best for Ron are stories and illustrations; no one does them better."

While I rushed against the clock on the Bitburg edits, Deaver called from Germany to say I needed to visit with Rabbi Marc Tanenbaum, director of international affairs for the American Jewish Committee. He wanted to share language for the president's Bergen-Belsen speech. I pleaded: "C'mon, Mike, the damn thing is finished; it's going to the president soon, and there isn't room for any more input." Mike wasn't in a mood to negotiate. "Ken, he's coming to the White House, and you'll meet him in my office. Hear him out. We can't afford to have him criticize us. Whatever he has to offer, be polite and accept it. You're doing this for the president; not me." That was bullshit; the rabbi was just another person Mike had to placate in atonement for igniting the Bitburg fire.

With my final draft already in circulation, I sat down with Tanenbaum to hear out his recommended language—a tribute to Konrad Adenauer, the first chancellor of the Federal Republic of Germany, and addressed confidentially to Deaver. Everyone else wanted to help—from the secretary of interior to former colleagues and outside speechwriters. Why not the rabbi? I didn't have the heart to tell him there wasn't room for changes. Still, it was important to hear him express, on behalf of his faith, that "Bergen-Belsen is a rejection of the basic values of both Judaism and Christianity—both of which sanctify life and human beings." There wasn't going to be space in the speech for his favorite line, "the miracle of peace."

NOON, APRIL 30

Reagan finally got a chance to look at his speech, and in the entire text made only three changes. He removed the words, "Adolph Hitler," as if they were epithets, and replaced them with "one man." After the phrase, "we can never understand as the victims did," he added this sentence: *"Nor with all our compassion can we feel what the survivors feel to this day and what they will feel as long as they live."* Then, at the very end, he changed, for emphasis and location, the words: *"We can and must pledge.—Never Again."*

1:18 P.M.

The president shoved his minimally edited copy across the desk to me, thanked me and said he would probably work on them again when he arrived in Germany. We visited briefly, and by 1:35 we were done. I returned to have the clean copy prepared, and it was circulated only to four others on the staff with the notation: "The attached version reflects the president's edits." Translation: mess with this at your peril.

It had been eight days since Deaver's phone call and four from my first visit with the president. There wasn't any more I could do; he was off to Bonn that night. For the most consequential speech of his presidency since he entered office in 1981, he had allotted me only forty-two minutes of personal guidance. It also appears he devoted very little of his own time. We both had to get it right.

I set my alarm in California to watch the president and First Lady walk slowly into Bergen-Belsen's bleak and stark surroundings. This was my first real-time view of what heretofore I was only able to picture in my mind's eye based on Henkel's descriptions. Reagan slowly stepped up to a free-standing microphone, absent a presidential seal. Deaver must have ruled out a teleprompter. Good—that would have made him seem distant and cold on such a solemn occasion. With only the lectern's top to place his notes, it seemed appropriately bare to match the mood and the backdrop.

Because the first paragraph included words he dictated to me, Reagan was comfortable with the text on his half sheets: *"No one of the rest of us can fully understand the enormity of the feelings carried by the victims of these camps."* In the cold air, and possibly shaken from the camp's tour he just completed, his voice appeared to carry the pain of the previous three weeks. He wore a heavy overcoat (perhaps bulletproof), making his movements seem difficult and awkward. I needn't have worried; soon he was smoothly working into the message I hoped would quell the crisis.

> *For year after year, until that man and his evil were destroyed, hell yawned forth its awful contents....*
>
> *What of the youngsters who died at this dark stalag? All was gone for them forever—not to feel again the warmth of life's sunshine and promise, not the laughter and the splendid ache of growing up, nor the consoling embrace of a family. Try to think of being young and never having a day without searing emotional and physical pain—desolate, unrelieved pain....*
>
> *Here, death ruled, but we've learned something as well. Because of what happened, we found that death cannot rule forever, and that's why we're here today. We're here because humanity refuses to accept that freedom of the spirit of man can ever be extinguished. We're here to commemorate that life triumphed over the tragedy and the death of the Holocaust— overcame the suffering, the sickness, the testing and, yes, the gassings. We're here today to confirm that the horror cannot outlast hope, and that even from the worst of all things, the best may come forth. Therefore, even out of this overwhelming sadness, there must be some purpose and there is. It comes to us through the transforming love of God....*

Yes, out of this sickness—as crushing and cruel as it was—there was hope for the world as well as for the world to come. Out of the ashes—hope, and from all the pain—promise....

As we flew here from Hanover, low over the greening farms and the emerging springtime of the lovely German country-side, I reflected, and there must have been a time when the prisoners at Bergen-Belsen and those of every other camp must have felt the springtime was gone forever from their lives. Surely, we can understand that when we see what is around us—all these children of God under bleak and life-less mounds, the plainness of which does not even hint at the unspeakable acts that created them. Here they lie, never to hope, never to pray, never to love, never to heal, never to laugh, never to cry....

Nothing illustrates this better than the story of a young girl who died here at Bergen-Belsen...Somewhere here lies Anne Frank. Everywhere here are memories—pulling us, touch-ing us, making us understand that they can never be erased. Such memories take us where God intended His children to go—toward learning, toward healing, and, above all, toward redemption. They beckon us through the endless stretches of our heart to the knowing commitment that the life of each individual can change the world and make it better.

We're all witnesses; we share the glistening hope that rests in every human soul. Hope leads us, if we're prepared to trust it, toward what our President Lincoln called the better angels of our nature. And then, rising above all this cruelty, out of this tragic and nightmarish time, beyond the anguish, the pain and the suffering for all time, we can and must pledge:

"Never again."

Laying in my pajamas, I followed him from my copy of the text as each phrase resonated through the chill air. He pulled it off! No one watching his performance could deny Reagan had successfully confronted the political and diplomatic stumbles that bred this mess, and I hoped the end of the day would see him closing this dreadful chapter.

He wrote in his diary:

> *[W]e helicoptered to Bergen-Belsen Concentration Camp. This was an emotional experience. We went through the small museum with the enlarged photos of the horrors there. Then we walked past the mounds planted with Heather each being a mass grave for five thousand or more of the people largely Jews but also many Christians, a number of Catholics Priests & Gypsys who had been slaughtered there or starved to death. Here I made the speech I hoped would refute the phony charges that had been made. I declared we must <u>not</u> forget & we must pledge, "<u>never again</u>.*"[205]

The newsweeklies and dailies that once had trumpeted Reagan's stumbles and proclaimed the irretrievability of his wounds changed their tone after his twin achievements at Bergen-Belsen and the air base. Wrote *Time Magazine*, "Reagan's speech at Bergen-Belsen was carefully crafted to acknowledge Nazi atrocities while also striking a note of amity with the Germans. The message delivered with obvious feeling, was a skillful exercise in both the art of eulogy and political damage control."[206] *Newsweek* was more grudging, but still couldn't help admiring, "His remarkable speech at Bergen-Belsen would go down in the history books, but so would all the unpleasantness that demanded such eloquence in the first place."[207]

Pestering Jim Hooley for those flight details from Hanover to Bergen-Belsen also appeared to pay off. In his *Washington Post* news analysis, Lou Cannon reported that Reagan read from a prepared text but "added one brief passage in which he said he had reflected, as he flew in from Hanover over the green countryside...."[208] That description was vivid enough that Cannon clearly believed that Reagan inserted the language in-flight, when in fact I had written it seven days earlier. The spontaneity I wanted to convey rewarded Hooley's legwork, and my homework. It is also a lesson in the craft of speechwriting and paralleled my use of the presidential monuments as "stagecraft" in Reagan's First Inaugural Address—creating word pictures that can prompt the eye as well as the ear.

The next morning, the *Los Angeles Times* was on our driveway, and I opened it to the review by its veteran Washington bureau chief, Jack Nelson. It was gratifying to read the bouquet in his final paragraph:

> The White House considered the speech so important that Kenneth Khachigian of San Clemente, Reagan's former chief speech writer and a one-time speech writer for Presidents Richard M. Nixon and Gerald R. Ford, was brought back to Washington 10 days ago to write it. Khachigian turned out a powerful and moving message of horror and hope that the president delivered flawlessly and with great solemnity.[209]

Returning to the capital, Reagan's sensitivity to the affair's reportage continued to rankle, as reflected in this diary entry:

> *An early meeting with a bipartisan group of Congress leaders—minus Tip O'Neill & Jim Wright. We reported on the trip which was a different story than they've been getting in the press who are determined to picture a very successful trip as a failure. Bad cess to them!* [210]

By July, the Gallup poll would have Reagan's approval/disapproval rating back at sixty-three to twenty-eight—a seventeen-point gain from the depths of the controversy. The fire was out, mission accomplished. Settled back home, an envelope arrived from Pat Buchanan. Inside was a letter addressed from Brooklyn, New York, to which Pat appended a note to "Rabbi Khachigian." Pat wrote that he heard I "just bought a new house and could use some extra money."

> *To the Office of the president*
>
> *Gentlemen:*
>
> *I listened to the president's speech over the radio early on Sunday morning, May 5, 1985, from Bergen-Belsen.*
>
> *On Monday, May 6, 1985, I read it in the morning papers.*

I would appreciate knowing who did the research for it—it must have been done by a scholar versed in Judaica.

If he happens to be a rabbi, and interested in a pulpit in Brooklyn—our congregation will have an opening after the summer—and of course, the price has to be right.

Sincerely yours,
/s/
Abraham Hoffman

JUNE 4, 1:40 P.M.

"Mr. Khachigian, please hold for the president."

It was the smooth, professional voice of the White House operator.

"Hello, Ken, how are you?" Sunshine traveling over a phone line. "I should have called sooner, but I want you to know how grateful I am for the help you gave with the speeches on the European trip."

"That was a pleasure, sir. From everything I heard, everything turned out okay."

"Well…" that famous stage pause. "Helmut couldn't have been more pleased." He chuckled. "Can you keep a secret? I think I could've been elected president of Germany!"

We both earned the hearty laugh that followed.

"There were a few days there when I wasn't so sure it would turn out well, but we did the right thing."

"Now I don't want to take up any more of your time, but thanks again for pitching in."

"Of course, sir. Any time."

"All right; so long, Ken."

On this call, he was back in top form, and his voice bore no resemblance to the sorrowful one in April seeking a lifeline in a sea of attacks against his honor. I rewarded myself with a smile of self-satisfaction. It was the first time he called to thank me for one of my long-distance contributions to his speeches—a measure of what had been at stake.

Chapter 21

GORBACHEV'S THREE LADY FRIENDS

Addressing the National Association of Evangelicals in 1983, Reagan didn't want it to remain neutral on whether the US should join the Soviet Union to freeze the world's nuclear arsenals. "...I urge you to beware the temptation of pride—the temptation of blithely declaring yourselves above it all and label both sides equally at fault, to ignore the facts of history and the aggressive impulses of an *evil empire*, to simply call the arms race a giant misunderstanding and thereby remove yourself from *the struggle between right and wrong and good and evil*."[211]

The tough language faithfully reflected more than three decades of Reagan's views of communism—not just a speechwriter's pen. They were the same sentiments Reagan debuted nationally at the 1964 GOP Convention, where he cautioned against US retreat "under the pressure of the Cold War," while charging Democrats that their "policy of accommodation is appeasement" with the Soviet Union.[212]

In the fall of 1985, Reagan set out to remove the harsh edges from those views and brought me in from California for the soft landing. The chosen forum was a major policy address to the United Nations General Assembly. Four weeks after the UN address, Reagan was scheduled for his first summit meeting with his newly designated Soviet counterpart, General Secretary Mikhail Gorbachev. Mrs. Reagan had a special interest in her husband's new "peace" image and wanted the UN speech to frame the Geneva Summit and asked that I assist Reagan with preparing his remarks.

As head of the speechwriting office, Ben Elliott would take the lead in writing Reagan's remarks, and it was logical for him to incorporate the president's historical views of America's communist adversary. Based on two presidential campaigns and sitting with Reagan in dozens of meetings, I was reflexively prepared for my contribution to also mirror Reagan's Cold

Warrior temperament. I was wrong. Behind the noniron curtain, there were three unseen women at work—with Nancy Reagan in the leading role.

Aboard Air Force One briefing for '85 UN General Assembly Speech, National Security Adviser Bud McFarlane on the phone. From the top: Dep. Press Secretary Larry Speakes, Chief of Staff Don Regan, Director of Presidential Speechwriting Ben Elliott, Assistant to the President for Communications Pat Buchanan.

Ronald Reagan's speech before the UN General Assembly on October 24, 1985, has never received its deserved recognition for marking a turning point in the history of the Cold War. The words he delivered at the UN were unlike anything spoken in his long private and public career and would set the tone of the talks with Gorbachev in Geneva.

Reagan was divided regarding the Soviet Union—a tough guy on the outside who yearned to demonstrate his inner peace seeker. That was precisely the kind of language used in his 1980 campaign television address, A Strategy of Peace for the '80s: "We need to remove their [Soviets'] incentive to race ahead by making it clear to them that we can and will compete if need be, at the same time we tell them that we prefer to halt this competition and reduce the nuclear arsenals by patient negotiation."[213]

The same philosophical poles were reflected in his First Inaugural Address when he reminded potential adversaries that "peace is the highest aspiration of the American people," but then quickly added: "We will negotiate for it, sacrifice for it; we will not surrender for it, now or ever."[214] Nevertheless, in the opening weeks of his presidency, Reagan handwrote to Soviet General Secretary Leonid Brezhnev hoping for a "meaningful and constructive dialogue which will assist us in fulfilling our joint obligation to find lasting peace."[215]

Gorbachev's gang gained the propaganda jump when the General Secretary wrote a very long letter to Reagan on September 12, 1985, with boilerplate warnings against the perils of nuclear war and goaded Reagan about whether he had a "true desire to halt the nuclear arms race." Gorbachev proposed that "the two sides agree to a complete ban on space attack weapons and a truly radical reduction, say by fifty percent, of their corresponding nuclear arms."[216] The Soviets made sure the international media played up Gorbachev's new initiatives.

At the White House, an intense effort began to shape a communications strategy to counter Gorbachev's ploys and set a positive stage for Reagan's meetings. Mike Deaver was brought back from the private sector for counsel, and Dick Wirthlin hauled in his massive binders of polling data that in the end would have no effect on what the president would say. We had two separate meetings in the Situation Room to include Pat Buchanan, national security adviser Bud McFarlane and his deputy, John Poindexter. The impish Buchanan summed up our goal with a laugh, "The basic objective is to have the president looking good, no matter what happens."

The bad guys appeared to be doing a better PR job because Gorbachev's public speeches touting his proposal for a mutual 50 percent nuclear arms reduction soaked up public attention, placed focus on the summit and got under Reagan's skin. He made this diary entry on October 7:

> *Meeting with Lord Carrington N.A.T.O. Sec. General. He was positive & optimistic about our relationship with our European allies. In other words, Gorbachev propaganda hasn't succeeded in splitting the N.A.T.O. nations from us.*[217]

OCTOBER 10, 1985

With stakes rising, I was summoned to join the president in the staff cabin of Air Force One on his return visit from Chicago to DC along with Don Regan, Buchanan, McFarlane, Larry Speakes, and Ben Elliott. While Reagan told me he attached high importance to the UN remarks as a summit curtain-raiser, he offered little guidance during the brief flight and said nothing that gave me or Ben Elliott reasons to believe he wanted to alert the Soviets he had softened his views. The purpose of my thirty-six-hour turn-around trip from California for minimally effective face time with Reagan appeared to be one of providing the president with additional assurance that a familiar face was engaged ahead of the first meeting with Gorbachev.

OCTOBER 14

With Ben Elliott's on-site access to the NSC and State Department, it was logical for him to undertake the major lifting on the first draft, and upon my return to DC, I had a draft to review—one that had gone through edits by Buchanan. Mrs. Reagan and Buchanan both made it clear they expected my imprint on the speech, and when I took my first look, Ben's draft was consistent with what all of us believed was Reagan's long-held policy views toward the Soviet Union—an "evil empire" without using those words.

I rearranged a few of the paragraphs, rewrote and toughened up Ben's already aggressive language, and then worked on a lengthy peroration to oblige "Reagan the performer." The drabness of international politics deserves colorful prose, and so I rewrote into the early hours of October 16. Nance Roberts typed up a clean draft, and the circulation process began all over again. After Elliott, the NSC, and Buchanan put in their touch-ups, the president's clean "master" was ready for his night reading on October 17.

OCTOBER 18, 11:00 A.M.

Henry Kissinger walked out as I walked in to hear the president's review. I assumed he would have very minor suggestions, and I would quickly work in his changes, take a leisurely lunch and head for the airport for my 5:15 departure.

Something was wrong; the Gipper's greeting was cool, perfunctory, and there sure as hell was no twinkle in his eye. I had the "dignitary's chair" to the president's left, and nearby were Buchanan, McFarlane, Poindexter, and Regan. I was hoping for a nice "attaboy" for the peroration on which I sweated bullets. Instead, the boss served up a gut punch by making it clear he wasn't happy with the speech's tone. I shot a deer-in-the-headlights glance at Buchanan, and we both wrote down the scolding. Here is a combination of our notetaking:

> *Ken, we can achieve the same purpose where we just say where the societies differ. Let's try more of the tone, "we're not out to threaten or change their system." We need to live in the world together, and we are the only two great nations that can cause, or prevent, a great war. We [America] don't start wars. If they mean that they want peace, they can quit their expansionist policy.*

> *The best way to draw the distinction between us is to let the facts speak for themselves. It's impossible for us to understand a system where there is not freedom of speech and of movement. They're not going to change our system; we're not going to change theirs. We can say, "here are the differences, and it is hard to reconcile those differences, but in spite of those differences we can still talk and communicate."*

> *I could just see the press and our allies picking on the tone of the speech and reacting negatively. We seem to be saying "what a bunch of bastards they [Soviets] are," and we would be hit with the "evil empire" comments. We can let their words and deeds speak for themselves without antagonizing our allies.*

Reagan's body language was icier than our notes. The "evil empire" tone he interpreted was clearly what he did *not* want used. Even though much of the language was Ben Elliott's, my name was also on the copy. I approved every word, and I was the face in the room. Not since the '80 campaign had Reagan received me so coolly, nor were remarks I submitted reviewed so negatively. In his diary that night he wrote: "*Friday Oct. 18th—A huddle on the speech to the UN next week. Some wanted it more harsh toward the Soviets than I think it should be. I won.*"[218]

Pat's summary memo to me ended: "As George Wallace used to say, 'A detenteing we will go.'" Ben was lucky he wasn't invited.

The president left without formal goodbyes, and I followed Pat to his office asking who "rolled" me. I had taken it personally. Was it McFarlane? Poindexter? The draft had gone through several reviews by their staffs, and they were silent in the meeting, so I immediately suspected a double cross at the NSC. That was an unfair assessment. I just couldn't grasp that Reagan had suddenly gone "soft on communism." In my emotional state, that's how I interpreted it.

I had only a few hours to make Reagan's changes before going home. In place of a leisurely lunch basking in the Gipper's praise, it was back to my cubby hole to navigate his new warmth toward the Commies into the structure of the speech Ben and I had carefully crafted. We had to come up with language to satisfy Reagan without crippling the integrity of the overall message. Only three decades later was I able to identify the culprits who influenced his retreat from the barricades.

The following information is important to Cold War scholars who can review important changes made to Reagan's UN speech to understand how the president tried to use precise language to send Moscow a message that he was open to progress in Geneva. The sentences and paragraphs in italics are those that I struck out of the draft that Reagan disliked, and the wording in bold type represents changes the president ultimately approved and used in his final remarks.

Reagan was okay with the original sentence that introduced the theme of the US/Soviet divide: "The differences between America and the Soviet Union are deep and abiding." But complying with his instructions, it was wise to strike two sentences that followed closely after: *"We are not, as some suggest, simply two camps, East and West, two superpowers, vying for dominion."* And: *"Nor do we head any bloc of subservient states."*

In their place, I added: **"And as deeply as we cherish our beliefs, we do not seek to compel others to share them."**

The next change raised a bigger challenge. I had to soften Reagan's tone but maintain his credibility regarding the darker side of the Soviet system. I decided to remove the following paragraphs Reagan found offensive:

> *What is called the East is a tightly controlled political entity directed from the Soviet Union. The Soviet Union is a*

self-professed dictatorship with a unique and distinguishing feature—it is totalitarian. It not only seeks to control each institution and every facet of its citizens' lives—from the expression of their beliefs, to their movements, to their contacts with the outside world—it reserves to itself the right to expand and use force to impose its system on other nations.

No Soviet leader has ever repudiated Lenin's dictum that..."Soviet power must necessarily, inevitably, and in the not distant future, triumph all over the world."

I replaced them with:

When we enjoy these vast freedoms as we do, it's difficult for us to understand the restrictions of dictatorships which seek to control each institution and every facet of people's lives—the expression of their beliefs, their movements, and their contacts with the outside world. It's difficult for us to understand the ideological premise that force is an acceptable way to expand a political system.

The next paragraphs I deleted required removal of provocative language and the addition of more subtle wording. Here is what I removed:

In 1972, for example, we negotiated in good faith a ban on biological and chemical weapons. Yet, today, deadly chemicals of war victimize helpless human beings.

In 1975, we negotiated the Helsinki accords. Yet, the promised human rights and freedoms have never been realized, and those who sought to monitor the accords languish in prison.

During the decade just past, we also negotiated several agreements on strategic weapons, but Soviet violations openly undermine their original promise.

This record does not induce the confidence of the American people in future agreements.

With the help of the NSC, I replaced them with:

> **For example, in 1972, the international commu-
> nity negotiated in good faith a ban on biological and
> toxin weapons.**
>
> **In 1975, we negotiated the Helsinki accords on human
> rights and freedoms.**
>
> **And during the decade just past, the United States and
> the Soviet Union negotiated several agreements on
> strategic weapons.**
>
> **And yet we feel it will be necessary at Geneva to discuss
> with the Soviet Union what we believe are violations
> of a number of provisions in all of these agreements.
> Indeed, this is why it is important that we have this
> opportunity to air our differences through face-to-
> face meetings, to let frank talk substitute for anger
> and tension.**

Despite Reagan's desire to back away from "evil empire" rhetoric, the Soviet Union's adventurism—in Afghanistan, Ethiopia, Cambodia, Angola, and Nicaragua—was too egregious to overlook. An earlier draft of the speech had skewered Gorbachev for laughably claiming his country was *"doing and will continue to do everything to ensure that it lives in peace with states belonging to other systems."* I gave Reagan language to turn the other cheek with a mellower response: **"I am not here to challenge the good faith of what they say. But isn't it important for us to weigh the record as well?"**

I was satisfied that my edits on the first two-thirds of the speech complied with Reagan's directives. The National Security Council staff also took a final look, and Steve Sestanovich, its director of political-military affairs, added conciliatory language regarding the Soviet Union's engagement in the above-referenced regional conflicts:

> **During the past decade, these wars played a large role
> in building suspicions and tensions in my country over
> the purposes of Soviet policy. This gives us an extra rea-
> son to address them seriously today.**

Last year, I proposed from this podium that the United States and Soviet Union hold discussions on some of these issues, and we have done so. But I believe these problems need more than talk.[219]

Editorial reviews were mixed, but most major news stories included important conciliatory language that should have pleased Reagan. One was the phrase "fresh start"—included in all of Ben Elliott's initial drafts. Another was referred to Soviet counterproposals regarding nuclear weaponry about which the president wrote, "There are seeds which we should nurture, and in the coming weeks we will seek to establish a genuine process of give and take." The president himself added that key wording because it showed up only after the staff completed their editorial changes.

Others did not seem to pick up on Reagan's "change in tone." The *New York Times* editorialized: "To a world eager for progress toward peace at Geneva, President Reagan yesterday offered a combative sermon...."[220] After quoting a particularly tough line from the speech, the *Wall Street Journal* opined: "Do those sound like the words of a man who plans to be mushy when he confronts Mikhail Gorbachev in Geneva in four weeks? Of course not..."[221] A typical response was recorded in Robert Timberg's *Baltimore Sun* news account: "Soviet Foreign Minister Eduard A. Shevardnadze sat impassively through Mr. Reagan's speech and did not applaud at the end."[222]

An important review was in Reagan's diary:

> *My speech went over extremely well. In fact veterans at the U.N. said no western speaker had ever gotten such a warm applause. It was broadcast live & we all agreed the crowds on the street had been affected by it—they were cheering like for a Super Bowl.*[223]

A week later, I received a letter on his special presidential stationery—a rare acknowledgment from the boss. Some of it may have been written by staff, but the two postscripts were vintage Reagan, and it ended with his personalized signature, "Ron."

THE WHITE HOUSE

WASHINGTON

October 28, 1985

Dear Ken:

Thank you for the stellar job you did on the
speech I delivered last Thursday at the United
Nations. If I may adapt a quotation I'm fond
of using, it's part of our responsibility to
"bear witness to the truth" about the world
situation no matter how unpleasant it may be
for some to hear it.

Nothing is more difficult in the public forum
than plain speech and the simple truth. I
deeply appreciate the craft and wisdom you
brought to this task, but, above all, I am
truly thankful for the love of our country's
values and ideals that you helped infuse in
my remarks on this historic occasion. In the
years to come, we will find, I pray, that these
words helped bring about the concrete deeds for
peace and freedom that we seek for the benefit
of all the world's people.

With my personal gratitude,

Sincerely,

Ron

P.S.S. What the above means Ken is that
you done d-m good & I'm real grateful

Mr. Kenneth L. Khachigian
Suite 203
209 Avenida Del Mar
San Clemente, California 92672

P.S. One measure of the effectiveness of a
speech is whether everyone applauds it.
I think the best measure of the success
of this address is the ones who didn't.

305

The typewritten postscript reflected Reagan's divided views toward the Soviet system. The president's original goal was to ensure that his new, more reasonable tone prevailed at the UN. But judged by his "P.S.," it pleased him even more that he pissed off the Soviet foreign minister.

A quarter century later, Buchanan and I were on a shuttle returning from our annual Nixon staff reunion dinner. I joked with Pat about our shock with Reagan's reversal of views toward the Commies. From a seat or two away, Bud McFarlane overheard me, and in his low, impassive voice said: "It was Margaret Thatcher." I whipped my head around. "What?" He repeated: "It was Thatcher."

McFarlane was present at Margaret Thatcher's December 1984 Camp David visit with Reagan. "Thatcher," Bud told us, "had just recently met with Gorbachev in London and painted a wholly different picture of him as not being hardline like his predecessors." The since-declassified "Secret Memorandum of Conversation" confirms McFarlane's informal shuttle chatter: "Mrs. Thatcher said he [Gorbachev] was an unusual Russian in that he was less constrained, more charming, open to discussion and debate, and did not stick to prepared notes.... He also indicated the Soviets would come to Geneva with serious proposals." She reiterated later in the long meeting with Reagan that "Gorbachev was both willing and able to openly discuss and debate issues."[224]

Later, Bud filled in the blanks.

> Thatcher was extremely critical of Reagan's support for SDI (the Strategic Defense Initiative—a missile defense system designed to intercept and destroy intercontinental ballistic missiles approaching the US). Thatcher believed it disrupted the concept of strategic deterrence. I convinced her in a meeting at 10 Downing Street that President Reagan really wanted her support in his second term to open a dialogue with the Russians if Gorbachev was up to it, along with meeting standards of human rights and arms control. And that pleased her, so she agreed to soften her rhetoric on SDI and, later, at the UN General Assembly

session, was responsible for organizing the allies—France, Italy, Germany, and Japan—behind Reagan.

McFarlane related "it was because of Thatcher's efforts behind the scenes that the president didn't want our allies carping about a hardline speech." Bud also revealed another lady who may have played a more important role than Mrs. Thatcher in pressing "Ronnie" to lighten up on the tough talk. "Of course, Ken, you know that Nancy and Deaver came to the conclusion that Reagan had to be known for something other than domestic successes, and that his reputation as president also would be shaped by international successes and peace."[225]

Nancy didn't succeed in changing Ronnie's mind over Bitburg, but she had a longer game plan that was best described in her own memoir:

> I was somewhat more successful in encouraging Ronnie to consider a more conciliatory relationship with the Soviet Union. For years it had troubled me that my husband was always being portrayed by his opponents as a warmonger, simply because he believed, quite properly, in strengthening our defenses....
>
> I knew that "warmonger" was never a fair description of Ronnie's position, but I also felt that his calling the Soviet Union an evil empire was not particularly helpful in establishing a dialogue with the other side. The world had become too small for the two superpowers not to be on speaking terms, and unless that old perception about Ronnie could be revised, nothing positive was likely to happen. *Some of his advisers wanted him to keep up the tough rhetoric, but I argued against it and suggested that he tone it down.* [emphasis added] As always, Ronnie listened to various points of view and then made the decision that he thought was best.[226]

Karen Tumulty, the insightful biographer of Nancy Reagan, extensively reviewed the First Lady's role and describes how Nancy worked with secretary of state George Shultz to ensure that Ronnie wanted a dialogue with the Soviet Union. "Nancy and Shultz saw eye to eye on their distaste for some of the president's advisers."[227] These efforts included a dinner where

Nancy's goal was for Shultz to begin to understand, "Ronnie was more willing to press forward in developing relations with the Communist world— even travel there—than the secretary of state had previously believed."[228] Reciprocally, Shultz encouraged Mrs. Reagan to flirt with Soviet foreign minister Andrei Gromyko at a White House social event to soften up the longtime Kremlin hardliner in believing that "peace" was a constant on Reagan's mind.[229]

It's impossible to assess Nancy Reagan's influence in lobbying Ronnie to bid adieu to the '60s and '70s Cold Warrior without introducing the third actor's role in the melodrama. Playing a bit part was Mrs. Reagan's astrological counselor and confidante, Joan Quigley.

Don Regan's memoir asserts that Mrs. Reagan influenced virtually all major decisions as guided by "a woman in San Francisco who drew up horoscopes to make certain that the planets were in favorable alignment for the enterprise."[230] Once Regan blew the whistle, Nancy decided to discuss the relationship openly, devoting a portion of her book to it and saying it began as a "crutch" after the assassination attempt made her fear for Ronnie's safety. The conversations with Joan Quigley turned to her helping with scheduling, and Quigley said, "Why don't you let me know when the president plans to go out? I could tell you if those are good or bad days."[231] Mrs. Reagan minimized Ms. Quigley's influence as "nothing other than Ronnie's schedule was affected by astrology," and it was her way of coping with trauma and grief.[232]

According to Mike Deaver, Nancy's description of Quigley's help with scheduling was considerably understated. Instead, the changes in plans could be massive and outrageous. "All of a sudden, we'd have to change our schedules at the eleventh hour. We couldn't fly at night; we couldn't fly on a Monday." Deaver took to calling Quigley "Madame Zorba."[233] Bill Henkel, Mike Deaver's deputy, was on the Bitburg trip and "was himself becoming crazed by the unexplained last-minute changes, all of which required a complex overhaul in security procedures and clearance with the Germans."[234]

Henkel was a convincing witness to Quigley's influence in advance of the Gorbachev summit. After Quigley advised the First Lady that Gorbachev's sign, Pisces, aligned well with Ronnie's, Henkel recalled to Tumulty that Nancy "came back saying, 'These two have some coincidental things.' It was a very favorable thing in terms of these two people have by the stars, some good vibes."[235] In her own book, Quigley recounts conversations with Mrs. Reagan prior to the Geneva summit—allaying the First Lady's concerns that Gorbachev might be a Stalinist. The astrologer reassured her that "Gorbachev's chart leads me to believe that he is different…. I warned her repeatedly that it would be disastrous for Ronnie to go to Geneva with mistaken preconceptions and his old outmoded bias. 'Ronnie's "Evil Empire" attitude has to go before he can meet with Mikhail Gorbachev at Geneva.'"[236]

Before the first Geneva Summit, Reagan changes the tone of the speech to the UN General Assembly in key Oval Office meeting. Left is Chief of Staff Don Regan and Assistant to the President for Communications Pat Buchanan. Forefront right is Dep. National Security Adviser, Admiral John Poindexter, seated next to National Security Adviser Bud McFarlane.

Mrs. Reagan yearned to lift the "warmonger" label from Ronnie and for him to leave office with a world less exposed to nuclear destruction and maybe even win the Nobel Peace Prize. Claiming that astrology was critical in Reagan's decision to lighten up on anti-Soviet rhetoric would be a vast overstatement. Nevertheless, it's also clear that the "stars" were more than mere emotional crutches for Mrs. Reagan to make changes in the presidential schedule. The record, including her own, demonstrates how charts and stars bent her decisions to leverage the president. From the beginning of his presidency Nancy unquestionably leaned toward pushing her husband to a more congenial view of the Soviet Union. Joan Quigley's signs simply gave her the comfort to reinforce her instincts.

Nancy's clout in Reagan's orbit was clear early in our relationship—beginning when Jim Brady and I briefed Reagan for the Barbara Walters ABC News interview in the 1980 campaign. As I related in detail in that earlier chapter, Mrs. Reagan was affixed to her husband while Brady and I offered answers to Walters' potential questions. That was when she interjected two or three times to say: "Ken's answer here is good, Ronnie, and you should listen to it." She prodded to ensure his focus, and he paid attention.

Days later in that campaign, I recall when I sat with Reagan to discuss the campaign's "peace speech"—the half-hour televised campaign address on foreign and defense policy. Nancy was right there listening closely when I suggested inserting the concept of SALT III as an extension of the existing SALT II agreement. The exact words I dictated into my diary are: "She was very pleased with this and thought it was very positive." Nancy's interest in leavening his "warmonger" image was obvious, and she wasn't shy about encouraging its use in a major campaign policy speech. Nancy exerted strong clout in her husband's messaging—whether on buses, airplanes, or over TV tray tables and pillow talk.

Reagan caught me by surprise with his sudden change in tone in rhetoric regarding the Soviet Regime, but it was clear he firmly decided to change the diplomatic dialogue in his UN General Assembly Speech on October 24, 1985. Even though Foreign Minister Shevardnadze had a sour look that day, analysts in Moscow could not have overlooked the subtleties in Reagan's change in direction. He wanted an escape from the "evil empire" tag line and to open lines of communication. My view is these changes didn't emerge solely from State Department and National Security Council consultations, but also included a potent brew of diplomacy distilled from the influence of Maggie Thatcher and the intricate pressures of the First Lady with added guidance by Madame Zorba's charts of Gorby.

Reagan and Gorbachev met twice after Geneva—in Reykjavik, Iceland, in 1986, and in Washington, DC, in 1987. My other former boss, Richard Nixon, was not enamored with how their relationship was evolving. I had written two opinion columns that provoked Nixon to send me letters that I've excerpted. Now, decades later, Nixon's observations add perspective to the Reagan/Shultz diplomacy.

In a May 10, 1987, *Los Angeles Times* column, I opined that General Secretary Gorbachev was winning an international public relations campaign enabling him to appear to stake the high ground of "peacemaker," and manipulating himself into having perceived advantages preparing for an arms-control deal at the fall summit. I suggested that Reagan and his team needed to put together an operation to counter the Soviet leader by orchestrating spokespersons to engage in broad refutation, lest Reagan have a weakened negotiating position.

On May 28, Nixon replied in agreement, hoping that the White House would "set up such an operation on a crash basis. However, I fear that the general philosophy at the White House at this time is to be conciliatory rather than confrontational with the media, Congress, and the critics generally. I think this is a mistake," Nixon wrote, leading him to share his deeper concerns about the pending meetings with the Russian.

> I fear the zero option deal,[237] due to strong lobbying by Shultz, will now be accepted by Reagan and jointly signed by Gorbachev at a summit this fall.... I have doubts about the political wisdom of going forward with the deal without adequately addressing the problems of the huge Soviet conventional superiority and regional issues like Afghanistan and Central America. I know that Nancy and other close advisers believe that this will assure Reagan's place in history as a "peacemaker..." I will have to admit that the huge publicity blitz of Reagan and Gorbachev signing the first arms reduction in history, toasting each other, traveling around the country visiting shopping centers and Disneyland...and the like will result in a boost in the polls. But I fear it will be temporary, particularly if perception develops that Reagan of "evil empire fame" got snookered by Gorbachev.

Nixon was unhappy with George Shultz's assertion that the Soviets' acceptance of an American offer where the Soviets gave up four or five times as many warheads as the US did was "a wonderful box to be in." Acidly, he wrote,

> Gorbachev is not a philanthropist. Why did he make such an unequal offer? One of the foreign ministers on my recent trip put it very bluntly. With his offer, Gorbachev killed three birds with one stone; he divided Europe from the United States; he divided the Europeans against each other, and he divided the German coalition. He could have added that there was a fourth bird—the weakening of support for SDI and other strong defense measures in the Congress because of fear of "poisoning the atmosphere" created by Gorbachev's generous arms control initiative.

> Writing to you like this is only the preacher talking to the choir. However, it does me good to get it off my chest!

> *Sincerely,*
> *RN*

Then in October 1987, I wrote again in the *Los Angeles Times* regarding the sudden confluence of adversity that seemed to be gathering around President Reagan. Congress challenged his actions in the Persian Gulf; the Black Monday stock market crash occurred; the US Senate rejected Robert Bork for the Supreme Court; and funding for the Contras in Nicaragua was in jeopardy. His presidency appeared to be under siege, so I listed a variety of ways for Reagan to get back on the offensive.

On November 5, 1987, another letter arrived from Nixon.

"Dear Ken, Your column of October 25th was a bell ringer. I hope our mutual friends in the White House read it and follow your advice, but I am not optimistic that that will happen." Nixon's real interest was to vent about the likely results coming out of the December summit:

> I see a huge wave of euphoria engulfing the Washington establishment as a result of the Reagan/Gorbachev summit on December 7th. By signing an arms control agreement, Gorbachev to the gullible (and that is most of your

friends in the press corps) will have demonstrated that he is a man of peace. Anyone who dares to criticize his repression at home and his destruction of freedom abroad will be accused of "poisoning the atmosphere." What you should watch for is an agreement which will give lip service to SDI but will sink it by concessions that are made to Gorbachev on testing under the ABM treaty. Just like the Reagan(Wright)/compromise sank the Contras, what I fear is that the Reagan(Shultz)/Gorbachev compromise will sink SDI. It hasn't happened yet, but unless [Secretary of Defense Caspar "Cap"] Weinberger comes out of the cocoon he seems to be in…I fear it could happen.

He concluded by saying that, in expressing these concerns, "I have no reason to believe that the president wants this to happen." Still, Nixon had concerns with Shultz being Reagan's dominant adviser on foreign policy, with no one strong enough to give contrary views. Then, on the very day he signed the letter, Weinberger resigned as Secretary of Defense, so Nixon added in handwriting at the bottom:

…and now Cap is not going to be there when we need him!

Sincerely,
RN

Just before Christmas 1987, Nixon called to wish holiday good wishes and exchange views on the political landscape. He segued into a discussion of the recently concluded summit between Gorbachev and Reagan: "Don't go for all the euphoria on the Washington Summit. Gorbachev can't be General Secretary and give up the goal of world domination." Then he launched into a discussion of "warhead to target" ratios, the kind of thing he would be discussing in his upcoming book *1999*; telling me, "Wait for it to come out in March." He continued to worry that Reagan and Shultz were going in the wrong direction. He surmised I didn't want to hear about warheads during Christmas, so finished with another look at the upcoming presidential campaign and a fond report on his precocious nine-year-old granddaughter, Jennie Eisenhower.

Five years later, Richard Nixon viewed Ronald Reagan and east-west relations through a very different lens. The Soviet Union had fallen; the Berlin wall was down; Eastern Europe was liberated. Nixon's words from his final book operate as a tribute to Reagan's Oval Office 1985 remonstrations to me—that "we need to live in the world together, and we are the only two great nations that can cause, or prevent, a great war."

Nixon wrote:

> For the United States, the great ideological and geopolitical rivalry with the Soviet Union has ended. The only power able to destroy the United States is now in the midst of a sweeping democratic revolution. We can now work with our former rival to eliminate the fear of war and reduce the burden of arms.
>
> For the world, the superpower that has been the principal source of aggression for most of this century can now become a force for peace....
>
> With the collapse of the Communist Soviet empire, we should no longer view Moscow or the former Soviet republics as permanent adversaries....[238]

The two Cold Warriors of the twentieth century had come around to see eye to eye on the preeminent foreign policy and defense issue of their generation.

Chapter 22

THE FIRST LADY'S WAR ON DRUGS

My relationship with Mrs. Reagan was smooth so long as the president approved my work. If Ronnie was happy, Nancy was happy. When we filmed the campaign commercials at Camp David, she was charming and flirtatious. Months later, she was icy on Air Force One when, after Mondale's slashing political attacks, she mistakenly believed I was responsible for omitting Mondale's name from Reagan's speeches. It was the same scolding I received when I wouldn't return full time to the White House staff in 1981 when she felt Ronnie "needed" me.

I grew to understand the wariness that shielded her from creating close relationships with those who worked with her husband. Frankly, it wasn't my goal to become a "pal" of the boss's wife, but to take advantage of the information she intentionally, or unintentionally, transmitted about her husband—all of which helped me understand him better and improve our collaboration.

Three-quarters into his presidency, Reagan's diary confirmed we were still on good terms:

> *Nancy is housekeeping & I'm doing homework. Lunch with Ken Khachigian who is going to help with our speech on drugs—Sept. 14. I'm glad—he's very good. Nancy and I are doing the speech together.*

His reference to "our speech on drugs" was a special project in 1986 that aimed to engage the country in the work of Mrs. Reagan's signature issue.

Early media perceptions of the First Lady were negative because they focused on her designer wardrobe and expensive dining room china. Moreover, in times of economic distress, she touched sensitive nerves by staying in touch with her California socialite friends—without recognition from the media or the public that this was also a reflection of her personal need to mitigate against the isolation of the White House. She lacked her husband's sunny disposition, and despite a surprise appearance to charmingly make fun of herself in a garish costume at the annual Gridiron Club Dinner, her public image needed help. So, she chose one close to home—the War on Drug Abuse.

The "War on Drugs" was first launched in the Nixon White House under the leadership of my friend and Domestic Council deputy Bud Krogh. Nixon later created the Office of Drug Abuse Law Enforcement. Mrs. Reagan's version made a toehold during the 1980 campaign, when she stopped at Daytop Village in New York City, where they attempted to educate kids about the growing threat of drug abuse. The phrase "Just Say No," originated in 1982 at Longfellow Elementary School in Oakland, California, when a child asked the First Lady what to say when approached about the use of drugs, and she replied, "Just say 'no.'" Her efforts grew as "Just Say No" clubs grew across America, and she continued to remain active as a spokesperson for drug prevention and returned to Daytop Village as First Lady.

In 1986, I was busy as head of communications and strategy for Governor George Deukmejian's reelection and even turned down famed actor Clint Eastwood when he personally phoned me with a request to run his mayoral campaign in Carmel. With the national midterm election outlook looking bleak with twenty-two GOP Senate seats up, compared to twelve for the Democrats, someone came up with the idea it might help boost Republican prospects to elevate the issue of fighting drug abuse if the president and First Lady promoted the cause in a joint appearance on television. Despite juggling Duke's reelect, I immediately accepted when I was invited to meet with the Reagans to discuss assisting on their brief address.

Jim Kuhn, Reagan's personal aide, alerted me that Mrs. Reagan would be a few minutes late for our scheduled lunch when he ushered me into Century Plaza's Presidential Suite on August 29. We walked in along with White House photographer Pete Souza and saw the president in Levis, with cowboy belt buckle and western shirt—prepared to head for the ranch after our visit. He was folding a piece of paper and tore off a little piece as we quizzically looked on. "Well, hi, I was just getting ready to test this out." It became clear that the "piece of paper" was a paper airplane. He looked over at Souza, "You better not take pictures; this is probably illegal, using White House stationery and all." Reagan grinned mischievously as the photog

Souza defied, saying, "This is too good to pass up." The four of us craned necks over the balcony as Reagan pitched his airship and watched it drift in a beautiful arc nineteen floors down to a construction site below—the former 20th Century Fox movie lot. He wasn't America's commander in chief that day. He was Dutch Reagan, having the kind of fun he had growing up in Dixon, Illinois.

The President captures his youth, flying paper airplanes off the Century Plaza Hotel's balcony while we await Mrs. Reagan's arrival for lunch, August 1986.

Over shrimp salad and iced tea, the Reagans were not only passionate about the subject but had given much thought to their message. They pressed me to ensure their remarks would reflect fidelity to their thinking in an address that would be a combination of a speech and a conversation between the first family and the rest of the country. On the president's end, it required mixing warmth with substance, policy, and politics. I wasn't accustomed to writing for Mrs. Reagan, normally the province of my protégé, Landon

Parvin, and so my challenge was finding words that best fit her plea for engagement.

The president wanted to focus on his record and the efforts being made by his administration, and to ensure that he would be giving ample credit to Nancy's effort to turn "customers away from the providers" of drugs. Reagan was intrigued by using this opportunity to return to a favorite theme: "What's needed, Ken, is a kind of a crusade; the all-American thing that everyone does, to include businesses and schools across the country. It's like a war; after Pearl Harbor, we just didn't leave it to the fellas flying the planes, we needed the efforts back home. It's the crusade aspect to turn people on wherever they are, in clubs, churches or neighborhoods. 'Let's do something about this problem.'"

Mrs. Reagan stopped eating, and I was drawn to a look of sadness to which I was unaccustomed—something more hurtful and personal than just a national issue. "Ken, you know, sometimes I've felt all alone these last five years trying to bring the issue of drug abuse to the point of awareness, so first, we have to make people aware. Now if they are aware, so now what? They must all take a moral position; they may lose friends and be unpopular, but it's the only way to solve it."

Her voice edged to anger. "Do you realize there are 9-year-old kids out there—very sophisticated—that have beepers in their pockets in school rooms? And they make sales, learning from older pushers." Her core message was clear in her own words, "Life can be great, but not when you can't see it. Make your life count and live it to the fullest." I had nine pages of handwritten notes on legal-size paper and now turned to Mitch Daniels, who was running the political shop as well as managing public liaison, and asked if he could turn loose the White House resources to assist with background on the administration's antidrug efforts. Working around two of my political campaign assignments in California, I set a goal to get a draft to the Reagans at the ranch while they were on vacation.

I also recommended to Don Regan that the Reagans should deliver the remarks from somewhere in the residence to add intimacy instead of coming from the formality of the Oval Office. Inasmuch as they were sending a message into American homes to American families, it would be much more appropriate if the first family delivered it as a family from *their* home, and not from Dad's office, and that's how the "Just Say No" joint address originated from the West Hall in the residence.

Because of my commitments in California, I wasn't going to be on site, so I recommended bringing in a professional director to oversee camera placement and infuse confidence in Mrs. Reagan, who was less comfortable than the president with prime-time presentations. Larry Speakes suggested using our campaign friend, Bill Carruthers, but I recommended someone else I believed perfect for this occasion: Roger Ailes.

I didn't meet Ailes in Nixon's '68 campaign when, as an up-and-coming television producer, he convinced Nixon that the television medium was not an enemy. Roger created for RN the concept of "the man in the arena." Those productions helped Nixon get his message across in a softer, more relaxed environment. In 1984, Ailes and I shared a few Tuesday Team meetings during the initial planning, but Roger didn't stick around for the summer and fall nor help on production of key spots. However, after the disastrous first debate in Louisville, Ailes was brought in to coach Reagan prior to the second Mondale debate, and combined with omitting Baker's team, Roger's more professional help contributed to a successful turnaround.

Ailes's other political client in 1984 was an upstart county judge/executive named Mitch McConnell, seeking to unseat Kentucky Senator Walter "Dee" Huddleston. When McConnell squeaked by with under a six-thousand-vote margin, it was largely due to creative ads by Ailes and his innovative, sharp-witted partner, Larry McCarthy. Huddleston had a poor attendance record, and the ads featured a Kentucky "good-old-boy" restraining four bloodhounds while scouring the continent for the junketing Senator.

When Deukmejian formed his 1986 reelection team, he asked my advice on media advisers. With more resources than in his first race, Duke wanted the most professional media team possible. I recalled Tuesday Team meetings with Ailes, but more importantly, I was struck by the creativity of the "bloodhound" spots, and suggested that George meet with Ailes, after which we retained Ailes Communications for the reelection. Ailes and our campaign team began an association throughout 1986 that culminated in a massive landslide over LA mayor Tom Bradley.

Roger and I also became very good friends, and he was entertaining, full of energy, good humor, and great company over drinks and dinner. He displayed plenty of the strong ego for which he became famous, but he also did not resist when I offered up creative input for one of the most effective commercials in the '86 cycle. His production team, which included Jesse Raiford, added to the lightheartedness of an easy victory; and with the help of campaign manager Larry Thomas and aide, Greg Kahwajian, it involved nonstop teasing of our pollster, Lance Tarrance.

In 1988 when I accompanied Dan Quayle as speechwriter and senior adviser in the Bush–Dukakis match-up, Ailes' role as Bush's lead ad man and producer created a little edge—especially given Roger's impatience with the heat Quayle was taking in the campaign. Three years later, the "little edge" snapped like the flip of a switch while I was running Bruce Herschensohn's California US Senate campaign. I was reluctant to get involved in another statewide contest after being drained and exhausted from managing Dan Lungren's successful race for California attorney general. However, I couldn't say no to Bruce, a longtime friend and Nixon loyalist, and before I could take charge, Bruce had already made staff commitments, including hiring a producer for television commercials whom Herschensohn would not allow me to replace. As our campaign ramped up, Ailes phoned, and after brief banter pressed me to hire him to produce our ads, knowing ours would be the highest-profile and possibly most lucrative Senate race in the country. "I'm sorry, Roger, Bruce already committed the media contract, and I don't have the flexibility to make changes."

Ailes' mood abruptly shifted. "Ken, you're running the campaign. Just get rid of the other guy. You know I can do a better job. Don't give me bullshit that you can't hire me."

I replied, "Roger, I'm truly sorry, but Bruce's decision was set in stone. I can't break a commitment, and I don't have a choice. You know I would have hired you in an instant, but I can't."

Ailes erupted. "I'm warning you; I'll go out and find a campaign to run against you!"

I reiterated that it was out of my hands, and he could do what he had to do. With that, he slammed the phone down. Years later, I was at Fox News Studios in New York for an interview, and I asked to see Roger—hoping we could restore our relationship. He refused, and I never saw or heard from him again.

When the Reagans returned to Washington after their stay in California, I hitched a ride on Air Force One to visit about their speech. As I suspected, they hadn't given much thought to the draft I sent to the Santa Barbara ranch, and Mrs. Reagan's main comment was she hoped her portion of the remarks could be expanded. I was so accustomed to being responsive to presidential addresses, I had unintentionally reduced her contribution. That was an easy fix. Don Regan and his staff hovered, so a serious back-and-forth editing session with them wasn't in the works. Back in DC, I added in all the policy-oriented contributions, the kind of edits that were out of my control. Mrs. Reagan made two very small additions in wording, and upon review, I saw the president made no changes to my final draft. They delivered the speech on my birthday, and prior to a quiet celebration, I watched Mrs. Reagan make her co-starring debut—dubbed by Donnie Radcliffe of the *Washington Post* as "The Great Communicatrix".[239]

The camera opened on them in the residence, with Dutch in a navy-blue blazer holding Nancy's hand, as she sat at his side in classic red with white blouse. The president looked comfortable with the camera, but I initially worried that Mrs. Reagan—with a wan, almost sad look on her face—might be having a case of stage fright or opening night jitters. It appeared that Ailes might not have directed her where to look, and she may have been peeking at her husband in the monitor. Things soon returned to normal as the camera panned into a close-up of the president. Here are excerpts:

> **RR:** *…Nancy's joining me because the message this evening is not my message but ours. And we speak to you not simply as fellow citizens but as fellow parents and grandparents and as concerned neighbors…. Drugs are menacing our society. They're threatening our values and undercutting our institutions. They're killing our children….*
>
> *From the early days of our administration, Nancy has been intensely involved in the effort to fight drug abuse. She has since traveled over one hundred thousand miles to fifty-five cities in twenty-eight states and six foreign countries to fight school-age drug and alcohol abuse…Her personal observations and efforts have given her such dramatic insights that I wanted her to share them with you this evening.*

NR: ...*Today there's a drug and alcohol abuse epidemic in this country, and no one is safe from it—not you, not me, and certainly not our children, because this epidemic has their names written on it... Drugs steal away so much. They take and take, until finally every time a drug goes into a child, something else is forced out—like love and hope and trust and confidence. Drugs take away the dream from every child's heart and replace it with a nightmare, and it's time we in America stand up and replace those dreams....*

Our young people are helping us lead the way. Not long ago, in Oakland, California, I was asked by a group of children what to do if they were offered drugs, and I answered, "Just say no." Soon after that, those children in Oakland formed a Just Say No club, and now there are over ten thousand such clubs all over the country...[T]o young people watching or listening, I have a very personal message for you: There's a big, wonderful world out there for you. It belongs to you. It's exciting and stimulating and rewarding. Don't cheat yourselves out of this promise. Our country needs you, but it needs you to be clear-eyed and clear-minded....

RR: *I think you can see why Nancy has been such a positive influence on all that we're trying to do. The job ahead of us is very clear. Nancy's personal crusade, like that of so many other wonderful individuals, should become our national crusade... My generation will remember how America swung into action when we were attacked in World War II.... Well, now we're in another war for our freedom, and it's time for all of us to pull together again. So, for example, if your friend or neighbor or a family member has a drug or alcohol problem, don't turn the other way... It's time, as Nancy said, for America to "just say no" to drugs....*

In this crusade, let us not forget who we are. Drug abuse is a repudiation of everything America is. The destructiveness and human wreckage mock our heritage. Think for a moment how special it is to be an American...The revolution out of which our liberty was conceived signaled an historical call to an entire world seeking hope. Each new arrival of immigrants rode the crest of that hope... They all came to taste the air redolent and rich with the freedom that is ours. What an insult it will be to what we are and whence we came if we do not rise up together in defiance against this cancer of drugs....

NR: *Now we go on to the next stop: making a final commitment not to tolerate drugs by anyone, anytime, anyplace. So, won't you join us in this great, new national crusade?*

The White House kept me posted on the returns, and based on all media reports, the Reagans received either a strong thumbs-up or a nicely straightforward review of their evening performance. In all the major papers, their effort made headlines—if for no other reason for the unique nature of their joint appearance. For the First Lady, the effort not only boosted a cause of great importance to her, it also contributed invaluably to lifting much of her negative image burdens.

Characteristic was this review by the editors of the *Christian Science Monitor*:

> The speech from the White House on Sunday night is an example of the kind of moral direction the president, and in this case, the First Lady, Mrs. Reagan, can provide in the nettlesome matter of drug abuse. Particularly heartening is Mrs. Reagan's focus on individual responsibility, on fostering development in young people—especially in the strength to say no.[240]

A Los Angeles entertainment writer was partially tongue-in-cheek about the "Ron and Nancy Show," asking, did "Alfred Lunt and Lynn Fontanne come back to life?" But then confessed:

> As the program progressed, visions of the Lunts gave way to Robert Young and Jane Wyatt solving family problems...a sober-sided presentation intended more to alarm than to charm. Nancy was participating, her spouse told

us at the outset, because "the message isn't my message, but ours." He might as well have said *hers*.[241]

It was all a long way from the portrayal of the First Lady as tied only to fancy clothes and elite friends and disconnected from the lives of Americans. Given his growing rocky relationship with Nancy, Don Regan's follow-up letter suggested he may have appreciated the outcome of the speech even more.

> *From the president and Mrs. Reagan to the White House staff to phone calls and Wirthlin polls, all reviews are outstanding…Dick Wirthlin's analysis indicates that never have reactions to one of the president's speeches been more favorable! Again, thanks for your great work, and I hope we can call you again.*

And three months later, they did….

Chapter 23

IRAN–CONTRA ERUPTS

T he fall election went well for George Deukmejian in California where he won in a massive landslide over Tom Bradley, but the GOP gave up the Senate majority after six years and lost nine net seats in the House. Congress was handed to the most partisan Democrats—West Virginia senator Robert Byrd and Tip O'Neill's successor as Speaker, Texan James Wright. Despite a preelection approval rating of 63 percent, Reagan's life turned upside down when US newspapers confirmed a Lebanese journal's election-week account of Iran's release of hostages in return for American arms shipments.[242] The arms payments were diverted to support anticommunist Contras in Nicaragua—a poke in the eye to the Democratic Party leadership that vigorously opposed more US aid to the Contras.

Reagan initially fumbled in his responses, and Admiral John Poindexter resigned as national security adviser while the president fired Colonel Oliver North, the mastermind of the diversion. Bad news emerged daily, and the president couldn't escape embroilment because he had approved the sale of the Hawk and Tow missiles to Iran. Secretary of state George Shultz claimed no detailed knowledge, and with Shultz's blessings, deputy secretary of state John Whitehead told Congress the president "may have been poorly advised." He piled on, adding, "We at the State Department find it difficult to cope with NSC operational activities…" The *Wall Street Journal* headline said it all: "Shultz's Top Aide Blasts Reagan Staff on Iran Sales…Escalating Public Feud."[243]

Two weeks after Whitehead's testimony, Nixon called me with serious concerns about White House crisis management. Days earlier, the Old Man had phoned Reagan to offer counsel, and Reagan told him if he had any advice to send it along. Nixon was enraged at Shultz's distancing himself—

believing it was not only an act of disloyalty but reflected RN's long held belief that in the political rough-and-tumble, George Shultz always looked out for himself and wouldn't take a bullet for the president.

> Ken, it's the height of unfairness they're going after Ollie North and Shultz isn't touched for publicly breaking ranks. John Whitehead should have been fired the minute after he testified. Firing Haldeman and Ehrlichman didn't do a damn bit of good, and in retrospect it was a mistake.

Nixon rued sacking Haldeman and Ehrlichman and how it left him without two key aides while simultaneously gaining him no public support. "You know, Ken, Reagan's a very sensitive man. He's a very loyal man, and that's how he got in trouble." Nixon's voice drifted off, a tone of remorse in replaying a scene from his own life, and then quickly switched subjects to the politics of the new Congress.

I was unaware of growing discord between the First Lady and Don Regan as well as her unhappiness with my valued friend and mentor Pat Buchanan because she preferred that Ronnie not bend to his conservative constituency. She passed the word to Regan that she didn't want Pat working on the '87 State of the Union and told Regan to reach out to me.[244] As Pat's acolyte, I shared many of his conservative views, but I also never believed my speechwriting role endowed me with rights to press my personal views on the president.

The White House playbook was familiar—assuming that the president's friends are always available to drop everything else to work on the demands of the first family. So, again I put aside everything else to take on my new assignment to help prepare Reagan's 1987 State of the Union Address. I would soon discover that the knives were not only out for Reagan, but they would be out for me as well.

5:13 P.M. NEW YEAR'S EVE, 1986

The White House operator placed Nancy Reagan on the line. "Thanks, for the wire, Ken, and Happy New Year to you and your family"—a perfunctory response to the "holiday wishes" telegram I sent. The president was scheduled for prostate surgery in a few days...end-of-the-year news stories were filled with negative Iran–Contra reviews... and Ronnie's polls were down. So, she only had the SOTU on her mind. There was an edgy tension in her voice, and she didn't waste time, "Ken, what's your plan?"

"Ma'am, I'm on the president's calendar for the 12th to get his guidance, I've started to make some notes. One thing I'm going to suggest is we don't focus on having 'heroes' in the gallery to play for television because the times are not right." She agreed about discarding the "heroes" reference and continued curtly. "We've done it before, and now it's time for a change. Ken, mostly I want you to know that I'm concerned that you're not coming back before January 12. We really need you here earlier. We have big problems."

Before I could respond, the president rescued me by interrupting her. They were in Palm Springs with Southern California friends for their annual New Year's party. The Gipper's voice was cheerful, as if there were no dark clouds hovering. "I just played my annual game of golf, and George Shultz and I beat Bill Smith and Charlie Price by a hole," and the state of the union wasn't on the top of his mind.[xi]

Still, he tossed in one idea—"On the drug issue, that's one area where Congress has done a lot, and we should mention that." With that, he turned the phone back to Mrs. Reagan, and we ended with mutual New Year's greetings, and another push by her that I start the speech and spend more time in Washington. Ronnie was always her only priority, and I couldn't bring myself to tell her that I had big plans for a round of parties at Deukmejian's second inaugural. Plus, I had at least one business trip and another commitment to raise money in Florida for an Armenian American advocacy organization. Only then could I focus on assisting with the State of the Union address.

If the First Lady and Don Regan wanted me to tackle another "firefighting" operation, I wanted control. So, the first call I made was to Dennis Thomas, in whom Regan had vested a role that paralleled Darman's. Dennis was Regan's Treasury aide where, during my earlier stints, he sometimes gave me legislative counsel on tax policy. But now in the West Wing, he and other Regan colleagues were smitten with the disease of proximity to the Oval Office: power—the lethal drug I described in Chapter 16. Regan

---

xi   **William French Smith, former US attorney general and Charles Price, US ambassador to the United Kingdom**

asked Thomas to coordinate the SOTU's paper flow and update me on domestic and foreign policy initiatives. I reviewed previous "process" memoranda between the two of them because Regan demanded the kind of operational control that worked well as a Wall Street CEO. That "process" didn't work well with me drafting Reagan's speeches, but I wanted to be a team player and took Thomas's calls regarding guidance for the speech.

I informed Thomas of several key themes that could work and decided to check in with my trusted friend Pat Buchanan to get my thoughts in order before meeting with the president. Buchanan summed it precisely: the speech had to be big and bold, showing "Reagan's back and it really counts." Pat also advocated Reagan taking a tough line for his actions. "KK, there are two questions for the Congress. One is the matter of free elections for the people of Nicaragua; two, do we want a permanent Soviet beachhead in Latin America?" Thomas began lobbying me to incorporate proposals from two cabinet members, education secretary Bill Bennett and labor secretary Bill Brock, with special emphasis on excellence in education and a more competitive workforce.

Don Regan pressed me on what he wanted in the speech by saying, "It's a little late for *real* new initiatives." Relaxed across his conference table with the perfect mien of his former roles as Merrill Lynch CEO and Marine officer, Regan appeared to be reading Thomas's briefing paper developed from dialogues with Bennett and Brock. "The '60s and '70s kind of education for our children is not the education for the 20th century. Today's student needs more science more math." Then he said, "with regard to labor, not only do we need training and retraining in jobs, but a different attitude and a willingness to work hard for the team."

"Ken, if we hit the twin themes of future, education, and the worker on one side and jobs, economy, and new attitudes on the other hand, we will make for a stronger America. On right to life, just put in a sentence or two, not five minutes." Mention privatization, but don't dwell on it. Regan suggested I could talk about holding down federal spending, but not make it the main theme. This was déjà vu—like Baker cautioning me not to have the president sound like a Bill Buckley lecture.

What national security adviser Frank Carlucci had to say about Iran–Contra was very important. "We need to launch an offensive on the Contra issue. The president has a good case and should continue to press it. So, he should make a preemptive attack on the Contras to galvanize our allies in Latin America." Carlucci wanted an aggressive position on national defense with Reagan saying to Congress, "You've cut our budget, and the Soviets expanded theirs." Carlucci wanted me to try out a theme when I meet with the president. "If he could, please tell the Congress it is systematically depriving the presidency of the tools to carry out foreign policy. They cut our assistance by twenty-two percent. Tell them we won't compromise on national security."

The day ended in the Roosevelt Room with Bill Bennett, Bill Brock, Senior White House Staff and Domestic Council Staff. But Bennett and Brock led with their favored themes of excellence, competitiveness, and a revolution of ideas. Bill Bennett provided a muscular intellect and strong personality that created a powerful voice to improve America's education. His desire to link labor and education as interdependent goals to remove illiteracy was on the mark. Bill Brock was influential in rebuilding the Republican Party and as Labor Secretary sought strong reforms. "We need lifetime education, he argued, "and a restoration of pride. This can't be a pass-the-buck speech. Reagan needs to tell the Congress it's not a money issue; it's a leadership issue."

Dick Wirthlin attended with his poll books to argue that: "Deficits are the key issue with which to confront Congress. Drugs are a separate element. We need measurable goals with a payoff that is consistent with our philosophy." I made note of everything I heard and wondered how these ideas, concepts and individual agendas were going to fit into a speech the purpose of which was to restore Ronald Reagan's status of respect and trust with the American people.

The following day, I sorted notes in my West Basement hideaway office when Nixon reached me. The Old Man's shrewd advice would be especially important now, so I scrambled faithfully to record his words:

> *Competitive—non-starter*
>
> *Catastrophic health—non-starter*
>
> *Laundry list—won't fly.*
>
> *Look good—feel good—mood more imp than words*
>
> *25-28 minutes*
>
> *Still, stand on the Contra thing—don't give ground*

Don't indicate Reykjavik formula will work

Iran—We look back over 6 years. We've had great successes and some not too successful. But you take risks to achieve great goals. Execution may not be admirable—But you don't quit trying new initiatives.

Good, eloquent—short to the point. Be aggressive and strong

We have had many differences in past years—but one thing no difference—inviolability of Western Hemisphere

I took final calls from Treasury Secretary, Jim Baker and from Senator Pete Wilson, my California friend who was a strong proponent of deploying the Strategic Defense Initiative as a way of Reagan "reasserting leadership." Baker had a crisp and succinct case on Iran–Contra. "The president shouldn't justify his position. He should say at the very first that we made mistakes. 'The idea of sending arms to Iran was a mistake. I was well-motivated. Mistakes were made. My response is to get the full story out, and I pledge to continue to get the full story out. Now it's over. Let's move on the trail.' Khachigian, don't try to use this speech to justify the policy."

JANUARY 13, 1987

The chatter and counsel from the "committee" was subordinate to what Reagan wanted as we met for thirty-five minutes as a waning winter sun shuttered the afternoon. Don Regan hovered on my left—hoping to imprint the message while protecting his image against increasing rumors of his precarious status with Mrs. Reagan. Visitors to the Oval were accustomed to the amiable Gipper, and except for rare moments in campaigns, the public saw rare glimpses of his edges, and today he seemed irritable, and after perfunctory greetings, Reagan made his first point clear. "I don't want any laundry list, Ken." He was feisty and annoyed at news accounts, and his words projected combat. He was assertive about his own ideas and unhappy with the roasting he'd received, not only by Democrats, but by many in his own party and "unnamed" sources within his staff and administration. "There's been a concerted effort to portray us having failed, like our continued deficits—that we're dead for the next two years and nothing will get accomplished. So, what I want to do with this speech is basically raise the question: What is the state of the union? Where do we stand? And then state where we are."

"The task now before us, within the structure of government, is to make those changes which are necessary to ensure that the state of the union will sustain." There were scattered papers on his desks, proving he'd done his homework. "For example, we need to have a budget process that once and for all removes the threat that we've had over the last fifty-six years where this country has operated on a basis of planned deficit spending, and now it's out of control. But the deficit is in a declining pattern, and we can start a budget process aided and abetted by a constitutional process which will prevent deficits in the future."

This was déjà vu to January 1981 in the cabinet room. It was the "crusade" I heard over and over again, a philosophy set forth in his precise handwriting at nights in lonely hotel rooms for General Electric, and never fully embraced or understood by the "power players" who wanted Reagan to play by the capital city's rules. After six years in Washington, the "fellas" still didn't have a feel for Dutch. He continued. "All right, the balance of what I'll have to say is they're portraying our foreign policy as one in shambles, but it's not." He nodded, then looked up straight at me, "At Reykjavik it was the first time the Soviet Union was willing to put on the table an actual reduction of weapons systems. That's never before been done. In Central and Latin America, things are on a sounder basis than they've ever been, and we're not imposing our will."

Don Regan interrupted with reminders that there was more harmony now among the Big Seven in the international economy—with the president on a first-name basis with all of those in the Big Seven.[xii]

The president replied, "Well, in my first meeting with them at the Ottawa Summit, I was the new kid, and no one got around to introducing me, so when it came to me, I just said, 'My name is Ron.'"

Back to the crusade.

"On the domestic front, I want to emphasize the power of this system of ours. The people were freed from unnecessary regulation and taxation. We have the highest percentage of potential workers in the labor force in the US employed—more than ever before. More than sixty percent of

---

xii Big Seven or Group of Seven originated in the early '70s with leadership of US, UK, France, Germany, and Japan to discuss international recession and oil crisis. Italy and Canada were added in the mid-'70s.

everyone in the US, male or female, sixteen years or older, are employed. As for the recession, we came into office without a budget in place, and none of our initiatives put into action until 1983. You might want to check the facts, but I think we've had the longest recovery or the second longest recovery in history—now in the fiftieth month."

Reagan turned to the speech's structure. "Let's plan on being there about thirty minutes—of which twenty to twenty-two minutes will be the actual speech. And, Ken, what if we have a section where we have some pretty good licks?" That term, "pretty good licks," reminded me how pleased he was in 1984 when he "laid into Mondale" for the "first time." Now, he was telling me that it was time he "laid into" his critics." He had Iran–Contra in mind. "Here's what we can say, 'Shortly, I will be speaking to you, the American public, on foreign policy. Ninety percent of Latin America is living in democracy; this was unheard of years ago. We haven't lost a single country, and we restored one—Grenada.'"

I proposed one theme Reagan might focus on that would get no disagreement in Congress—the two hundredth anniversary year of the US Constitution. This triggered a response, and he looked down at my notepad to ensure I was writing. "On a number of occasions in talking to young people regarding the Constitution, I've emphasized its importance to America. I've read the constitutions of many countries, including the Soviet Union's. Most supposedly claim freedoms granted to the people—freedom of speech, assembly, etc. If this is true, why is ours so exceptional?"

He paused for the rhetorical question to sink in.

> Well, the difference is so small, it almost escapes you, but it's so great that you can't miss it. It's right there... in three words: "We the people." In all other constitutions, the government tells the people what they can do. In our Constitution, people tell the government what *it* can do, and none other than what's listed in the document. Virtually every other revolution exchanged one set of rulers for another. Our government is the first where we said the government is the servant of the people, not the master.

Reagan's monologue ended, and except for his brief reference to the Group of Seven, Don Regan made no effort to bring up the previous day's education and labor themes. Otherwise, he sat with hands folded neatly over his briefing book listening without objection.

With my marching orders, I retreated to my West Basement lair and revved up the IBM Selectric. The speechwriting research staff and NSC provided substance to defend Reagan's record against the pounding he'd been taking, and the president's guidance and my collected notes gave me a thematic outline. All that remained was addressing Iran–Contra's deepening quagmire. Each day's front-page story spun a new version. During Watergate, Pat Buchanan's black humor regarding explosive daily disclosures was about hearing the "whump" of the *Washington Post* at his front door's threshold—and then racing his cat to see who got there first!

Initially, the Baker/Regan transition freed me from Darman's interference in writing assignments—such as helping the Reagans during the Bitburg Crisis and with their antidrug appearance. Alas, after two years in the West Wing, Regan's team had been lured with the same power aphrodisiac that seduced Baker's. Dennis Thomas's ascent took him from being a former congressional aide and assistant secretary at treasury to sudden elevation in a West Wing aerie with daily access to the chief and sporadic exposure to Reagan. Thomas assumed—like Darman—that he enjoyed a roving portfolio as a jack-of-all trades insider.

For the next two weeks, Thomas became a royal pain in the ass by assigning himself speechwriting skills of which the first family had heretofore been unaware. His periodic accomplice was David Chew, the staff secretary who acted as Dennis's paper-pusher when Thomas declined the chore. With Thomas, Chew was one of the handful of Regan's staff dubbed "the Mice." The rodent appellation was apparently bestowed by an OMB official after Peggy Noonan shared with him a disagreement with Chew, and the OMB'er disabused Noonan of concerns with assurances that Regan's staff were nothing more than "the three blind mice."[245]

As I worked on my draft, Thomas frequently walked in to interrupt and with an edge of condescension would ask, "Ken, what's the lede?" He also thought I should consider the thoughts of another "speechwriter"— his boss. On the day of our meeting with the president, Regan penned a page and a half of suggested SOTU language to Thomas, and Thomas forwarded it to me with a cover note saying, "I think it's very good."[246] However, Regan was just another wannabe speechwriter who didn't have the stomach to submit the "very good," language directly to the president. I took a quick look at Regan's prose: "We are a nation undivided, inspired by divine guidance, in search of our past, in pursuit of a goal, a goal we once had, and by the Lord, we'll have again, a goal of excellence!... America equals excellence. Big 'E,' a national goal, not easily accomplished but attainable.... From here the trumpet sounds—here is our program to make America better, to excel, do better, be better, live better, grow better, make America better!..." It continued with the more of the same stale clichés, so I disregarded them and reassured Thomas he had satisfied his duty.

Here the connivance began.

Without informing me, Thomas and Chew back channeled the circulation of a second version by Tony Dolan and his speechwriting staff, and Thomas continued to confer with Dick Wirthlin, Bill Brock, and Bill Bennett as the two Bills kept pressing their respective agency agendas with the aid of Numbers' data distillate. I didn't fault Brock and Bennett for seeking change but didn't appreciate their attempts to shape Reagan's agenda through a speech rather than normal policy channels for cabinet officers. There was no sensible reason to follow Wirthlin's advice, just as Stu Spencer ignored him in 1980, and I did in 1984. In a spirit of cooperation, I showed my SOTU rough drafts to Thomas; a judgment error that perpetuated his patronizing questions of: "What's the lede?" My patience wore thin. "Dennis, fortune-telling isn't in my job description, and please leave me alone so I can finish." In the media feeding frenzy surrounding Iran–Contra, it was stupid to think that anyone could be prescient about the direction of a news story two weeks in advance. I wrapped up my first draft on January 17 and returned to California.

Forty-eight hours later, I received a "revised draft" with an FYI note from Mouse Chew. "We have done a little bit of editing and sharpening of the focus on excellence. What do you think?" In the White House speechwriting process, authorship of drafts is denoted on the top right corner of each version. In this case, my "Khachigian" version was totally reedited and signed *"(Thomas/Khachigian/Dolan), January 19, 1987, 3:00 p.m."* Obviously, their cabal planned this "committee" version from the outset, so they waited to surface it when I was in California, where it would be difficult to push back.

Without copying me, Thomas sent the bastardized draft to Don Regan with a cover memo claiming that he didn't want to be seen as "committing the sin of criticizing and not offering an alternative." Thomas assured Regan his rewrite was "based upon Dick Wirthlin's paper outlining what he felt and we agreed should be in the SOTU. I have deliberately tried to bring focus on jobs, education, catastrophic illness and those issues suggested in Dick's paper." Thomas, and now Wirthlin, were meddling in territory that wasn't theirs and hijacking a responsibility Nancy Reagan specifically asked me to undertake.

As chief of staff, Jim Baker depended less and less on Wirthlin when he discovered that Dick's prolific memo writing was selectively useful, especially after Stu Spencer showed up to take over campaign strategy. But Regan and team mistakenly believed Wirthlin had a Svengali role in guiding Ronald Reagan's messages. Reagan enjoyed Wirthlin's briefings for approval ratings or about positive campaign numbers, but Reagan relied on Stu Spencer or his own instincts, as well as on me, for political positioning and messaging in his '80 and '84 campaigns—not Wirthlin.

Thomas's memo offered a general critique of my draft, proposed four headlines that would flow from his "alternative," and closed with an understatement: "This draft is truly a meld—of Ken's, Tony's, Brock's, and Bennett's. Perhaps it, like all things built by Committee, is a rhetorical camel—but I believe it is an improvement." Thomas covered his ass by concluding he had not circulated the draft and would only do so "unless you determine it useful,"[247] and included a separate side-by-side comparison of his "camel" draft and mine—arguing that my submission had "no theme/ not based on Wirthlin's findings."[248]

One of my deepest regrets while serving Reagan is that I did not forcefully disagree with him on his 1982 tax increase—especially when he violated his own heated rebuke to Margaret Thatcher's backpedaling on her "no tax increase" pledge. I muted any objections out of a sense of loyalty and to maintain working relationships with colleagues. I repeated my mistake in 1987 regarding the SOTU. I was wrong to accommodate in 1982, and again in 1987. While angry over the duplicity and underhanded conduct of little men swaggering in oversized shoes, I tried to be a team player and didn't take appropriate action to end their charade. I should have pushed back and told Don Regan I didn't need speechwriting help from him or his staff. If Regan didn't stop the end run by his poseurs, I could have gone to Nancy—the one person who had been desperate for my participation.

I didn't know it, but the First Lady was getting engaged on her own.

Without knowledge of Thomas's intermeddling, I quickly edited and returned another version with new language that Reagan requested to rebut an NBC News "doom-and-gloom" commentary by John Chancellor. Regan alerted the president to disagreement in the ranks, and that filtered up to Nancy, who quickly tracked me down. "Ken, Ronnie just can't take this. He's gotten three drafts of his speech and says, 'What do the fellas expect me to do?' You need to get back here now and take charge." The next call was from Don Regan, who said the president wanted me up to Camp David to resolve differences. Meredith had never been there, and I asked if she could accompany me.

Reagan made a diary entry on January 23:

> *We have a little friction between policy makers & speech writers on St. of the U. Address. I'm going to have Ken K. come up to Camp D. for a little talk.*[249]

Thomas wouldn't relent. Just before my arrival in DC, he submitted his new version at 4:30 p.m., and asked Regan to have the president consider the language. I entered the White House early Saturday morning with my clean version and a cover memorandum to the chief of staff telling him "I tried my best to incorporate the elements that you have asked for—the key issues—some of the initiatives and reforms and many of the proposals the president will send up. But I did not do it in the format of the other draft [i.e., Thomas's] quite simply because of my judgment that that won't work."[250]

We arrived at Camp David just after 1:00 p.m., on January 24, and I joined the president in Aspen Lodge, where he made clear we would work only from the draft I prepared. Regan continued to ask if I would do my best to work in some of his staff's changes. Too late. Reagan already had my clean copy and started editing it before we arrived. I shouldn't have, but I brought the competing draft. Reagan glanced over it, looked up, and scowled, "Did the damned committee get a hold of this again?"

He wrote in his diary, *"Ken K & I had a working lunch—St. of the Union. He spent the afternoon in the office here at Aspen working on the latest draft & and I did the same in the living room. Both of us were working to shorten it...I think K & I pretty much finished the speech."*[251]

In a throwback to his days of script editing to meet time requirements for his radio shows, Reagan placed word counts in the margins of the text, noting the total of the words he took out and the number of words he added. For example, he heavily edited the paragraph on Iran–Contra so that he removed ninety words and added eighty-seven, for a net minus three. For history's sake, I have copied and pasted in the entirety of the president's initial edits on my proposed Iran–Contra language. We continued to struggle in later iterations, and the version below did not survive.

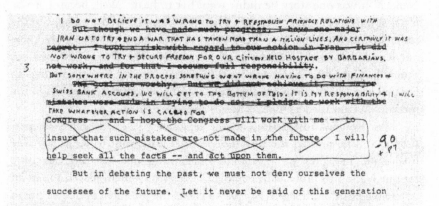

Mrs. Reagan phoned Regan that she was pleased I was working on it, but told Don, despite Ronnie's request, "The parts about abortion have got to come out."[252] Her call may have accounted for the handwritten question mark I found in the margin of the copy Reagan worked from—where it read: "The time has come for our Nation to protect the unborn." I'm unsure whether the question mark was in the president's writing or Mrs. Reagan's. Either way, it must have been provoked by the First Lady's intervention.

In the meantime, I looked forward to dinner with Meredith at Laurel Lodge. I told her it would be a wonderful evening—snowed in at the lush beauty of Camp David's special location, with fine dining courtesy of the navy stewards, followed by a fireside movie. But the phone rang, and the Signal operator alerted us that President and Mrs. Reagan asked if we could join them for dinner. I wasn't sure whether to knock on the door or ring a doorbell. It turns out they were expecting us, and Mrs. Reagan welcomed us, and of all the sessions I had with the first couple, I only have two or three memories of that one. Reagan apologized for Nancy adding logs to the fire because the doctors ordered him not to lift anything after his surgery. Next, just as we were seated, the president asked, "I hope you like corned beef?" Of anything I could choose on any menu, short of starvation, corned beef would be *last*. Meredith loves it, and I falsely claimed it was one of my favorite foods.

I have a memory blank on the small talk of the evening except for one vivid recollection. The First Lady stepped out briefly, so I asked Reagan about his first screen kiss. He turned around with a sheepish look, "Where's Nancy?" It was one story he didn't want her to hear. "Well, because it was my first movie [*Love Is on the Air*], I had never been in a love scene, and the script included kissing June Travis who played opposite me. I only knew one way to kiss, so I planted a good one on her. The director jumped up, shouted, 'Cut, cut. What do you think you're doing? You're messing up her makeup.' So that was my first kiss, and my lesson in how to kiss in the movies." We muffled a laugh as Mrs. Reagan returned.

Mrs. Reagan's instructions to the beleaguered Don Regan were persistent, and he pressed me to remove words important to Reagan in the final draft: "to express care when life is beginning" and "the time has come for our Nation to protect the unborn." The two of them placed me in an untenable position. It wasn't my job to create the president's policy; only to put *his* policy into words. Nancy didn't want to have to debate Ronnie in the residence, so she pressured Regan to do the job, and he, in turn, passed the instructions on to me. I acceded.

MONDAY, JANUARY 26

That afternoon Reagan and I met in the Residence, spending forty minutes polishing the final copy. Mrs. Reagan was in the room, trying to appear innocuous as we worked toward completion, but from the time of our New Year's Eve phone call to this moment, Mrs. Reagan had been on top of the process.

Reagan stood up, "Well, we've finally put this to bed. We'll see how it goes when the curtain goes up." Then, he paused, pointed down at the text in his hand, and gave me a worried look. "The only thing I'm wondering, Ken; I'm reviewing this, and we don't have anything in here about abortion or the life of the unborn. I just wonder what our people are going to think if I leave that out; it's a very important issue to them." I looked at Reagan and glanced over his shoulder at Nancy staring at me. She began shaking her head furiously, waving her hand and mouthing the words, "No, no."

He wanted the antiabortion language in, but if I acquiesced, the First Lady would arrange for my removal from the island with the alacrity she arranged for others. No one elected me to set social policy; only the president could. Still, Mrs. Reagan's icy look was unmistakable, and I've always felt remorse at weakly fumbling with words to shield myself from her wrath while comforting the president for being unresponsive to his principles.

I searched for a convincing voice. "Mr. President, you've already made your position very clear, and those folks know how strongly you feel. With Iran–Contra in the forefront and all the other pressing issues, this is an occasion where I think it's harder to find the appropriate context for that language. I'm sure you'll be forgiven this one time, and there will be many more opportunities to make your views known about right to life matters." Reagan looked tired and worn from the tortuous path of the speech's preparation and didn't want to argue. He nodded assent, thanked me, and I looked to Mrs. Reagan as if nothing out of the ordinary had taken place. She gave me a brief hug and I walked out after muttering a goofy "Break a leg."

Thomas didn't confine his petty jousting to the executive mansion. He joined with Wirthlin to undermine the president's direction by leaking their versions to the press. Wirthlin had access to each speech draft and unfettered rein to shape his and Thomas's contrary messages. Don Regan had conceded discipline of his operation and allowed leaks that fueled reports of White House dissensions and divisions destructive to Reagan's interests even as the president struggled to emerge from scandal and illness.

A week before the SOTU, Wirthlin sat down with reporters and "predicted" the points Reagan would make in his speech and added a condescending lecture on how the president "must also 'block out in a credible fashion three of four major goals he wants to reach'" in the final two years of office. Adding to Reagan's Iran–Contra woes with a backstab, Wirthlin told *New York Times*'s reporter Phil Gailey, "'Clearly, the public wants to know' all the details, he said, adding that a 'high priority in the public mind' was to know whether there had been a White House cover-up."[253]

With the unconstrained flow of leaks, I wondered if Don Regan violated his fealty as staff chief and collaborated with the dissenting voices.

Wirthlin profited handsomely from the president's goodwill, so it was indefensible for Regan to allow the pollster to freelance in the media with inside information and damning insinuations of a "cover-up." By setting a high bar for Reagan's success, Dick positioned himself to win brownie points with his media constituency by claiming "I-told-you-so" if his advice wasn't followed.

Like Dick Darman, Regan and Thomas were beguiled by Wirthlin's data. Reporters Jane Mayer and Doyle McManus observed that "Regan, whose background was in sales, was simply fascinated by the numbers. Just as new computers allowed him and his staff to follow the financial markets, so Wirthlin allowed them to follow the political markets. Regan's staff would soon talk about who was following the welfare 'account' and how to 'invest the president's political capital.' And inevitably Regan and those around him would think and talk about Reagan's popularity as the 'bottom line.'"[254]

Wirthlin's business plan conformed perfectly with Washington's political success scheme as another establishment "power player." Though his million dollar–plus budgets were paid by the Republican National Committee, his contracts were owed entirely to Ronald Reagan's political benevolence. His data, analyses, and polling information belonged to the White House—along with the extraordinary entrée he gained to its internal communications. Dick was given a trust that demanded secrecy and discretion, especially when he had custody of confidential surveys for the sole use of the White House. Instead, he used his privileged West Wing access and subsidized polling data as coinage to advance himself as a Reagan confidant and White House political and message guru—a plum target for the national media to mine for confidential information. Wirthlin's shameless leaking, self-promotion and advance revealing of presidential speeches and initiatives were tolerated in the Baker years because Baker and his team did the same. Owning details of the 1987 SOTU speechwriting process along with Iran–Contra polling data, Wirthlin was loaded for negative comments if his advice was rejected.

The *Washington Post* believed Reagan was out of touch on Iran–Contra, and in Dick Wirthlin they found the perfect "insider" to "keep [Reagan] in touch with the real world." In advance of the SOTU, the *Post*'s Lou Cannon piggybacked on Wirthlin to conclude that the "disquieting thought, reflected in the fine print of the polls is that Reagan is not as much in touch as he should be." Pointedly, Cannon wrote, "Wirthlin observes that even those who do not pay attention to every twist and turn of the controversy *question whether the president is telling the truth or doing all he can to bring out the facts.*" [emphasis added][255]

It was Cannon's job as a reporter to find a credible source for his story line about Reagan and Iran–Contra. In Wirthlin he found a willing member of the "Reagan team" to crap on his own patron by offering privileged polling data to support the notion that the boss might be lying and withholding information. Whether Reagan was out of touch should never have received an endorsement from someone who enjoyed political and social prominence as an ally.

Additional serious damage emerged from a lengthy pre-SOTU piece under the bylines of David Hoffman and Lou Cannon in Sunday's *Washington Post*—one I had not read until I returned from Camp David. With its hard-edged and acid tone and Hoffman's name in the lead, I suspected he did most of the writing with reporting contributed by Cannon. It was the *Post*'s lead news article but should have been labeled "news analysis." They quoted only two sources directly, former senator Paul Laxalt and Dick Wirthlin. Once again, Dick provided exactly the quotes they wanted by saying "the speech 'will challenge the president' as few speeches have." And, "Iran does cast somewhat of a shadow over his presidency…"[256] These were the tainted comments reporters loved to hear from one purportedly close to the president, and again raised the question why Wirthlin was given his privileged access. It proved the adage: "With friends like this, who needs enemies?"

In describing Reagan's preparation for the SOTU, the article cited no other direct sources. Instead, in twenty-nine different places, it quoted "senior officials," "one adviser," "intimates," "White House officials," "sources," "senior administration officials," and other similar sources with assorted opinions and criticisms of internal White House struggles and conflicts. Hoffman's dark language foretold what he would write in his postspeech analysis: "His primary objective in the speech is to address the growing perception that his presidency has been impaired by the Iran-contra [sic] scandal and that he has grown too old, too out of touch and too dependent on his aides, according to senior White House officials and intimates of the president."[257]

The duo's reporting was uncharacteristically sloppy when they swallowed a wild fabrication from "senior advisers" to assert: "Reagan had dropped a confrontational reference to the 'poisonous influence' of the Soviet Union in world affairs contained in an original draft given him by

Khachigian."[258] Sore losers fed them this contemptible lie to undercut *my* credibility as well as the president's. I had plenty of headaches in the war with team Thomas, so in the rush of getting the speech done, it wasn't worth wasting energy to body-check Hoffman and Cannon, and I let it go.

To confirm my memory, I carefully researched the National Archives to see if speech drafts under my authorship included the phrase, "poisonous influence." Nothing submitted to Reagan under my name came back with his handwritten edits removing those words. "Poisonous influence" was never included in any draft where only my name appeared as author. I cannot speak for the other speechwriters.

JANUARY 27, 1987

Reagan walked into a chamber filled with angry Democrats who resented his six years of attempts to bleed the New Deal and Great Society. The congressional leadership was in the hands of extreme partisans unwilling to extend gestures of goodwill while Iran–Contra dominated the news. The night rivaled a South American soccer match, with Republicans leaping up to cheer Reagan's tough foreign policy talk and calls for smaller government. Their counterparts sat glumly and applauded politely, only when necessary, then jeered him when he called for a balance budget. Jim Wright was a portrait of boredom, taking out his hankie to clean his glasses, and offering dainty hand claps as if chasing away flies. Every member of Congress held an advanced text, so as the president spoke, each fingered through it in a neverland of apathy.

On live television, Reagan checked off at least one of Nixon's important goals—he "looked good and felt good" by energetically entering the House of Representative with a strong, jaunty demeanor just three weeks after prostate surgery. Nixon had emphasized that Reagan's "mood would be more important than his words." If the calls to the White House switchboard meant anything, 89 percent came in positive over negative. Despite CBS News's Bill Plante's observation that Reagan achieved his objective to "look strong, come out strong, look rested," most reporting focused on the president's limited Iran–Contra explanations.[xiii] The capital was in no

---

xiii Proving former Minnesota U.S. Senator Eugene McCarthy's wry illustration of media groupthink: "Newsmen are like blackbirds on a telephone line. When one flies away, they all fly away, and when one comes back, they all come back."

mood to cheerlead the Gipper's comeback. Realistically, there was no magic potion, verbiage, or rhetoric that was going to lift the anchor of the growing scandal weighing down the opening curtain of his last two years.

When Mrs. Reagan summoned me to help put out the growing fire of Iran–Contra, I was given a hose with little water. In advance of the SOTU, *Business Week* flattered me as a "master stylist who has helped Reagan out of many a jam in the past," but the magazine was also right on target when it added, "the Administration isn't giving him much to work with."[259] Reagan was sidelined over the holidays by his absence and surgery. Blended with Don Regan's teetering leadership, lack of focus on new initiatives, and a burgeoning scandal, I should have foreseen the potential of a toxic brew. The president's own detachment from creative policy development led him to retreat to the comfort of defending existing policies and promote new ones in broad context only. In their place, he would emphasize oratory that displayed renewed vigor and energy to dispel age and health issues.

After five years in Nixon's White House and bruises in two Reagan campaigns, I should have been insulated from any surprises in political Washington. But the rush from Reagan's ranks to deride and ridicule him illustrated a level of duplicity that gave good names to rats leaving the sinking ship. In the nation's capital, the scorned and aggrieved have ready sources to air resentment and anger, and the political press has a list of informants on speed dial who will conform to preset story lines. With its pre-SOTU article, the *Washington Post* signaled it was an open-air platform for dyspeptic White House or administration leakers whose advice the president rejected. The *Post's* David Hoffman quoted from a "high-ranking administration policy-maker" who whined: "They have finally achieved the content-free presidency." Another anonymous source used Hoffman to thrash Reagan's "lack of imagination and boldness," offering a budget recommendation that was "idiotic," and accused a White House suffering from an "utter absence" of strategy." All came from so-called "friends" of the president.[260]

David Broder joined with an abrasive opinion column about Reagan's "lost opportunity" and quoted one of the "more literary-minded members of the Administration" who described the SOTU as "the day the cheering stopped." Broder attacked the SOTU as a "themeless pudding" from a "rudderless White House"—largely because Reagan missed out on the "competitiveness initiative" that been fashioned by treasury secretary James

Baker's (and deputy secretary Dick Darman's) cabinet council on economic policy. Broder's view was that Reagan's omission of the Baker/Darman competitiveness program "exemplified the haplessness that is threatening to overwhelm this administration."[261]

It was easy to spot Darman's DNA on leaks. The reference to Reagan's management of a "content-free" administration was a pervasive theme in Darman's memoirs and dominated his view of our '84 strategy and wasn't the first time he chose ego over loyalty. Every one of those "intimates," "senior officials," "advisers," "White House officials," and other sources who cowered behind anonymity were tantrum throwers who with brazen alacrity betrayed the sitting president without whom they had no stature or career.

At least outside of Washington's swamp, several editorial bright spots lightened Reagan's news summary reading. "Vintage Ronald Reagan," wrote the *Dallas Times Herald*. "Reagan's Reagan Again," said the *New York Post*. From the *Chicago Sun-Times*, "President Still Alive, On Course." And, down in Atlanta, the *Journal*'s editorial was gracious, "The President Comes Back with a Fighting Speech," and closed with, "The State of the Union message gives us hope that the president can get both his administration and the nation moving again in the right direction, and soon."

I cared deeply about helping Reagan escape this mess, just like I did during Bitburg. I had nothing to do with the morass of the scandal and was given no exit or explanation on which I could hang an oratorical hat. Because Reagan was still unsure how to unravel Iran–Contra, the two of us were unprepared to confront it with language that would assuage a restive Congress, press and public. Moreover, Regan's Mice had been in place for two years, high on power's dopamine and ill-prepared to collaborate helpfully. The White House did not have a domestic policy director and lacked formulated policy initiatives while Regan allowed four different cabinet secretaries to compete randomly for elbow room to place their favored programs into the State of the Union. Combined with the officious intermeddling by speechwriter wannabe Dennis Thomas and message mechanic Dick Wirthlin in realms for which they had no true expertise, my antennae should have risen with warning signs. In the words of one of their own team members, Christopher Hicks, "We were implementers, not thinkers, organization guys, not policymakers."[262]

I take blame for not having set ground rules with Mrs. Reagan and Don Regan when I took the assignment. In addition to clear domestic and foreign policy objectives, I should have required a working environment that precluded interference by staff or Wirthlin. Drafting by committee never works, so I should have overruled my inclination for collegiality and teamwork and set forth an ultimatum with the First Lady: "It's them or me."

Still, the president met his central goal and delivered a speech with which he was comfortable—one underscoring that the responsibilities of the office were his, not theirs. Achieving status with a White House pass and a West Wing office doesn't bestow the power to command the fortunes of the nation. In the 1987 SOTU, he laid claim to his leadership and health. After study and reflection, he returned weeks later to resolve questions regarding Iran–Contra. The dire warnings of the end of his presidency proved empty as he renewed his crusade and moved forward to shatter the Soviet empire.

Chapter 24

SAYING GOODBYE

Ronald Reagan scorched Hollywood communists and refused to be upstaged by Errol Flynn. He dumped his staff in the 1980 primaries and refused to budge when I questioned a half-truth in his inaugural address. Tip O'Neill lost battles with the Gipper, and Mikhail Gorbachev couldn't move him. Don Regan was shown the door, and even Nancy couldn't overrule his stubbornness when he insisted on honoring his controversial Bitburg visit. When Reagan's deepest instincts were challenged, he resisted being told what to do or say. His career was littered with those who mistook the genial smile and affable demeanor for a rube who didn't know his own mind. That unshakable trait surfaced in the summer of 1988 when we met to collaborate on his last major speech as president and party leader to the Republican National Convention.

Nancy never liked his tough rhetoric and portrayal as hardline anti-communist and rigid conservative and wanted to shape the speech's tone as emotional, softer, warmer, and less political. She recruited Stu Spencer and chief of staff Ken Duberstein as allies to instruct me that a slashing political speech was a no-no. If that was what Reagan preferred, okay, but I never scripted anything he didn't want, and he knew exactly what he wished to convey to the GOP delegates. Based on his personal instructions and extensive edits of the draft I submitted, he achieved his goal.

After the '87 SOTU, word leaked that Tennessee senator Howard Baker accepted an offer to replace Don Regan as chief of staff, and Don tersely submitted his resignation, with the Mice scurrying behind. Baker brought along former Senate aide Tom Griscom to serve as director of communications to help Reagan move a new agenda after Iran–Contra. "Senator"

Baker wasn't accustomed to serving as a staffer and asked Ken Duberstein, a former Reagan legislative lobbyist, to return from the private sector to make the trains run on time. Duberstein fit comfortably with the capital's glad-handing pragmatists whose political philosophy drifted with prevailing winds. He came from New York's moderate GOP wing, was affable, leaked to the press with the best and provided Baker a malleable first family intermediary.

As the new year opened in 1988, Stu Spencer asked to meet in my office, and after small talk, Spencer broached his mission. "Hey, what would you think about taking a year off and helping Reagan with speeches?"

I paused, "You're kidding. He has a speechwriting staff. My business is going well, so why would I want to leave my family and everything behind and go back and deal with all the problems I just left?"

Stu laughed, and I said, "Okay, now I know where you're coming from. Whose idea is this? The president's, or Mommy's?" He grinned sheepishly and said, "Actually, it's Baker's and Duberstein's. They're having some problems with the process and internal operations, and Reagan would like a familiar face for the big speeches when he's walking out the door." When Reagan's diary was published in 2009, this was his entry for January 5, 1988, three days before my visit with Stu:

> *Staff meeting—discussed outline on planning major speeches*
> *for coming Year. We're thinking of sounding out Ken*
> *Khachigian as editor—if he can take a year off from his private life.*[263]

Stu knew it would be impossible for me to take off an entire year. With two teenage daughters and Meredith's appointment as a University of California regent, I couldn't add White House responsibilities. I told Stu I was honored to be asked, and he could pass along that I would make every effort to help make Reagan's exit a success. However, before I even considered making any commitments, I wanted personal contact with the White House to hear what their expectations would be. Tom Griscom faxed me a backgrounder with eight major speeches contemplated for Reagan's last year—from January's State of the Union through the farewell address. Baker, Duberstein, and Griscom had a small window in Los Angeles where Reagan would be attending a Lincoln's Day Republican fundraiser, and Tom followed up that Baker wanted me to drive up to discuss my availability.

Howard Baker had plenty of Tennessee charm and opened the conversation like his namesake Jim Baker, "Khachigian, we need to have you back to help your president; and we expect you to step up." That was the good cop. He turned things over to the bad cops. Tony Dolan was running the speechwriting shop and creating problems in pushing his agenda and trying to work around Griscom by resisting oversight. Duberstein already had the president's sign-off and looked for smoother sailing toward the end of the year with someone who could help without disrupting internal procedures.

Griscom's background paper set out a detailed and ambitious agenda through January 1989. Two of the events had already passed, so I would be responsible for six big speeches from March through the farewell address with the "last important policy speech" of the Reagan administration coming after the May Moscow summit. (See Appendix 14 for Griscom fax.) Duberstein pushed hard to close the sale, "We want you to finish with a bang-up farewell address that lays out the president's vision for America." I flipped the pages and responded, "Look, Tony was often a headache, and I wasn't happy when he back doored me on the State of the Union speech, but I'm not comfortable being used to push him out. So, I'll agree to do two or three of these big speeches and the farewell address. However, I can't take the whole year off." Griscom and I agreed to stay in touch and reached agreement on a time commitment. I didn't ask for a financial arrangement, and they didn't offer one. Working on Reagan's farewell address would be an honor and a fitting sequel to my collaboration on his inaugural address. Alpha and omega.

Exactly two months later, April 13, Tom Griscom called with his proposal. "Ken, here's the deal, we'll be going to Moscow at the end of May and first week of June. Post-Moscow, the president will get back into the political mode. I talked to Baker and the president, and I proposed that you take responsibility for two or three speeches—where *you* do them and no one else," and emphasized no interference in my working relationship with Reagan. "One will be the president's speech to the Republican National Convention—his valedictory to the delegates and support of the nominee. The second speech would be one in the fall on the lessons and guidelines he has learned in office. And the last speech you'll work with him will be his farewell address. I'll tell you, the president jumped on it pretty quick!"

"Tom, are you sure the president is on board?"

Griscom reiterated yes, and assured me that Ken Duberstein pinned it down that morning in a meeting with Reagan. I had pondered the proposal, and now they seemed to have come up with a workable middle ground. I wouldn't have to get involved with the messiness of shoving Tony aside and would retain the gratification of reaching home plate with Reagan after helping him get to first base in 1981.

The president confirmed it in his diary on April 13:

> *Ken [Duberstein] proposed Ken Khachigian as writer for three speeches that will face me before I'm through. I OK'd.*[264]

On June 14, 1988, Reagan made a related diary entry after meeting with Baker and Duberstein:

> *Then we had our short meeting—we're talking about Ken Khachigian doing my convention speech.*[265]

That was bizarre, because nine earlier weeks Reagan already signed off on my preparing "three speeches that will face" him before he left office, and I had been informed of that assignment. Not reminding the president that my "doing" his convention speech was a *fait acccompli*, was an unseen signal of Duberstein's loose management style to leave maneuvering room in case he wanted to change direction.

JUNE 16, 1988, 4:30 P.M.

A warm smile and "long-time-no-see" welcome in the Oval Office.

A year and a half passed since our last working meeting, and we met alone with none of the hovering that was such a bad memory from the days of Don Regan's gang. He was rankled about the Democrats' prattle about a "time for a change," and got to the point, "There's a theme I came up with, Ken. You'd think we're in the depths of depression when you hear it's 'time for a change.' Well, I've been thinking about using it. The change took place eight years ago when we took office. Still, it's time to *keep* a change." Reagan recited from his memory and notes—how the Democratic party had controlled Congress for so many years, and against their opposition, he still had huge accomplishments—all of which he wanted to defend in his speech. Creating 16.8 million new jobs, reducing inflation, and a long list of other achievements.

He was prepared to defend Bush. "I've always had the idea that the vice-president should be a part of the administration and not just sitting on the sidelines. George has been a part of everything we've done and ever accomplished. He headed up the task force to cut back regulations and the task force on drug reduction. He is going to 'keep the change' we started—on the economy and to build a strong national defense."

Reagan rattled off statistics, lamented about the deficit and its continuation without a presidential line item veto. He took down his half glasses and said sarcastically, "You know, Ken, when we hear about the war on poverty, the answer is: 'poverty won.'" Making sure I wrote down his words, he emphasized "Not one country has gone to the communists since I've been in office. When we got here 50 percent of our aircraft couldn't fly for lack of spare parts and 50 percent of vessels couldn't leave port."

With all the facts he wanted stuffed in, it was impossible to honor his request to keep it at twenty-five minutes. I managed only one suggestion, plugging how he left the Democrat Party based on fundamental freedoms like freedom of expression. We called it an evening after a good laugh at his jab at Ted Kennedy for never holding a real job.

JULY 5, 1988, 11:35 A.M.—12:03 P.M.

Dutch was wearing a light tan suit, blue shirt, blue tie, and brown shoes—prepared to check into central casting for leads in multiple leading roles. Country lawyer, college president, and royal prince came to mind. "Hi there. You kept me awake last night; I was thinking about correcting those numbers I gave"—slight errors regarding Democrats' control of both congressional houses over the past five decades. He detailed employment and unemployment numbers and taxes paid in different brackets after his tax reform cuts, then added, "Now, I don't want to get overboard with statistics."

I interrupted, "Sir, how do we weave Mrs. Reagan into the speech?" He bypassed and returned to his theme. "Change" began with his administration and would only continue with another Republican president and Republican leadership in the House and Senate. "Keep the change going; that's the point I want to get across." He stood, shook my hand, and left.

I think most speechwriters agree it's better to work on shorter deadlines. With too much time to prepare for a major national event, the tendency is to overthink and unnecessarily overdo with ideas and information. Once again, the intensity of preparation was enormous since Reagan had to motivate continuing support for his crusade while also creating a transitional tide to sweep in his successor. An equal burden was finding the perfect words to meet the conventioneers' expectations of Reagan's dazzling wizardry of communication. Above all, I was determined to be unwavering to Reagan's wishes. Though it was his night, not mine or anyone else's, two other voices jumped in to dispute the president's message primacy.

Stu Spencer tracked me to my Santa Barbara hotel as I prepared for the next day's visit to the Reagan Ranch. "What's up Stu?" He laughed, "Mommy called me and wanted me to pass along a message. She's not interested in a political speech per se. She's interested in what he's accomplished, but to make it personal, with a lot of vision. But include George Bush as well." It's not the first time I heard the bullshit about "vision" without anyone defining it.

"Okay," I replied, "but I don't know how the hell you go to a political convention and not give a political speech."

Stu was only the messenger. "Look, Khachigian, we need to humor her as much as we can. She wants vision—where this country is going with the base that has been built." Then, he got to Nancy's clear request. "She said, 'I hope it isn't a slashing partisan speech.'"

Then Duberstein called and asked to have coffee before I left and meandered through each cliché speechwriters hear—especially from people who never write speeches. "Reagan needs to tell his dream for America... Have accomplished so much, but more needs to be done...Then talk about the future; his vision for the future."

Duberstein claimed to speak for Reagan, but I knew his message came from Nancy. "What's off is a political speech which lambastes the Democrats. Contrast 'them with us' and then a positive look at: (1) what we wanted to do (2) what we accomplished (3) what we want America to be." He talked of Reagan's budget requests, how Democrats said "no" to change, and "we need George Bush."

With these admonitions, I was off to Rancho del Cielo. Reagan made note of the day in his diary:

> *Friday, July 22. We rode down to the old Eckert ranch through that property down to the spring fed lake we've known about but never seen...I had to get back for lunch with Ken Khachigian who is working on my speech for the convention. It was a working lunch & progress was made.*

12:15 P.M.

We sat down for a "working lunch" on the patio of their little house, and Mrs. Reagan joined us over grilled salmon salad and iced tea. Within minutes, I was placed uncomfortably in the middle of two separate views of the speech's tone. Reagan opened the discussion as I jotted notes in between bites.

"Well, when you recall, our theme when we came in was a 'new beginning,' and we should concentrate on a vision of the future. It *is* a new beginning, and it's still beginning." Mrs. Reagan cut in. "Ken, it has to be visionary and emotional—nobody can do that better than 'my friend.'" She looked over at her 'friend' with what the press called the "gaze." Her message hadn't changed since our ride to the Illinois hog farm in 1980: *"It's important to remember that Ronnie's at his best when he's emotional, and you need to reflect that in his speeches—to let him show emotion."* She turned to me, "This is not the place of a hard political speech, but to play on the emotions of the day and to show a lot of love—to focus on what's been done and what remains to be done."

She was shrewdly ambivalent regarding "Ronnie's" communications. When Mondale humiliated her "friend" in '84, Nancy pounced on Jim Baker for his embrace of "white picket fence" speeches and ordered hardball. She disliked the rough-and-tumble and portrayals of Ronnie as a hard-hitting conservative or hardline on social issues except when it was functionally necessary. Once her "friend" attained the summit, she opted for reversion to the "shining city on the hill." At today's lunch, she was sending signals for *Mister Rogers' Neighborhood*.

I could write it either way, but it was contradictory to deliver a nonpolitical speech at a political convention, especially when the president clearly wanted a vigorous defense against the failure of his Democrat critics. I didn't invent Reagan the "tough guy." His indignation and combativeness for issues about which he cared were honed on the mashed potato circuit and first displayed in "The Speech" for Goldwater. Nancy hoped she and I would team up to tamp down her husband's instincts. I changed the subject and suggested the president consider shaping his political exit as the opposite of his sunset years—as a sunrise where Bush would continue his crusade. Reagan agreed and spoke of how Bush reduced regulations on businesses.

RR: He was the man who oversaw those efforts and played a part in everything we accomplished.

NR: Ken, it's a fine line we walk. Ronnie can talk about what he's accomplished in domestic and foreign policy. But Ronnie can't emasculate George.

RR: He hasn't just sat on the sidelines as vice president.

NR: You need to be visionary and emotional.

Hmm...Just in case I didn't get her point on the "vision thing."

RR: Look, the president can't spend a dime. That's the legitimate thing of plugging George Bush—he must be elected for everything we did to continue. On the deficit, the president can't spend a dime; that's pure Democratic cant from way back. Upper wage earners are paying a bigger percentage of revenue than ever before. The Democrats controlled Congress for fifty years. The president can't spend a dime, only that which Congress authorizes, and they add billions more money the agencies have to spend.

He was beginning to sound like the O&W from the '80 campaign trail—spinning yarns of bloated government, excessive taxation, and out-of-control spending. He wanted to retell the stories to his base, so Mrs. Reagan interrupted to change the subject.

NR: You often talk about your faith in people.

RR: I said we merely got out of *your* way.

NR: That would be ending after your talk about where you want to go for the good of the people.

There was mild annoyance in Dutch's voice, and I wondered if he preferred our standard one-on-one prep meetings. It wasn't comfortable being caught between them when the president shook his head at the First Lady.

RR: But, honey...facts...not just platitudes. Facts are the soul of credibility. Michael Dukakis created an image for their party that they'll correct a lot of things. But we should paint a different picture that includes our accomplishments. But isn't this worth continuing?

The Gipper was riled because the night before, he watched the Democrats' presidential nominee rip him by telling America that the "Reagan era is over." Dukakis accused the president of limiting the American dream to the "privileged few" and promised to exchange "voodoo economics for can-do economics." He piled on by blasting Reagan's administration for running up "more debt in this country in the last eight years than we did in the previous 200."[266]

Reagan virtually ignored Nancy when she offered, "You should say how *you* see your vision of the next 10 years."

Dukakis's budget jabs had gotten under his skin, and he was more agitated. "Yes, the first budget I had would have been $207 billion less if they had passed the first one. They did want to cut defense, but when we got here, fifty percent of the planes couldn't fly, and fifty percent of the ships couldn't leave port. They cut $125 billion out of what we recommended, and they added $250 billion in domestic programs." He restated his unhappiness for his "big mistake" on the 1982 tax increase compromise.

Mrs. Reagan began to read her "friend's" thinking, and it was unlikely she would change his mind, so slightly shifted gears—adopting his theme, but reducing the heat.

> **NR:** I don't think you name any names. You take the high road when you talk about your accomplishments. Just don't get down to the level of naming the other side.

> **RR:** I could use FDR; he's their hero. His platform in 1932 was to return to the states authority that was unjustly taken from them. That's one of the things we've done...is to return power to the states.

> **NR:** We're in better shape with our foreign friends then we were eight years ago.

> **RR:** Yes, I told the head of state of Malta during a recent visit, "You've set the pattern for the whole world."

After their banter, I wasn't sure what the hell to write. One thing was clear; Reagan wanted to put the onus on Democrats for his inherited mess, and the "great value in letting people know that for past 58 years, the Democrats have controlled the House of Representatives for 54 years and both Houses of Congress for 54 years. We only had the majority in the Senate for six years to help pass our program.[xiv] That's why we need change."

Mrs. Reagan didn't dispute, and offered, "You can point to the economic conditions in 1976."

> **RR:** We can point out that the 'misery index' (combining inflation and unemployment rates) in 1976 was 12.5 percent, and Jimmy Carter said that no one had the right to run for president with the numbers at those levels. It was over 20 percent in 1980, so they didn't mention it.

I finally got in a word edgewise: "Mr. President, in 1980, they didn't mention the misery index because it was too high, and in 1988 they don't mention it because it's too low. We might want to use that line."

Over dessert, Reagan finished talking about job training numbers and segued into a possible speech ending that thanked the delegates and the audience "out there" watching on television—"not about making me president but giving me temporary custody of an institution called the presidency—one that was entrusted to me. Our dream was that we sought a shining city on the hill. And maybe we can come up with a surprise about the six hundred million man-hours of labor...and that man was George Bush."

That was awkward, so I countered with Reagan speaking directly to Bush about winning the campaign and carrying the message of change, etc.

Mrs. Reagan chimed in forcefully, "Ronnie could look into the camera: 'George, I hope you'll make it one more for the Gipper. Because wherever I am....'" Her voice drifted off, and we knew what she meant. It wouldn't be difficult to finish her sentence. She added a final endorsement of the need for an international dialogue because the world has gotten much smaller.

Reagan was anxious to get back to horse riding and cutting wood, and his final suggestion was about the "need for dialogue. Ken, we only get

---

xiv   The Democrats controlled the House of Representatives for 52 out of the last 56 years and controlled the Senate for 46 out of the last 56 years. The numbers he used in his speech.

peace through strength. That was illustrated with the Soviets' SS-20s. The Soviets wouldn't remove them from their multiple locations until we put in our Pershings and GLCMs in Europe.[xv] One day after months had gone by, they said to us: 'We want zero, zero.'" Reagan paused, and winked like he just leaked a code-red alert, "But, this is not to be used in the speech. People aren't armed because they mistrust each other. They mistrust each other because they are armed. In my first meeting with Gorbachev, I proposed a reduction in our arms race; I told him we need to do that because 'You know you can't win.'"

The First Lady departed, and the president guided me to their little house where he eagerly pointed to his personal woodwork and floor tiling. "Look, see how perfect this fits in with the rest of the wall and flooring. I did this all myself." He was pumped up with pride, and I think those few minutes outweighed everything else we discussed.

Reagan reluctantly left this cherished environment for the turmoil and discontent of the capital's mire—a galaxy away from the scrub, dust, and sweat of horses, tractors, and his beat-up Jeep. A photo captured Reagan and me when I arrived at Rancho del Cielo, he in his jeans and worn hat and sweaty shirt and me carrying a briefcase and flashing designer sunglasses. He sent it to me inscribed:

> *Dear Ken—Come on—we're sawing wood just up ahead. You are just in time. Very Best Wishes Ken & Warmest Friendship*
>
> *Ronald Reagan*

I missed my chance to tell him I wasn't that slick city boy—the one in our West Wing meetings wearing nice suits with pocket squares—but instead, that we shared small-town Americana. My hometown Visalia and his, Dixon, Illinois, could have been twin cities. My upbringing identified with the one Dutch loved at Rancho del Cielo. I grew up driving tractors, clearing away pruned wood, feeding farm animals, and thriving on do-it-yourself "fix-it and repair" farm culture. When the free world's leader knelt to demonstrate his talent in laying floors in a modest country house,

---

xv   "SS-20" - Russian two-stage nuclear ballistic missile system with multiple independently targeted re-entry warheads. "Pershing" – American nuclear two-stage medium range ballistic missile system. "GLCM - Ground Launched Cruise Missile," ground-to-ground nuclear missile with a range of roughly 1500 miles.

he informed me as much about his character as all his magnificent orations. I wasn't as gifted with words, or as well read as others in my generation, but Reagan and I bonded in ways that turned out working well because we shared similar roots.

My secretary, Joni Johnson, faxed the first draft to Reagan's personal assistant Kathy Osborne, and I added humor by an outside consultant, Fleming Saunders, while the research office's Teresa Rosenberger helped me with fact-checking. I tried very hard to please both Reagans. The president was determined to combine the warmth of his "long goodbye" with a strong political defense of his administration's record, and the First Lady wanted to avoid a "slashing partisan speech" and apply the "vision thing." The White House staff didn't meddle, and Reagan had a free hand to edit in any way he wanted. I wasn't beside him to admonish about Stu's caution lights, and apparently Mrs. Reagan was unavailable to buzz in his ear about being visionary and emotional in place of political and factual.

His heavy editing started midway through the speech, adding in precisely what he described over lunch at the ranch: "Honey, facts, not platitudes." He was determined to set the record straight that runaway budgets began with the Democratic party's passage of the War on Poverty, so he hung budget deficits around Congress's neck. Under the guise of praise for Bush, he added a long, handwritten insert on reducing federal regulations, streamlining government, and a huge success in getting Soviets to remove SS-20 missiles while placing our Pershing missiles in NATO. A few pages later, he inserted a jab at FDR's pledge to return autonomy to the states. His initial "twenty-five-minute" speech lengthened as I reviewed his edits, but I wasn't going to argue. In a replay of his '84 convention speech, he took my draft and toughened it. Each change was triggered by outrage from the attacks on him at the Democratic convention. Dutch was competitive and ornery and responded accordingly when belittled or demeaned. Mondale made that blunder in '84 and awakened a sleeping giant. The Democrats reprised the mistake in '88.

He couldn't resist adding more pokes in his opponents' eyes when I returned a clean copy to him. He cited data regarding record economic growth into his final year, then added this line: "Funny...they don't call it Reaganomics anymore." He later added boasts about ending the Iran/Iraq war, possible peace in Southwest Africa, and removing Cuban forces from the region. He threw in everything but the White House kitchen china—hellbent on informing America that his eight years were successful, and the fellas on the other side were distorting history. With audience reaction, I figured he added another four minutes or more to his remarks. This would be his last opportunity on the national stage to get his licks in—something that everyone should have embraced. There was a time for the "shining city on the hill," and a time for roundhouse punches.

After a long video tribute to the president and Nancy, the delegates in the New Orleans Superdome were amped when Reagan opened with a tribute to his "very special lady who has been selfless, not just for our party, but for the entire nation. She is a strong, courageous, and compassionate woman… She makes us proud…But never more so than these last eight years."

He joked about his first GOP convention and how Abe Lincoln's speech sent tingles down his spine, and then laid the foundation for a successful eight years by reminding delegates of their mutual pledge in 1980 "to conduct a national crusade to make America great again…We met at a time when America was in economic chaos—and today, we meet in a time of economic promise. We met then in international distress and today with global hope."

He offered "a little review of that history" from 1980's election—high taxes, high interest rates, budget deficits, gas lines, factory shut-downs, a weak national defense and disrespect for America across the globe. The *Washington Post*'s David Broder laid aside daggers from his '84 convention speech analysis and offered a positive summation:

> Reagan enthusiastically fulfilled his part in the overall strategic design of making this first night of the convention a forceful reminder to American voters of how much (as Republicans see it) their lives have improved since the Democrats were driven from the White House.
>
> The emphasis was on 67 months of economic growth and progress in curing world trouble spots from Afghanistan to the Persian Gulf.[267]

The Gipper embraced Bush, related America's values of love of country, prayer in schools, and protecting the unborn. Toward the end, he unwrapped the "vision" thing.

> *It's our gift to have visions...That's America. Everyone with his or her vision of the American promise. That's why we're a magnet for the world—for those who dodged bullets and gave their lives coming over the Berlin Wall and others, only a few of whom avoided death, coming in tiny boats on turbulent oceans.*

> *This land, its people, the dreams that unfold here and the freedom to bring it all together—well, these are what make America soar—up where you can see hope billowing in those freedom winds.*

> *When our children turn the pages of our lives, I hope they'll see that we had a vision to pass forward a nation as nearly perfect as we could. Where there's decency, tolerance, generosity, honesty, courage, common sense, fairness, and piety.*

After quoting H. G. Wells about the "past is but the beginning of a beginning," the president looked out to the vast sea of adoring party activists:

> *That's a new day—our sunlit new day—to keep alive the fire so that when we look back at the time of choosing, we can say that we did all that could be done. Never less.*

Broder mentioned, and understated, one problem. He noted a sign in the audience, "Reagan for King," and wrote if the Constitution had permitted, "this crowd was ready to crown its hero. All that kept it from happening was the acoustics in the hall—a problem that Reagan managed only occasionally to overcome."[268]

My daughter Merissa and I were seated in risers above the convention floor, and with Reagan's first words, I heard dissonant feedback from the sound system. With each passing paragraph, the Great Communicator was getting screwed by the sound and lighting experts who were so critical to his prior trade's success.

The *Los Angeles Times* reported the nightmare in detail. "'This is the worst convention I've been to,' said Arizona Senator Barry Goldwater, who is attending his ninth. He was sitting in the Bush family box for the president's address, but 'I couldn't hear a word of the speech,' Goldwater told NBC in a televised interview."[269] The *Times* also cited an LA sound consultant, Stanley Miller who said of the vast New Orleans Superdome, "it's an acoustical disaster area."[270]

Television wasn't affected because "networks get their sound through direct electronic cable." But "in parts of the great hall, the echo has proven so severe the delegates can barely hear what speakers are saying." Worse still, the *Times* continued, "[T]he Reagan video was so loud on Monday night that when the president spoke afterward he seemed diminutive in person." Poor lighting was confirmed by the reporters' quick trip to the floor where they observed "that the delegates must squint because those 1,800 bulbs point right at them, and VIPs in the sky boxes must watch the proceedings through the lighting grid."[271]

The *New York Times* piled on. "It's so hard to hear in the cavernous Louisiana Superdome that some delegates have gone to their hotel rooms to find out what is happening by watching television."[272] The cause of the problem, according to Joseph Angotti, vice president of NBC News, was "the hall is so vast things are getting lost." Angotti further observed that, "Speeches don't have the impact they normally would. It affects the viewers less than it does someone sitting in the hall. But even what goes out over television seems to have less impact." CBS's senior producer in charge of convention coverage, Lane Venardos, agreed. "He was puzzled that the crowd did not appear 'as enthusiastic as you'd expect it to be.'"[273]

Nancy, sitting in a nearby box to Goldwater, wouldn't have been immune to the same problems—having trouble hearing Ronnie and likely squinting with others through the lighting grid. Reagan didn't appear quite on his game and stumbled a couple of times—saying "facts are stupid things," where the script read "facts are stubborn things." He got a bounce from the acoustics, and the audience feedback upon which he had grown to depend was uneven and ragged.

On the bright side was praise from Nixon's letter to me, "The fact that even the anchor men praised the president's speech last night was a great tribute to him, but also an equally great tribute to you." It was the first of many nice letters and calls from television viewers. The *Wall Street Journal* editorialized, "Mr. Reagan's speech was an aggressive, concrete defense of his legacy and attack on his opponents. It was written by speechwriters, the one remaining political class that tends to despise what the consultants are doing to politics."[274]

However, the most important viewer was not in the television audience; she was in the sky box hearing distorted sound through bad visuals. Worse, without her knowledge, her "friend" had laden the address with language and facts to defend his two terms in a way that reduced the "vision thing." Reagan entered in his diary, "My speech was well received..." But his insistence on a heavy political speech combined with the horrible acoustics and visuals may not have been "well received" at home. I couldn't overrule what the president wanted to do with his remarks. At evening's end, I was caught in the crossfire of falling short on the First Lady's wishes and lousy mechanics in the Superdome.

Nevertheless, Reagan's instincts were mostly correct in defending even the minutiae of his eight-year record. His approval ratings in the NBC/ *Wall Street Journal* poll enjoyed a net gain of twelve points, to a fifty-seven to thirty-three positive rating. The post-mortem was summarized in a significant political newsletter of the day, The American Political Report from editor/publisher Kevin Phillips:

> After several months of minimal movement.... President Reagan's job approval is up again—and also strategically relevant...Part of the president's surge, we think, reflects the way his party farewell speech recaptured his successful early years instead of the more troubled circumstances of 1987-88... [N]ot only did Reagan's convention speech lift Bush's own ratings/trial heat scores, but it's a generally accepted rule of thumb that retiring presidents with ratings over 50% help their party's candidate.[275]

Reagan escaped to his Ranch, and I had three nights to enjoy New Orleans' cuisine with Merissa and my brother Luther, a California delegate. At week's end, I joined Dan Quayle's campaign as his speechwriter after the feckless announcement of his addition to Bush's ticket. In the meantime, the convention technicians got the message as well as a deserved scolding from

Bush's team, who couldn't afford to have the vice-president's debut marred by defective sound and lighting. I looked forward to his acceptance speech.

The veep delivered a bravura performance well coached by Roger Ailes and with artfully crafted words by Peggy Noonan—sharing Reagan's record with a "no new taxes pledges" while setting sights on his own. He offered enough poetry to show that George Bush had a feel for his country and a portrait of what America could be if its fate was placed in his hands.

Standing on the convention floor, I had writer's envy and respect for the metaphor that stood out in capturing the delegates' hearts—language to be chiseled in the speechwriting hall of fame: "*A thousand points of light in a broad and peaceful sky.*" Its imagery became embedded in Bush's campaign messages and subsequently within his administration and through the Points of Light Foundation. Among the reasons that figure of speech resonated so dramatically and forcefully into Republican hearts was how its lyricism seemed so Reaganesque.

It turns out there is a very good reason it sounded like Reagan because the elegiac "points of light" *was* used by President Ronald Reagan three and a half years prior to Bush's convention address. During the writing of this book, Dennis Cuddy, a Reagan-era education adviser, checked in to reminisce. During our visit, he inquired if I recalled Reagan's address to the Conference on Religious Liberty in 1985. I had not.

On April 16, 1985, Reagan was asked to address the Religious Liberty Conference on the history of religion and its impact on civilization. Cuddy's reminder was correct.

Included in his 1985 remarks, President Reagan expressed concern about attacks against religious freedom but found promise in its defense by groups of believers and reassured them, "*Points of light* flash out in the darkness, and God is honored once again." [emphasis added][276]

After Bush's convention speech, there was a running kerfuffle over the possible origin of his "thousand points of light." Did it come from C. S. Lewis? Van Gogh? Thomas Wolfe? A variety of pundits had their theories on "points of light."[277] They had to look no further than the presidential remarks of Ronald Reagan in April, 1985. The veep borrowed the Great Communicator's language, and by simply adding the number one thousand in front of Reagan's words, Bush boosted the wattage of his new version of "points of light" before an audience of millions—more than three years after the phrase had already been used.

George Bush trounced Michael Dukakis in the electoral vote, won the popular vote comfortably, and election night ended my thirty-three-state tour with running mate Dan Quayle. I was off to California less than forty-eight hours after polls closed. The only loose end was to honor my commitment to Reagan to write his farewell address after Tom Griscom confirmed that Reagan wanted me and "no one else" to work on his last two or three speeches—including the farewell address. With the assurance from Griscom that Reagan had "jumped on it pretty quick" when Howard Baker and he offered my services for his last speech, I opened a "Farewell Address" file and began scribbling notes and ideas. The holidays approached, and I became concerned about my schedule. I called Griscom's replacement as head of communications, Mari Maseng. I mentored Mari from the administration's first days, and we remained close. "Mari, what's going on? If I'm going to prepare his farewell remarks, I need to get moving, and need a meeting." There was awkward silence.

"Ken, I'm sorry, Duberstein told me to call Peggy Noonan to bring her in for the farewell address." I was baffled and angry and detailed the meetings with Baker, Duberstein, and Griscom; the effort to use me to push aside Tony Dolan; the memorandum from Griscom; the meetings they had with Reagan and his eagerness for my involvement; and, not least, the commitment, preparation, and anticipation involved on my part. "That's nuts. Mari, are you also aware the president wanted me 'to take a year off my private life' to edit his final speeches in 1988?"

Mari hesitated. No one had briefed her about those discussions, and she was blindsided. She knew Peggy didn't match my close relationship and bond with Reagan, nor spent long private hours with him—those that offered Reagan a familiar face and comfort levels when collaborating. I tried calling Duberstein, and he didn't take my call. Mari was remorseful at her inability to change things. There appeared to be hidden reasons about which she couldn't speak. All she could say is that the decision was final because it came from the chief of staff.

While I was writing this book, Mari reported the story she couldn't tell me back in 1988. "Ken, the decision came from Mrs. Reagan. Duberstein passed it along to me, so that's when I called Peggy to bring her aboard. It was part of Mrs. Reagan's whole legacy strategy that she pressed on us. She was fixated on the idea that he needed to leave behind a vision of his years in office that would define his legacy. Even though you were my mentor and friend, I couldn't spill the beans, and I regret being forced to withhold the facts."[278]

Obviously, the First Lady was unaware of the mutual commitments between me, the president, and his staff. But Duberstein knew, and he made no effort to inform Mrs. Reagan. Ken knew it was in Reagan's character not to renege on a pact. He could have slipped a reminder to the president to overrule the First Lady: "Remember, Mr. President, back in April, we checked a box by convincing Ken Khachigian to carve out his schedule to work on three of your most important final speeches—including your salute at the GOP convention and your farewell address." Duberstein lacked cultural affiliation with Reagan. He was a moderate Republican from New York who fell out of the sky into the lucky bush as the placeholder chief for Reagan's final half year. He wasn't with those of us who fueled the revolution, helped in crises, wrestled as political road-warriors, and didn't leak to play against Reagan's agenda. Betraying a commitment was an easy out for Duberstein—pocket change in power poker.

Mari's unfolding secret took me back to two events. The disaster of the sound and lighting at the convention that marred Reagan's presentation in the Superdome was one. However, of more significance was the luncheon at the ranch when Nancy debated Ronnie over the style of his convention speech. She wanted him to be "visionary and emotional," and "to show a lot of love." Over lunch, Reagan talked about facts and rebutting the Democrats, and she said, "this is not the place for a hard political speech." He argued for "facts, not platitudes."

In New Orleans, Reagan did everything Nancy didn't want, and combined with the horrible sound and lights, the First Lady's takeaway may have resulted in blaming the speechwriter, not the speech giver or speech setting. When a couple of nights later the media lit up with Bush's "kinder, gentler nation" performance in an improved Hollywood set, Nancy discovered the combination she wanted for her "vision legacy." The GOP convention in 1988 was a political affair, but in her mind that was no excuse for Ronnie's "lambasting" the Democrats for their attacks on him. Political or not, she wanted roses, not guns.

Editing on Air Force One—Final Touches for his '88 Convention Farewell.

Still, whatever pressures came from the First Lady, they were no excuse for Duberstein's behavior. Mari Maseng was unaware of my prior agreements and not positioned to question the president, but Duberstein knew the full record and with the bare minimum of integrity should have repeated to Reagan that I had already been asked to write the farewell address. He had an obligation to hear from the president directly that he, Reagan, was aware that the commitment to me was being withdrawn—and that I should be informed. Instead, Duberstein took the craven's route of silence. I wrote Duberstein, scolding him for abusing my goodwill and his "failure of professional courtesy." He never responded. I'll concede to Dick Darman that he wielded his knives frontally in open daylight. Duberstein preferred to slide the stiletto in the still of night.

When Barack Obama's 2008 election victory was a sure thing four days before the vote, Duberstein's duplicity was on full display when he endorsed Obama over John McCain, a personal friend. Paul Gigot captured the sellout perfectly in his *Wall Street Journal* note.

> *An old British quip is that the passengers jumped ship so fast that even the rats were left gaping in admiration. Rats everywhere in Washington are no doubt admiring Ken Duberstein's*

decision late last week to dump his old friend John McCain and endorse Barack Obama. The media gave his endorsement fulsome play, citing Mr. Duberstein as a former chief of staff to Ronald Reagan to play up the story about one more Republican defection to Mr. Obama.

The truth is that Mr. Duberstein is a perfect Washington weathervane, a Beltway fixer who makes his living from influence peddling... The betrayal of an old friend can be written off as a cost of doing business in Washington...[279]

Four days before he left office, I wrote Reagan to thank him for the opportunity to be at the center of his historic presidency. Toward the end I added:

> *[H]ow disappointed I was not to be able to collaborate with you on your Farewell Address. If that was your personal choice, I can understand. But—just so you know—I was fully prepared to help out on this final project, having made that commitment upon your request nearly a year ago. Frankly, I am concerned that you might have been told differently—that you might have thought I didn't have time or did not want to help out. Not so. Fact is, I was prepared and ready. It is important for me to let you know that.*

At 2:15 p.m. on January 31, 1989, Reagan called. I wasn't expecting him to respond to my letter. I added the language only to ensure he hadn't been misled. He displayed far more character than his former chief of staff.

> **RR:** *Hi Ken, I got your letter. Thank you, and it was good to hear from you.*

> **KK:** *Welcome home, sir. It's great to have you back in California.*

> **RR:** *I just want you to understand what happened with regard to the speech. I wasn't avoiding you for any other reason. I would have felt guilty dragooning you into another project. I just didn't want to impose on you again.*

Reagan disliked personal confrontation, and the call was awkward. He searched for a way to reflect remorse, and one way was to seek a rationale he thought I could accept.

> **RR:** *I did most of the work on the speech myself. I got a little help in typing from that young girl. She happened to be around* [referring to Peggy Noonan].

That was a stretch—contrition by way of a fib. While Noonan is gifted and creative with words, I'm confident he *did* put a strong personal imprint on the farewell address, just as he did on his inaugural address. I learned over eight years how his storytelling worked, and I accepted Reagan's going outside the boundaries to salve my wounds. He quickly changed subjects.

> **RR:** *My hand is healing well from an operation on my finger, and I have a nice view looking out the window, though it's a little hazy over the ocean today. We're unpacking, and it's getting to be tiring. Our office here looks out on the 20th Century Fox lot below.*

It was uncomfortable dragging the conversation out, so I brought it to an end.

> **KK:** *Mr. President, there's probably one thing you haven't realized. Tom Wolfe was wrong. You* can *go home again. Hope to see you soon.*

Chapter 25

THE LIONS GATHER

Between the fall of the Berlin Wall and the Soviet Union's collapse, Richard Nixon and Ronald Reagan sat for a private talk about nuclear arms control, their assessment of Soviet leader Gorbachev, and the future shape of Eastern Europe. I attended and made detailed notes of this extraordinary meeting between the presidential legends who presided over the Cold War.

Nixon was in California for the July 19, 1990, dedication of his presidential library for which RN gave me responsibility of overseeing. I had completed my former White House colleague John Whitaker's pioneering work with the facility's site selection, and the library was conveniently adjacent to Nixon's Yorba Linda birthplace home. Nixon asked me to accompany him on the courtesy call to Reagan because of my mutual associations, and he also knew I would find the history of their visit fascinating.

I left San Clemente early on July 17 to preside over a "countdown meeting," where Nixon's former chief of advance, Ron Walker, laid out his plans for managing the library's opening day, and the young executive director, Hugh Hewitt, fresh out of Reagan's White House counsel's office, ran through guest lists and timelines. I later met Nixon for lunch at the Century Plaza from which, after a five-minute ride, Reagan greeted us at his Fox Plaza office, joined by his genial chief of staff, Fred Ryan, and public affairs assistant, Mark Weinberg.

I had not seen the Gipper since the New Orleans convention and our last visit was over the awkward phone call when he manufactured the transparent cover story about his farewell address and getting "a little help in typing from that young girl." That was the furthest thing from my mind when he cocked his head, flashed a broad, warm smile, and clasped my hand— like we expected to collaborate on the next State of the Union address. He wore a dark, chocolate-colored suit with two-tone brown tie held in place by a tie tack. It wasn't the latest Westside fashion and an ensemble only he could pull off. However, with not a hair out of place, he still looked like he could step onto the set to host *General Electric Theatre*—television's third most popular show in the mid-1950s. Nixon looked relaxed with good color and wore a standard blue-gray pinstriped suit and blue-checked tie.

Reagan gave RN a brief office tour, showing his many mementos—especially proud of four saddles gifted by Walter Annenberg, each representing, in succession, a study of the western saddle.[xvi] As Reagan beamed while his hands massaged the leathers, Nixon feigned interest, the kind of attentiveness politicians learn to master as protocol. The two of them shared a common bond of professional regard, but still occupied two disparate cultural galaxies.

Trying to read how Reagan viewed Nixon wasn't easy—no different than the difficulty I had over many years in reading his interactions with me, staff, or visitors. Nevertheless, I knew from the two presidential campaigns and in personal crises, Reagan appreciated the breadth of experience and wisdom his predecessor possessed. Nixon's advice was faithfully solicited and absorbed in those key situations. That day, I saw a certain deference in the way Reagan engaged with Nixon—only perceptible to one looking for it, and probably owing to the senior status Nixon had earned from decades in politics, government, and diplomacy. Putting it in perspective: The summer that Ron Reagan was playing Grover Cleveland Alexander with costar Doris Day in Warner Brothers' *The Winning Team*, Dick Nixon was accepting the nomination as Dwight Eisenhower's running mate as vice president of the United States.

I knew from our dozens of conversations that Nixon's opinion of Reagan was mixed. He didn't think of Reagan as a student or deep thinker, but unlike his peers in the '60s and '70s, Nixon never underestimated him and praised Reagan's flexible mind. He spoke with great respect—and a little envy—about Reagan's communications skills, breaking down for me how Reagan's word pictures and the timbre of his voice could affect entire movements. Nixon also paid Reagan the ultimate compliment; he viewed him as a potentially dangerous political rival in 1968, the one person capa-

---

xvi Annenberg was Nixon's Ambassador to the Court of St. James, and his wife, Lenore, served briefly as Reagan's Chief of Protocol of the United States. The couple were strong political and financial supporters of both presidents.

ble of disrupting his path to the nomination. Paying this courtesy call was more than a gesture, it reflected Nixon's admiration for Reagan's presidency and how he emerged revered by his fellow citizens.

As they began their forty-six-minute visit, I scribbled notes as verbatim as possible—the closest transcript existing of their historic dialogue.

Nixon broke the ice with small talk: "When's your library going to open?"

Ryan answered for his boss: "Next November."

> **RN:** I want to come to your library's opening; just let me know.

Reagan chuckled: "I saw Carter's library and visited him there, and it was strange, he said: 'don't kick me out of your dedication.'"

Nixon shook his head, "Jimmy Carter's strange, isn't he? I talked him out of selling Camp David. He actually wanted to sell Camp David. The Camp David Accords [agreements signed by Egyptian president Anwar Sadat and Israeli prime minister Menachem Begin] were the only positive thing in his administration."

> **RR:** I loved Camp David. It was like living in a ranch house again.

> **RN:** I got more constructive work there than almost anywhere else. There, and the Lincoln Sitting Room.

There was a brief pause, and I looked to reflect on yet another cultural chasm between the two. Nixon went to Camp David to work, contemplate, write, and make policy. While he sometimes went for walks or used the bowling alley, Camp David was the Old Man's place to think out his presidency. For Reagan, Camp David was his East Coast ranch—to don jodhpurs and riding boots in the daytime and watch movies in Aspen Lodge at night. There were many occasions he worked there, such as on the 1981 economic speech to Congress or the '87 SOTU, but he clearly viewed the retreat through a different lens than Nixon.

Nixon asked, "Do you still ride? How do you do it?"

That was the kind of question the Gipper liked, and he smiled. "I just got back from the ranch four days ago. I learned how to ride while doing Des Moines radio and was attached to the Horse Cavalry. Horses are used as great therapy for children." I mouthed Reagan's next line quietly because

I had heard him say it dozens of times: "There's nothing so good for the inside of a man as the outside of a horse."[xvii]

> **RN:** Let me say, Ron, I really appreciate you and Nancy coming to my library opening. It's so good that you're coming. It's the first time ever that four presidents will be at the opening of a presidential library. [Laughing] For sure the first time four First Ladies!

> **RR:** From a scholarly point of view, it's a place where real students can find the truth.

Revealing a few decades of bruises, Nixon replied: "It's a place where you'll find balance, for sure, because you shouldn't leave the verdict of history just to professional historians, and history involves much more than instant historians."

Reagan changed subjects. "Thanks for sending me your book; it's just tremendous."[280] Of all RN's postpresidential books, this one was among the most interesting and revealing—certainly since his memoirs were published a dozen years earlier. It was not as policy centered as the others, and perhaps the personal element was a factor in triggering Reagan's interest.

> **RN:** Let me say, I know you're working on your book.[281]
> Writing a book is worse than having a baby.

RN caught himself in the awkward statement and sheepishly added, "although I've never had a baby." We all laughed, and Nixon moved on, "You may use anything I've written and use it in your book. You might find some of the information there useful to round things off."

Then, Nixon quoted Churchill: "History will treat me well because I intend to write it." Reagan threw his head back and laughed at the recital of one of Churchill's most repeated quotes. The small talk of writing books droned on, led by RN. "I've had six national bestsellers, and none got a

---

xvii It was additional proof Reagan's life was shaped by Hollywood. It appears that he cribbed that line from the 1964 Alfred Hitchcock movie, "Marnie." There were three screenwriters on that adaptation of the Winston Graham novel, so I'm unsure if the credit goes to the novelist or the screenwriters. But those exact words are spoken by the character Mark (played by Sean Connery) to Marnie (played by Tippie Hedren) while riding alongside her.

positive review in the *New York Times*. Let me tell you, Ron; what we have going for us is that there is a fair-mind sentiment out there which is not affected by the bias."

Reagan's press coverage wasn't unanimously positive over the years, so it was unsurprising when he jumped in with his own experience: "When I was speaking for G.E., I was often interviewed by the press in the late '50s and early '60s, and there had never been such a hostile gathering as the one I had at the *New York Times*."

I decided it was time to change the subject. I was curious how they first met, and I interrupted to ask: "Do either, or both of you, recall when you first met, and what those circumstances were?"

> **RN:** I had seen your movies, and the first time in person was when you were President of the Screen Actors Guild, and you came to testify before the House Committee on Un-American Activities. I remember you came and appeared at our "Hollywood hearings" regarding possible communist infiltration in the film industry. I checked the record; I didn't ask one question.

> **RR:** I was a diehard Democrat.

Indeed, Reagan had campaigned for Nixon's 1950 Senate opponent, the congresswoman and former Hollywood actress Helen Gahagan Douglas. Reagan continued, "But you had one friend there you never knew about, and that was Ralph Cordiner, the head of General Electric. I gave speeches attacking the TVA [Tennessee Valley Authority]. When I did that, the TVA threatened to take $50 million a year from G.E. So, I called up Cordiner and wondered if I had gone too far. And he defended me; took me aside and said, 'I've never told an employee of G.E. what to say, and I'm not going to start now.'"

Nixon interrupted. "A lot of business guys today have no guts."

> **RR:** Cordiner knew I was a Democrat, and when I was going to run for office, Ralph told me all about you [gesturing toward RN], and how you did things. So, I went to you and told you I was going to become a Republican and support you. And you told me to wait until after the elec-

tion to change my party affiliation—it would be better that way. [A reference to the 1960 presidential campaign.]

That was shrewd on Nixon's part. He knew Reagan would be more effective campaigning for him as a "Democrat who saw the light" rather than as a newly minted partisan Republican.

The Old Man was chafing at the continued small talk, and he shifted gears.

RN: It's interesting to see how the world is changing.

On cue, Reagan provided the precise opening Nixon sought, and asked him, "Have you met Gorbachev?"

RN: I met him in 1986. What's interesting is because when he first went in, he wasn't a reformer. In '86 we talked about arms control, and I told him how important it was to have proper relations with you. I would never criticize the president because—as you know from sitting there—he sees things we don't see.

RR: He [Gorbachev] had an economic basket case because of military spending.

RN: Gorbachev is no closet democrat. And regarding financing Perestroika:[xviii] Number one, Gorbachev should finance it by stopping subsidies of communists in the third world, saving $15 billion a year. And number two, Gorbachev could cut his military budget.

Nixon was in his element, and from time to time glanced over to look for reactions from the three of us observers. "There is an excellent book I just read, by Judy Shelton at the Hoover Institution. And she points out that even after cuts, the Soviets are spending twenty percent of their GNP on the military!"

RR: We should rely on deeds and not words. Gorbachev is the first leader in Soviet history to actually destroy weapons.

---

xviii Perestroika was the policy or practice of reforming the political and economic system in the Soviet Union in the 1980s and '90s.

RN: Well, it's an awesome power they have.

RR: In the first summit in Geneva, I suggested we take a walk and Gorbachev jumped out of his chair. We found a fireside in the boathouse and sat down. I said to him, "We're the only two men who could start World War III, and the only two who could bring world peace. If we don't find a way to reduce arms, then we'll start an arms race all over again, and that's one race you can't win." [Then shaking his head] But, how the hell do you convert all those factories?

Reagan had just referred to the Russians' challenge in converting their military economy to peaceful uses, and Nixon took up the theme. "Eastern Europe wouldn't have free markets overnight. The problem is that those who are experienced in running things are out. So, who's going to run it now? Who will run the system if they try to convert the economy? Remember World War II? Under the Morgenthau Plan, no one in the old German government could have a place in the new one. Henry Morgenthau, Jr. was Secretary of Treasury under FDR. But you had to have some of them from the old regime to make it work to do it. That was the cause for the German miracle after the war. So, it's the same problem for the Soviets. They got rid of the old ones, but then now who's going to run things?"

I spent a decade and a half in close, confidential contact with these two presidents. It would have been easy to be jaded about my relationships—whether hearing about history or making it. Today's occasion was different. It was the first time I was with them together, and they talked of serious things. Sure, I had heard many of these stories before, but in exchange with one another changed the level of the playing field. What if at another time, I was in a meeting between FDR and Truman? Or Eisenhower and Kennedy? I was with the presidential giants of modern America who, in sequential decades, had negotiated with the world's other great superpowers, and at this moment, they were sharing some of their extraordinary experiences in my presence. I managed a glance over at Ryan and Weinberg, whose faces had the look of two choirboys thrust into a Vatican audience. I was also reminded one more time of the distance traveled from my country school and dusty farm.

RR: Bismarck[xix] made everyone shareholders. It was his way of privatizing. Gorbachev's talked about leaseholds for farmers—learning from the Chinese. It's easier than trying to turn everything around. In the United States, we did it with land grants.

RN: You remember the Homestead Act.[xx] The Poles are trying to do it by giving people stock. But getting back to Gorbachev's problem. He looks at Eastern Europe, and even the reformers get thrown out. Gorbachev has the same problem. He can't leave the Communist Party because he doesn't have the base. But if he remains in the Communist Party, will he still be a reformer?

RR: Well, instead, of opposing sovereignty, Gorbachev should support a collection of states, like the United States.

RN: You mean federalize it?

RR: Yes. When I met him, I knew there was a chemistry. We could go nose to nose, but then go out arm in arm. He gave me a bear hug in San Francisco when I saw him last month. Gorbachev is different from all the others.

Nixon rose, and a photographer came in to memorialize the visit, with each former president jovial and relaxed. Separated by only two years in age and so different from one another, these legends had shaped three decades of the twentieth century. On the short drive back, the Old Man's assessment was how "interesting" he found Reagan, and how he had changed from

---

xix   Otto von Bismarck, 19th century German Chancellor
xx   1862—public land given to homesteaders opening the west

the days he knew him as governor and candidate. "Ken, he grew in the presidency." The rush hour traffic on the 405 Freeway allowed me plenty of time to absorb what I witnessed.

The social call that brought Richard Nixon and Ronald Reagan together aptly summarizes my political adventure. They represented, in equal proportions, exhilarating highs and devastating lows in my professional life—connecting threads in my personal journey. What has been underobserved and unappreciated by historians is the positive connectivity in their careers. Their lives were shaped by the '20s, '30s, and '40s, but their educations, grasps of politics, and visions for America and the world found different pathways in their callings. They followed each other, learned from one another, and even shared staffs over the years. In that July 1990 meeting, I learned that early in his career, Reagan was mentored by Nixon at the urging of Ralph Cordiner. I also know that Nixon's frequent references to Reagan's communications methods proved that he sought to adopt them in his own speeches.

No one disputes they were wholly different in style, in outside interests, and in how they approached politics. Despite being shaped by different perspectives, their conversation on Fox Plaza's thirty-fourth floor underscored my conviction that during the Reagan presidency, the two lions converged in the kind of unity reflective of a better time. As a political junkie, I wondered who would have prevailed in a one-on-one campaign. Nixon might have underestimated Reagan's toughness. Reagan would have underestimated Nixon's communication skills. An epic contest.

What wonderful good fortune for me to have been at their service, and, for the country, for each of them to have served.

Appendix

APPENDIX 1

RICHARD NIXON

September 12, 1980

Dear Ron,

    I can imagine that you are getting all
kinds of advice on the debates.... I hesitate
to burden you but I thought it might be useful
if I passed on some observations based on my
experience in 1960 with Kennedy and my analysis
of the situation you face.

    You should continue to insist that Anderson
be included in the first debate. Under no
circumstances should you agree to a one on
one with Carter until after he appears in a
debate with Anderson. In 1960 the press agreed
that I won the last three debates but because
I looked so bad I lost the first and it was
the one with the biggest audience.

    I strongly urge that you take off at
least two full days before the first debate
for preparation. If events have been scheduled
let Bush fill in for you and also have him try
to make major news in that period. One effective
move would be for him to demand that Carter
answer five or six tough questions in the
debate - which your staff should prepare.

    On the day of the debate I would suggest
that you allow no interruption except for a
fast breaking news story or for checking out
a fact where you feel the need to do so. You
know what I learned the hard way in 1960 - that
how you look is if anything more important than
what you say. Let Carter come over up tight,
nitpicking and mean. You should be a contrast -
strong but not shrill; in command, poised -
the big man versus the little man.

    If you have not made other plans I strongly
recommend that Pat Buchanan be asked to prepare
the briefing book. He is smart, quick and brief.

- 2 -

He will come up with some good lines. Some of
his rhetoric may be too tough but you can tone
it down. There is no one on the scene who can
do it half as well as he can except for Bill
Safire and of course he would not be available.
Most important, as you know, Pat is a long time
Reagan loyalist.

Prior to the debate I would hope your staff
could get our media "friends" to paint you as
the underdog. I believe you will do better than
Carter but you will appear much better if the
public has been conditioned to expect Carter
to win.

A tactic Kennedy used effectively was to
virtually ignore a question where he had no
good answer and to make points he wanted made.
I would suggest you ask your shrewdest advisors,
including Buchanan who is very good at it, to
list eight or ten points they would like to
see you make. Then make them even if the
questions do not call directly for that kind
of answer.

During the debate take on Carter and slough
off questions which would try to get you to
fight with Anderson. Let Carter take on
Anderson.

I have a couple of suggestions on issues.
Carter's greatest weakness from the standpoint
of the average voter is his economic policy.
Even with the latest slight down turn in August,
there are more people unemployed today, over
8,000,000, than at any time in the last 40 years
and 200,000 more than when he took office.
Always talk about the number unemployed rather
than the percentage.

But the bigger issue is inflation. Unemployment affects only those who have lost their
jobs or who are afraid they will lose their jobs.
Inflation affects everybody. If someone saved
$100 in January 1977 and put it into life
insurance or a pension, the Carter inflation

- 3 -

<u>tax</u> has reduced that to $70 in 1980. After
four more years of Carter that $100 will be
worth only $40.

Looking at the wage earner, the average
weekly wage when Carter took office was $176.
Today it is $232. But today's $232 will buy
$20 less than the $176 could buy in 1977.

You probably have better examples but I
would urge you to always put it in terms of
the average worker or saver. In that connection
with food prices skyrocketing ask Pete Daily
to prepare one of those market basket T.V.
commercials. This is what people can understand.
They care about the size of the federal budget
only when they can relate it to the size of
the family budget.

Despite the Carter surge in the polls which
was predictable I am confident that you will
win. In the final analysis in a close election
it comes down to how people look at the two
men. You come over on T.V. like gangbusters
and despite his glibness with facts and figures
he comes over like a little man. That is why
I have told people that while he might win the
debate, which I would question, you will certainly
win the audience.

Pat and I will be watching and counting
our Chinese good luck beads!

Best regards to Nancy.

Sincerely,

Richard Nixon

The Honorable
Ronald Reagan

APPENDIX 2

RICHARD NIXON
October 22, 1980

MEMO FOR: Governor Reagan

The following observations reflect some thoughts Ray Price and I have developed with regard to the decisive last two weeks of the campaign.

Analysis

The four principal needs now are: 1) to reassure possible Reagan voters that he is not an ogre, an imbecile, or one who will blunder us into war; 2) to continue the erosion of Carter's "good guy," "trustworthy and true" public image; 3) to remind the voters of what a disaster the Carter presidency has been, for them personally and for the country; and 4) to give the voters not only a negative reason to vote against Carter, but also a positive reason to vote for Reagan.

Given what appear to be the dominant present attitudes, in the final analysis the election is probably going to turn principally on how the voters balance their doubts. We want to soften the doubts about Reagan, while hardening the doubts about Carter.

In Carter's case, we want to harden their doubts about:

- Character
- Competence
- Handling the economy
- Naivete about defense and foreign policy

In Reagan's case, we want to soften doubts about:

- Competence
- "He'll get us into war"

- 2 -

Reagan needs a strong finish -- a determined drive to the wire, not to protect a fragile lead but to lead a frazzled country.

Those people out there in never-never land where the verbal artillery barrages are dropping, and who are saying "never, never" to both sides, need a reason to vote for Reagan. They need at least a glimmering of faith that he can and will provide that sense of direction that the country has lost and yearns for.

In these final weeks, Reagan needs to come across as a man with a mission -- as the leader of a "crusade," as Eisenhower was both portrayed and perceived in 1952.

This isn't just a narrow ideological crusade; Carter's not that identifiable an ideological target. It's a crusade to replace incompetence with competence, polls with soul, drift with direction.

Carterism means Billy and the rest of the Carters slopping around the hog trough, while Jimmy bares his teeth, ices his eyes and prates of his virtue.

It means a Georgia gang that know everything about below-the-belt campaigning, and nothing about running the country.

It means a slander and sanctimony, hypocrisy and hyperbole, meanness and mediocrity.

If Carter were competent, perhaps we could forgive him his personal failures. But his sole claim to the office was that he was somehow, personally, better than the rest of us, that he was holier-than-thou, more good, kind, loving, honest selfless, ethical -- but now he has exposed himself. On the campaign trail he's opened his overcoat to show us Jimmy, Jimmy the mean-spirited, the small-minded, the vicious. He's shown us that Carter the man is, after all, no better than the dismal record of Carter the President.

- 3 -

We've had four years of leadership by a man
who wanted desperately' to be President, but who
had no coherent idea of what he wanted to do with
the Presidency; and now that he sees the prospect
that his precious Presidential seal is about to
be ripped from his hands, he's getting mean and
desperate -- but still showing no sense of purpose
beyond his own ambition, his own ego, his own stubbor
pride.

Carter has come to identify himself with the
Presidency, in an almost imperial and certainly
imperious way, but as a mantle for himself, not
as an office to be used in the service of a larger
mission. Reagan has a mission; he views the
office as a means of pursuing that mission.

The Reagan "crusade" has two aspects. One
is the negative view of what these next few years
will bring if we don't get rid of Carter. The
other is Reagan's own positive view of America
and its future. The negative view is of the
meanness, the scheming, the manipulation, the
self-service, of the Georgia gang, and the cost
to the nation of weakness and drift. The positive
view is one of unlocking the nation's -- and the
people's -- potential, of renewing the upward climb,
getting us back on track, enlisting our energies
and energizing our hopes, fulfilling our dreams,
restoring our strength and ensuring our security.

An important theme to get across is this:

As the campaign winds down to its final days,
both pundits and people are calling it empty and
bewailing the frailties of both major candidates.
This of course is in large part due to the nature
of media, and especially television coverage, which
would reduce any candidate to rubble. But it does
reflect the fact that most people are still not
persuaded that either candidate has the self-evident
stature one would hope for from the prospective
leader of the free world at a time of maximum crisis.

Yet there is a choice -- a clear choice.
Carter has demonstrated clearly for the past four
years what we can expect from him if we give him

- 4 -

another four. Reagan has, over the years, given
a consistent picture of the direction from which
he would approach a president's tasks, the philosophical orientation that would guide his choices -
but also has demonstrated the flexibility to adapt
that philosophical orientation to changing circumstances, and the capacity to compromise where
necessary. Thus we can't predict with certainty
just what his reaction in a given situation would
be, but we can be pretty well aware of the kinds
of considerations that would guide him.

Reagan wouldn't dismantle the Federal government, but he would place the burden of proof on
those who want more government rather than less.

Reagan wouldn't launch us willy-nilly into
an all-out arms race, but he would place the burden
of proof on those who say we should have fewer
arms rather than more.

Reagan wouldn't send our armed forces careening
to every trouble-spot around the globe, but he
would be readier than Carter to use the credible
threat of force in situations where our interests
were directly threatened. This is the only way
to defend our interests and deter the use of force
by our enemies. In a nutshell, Reagan stands for
power not because he wants war but because this
is the only way to keep the peace.

These are important differences. And, at a
time when the Soviets are rapidly surpassing us
in military power, and when every tinhorn dictator
in the world is learning to treat the United States
as fair game for mischief-making, they could, in
the most precise and sobering sense of the word,
be vital differences.

Tactics

The economy is Reagan's issue because Carter
has no answer for the inflation and unemployment
his policies have created. Foreign policy is Carter's
best issue because of the fears he has been able
to raise on Reagan. If voters are thinking primarily
of the pocketbook issue when they vote, Reagan will

win. If they are thinking primarily of the
fear of war, Carter will win.

The tactics become obvious. For the last two
weeks Reagan, Bush, the surrogates, and the ads
must keep inflation and unemployment front and
center and address foreign policy only to the
extent necessary to reassure voters who have fears
about Reagan. I believe the debate will have a
very positive effect on that score.

The practice of having a different speech
each day should be discarded for this period.
Repeat over and over again the inflation and
unemployment themes. Don't give the media a
chance to report on other issues. They will
desperately try to avoid reporting on the eco-
comic issue not because they think it is an old
story(which they will contend) but because deep
down they know it helps Reagan and hurts Carter.
Don't let them get away with it.

In these last two weeks big crowds and
audience enthusiasm is essential. I urge again
that you over rule the P.R. types who want out-
door rallies for "color" purposes. Packed halls
where they can't say that crowds were less than
expected are essential. In addition, the applause
factor is at least three times as great in a
hall as it is outdoors.

In this period, use your best cheer lines
even if you are tired of them. The time is past
for reading important but dull lines prepared by
speech writers. Hammer the same themes so that
the voters are forced to focus on your issues and
avoid scattering your shots. Otherwise, undecided
voters will not be motivated to vote for a change
and will vote for the incumbent. Hit hard. Excite
people. A complacent electorate always votes for
the incumbent.

In the debate, let the visual and verbal
image be the contrast between a small man in a
big job and a big man for a big job.

- 6 -

Possible Quotes(some for surrogates; others for Reagan)

"If Carter's energy policy is, as he once
boasted, the moral equivalent of war, I'd hate
to think how he'd perform as Commander-in-Chief.
If his military performance was the moral equivalent of his energy policies, he'd probably be
bombing our own cities."

_____   _____

"Why do I care so deeply about winning this
election? Because I don't think America can afford
to continue for four more years on the course that
it's on."

"We can't afford to continue the shameful
neglect of our defenses. We can't afford to
continue waffling and wobbling and wavering in
our foreign policy, so that our allies don't
trust us, our adversaries don't fear us and nobody respects us."

"What has increased the danger of war has
been a consistent pattern of inconsistency, a
weakening of our defenses against war, a failure
to recognize that strength is the surest guardian
of peace."

"If we continue on that course, then within
the next four years we'll either be at war or be
well on our way to defeat without war."

_____   _____

"I didn't get into politics and then search
for something I could point to as a set of beliefs.
I developed a set of beliefs, and then these led
me into politics. That's one of the fundamental
differences between us."

"I've been advocating these principles for
20 years -- on the lecture circuit, in radio and
newspaper commentaries, in the political arena --
for eight years as Governor of the nation's largest
and most diverse state, and in three campaigns
for my party's presidential nomination. I've
adapted to changing circumstances, I've made those

- 7 -

compromises that are the essence of a democratic
system, I've sometimes signed legislation that
I didn't agree with as part of the give-and-take
of a free society. But on the basic principles,
my record has been consistent over these 20 years."

"Anyone who would take casual, off-hand
remarks that someone made 10 or 15 years ago,
rip them out of context and try to sell them to
the American public as if they were considered
statements of policy isn't just being dishonest
toward his opponent. He's being dishonest toward
the American people."

"In his repeated distortions of my positions,
President Carter is not just lying about me. He's
lying to the American people, and that's a much
more serious thing.

"The only President in the whole 20th Century
who served two full terms and who didn't get the
country into war was Dwight D. Eisenhower. During
his first months in office Eisenhower ended the
war in Korea, and he kept the peace for the rest
of his eight years in office."

"How did he do it?"

"By weakness? No. By waffling? No. By
truckling to the truculent? No."

"He did it by keeping the United States strong,
consistent and respected -- whereas under Carter
America has become weak, waffling and held in contempt."

(If some version of this is used, note that
the precise wording is important. We cannot say
"who served two full terms without getting the
country into war;" the U.S. didn't enter World
War II until FDR was in his third term.)

387

- 8 -

"Where others have a soul, Carter has a poll."

"Carter vs. Reagan: a man with ambition vs. a man with a mission."

"Carter has blown so much smoke in his campaign speeches that they're going to give him this year's Oscar for special effects."

"It's funny that a saint would be surrounded by so many sinners."

"The question is not whether we're going to stumble into a shooting war. It's whether we're going to continue drifting toward defeat in a non-shooting war."

"It's time for the people of America to take this country back again -- to take it back from the politicians, take it back from the bureaucracy, and claim it as their own again."

"Those pioneers who crossed the ocean from Europe 300 years ago, 200 years ago, 100 years ago, and who crossed the land itself in covered wagons -- they made this country their own. They created something new in human experience -- a land born in freedom, built on liberty, a land that belonged to its people. And because of this, America thrived and grew, and became the richest, the strongest, most respected nation on earth."

- 9 -

"But then something happened. We turned to
the Federal government to meet more and more of
our needs, to satisfy more and more of our wants --
and for a while, this seemed to work. But then
the government got bigger and bigger, more powerful,
more intrusive. Taxes got higher and higher, and
the government spent more and more, and inflation
ate away at our currency and at our incomes. And
as all this was happening, people began to feel
powerless, to feel no longer in control of their
lives, to be uneasy, fretful, fearful, insecure --
in a word, dependent, rather than independent --
dependent on the whims of Federal workers, on the
dictates of Federal courts, and trapped in a maze
of laws and regulations so vast and so tangled
that no one could even read them all in a lifetime,
much less understand them."

"This has gove too far. If I'm elected, I'm
not going to dismantle the Federal government. But
I'm darn sure going to whittle away at it every
chance that I get. And I'm going to do everything
I can to turn power back to the people, recognizing
of course that it takes time to adapt to new ways
of doing things. But the direction of change is
going to be away from bigger government, and toward
freer people, away from arrogance in Washington and
toward independence on Main Street."

"I don't question Mr. Carter's sincerity when
he says he believes his policies will lead to peace."

"I am sure he sincerely believed that when
he cut out the BI and delayed other weapon programs,
the Soviet Union would respond by cutting back
their defense programs."

"I am sure he was sincere when he said we
should not have an inordinate fear of communism
and that Mr. Brezhnev wanted peace just as we do."

"I am sure he is sincere when he approves
going ahead with arms control in spite of Soviet
aggression in Afghanistan, their conquest of Angola,
Ethiopia and South Yemem, and their brigade in Cuba."

- 10 -

"I don't question his sincerity. What concerns me is that he believes so sincerely in the wrong things."

"During his presidency, over 100,000,000 people have come under communist control or have been lost to the West. The Soviet Union has become number one in military power and the United States has slipped to number two. We simply can't take the terrible risk of four more years of Jimmy Carter in the White House. It is time to stop the retreat and defeat which could inevitably lead us to war or defeat without war."

_____   _____

"There is nothing wrong with America that new leadership can't cure. After campaigning across this great land of ours and looking into the faces of millions of great people, I say the heart of America is sound. What America needs is a new head."

_____   _____

"The Jimmying of the economic statistics by the liberal bureaucrats in the department of labor isn't fooling the American people. America knows that Carter's inflation is making it impossible to balance the family budget, they know that Carter's high interest is destroying the ability of young Americans to realize their dreams of owning their own homes. 8,000,000 unemployed Americans want jobs -- not phony-statistics which tell them things are getting better."

"Based on his record of failure, four more years of Carter's policies means four more years of higher unemployment, higher prices, higher interest rates and a lower standard of living for millions of Americans."

"He has had his chance and he has struck out on all fronts. It's time to bench him and to get a new batter up to the plate."

_____   _____

- 11 -

"The October surprise which the Carter crowd
has been desperately trying to pull off is not
going to work. It's too late and whatever they
pull, it will be too little. The American people
are too smart to be fooled by such a shabby
trick."

"A last minute gimmick cannot cover up the
abject failure of the Carter administration at
home and abroad. Millions who can't make ends
meet aren't going to be fooled. Millions who
have lost their jobs aren't going to be fooled.
Millions who see America losing strength and
respect around the world aren't going to be
fooled."

"He was able to sell that peanut oil cure-
all once. But people now know it won't work
and they aren't going to buy it again."

Sincerely,

Richard Nixon

The Honorable
Ronald Reagan

Pat joins me in
sending our best wishes for
what we confidently believe
will be many happy returns
for Nancy & you on November 4.

RN

APPENDIX 3

Richard Nixon

10-31-80

Dear Ken,

In the critical days after
the debate – at least one
excerpt should be "The choice"

The "grin & bear it line"
sums up Carter's economic program
in a subtle & effective way.

Now is the time to hit
clean – but hard.

Above all provide lines
which will radiate
strength & confidence –

Warm regards

RN

P.S.
also try a hard hitting
Halloween release – on the
most shocking campaign of
"fear & smear" in our history

RN

392

BEHIND CLOSED DOORS

RICHARD NIXON

October 27, 1980

Possible Debate Questions

Flip-Flop

    The question may well mention a half a a dozen instances in which the Governor has changed his position. It will not be possible to adequately answer each of the charges. The following answer might be a good way to cover the whole subject.

    "Well I hope we don't have a double standard here. As I recall candidate Carter in 1976 said that we should reduce our defense expenditures and in 1980 he says we should increase them. I believe he was wrong then and right now."

    "As far as I am concerned, I believe that anyone who refuses to change his mind when confronted with new facts or a changed situation, isn't fit to be President. Let me emphasize, however, I have not and will not compromise my principles. For example, I believe deeply in private enterprise and generally take a dim view of big government solutions to problems. That is why I originally opposed massive federal aid to New York City and the Chrysler Corporation. However, when I found that Mayor Koch in New York and Lee Iacocca of Chrysler had instituted financially responsible programs which gave real promise of recovery, I decided to support federal aid. I did this because I believe government should help those who demonstrate that they are trying to help themselves. In other words I have changed my position, but not my principle."

The Use of Force

"In dealing with a self-proclaimed aggressive
power, I believe weakness leads to war or surrender
and that strength, wisely maintained and used,
will preserve the peace. History tells us that
time after time since World War II American Presidents
have used the credible threat of force to prevent
war and preserve peace."

"In 1958, President Eisenhower sent Marines
into Lebanon. That action did not lead to war.
It diffused an explosive situation and detered
the Soviet Union from intervening in that area."

"In 1962 when the Russians put missiles in
Cuba, President Kennedy ordered a blockade. There
was no war. Khrushchev backed down and removed
the missiles. That incidentally is in stark
contrast to what happened in 1978. The Russians
put a combat brigade into Cuba. President Carter
protested but did nothing. The brigade is still
there."

"In 1973 when the Soviets threatened to intervene unilaterally in the Mideast war, President
Nixon ordered an alert of our conventional and
nuclear forces. The Soviet troop transports turned
back and the foundation was laid for negotiating
peace."

"I believe that a President has no more
sacred duty than to preserve peace and defend
freedom. I will only use force as a very last
resort after all diplomatic options have been
exhausted. It might be politically popular to rule
out the use of force unless we are directly attacked.
It would be totally irresponsible to do so. We
must recognize that we live in a dangerous world.
Aggressors small and large are on the loose. If
they are not checked, war will be inevitable. That
is the tragic story of Hitler in World War II. Lets
not let it happen again. We should not act as the
world's policeman, but when our interests are
directly threatened, we must make it clear that
we are prepared to defend them. This kind of a
policy will not lead to war. It is the only way
to prevent war, keep the peace, and avoid surrender."

- 3 -

Arms Control - SALT II

"Let us get to the heart of the question. The question is not <u>whether</u> Jimmy Carter or I am for arms control but <u>how</u> we can <u>get</u> arms control. His position is that <u>he</u> will resubmit SALT II to the next Senate. I believe that SALT II is not a good agreement for the United States, but leaving that point aside, even if it were, President Carter did not have the votes to get SALT II through the Senate last year. And he is going to have less support in the next Senate where at least three Senators who supported President Carter on SALT II will have been defeated. To put it bluntly, President Carter's proposal for arms control is a dud. SALT II has no chance whatever to be approved."

"And so the question is how do we get a new agreement? Now I don't want an arms race. However, the difficulty is that for the past few years the Russians have been racing and we haven't. We must make it clear that if there is an arms race we will win. This ironically is the way to avoid an arms race and to get an arms control agreement."

"SALT I is an example. By a margin of one vote the Senate approved an anti-ballistic missile system for the United States. The Soviet Union already had one. Those who voted against ABM said that it would torpedo any chances for the negotiation of arms control. Exactly the opposite proved to be the case and an aggreement limiting both offensive and defensive missiles was negotiated. But if President Nixon and Dr. Kissinger had not had the ABM program in hand at the negotiating table, there would have been no chance whatever to get an agreement. In all walks of life and in international diplomacy, there is one undeniable truth. To get something, you must have something to give."

"In my administration I shall make it clear at the very outset that the United States is prepared not only to limit nuclear arms but reduce them. We must make it clear however, that if we do not get an agreement, we will do what is necessary to restore the balance in nuclear strength which has been so ominously tilted in favor of the Soviets during the Carter years. I believe we will get an

- 4 -

arms agreement if we negotiate in that way. The
Soviets have a far greater incentive than we have.
They know that because of the greatly superior
economic power of the West, if there is an arms
race, they will lose it."

"And so on this whole subject of arms control,
President Carter advocates an approach in SALT II
which has absolutely no chance for success. I
am advocating a new approach which based on the
past record of our dealings with the Soviets has
a very good chance to succeed."

Arms Control - Linkage

"The purpose of arms control is to reduce the
danger of war. What we have to recognize is that
if war comes, it will be because of failure to
resolve political differences, rather than because
of arms buildup. If political differences are not
resolved, there are plenty of arms in the world
already even with the best arms control agreement
possible to blow up the world many times over. Consequently, an arms control agreement by itself
does not reduce the danger of war. That is why it
is essential why the United States make it clear
that while we want arms control we consider Soviet
adventurism to be totally inconsistent with the
overriding goal of avoiding nuclear war and preserving
peace."

Hostages

"All Americans are thankful that our hostages
are coming home. Because of the personal factor,
their tragic ordeal has understandably commanded
much of our attention these past few weeks and
months. Fortunately, their long ordeal is over.
How and why they had to endure it is an issue for
future discussion and debate. Now is the time for
all of us to turn our total attention to those great
issues which will determine our future and the Free
World's future for the next four years and thereafter.
Millions of Americans will be making a critical
decision this week; a decision that will effect

their own fate, the fate of the nation, and the fate
of free people everywhere for years to come."

"The choice could not be more clear. Jimmy
Carter offers no change from policies which at
home have brought us the highest unemployment,
the highest inflation, the highest interest rates
in forty years; and which abroad have made America
second to the Soviet Union in military strength
and have resulted in _____ million people coming
under communist domination or being lost to the
Free World. Four more years of Carter means four
more years of higher prices, higher unemployment,
higher interest rates at home and continued drift
into retreat and defeat abroad. The old leadership
and the old team has failed America on all fronts.
Now Jimmy Carter offers more of the same. He says,
"Tighten your belts, grin and bear it for four more
years." America has had enough of failure.
Americans are fed up to here with incompetence
and failure. That is why on November 4 they are
going to vote for new leadership, a new team, and
new ideas to restore our strength at home and our
prestige abroad."

"Jimmy Carter busting the federal budget is his
business. When his policies bust the family budgets
for millions of Americans it is their business.
The people are going to vote their pocketbooks on
November 4 and send to Washington new leaders who
will stop the rise in the cost of living, reduce
their taxes, and provide jobs for millions who
are unemployed."

"America is a sleeping giant. I have travelled
across this country for the past year. I have
looked into the faces of literally millions of our
fellow citizens in the great cities, in the countryside, in the small towns, on farms, in factories,
in schools and ghettos. I think I know what the
health of America is. The heart of America is
sound. What America needs is a new head. There
is nothing wrong with America that new leadership
won't cure."

- 6 -

Conclusion

"I have been deeply hurt and disappointed in the level of personal attacks in this Presidential campaign. President Carter has said that the choice this November 4 is between war and peace, between black and white, etc. Obviously I don't agree with his assessment of me but I will not respond in kind. There is no question in my mind that all three candidates for President want peace. All three want to bring America together rather than divide it. All three want a better life for the American people. The question is not goals, the question is means. I hope in these next few days we can all stay on the high road discussing the great issues which will effect our future rather than descend to the low road of attacking our opponents on a personal basis."

"President Carter has tried hard. He has worked hard. I don't question his sincerity. The problem is very simple; he sincerely believes in the wrong things."

"He constantly turns to government to solve our problems as contrasted with my position that we should first turn to private enterprise."

"He believes that the very policies which have brought us record high prices, high unemployment, and high interest rates in the past four years are good enough for the next four years. I believe that four years of failure is enough and that we need new policies and a new team."

"He believes that if we will set an example by cutting back our arms programs, the Soviet Union will do likewise. I say that's shockingly naive. The way to get the Soviet leaders to agree to arms control is to make it clear that if they don't agree, they will force us into an arms race that they will lose."

"Shortly before the war between the States, John Brown was riding on the back of a wagon through the Virginia countryside on his way to the gallows.

To no one in particular he said, "Isn't this a
beautiful country."

"This is a beautiful country. I have been
to the great cities of Europe and Asia. I have
enormous respect for the people of those countries
but every time I return to America, I realize that
this is the place. Sometimes people have asked
me why I would go through the ordeal of running
for President. After all I have everything that
any man could want; a loving wife, a fine family,
a beautiful home, a ranch in the beautiful state
of California. Certainly being Governor of the
first state of the Union should be enough to
satisfy any man's ambition.".

"Putting it very simply, America has been very
good to me. I want to do something for America.
I grew up in the depression. I remember when my
father lost his job. I have lived through four
wars. I consider my most sacred duty is to preserve
peace. I have benefited first hand from the fact
that America is a free country and provides opportunities for those who are willing to work hard to
achieve their goals. I want to preserve that
freedom and opportunity for my children and your
children in the years ahead."

"Yes, this is indeed a beautiful country. My
greatest goal in life is to contribute if I can to
making it possible for all Americans to realize
the American dream as I have realized it in my own
life."

Halloween Excerpt

"In a frantic effort to divert attention from
a dismal record of unprecedented incompetence and
failure, Jimmy Carter is trying to frighten people
to vote for him by waging a desperate campaign of
fear and smear."

"Halloween goblins may frighten little children
but the American voters are too smart to be fooled."

- 8 -

"It is time to rip off his mask of self-
righteousness and let people see the failed
leader he has proved himself to be."

APPENDIX 4

RICHARD NIXON
November 17, 1980

Memo to: President-elect Ronald Reagan

From: Richard Nixon

I begin this memo by observing that Nancy and
you have made all Americans proud again by your
conduct during and since the election campaign.
Because of your overwhelming victory and our gains
in the Senate and House, you have a clear mandate
to call them as you see them on both issues and
personnel without regard to the usual political
pressures.

As one who has been there and who seeks or
wants absolutely nothing except your success in
office, I would like to pass on to you some candid
observations based on past experience and on intimate knowledge of some of the people you are considering for major positions.

Priorities: As you know, I believed before the
election that, while foreign policy was to me the
most important issue of the campaign, the economic
issue was the one which would have the greatest
voter impact. Now I am convinced that decisive
action on the inflation front is by far the number
one priority. Unless you are able to shape up our
home base it will be almost impossible to conduct
an effective foreign policy.

Consequently, I would suggest that for at
least six months you not travel abroad and that
you focus the attention of your appointees, the
Congress and the people on your battle against inflation. Your meeting over the weekend with your economic advisors set exactly the right tone for the
months ahead. The time to take the heat for possibly
unpopular budget cuts is in 1981, not 1982 or 1984.

KEN KHACHIGIAN

November 17, 1980   -2-

This does not mean that foreign policy should
be ignored in this period. However, it will require
that you have experienced people in State and
Defense who reflect your views and will carry out
your policies until you can devote more of your
personal time to foreign policy matters.

Personnel Guidelines

There has been a lot of press speculation
about whether you should appoint Nixon-Ford people
or new people to top posts. I have very strong views
on this issue. Based on the foregoing analysis
you cannot afford on-the-job training for your
Secretaries of State and Defense. However, in all
other positions you should put in your own team
unless you conclude that someone who served in the
past is indispensable for your needs now. The
country voted for new leadership. New people will
make mistakes but they will move forward and not
simply play not to lose. I have enormous respect
for those who served in our Administration but many
are worn out; they are, as Disraeli once described
Gladstone, exhausted volcanoes. Washington needs
new men as well as new ideas. By your appointments,
you can give the country a sense of excitement, hope
and drive to government which we have not seen since
F.D.R.

State and Defense

These are the two positions where you have to
go with experience. However, in both cases at the
deputy level a vigorous new individual with proven
management capabilities and some understanding of
foreign and defense policy would be certainly acceptable and preferable to someone who would have so
many ties to the old establishment that he would be
reluctant to do the house cleaning that needs to be
done in both departments.

November 17, 1980   -3-

Based on press reports, I understand that
Kissinger is not under consideration for Secretary
of State. Because of his vast experience he should,
of course, be called upon for advice and to the
extent he is willing, should be asked to undertake
specific negotiating assignments. He is not only
an outstanding strategic thinker but, unlike most
intellectuals, he is a superb operator and negotiator and is a national asset which should not be
wasted.

Whoever is appointed as Secretary of State must
have a thorough understanding not only of Europe,
but of the Soviet Union, China, Japan, the Mideast,
Africa and Latin America. He must also share your
general views with regard to the Soviet threat and
foreign policy generally. These requirements pretty
much limit those who could be considered. Haig
meets them all. He would reassure the Europeans,
give pause to the Russians, and in addition, because
of over five years as Henry's deputy in the White
House and two years at NATO, he has acquired a
great deal of experience in dealing with the Chinese,
the Japanese, the various factions in the Mideast,
the Africans, and the Latin Americans. He is intelligent, strong, and generally shares your views on
foreign policy. Those who oppose him because they
think he is "soft" are either ignorant or stupid.
Others who raise the specter that he was somehow
involved in Watergate simply don't know the facts.
On the contrary, I can vouch from experience that
he did an outstanding job helping to keep the wheels
of government moving during the time we were under
such enormous assault in the Watergate period. He
would be personally loyal to you and would not back-
bite you on or off the record. He has one potential
weakness. Because he is a career man he might be
reluctant to clean house in the State Department to
the extent the situation demands. That is why, at
the deputy level, you might well appoint an administrative type who would come in with a big new broom.

I have noted that Jackson has been suggested
as a possibility for both State and Defense. Even
though I considered him in 1968, I would strongly
recommend against your appointing him in 1980.
He is a hawk on foreign and defense policy. On
the other hand, he is a partisan Democrat on economic and social policy. He campaigned for Bayh,
Church, Culver, et al. It would be necessary for
you to have him leave the room whenever politics
is discussed as it must be at times in Cabinet
meetings. I think he would be more valuable, frankly,
in the Senate rather than in the Administration.

George Shultz has done a superb job in every
government position to which I appointed him. However, I do not believe that he has the depth of
understanding of world issues generally and the
Soviet Union in particular that is needed for this
period.

Connally, next to Haig, understands the major
foreign policy issues and shares your views. He
would have one significant advantage over Haig -
he would clean house from top to bottom with great
enthusiasm. His disadvantage is that his appointment might send many in the American-Jewish community
up the wall.

Among career State Department types I vouch
for Joe Sisco and Walter Stoessel. Both are competent
and honorable. Both would loyally support your policy.
Either would be excellent for the Alexis Johnson
under secretary spot.

Defense

I have noted that Haig has also been suggested
for Defense. I think this would be a mistake. Not
only would it require a change in the law which you
could probably get, but you should avoid wherever
possible appointing someone who is part of an establishment to clean up an establishment. Like you, I
am a strong national defense man. But the Pentagon
should not be a sacred cow. Forty-six percent of
all civilian employees of the government work for
the Defense Department. When we talk about over-

lapping and fat in the bureaucracy you must have
in mind that not only is this the case in the new
agencies like HUD, etc., but that it is also the
case in old line agencies like Defense, Agriculture,
Interior, etc. I would strongly recommend, for
example, that an across-the-board 10% cut in civilian
employment in the Defense Department would result
in more efficient management and would make it much
easier to get support for similar cuts in the non-
defense areas. In going after fraud, for example.
I could not urge more strongly that the Defense
Department should not be considered off limits.

Coming down to specific names, if Haig were to
go to State, Connally, I think, would do an excellent
job for you in Defense. He is a former Secretary
of the Navy, he is an excellent manager, and he
would not be afraid to "tear up the pea patch."
Another off-beat suggestion is that George Shultz
could do an excellent job in this spot. His business
and budget experience would be invaluable in managing
what is the biggest business in the world next to
the total federal government itself.

Whoever gets the top spot here I urge that someone like Bill Clements or Dave Packard be appointed
as deputy. The man at the top can be a political
and strategy man only if the second man is a top
flight businessman.

Treasury

Here you have a number of good people to choose
from. While I think you would be well advised to
select someone entirely new, you could not go wrong
on Bill Simon. He believes as you do, he is an
effective public spokesman, he is a team player and
would be totally loyal. Some believe that he is
too emotional for such a cold-hearted position but
perhaps that could turn out to be an asset. If you
do not go with Simon, Walter Wriston from the outside certainly has to be one of your top choices.
Needless to say, George Shultz would be superb if
you could prevail upon him to take it again. The
same can be said of Connally. If Caspar Weinberger
does not take on Budget again or some other position, I believe he could serve you well in Treasury.

I do not believe you should select an economist. This is a management position and whoever
you appoint can employ plenty of economists. The
place for economists is in the Council for Economic
Advisors and not in the top position at Treasury.
In the event that none of those I have mentioned
meet your needs, one of the very best men from
past administrations is Charls Walker. You would
be extremely well-served to have him in the department as deputy because he is one of those rare tax
experts who would enthusiastically carry out your
views on tax cutting and tax reform.

Attorney General

This is one of your most important positions.
Above all, he must be a man whose personal loyalty
to you is unquestioned. In addition, of course,
he must be an outstanding lawyer and a good admin-
istrator. William French Smith fits the bill
above anyone else I can think of. As you probably
know, I strongly considered him for appointment to
the Supreme Court. He is a legal heavyweight with
impeccable credentials and has been one of your
devoted supporters for years. Another point that
should be made is that your Attorney General will
be making the recommendations to you for all judi-
cial appointments and particularly those to the
Supreme Court. The importance of this is obvious
when you consider the fact that you will probably
appoint at least four and maybe five Justices in
your first term. I very deliberately appointed
conservative Justices to the court who shared my
philosophy that it was the responsibility of the
Court to interpret the law rather than to make it.
Because he had a liberal Attorney General, Ford
appointed Stevens who has lined up with the liberals
on the Court in virtually every significant case.
With someone like Bill Smith advising you, I am
confident you would not make that mistake. You
will leave a great legacy both in your new approach
to economic policy and in your foreign policy. But
the most lasting legacy will be your impact on the
Supreme Court. That is why it is so important that
you appoint as Attorney General someone who shares
your conservative views about the role of the courts
in our system of government.

CIA

I have noted press reports to the effect that
Bill Casey is under consideration for CIA. If he
could take it, I think he would do an excellent job.
I would suggest that as a deputy, Dick Walters be
considered. He had the position before but under
directors who were part of the CIA establishment.
He knows the organization inside out and with a
man at the top to back him up, would do an outstanding job in reinvigorating an organization that has
been castrated by the Carter Administration. He
would probably be reluctant to take this position
since he had it before. In any event, I would
strongly urge that you or one of your top people
consult with him as to what needs to be done within
the agency. Even more than in State and Defense,
CIA needs an entirely new guard and a complete
house cleaning.

OMB

I have noted the reports that you intend to
set up an executive committee of the Cabinet. This
is an excellent idea but I would respectfully suggest
that if you can get someone with the qualifications
of Cap Weinberger for OMB, you should include him
in that group. I don't need to tell you that he is
a superb budget man. He also has a very broad understanding of other agencies of the government. He
is intelligent, he is wise and totally loyal. In
view of these qualifications, he would add greatly
to the breadth and depth of your top Cabinet committee. I would imagine Cap will be reluctant to
come back as Budget Director. But if you upgrade
the position in this way (and I would include him
also in the National Security Council meetings) I
think it would not only make it more attractive for
him but also it would be very much in your interest
as well.

One offbeat suggestion, if Cap is not available,
would be John Connally for OMB. With the job
restructured as I have outlined it he might take it.
He could handle it like gangbusters and would be
enormously helpful as a member of the Cabinet executive committee. Next to Secretary of State, I would
consider the head of OMB to be potentially the most
influential and powerful position in the government.

Energy

For the immediate future oil is the name of
the game. Since you have a Republican Senate, I
believe you should bite the bullet and put a hard-
nosed oil man like John Swearingen in charge. The
press would scream but results count and he would
make things happen. You cannot compromise on this
issue. Churchill once wrote that in war one can
have a policy of audacity or one of caution. Compromise between the two courts disaster. The energy
crisis calls for audacity.

GSA

While GSA is not a Cabinet position, it is
one of the most important appointments you will
make in the domestic area. The corruptio n and
inefficiency is rampant and I think we have seen
only the tip of the iceberg. Here is a spot for
one of your most vigorous, able and hard-charging
businessmen. Give him an absolutely free hand with
a mandate to clean house even though it may affect
some Republicans as well as Democrats. The procedures that he develops in his investigation might
then well be applied in the other government agencies
where there is bound to be fraud and atrocious
management at both high and low levels.

Sub-Cabinet

All deputies should be personally selected and
appointed by you with the guideline in mind of supple-
menting the qualifications of the Cabinet secretaries.
One mistake I made and that others before and since
have made was to allow Cabinet secretaries to bring
along their deputies. This does not mean that you
appoint someone who would not get along with the
Cabinet secretary. It does mean that you will have
someone who adds to what the Cabinet secretary brings
you, and is a voice and not just an echo of the top
man. In making these appointments you could turn
toward young people and new people who have fire in
their bellies. They would be given valuable experience for elevation to the top spot if that became
necessary. Also, they would be the follow-through
group for the top administrators.

November 17, 1980   -9-

        In this connection, I have an idea which is
novel and I think one which would appeal to you.
During the Eisenhower years and during my own term
in office, Cabinet officers often used to complain
to me that during Cabinet meetings the whole room
was filled with members of the White House staffers
who sat behind the Cabinet officers. Some of them
said that they did not like to talk freely with
all of the "pipsqueaks" there in the room. Some of
these complaints were unjustified but they have
some merit. I believe that you should make the
Cabinet meetings very special. Only your chief
substantive man, who I understand will be Ed Meese,
and your Chief of Staff, Jim Baker, and your press
secretary should be invited to attend Cabinet meetings. Other members of the White House staff should
come in only when a matter is up for discussion
affecting their particular area of responsibility
and then should leave the room immediately thereafter. Instead then of having members of the White
House staff sit in the chairs in back of the members
of the Cabinet, you could invite members of the sub-
Cabinet to sit there. This will build them up
enormously. They will then be in a position to
follow through when matters are assigned to Cabinet
secretaries and also they will have an opportunity
to present their own views. If you follow this
procedure, I think you may be able to upgrade deputy
positions to the point that good men and women will
be willing to take those positions almost as readily
as they would take the top Cabinet position. I
strongly urge that you consider this proposal and
whether it appeals to you or not, you should under
no circumstances allow too many members of the White
House staff believe that they have a right to be
present at all Cabinet meetings.

        For the sub-Cabinet, as well as the Cabinet,
I would urge that in addition to the usual minority
groups you consider for appointment representatives
of groups who make up your New Majority - Italians,
Eastern Europeans and Latins. It is time once and
for all to erase the image of the Republican Party
as white, Anglo Saxon and Protestant (WASP.)

Second Level Appointees

As you know, one of the major weaknesses of the Carter Administration was that, while his Cabinet people generally supported his point of view, at the second level the McGovernites totally took over his administration. I cannot urge too strongly that you follow through what I understand from the press is the present intention of cleaning out the second level bureaucrats lock, stock and barrel. You and the Cabinet secretaries will hear some heart-rending stories about how this one or that one has really been a "closet" supporter of yours or is a "true professional."

Two examples demonstrate the danger of being taken in by this line. Bob Finch brought Leon Panetta into HEW. Panetta opposed everything we stood for and eventually resigned and now is a liberal Democratic member of Congress. Henry Kissinger brought people like Morton Halperin, Tony Lake, etc. into the National Security Council staff. I often expressed my concerns to him about them. He assured me that, while they were more "dovish" than I was or he was, they were "professionals" and were honorable men. As you know, they have to a man turned on him and on me. Henry has admitted privately to me that that was one of the greatest mistakes he made. I would urge you not to let this happen again. Particularly in the State, Defense and CIA, don't take the eastern establishment types. There are plenty of intelligent conservatives from the mid-west, the south, and the far west as well as some in the east who can take these positions. What you were elected to do and you must do is to appoint a new breed - people who believe as you do and will carry out your policies. The liberal academics have had their chance and have failed. It is time to build a new establishment.

An example of what you should not for one moment consider doing is the suggestion made by even as good a supporter as U. S. News and World Report that you should retain John Sawhill and others appointed by Carter for the new synthetic energy program. This is nonsense and silly nonsense as well. Here is one place, incidentally, where instead of going to one with an academic background like Sawhill, you should put one of the best business people you could possibly find.

November 17, 1980   -11-

    I have not mentioned the Vice President's
role because I believe that essentially must be
worked out between you and him. He would be
excellent as Director of Congressional Relations,
as liaison with the various campaign committees
or as a special emissary on foreign assignments -
provided the Secretary of State approves.
And don't downgrade good will trips and even
attendance at funerals, inaugurals, etc. Speaking
from experience, I can say that he will learn a
lot and at the same time be in a unique position
to promote and defend the Administration's foreign
policy.

    I hope I have not been presumptuous in making
some of these suggestions. However, as Arthur Burns
once told me in 1969, the best advisors to Presidents
are those who told them what they need to hear
rather than what they want to hear. I hope that
I can always be that kind of advisor to you.

    As far as my own personal situation is con-
cerned, I do not, as you know, seek any official
position. However, I would welcome the opportunity to provide advice in areas where I have
special experience to you and to members of your
Cabinet and the White House staff where you deem
it appropriate. President Eisenhower said to me
when I visited him at Walter Reed Hospital after
the election of 1968, "I am yours to command."
I now say the same to you. I trust that that can
be our relationship in the years ahead.

APPENDIX 5

RICHARD NIXON

January 15, 1981

D. Mike,

I noted in the press that the Inaugural has been completed and I hesitate even to pass on some random thoughts which might be considered for inclusion. I would suggest, therefore, that you scan the attached memo and if you find a thought that is not already covered in the speech or one that you think might appeal to the President-Elect, pass them on to him. I am sending a copy of this to Ken Khachigian for his information in view of the fact that he as I understand it was responsible for coordinating the various suggestions that had been sent in.

In the event that the President-Elect feels comfortable with what he has, please don't bother him with this material. I have learned from experience that once a speech is wrapped up, last minute suggestions can be very irritating and not at all helpful.

With warm regards,

Sincerely,

Richard Nixon

Mr. Mike Deaver

Introduction

One problem in writing an inaugural is to set forth goals for the future without reflecting in an obvious way on the mistakes of the past since Carter will be on the platform.

If it is not already included, an informal grace note at the beginning along the following lines could be a ten strike in beginning the new administration in an atmosphere of good will. I would suggest that this should not be put in the advance text which is given to the press but that he ad-lib it somewhat as a thought that occurred to him on the platform. This way it will greatly increase press attention.

"On behalf of all Americans, I wish to express to President Carter and his First Lady the appreciation of the nation for his years of dedicated service in a difficult period."

"Nothing is more illustrative of the greatness of America than our ability, after debating our differences in a hard campaign, to join together in meeting the challenges we face. The problems we face are grave and urgent. We can solve them only if we are strong and united people. I am confident that President Carter and the millions who supported him will work with us in building a better future for all people at home and abroad."

Foreign Policy (alternate rough draft formulation of a theme)

"This is a time not just to defend freedom but to extend it to those who want it wherever they may be - not by the force of our arms, but by the power of our example."

413

"The hopes and dreams that we had at the
end of World War II for a world free from war
and fear and repression have been shattered.
The world today is spending $500 billion dollars
on arms per year. This is a crime against humanity.
Let us work to lift the burden of arms from the back
of mankind so that we can launch a winning crusade
against poverty, misery, and disease throughout
the world."

"Since World War II, the world has been
divided not because of differences between people
but differences between governments. It is time
for governments to listen to the voice of people
and to resolve our differences so that the burden
or war, poverty, misery, and disease may be lifted
from the back of mankind."

"As I have travelled over this great and good
country over the past 40 years, I have had the
privilege of speaking to and looking into the faces
of millions of Americans. We are a strong, peaceful, generous, and decent people. There is nothing
we desire more than to join with other men and
women of good will to launch a winning crusade
against poverty, misery, and disease throughout
the world."

"We had hoped that World War I was a war to
end all wars. We had prayed that the devastation
that followed World War II would be followed by an
era of unprecedented peace, with differences being
settled in a world forum. Our hopes and dreams
have been shattered. Wars and the fear of war have
plagued us over the past 30 years. The time is now
for total mobilization of our resources to bring the
world the blessings of peace, with the same dedication that we mobilized our efforts to wage war."

"Those who desire peace, freedom, progress, and justice for all people have nothing to fear from the United States."

"Two hundred years ago when the Declaration of Independence brought America into the world, Thomas Jefferson said, "We act not for ourselves alone, for all mankind." Let us consecrate ourselves today to the ideal which inspired us at our birth. Let a new America work with others who share our values to build a new world in which freedom from war, disease, hunger, repression becomes not just a hope, but a reality for all mankind."

"We are an idealistic people. We have come as far as we have because we have always been lifted by our hopes and have never been paralyzed by our fears. But let no one mistake our idealism for naivete or weakness. We are a realistic people. We know that millions have suffered in the past and suffer now from the pestilence of war and terror and despotism. It is our sacred duty to ourselves and future generations to bear the burden of world leadership which destiny has thrust upon us. We like our system. We shall never try to impose it on others who may prefer a different system. We do, however, declare that freedom from war, hunger, disease, and injustice and the God given freedom to choose shall always be our goal, not only for ourselves but for all mankind."

"The challenges we face at home and abroad are urgent and difficult. This is not a time for sappy optimism. But neither is it a time for hopeless pessimism. Americans are always at their best when the goings get toughest. There is nothing we can't accomplish if we commit our minds, our hearts, and our souls to the task."

APPENDIX 6

12-16-83

MEMORANDUM FOR THE PRESIDENT

FROM: Ken Khachigian

RE: Taxes/Contingency Taxes

I hope you'll forgive one more oar into the water on
the tax issue, but I've been a bit concerned about the signals
coming from "sources" in Washington to the effect that, ultimately,
you will have to raise taxes in order to subdue the deficit
monster. Your interview this week helped dampen such talk --
but I'm convinced it will rise again, given the enormous interest
your political adversaries have in seeing the government grow
unabated.

In my view, the tax issue ought to be put to bed -- period.
The fact is that the Congress has never come to grips with the
outrageous spending that marked the 1970s. Indeed, as you know,
budget outlays as a percentage of GNP continue to rise. These
deficits are Congressionally-mandated; they are the result of
liberals in Congress who are simply unwillingly to restrict the
largesse that has become their stock in trade.

Talk of taxes -- contingency or otherwise -- merely allows
your opposition to build a national debate around an agenda they
create instead of one determined by you. This is not unlike
what we went through with TEFRA some 16 months ago. But in that
instance, the Congress completely deceived the American public.
They have not given -- and they probably never intended to give --
the three dollars in spending cuts for every dollar of tax increase.

This is not really a debate over the deficit. It is just
a continuation of the epic struggle between those who want the
government to grow and smother the lives of individuals versus
those who seek economic freedom, opportunity, and expansion through
the miracle of the free market. It is really, once again, the
debate of 1980 -- wherein you made clear that individuals should
keep their money and spend it the way they want to rather than
have the government take their money and spend it the way it wants
to.

Politically, you have the winning side, and the right decision
will also be the best politics. But if we accept the concept of
a "possible" tax or "contingency tax," then I fear that is virtually
a guarantee that after you are re-elected the Congress will look
for an open season on the national treasury.

The Congress ought to have no safety net on this issue.
Beryl Sprinkel has written that the 1981 and 1982 tax cuts have
had the effect of leaving the average tax rate in 1984 essentially

page 2

the same as it was in 1980 -- due to countervailing effects of
higher social security taxes, indirect taxes and bracket creep.
To let this so-called tax-deficit debate drag on will only benefit
those who are practicing the deception that taxes were cut too
deeply in the past three years.

This issue truly defines the legacy of your presidency.
This is perhaps the only chance we'll have in this century to
turn back the juggernaut of government gone crazily out of control.
Combining the Grace Commission recommendations with some very
courageous decisions on entitlements, you can, I believe, recapture
the fervor and excitement of the crusade you led in 1980. And it
was a crusade -- one that rallied the country to something more
than the dreary acceptance of the discredited past.

Moreover, we already hear the Democrats saying that TEFRA
was an "admission" by you that the revolution of 1981 got out of
hand. The mere talk of possible taxes in '85 or '86 will only
fuel the doubt and uncertainty that your opponents are trying to
create. New taxes should not even be an option. When Senator Dole
leaves Washington, he'll find there is life after government --
that the force of America's good relies not on the faked genero-
sity of a Congress which hands out money but on ingenious individuals freed from the oppressive greed of the government.

My recommendation. This year's budget as tight and prudent
as it can be. Then, from January forward, we will carry the fight
to the Congress -- and to the country -- that this government, by
every device of reason and even-handedness shall be sliced and
whittled to dimensions that will ensure economic survival.

Some will tell you that this may be politically risky and
cuts across the national grain. But the answer is that your
leadership has never taken the conventional path; this is less a
risk than an historic opportunity. I'd much rather have us out
on the road boldly standing for a better future than weakly defending the sickness of the past. That's not political risk; that's
political good sense.

# # # #

417

APPENDIX 7

February 27, 1984

MEMORANDUM FOR THE PRESIDENT

FROM: Ken Khachigian

I believe the time has come for you to cut off the deficit talks with the Congress and go on the offensive with a plan that not only recaptures the policy ground for you, but also happens to be good politics as well.

After spending last week in Washington and witnessing the political antics of O'Neill, Wright et al. and their skillful use of your goodwill to blast you nightly, I became further convinced that these talks are pointless. Moreover, this continued fruitless negotiating with the Congress is not playing to the President's strengths, i.e., his ability to rise above the battle and exercise national leadership.

I shared these and other thoughts with Jim Baker last week, and Jim asked that I send you a brief note.

First, make a public announcement that you are disappointed with the Democratic Congressional Leadership's refusal to be realistic or fair. Their plans for new and higher taxes, a post-ponement of indexing, and massively dangerous cuts in the defense budget would put America back where it was four years ago and are plain unacceptable.

The President would then say that he will prepare a detailed downpayment on the deficit, and that he will present these ideas to the Congress and the Nation within 10 days. Remind the public of the fast one pulled by Congress in connection with TEFRA and the President's determination not only to save the recovery, but also to regain a sound financial footing which will keep inflation and interest rates down.

Second, the 10 days before the speech should include some careful preparation by which the American people clearly understand the President's commitment to this process. This must include, in my judgment, a clear and convincing effort by the President to take the initiative with regard to cuts in the Pentagon budget.

I believe, reluctantly, that the President must be visibly in front regarding defense cuts. I come to this conclusion because of my understanding that Congress not only has in mind deeper and more dangerous cuts, but that the Administration would likely have to swallow some of these cuts whether it wants to or not.

page 2

That being the case, why should the President have to take several months of partisan attack and then be forced to accept something that he could have lived with in the first place? If the President takes command of this situation, he would not only be more able to control the cuts, but also demonstrate clearly an ability to lead on a sensitive national concern.

However, defense cuts should not come merely by some vague public pronouncement, but from symbolic Presidential action. In 1981, the President built up great credibility about the budget and Economic Recovery program through conspicuous participation (with constant photo opportunities) in the process. We need to do the same, I believe, with the defense budget.

If the President agrees with this approach, then I believe he should quickly have briefing books prepared for him, and then schedule perhaps two consecutive days (a half day each) of briefings at the Pentagon. Each day the President should be seen on national television and in front page photographs, striding into the Pentagon carrying fat briefing books under each arm. There would be no public comment after each day.

There should be some tough questions for each service, briefings on various weapons systems, and deep discussions with the joint chiefs. Because of this very prominent look into the Defense budget, I'm convinced that the President will be more able to limit the cuts to those which cannot harm the national defense. The public, having witnessed his intense study of the issues, will be better able to accept the President's bottom line -- which, by the way, will reflect his willingness to achieve savings. (It's my under-standing that we are talking in terms of some $10 billion a year in outlays and a little more in obligations.)

Third, these cuts now can be combined with domestic spending cuts and loophole closures to start the effort to control the deficit. I'm told the revenue increases are strictly limited to those which do not inhibit the recovery, which protect the individual cuts and indexing at all costs, and which do not substantially affect the middle class or the poor. The bottom line: this far and no further. America cannot tax itself to prosperity and balanced budgets.

Fourth, this entire package, some ten days after the President announced it, should be presented in a televised Oval Office speech -- an educational speech like the President gave in February 1981. It will explain the cause of the deficit, the clear necessity to preserve the tax cuts, the need to gain control of government, the President's willingness to pare down the Defense budget with cuts that don't use a meat-ax, and the belief that this three-year $100 billion slice into the deficit is just the tonic necessary to keep inflation down, the recovery roaring, and perhaps even encourage interest rates to come down.

page 3

This is one speech that ought to be long enough to get every
argument in -- to set things out with great detail, sound argument
and superb documentation. The goal: to take away from Congress
their ability to determine this agenda, to use the bully pulpit
to put the President back in the pre-eminent leadership role, and
to stimulate public confidence which will preserve all that we have
achieved. And the President ought to make clear that he's acting
because the Congress wishes to politicize this issue.

This will not be sent up in the form of a new budget -- but
it will be our way of asking the Congress to make these changes.
On the other hand, once these recommendations are made, we must
keep the heat on the Congress -- insisting that the package be
as the President presented it, with no compromises on basic
principles and no reduction in the numbers. Follow-up over the
next few weeks is essential as is speaking with only one voice within
the White House. If necessary, for the period of this battle, one
economic spokesman could be designated.

The timing will be superb. This comes in mid-March; the
President's foreign travel, including China, begins in April --
and while the Democrats are flailing around, the President will be
strongly on top of every key public issue there is. These actions
could be a tonic for the Nation. And, with some discipline in GOP
ranks, could put the party as well as the President on a roll into
the Convention. But to repeat -- this entire process requires the
same kind of overriding commitment that was created in 1981. We're
close enough to the end that I'm confident it will all be worthwhile.

Privately, I believe this will give the President all the
latitude he needs to begin the second term with the kind of strong
sense of constancy that has been his strength as President, and
enable us to start phase two, in 1985, of controlling the
growth of government and expanding personal freedoms.

420

APPENDIX 8

THE SCHEDULE OF
PRESIDENT RONALD REAGAN

Tuesday, April 3, 1984

Staff Time *9:03 —* (Baker/Meese/Deaver) *9:23 B. Oglesby — 9:28*	Oval Office
Meeting with GOP *9:33* Congressional Leadership (Oglesby) (TAB A)	Cabinet Room
National Security Briefing *10:21 — 11:32* (McFarlane) *Amo. James Goodby Adelman Shultz* *Sgn. Craimer JB, Ed, Mike, McFarlane*	Oval Office
Personal Staff Time *Att Gen. Smith — 10:59 — 11:09*	Oval Office
Lunch and Personal Staff Time	Oval Office
Drop by Meeting of National Security Telecommunications Advisory Committee (McFarlane) (TAB B)	Indian Treaty Room
Pre-News Conference Briefing *2:04 —* (McManus/Speakes) *4:30 — Kenknachghan, Mkd*	Family Theater
N Private Appointment (Crispen)	Residence

Def

APPENDIX 9

RICHARD NIXON

26 FEDERAL PLAZA
NEW YORK CITY.

10-2-'84

Dear Ken —

Some random thoughts
which may not add to
present state of preparation.

The Econ Club Speech
has excellent lines which
should be repeated, if possible
in the debate.

Always remember — he
is not talking to the media —
but to millions who have
not heard the lines before.

If you get some foreign
policy question to me as
soon as possible I may be
able to provide some good lines.

Sincerely, RN

422

MEMORANDUM FOR KEN KHACHIGIAN

Instead of preparing suggested specific answers to the
questions you sent to me, I think what would be most helpful is
for me to pass on some general observations which might put the
whole event into what I believe is the proper context.

You may not agree with my first observation. I believe the
media and some of those advising the President are wildly
exaggerating the importance and impact of the debates. The reason
for this is that their historical perspective is skewed. Teddy
Kennedy, for example, on a recent TV program, claimed that his
brother overcame a 14-point deficit in the polls as the result of
the debates. Even Dave Gergen, who should have known better,
stated that I was ahead of Kennedy before the first debate and
behind him after. The facts, as you know from having researched
this for RN, are that Gallup showed Kennedy at 51-49 in
mid-September, before the first debate on September 26. He moved
up a point as a result of the first debate, but after three more
debates and thousands of miles of campaigning by both candidates,
it came out a dead heat. There is no question but that Kennedy
did better in the first debate than I did, but the others balanced
it out -- and in any event, even without the others the first
debate did not affect the polls in any decisive way.

In 1976, a case could be made for the proposition that Ford's
boo-boo on Poland, and his failure to correct it expeditiously,
cost him the election. On the other hand, again it should be
noted that Ford had pulled even with Carter at the time of that
debate and dropped only a point or two behind him as a result of
it -- which was enough to lose the election for him.

In 1980, media pundits who should know better have Reagan
even with Carter before the debate and winning a landslide as a
result of it. You may recall that Reagan had already passed
Carter the week before the debate. In fact, I made a statement at
that time predicting a landslide. The debate helped Reagan and
probably added two or three points to his margin of victory, but
it was not the decisive factor.

What this all adds up to is that debates can affect the
result, but only by two to three points -- not massively. With
all the polls indicating that Reagan is ahead now by between 15
and 20 points, there is no way the debate by itself will tighten
up the race significantly. While there is the possibility that
Reagan might make a slip or two, people always underestimate his
overall effectiveness. He can lose the debate on points with his
media critics, but he will win the TV audience going away because
of his style and his tone.

Mondale will be more formidable than Carter, and he has the
advantage, which Carter did not have, of being the challenger. He
has also had a lot of practice during the primaries. But because

he is so far behind, he will be desperate and probably uptight, since a "win" in the debates is absolutely indispensable to the survival of his candidacy. Reagan, on the other hand, could "lose" the debate decisively and still win going away. Consequently, Reagan should be encouraged to take the whole event in stride, adopt his very effective, relaxed, confident manner, and, above all, not worry about every miniscule debating point on the types of questions you suggest might be asked. He should treat Mondale almost gently, more in sorrow than in anger, and above all totally ignore Ferraro, no matter how the press comes at him on her. The net result of this will be that Mondale will undoubtedly come through as desperate, harried, and even disrespectful of Reagan. Reagan will come through as a confident, in-charge leader. What I am trying to get across here is that what matters in the debates is not so much the substance but the tone, and in this area Reagan will win going away and increase the margin he already has over Mondale in the leadership mystique, a quality everybody recognizes and no one can define.

As far as issues are concerned, the only one that really matters is the pocketbook. Consequently, Reagan's whole effort should be directed toward leaving in the minds of the viewers two fundamental impressions -- that they are better-off now than they were when he took over from Carter-Mondale, and that they will be better off in the future in a Reagan Administration than in a Mondale Administration. All the tiddlywink crap about the environment, etc. will make interesting columns for Reagan's unrelenting critics, but they pale into insignificance when put beside the economic issue.

For example, when the question of what each candidate would do about the deficit comes up, I think Reagan might consider answering along these lines: "This question raises the most profound irreconcilable difference between the two candidates. Mr. Mondale, very deeply and sincerely, believes that we should raise taxes in order to reduce the deficit. I just as deeply and sincerely believe that that would be a tragic mistake, and that rather than raising taxes we should continue policies which will increase revenues, and that rather than putting the emphasis as he does on cutting defense spending, we should put the emphasis on cutting domestic spending. The American people have a very clear choice. Based on his record in the past, while he served as Vice President and as a Senator, a Mondale Administration will lead to higher taxes, higher interest rates, slower growth, higher unemployment, and, inevitably, a recession. The policies I have adopted have made the United States the envy of the world as far as economic progress is concerned. The basic question is: Do the American people want to take a chance on Mondale's old economics, which brought us to the brink of disaster in 1980, or to continue with my new economic policies, which have brought unprecedented prosperity to the great majority of the American people?"

Another point that Reagan might make at some point during the debate, if a question is raised on some government program, he

might say, "I don't question Mr. Mondale's sincerity at all. He
sincerely believes that in meeting any problem we should increase
the role and the size of government. I just as sincerely believe
that we should reduce the role and size of government and increase
the opportunities for millions of Americans to lead their own
lives without government interference."

I doubt if these off-the-cuff observations are at all
helpful, but I am sure that after you hone down these thoughts if
you think they are worth pursuing, you may come up with a line or
two or a phrase or two that Reagan can use which will stick in
people's minds after 90 minutes of what I think will be an
excruciating and possibly boring discussion of the details of
domestic issues. You can't say it this way, but somehow it is
important to leave the impression that a vote for Mondale is a
vote for taking a chance on your future -- a vote for old ideas
that produced high taxes, high interest rates, and high
unemployment. A vote for Reagan is a vote for new ideas which
have been put in place in the last four years and which are paying
off in the pocketbooks of millions of Americans.

The President's Detroit Economic Club speech had some
excellent lines on these gut pocketbook issues. I strongly urge
that he use them again, particularly those that went over the best
before the audience. We have to get away from the media-inspired
concept that a line isn't good unless it is new. Lincoln, for
example, had made the "House Divided" speech at least 30 times
before it caught on when he made it in June, 1958. Kennedy had
used the line, "Ask not what your country can do for you but what
you can do for your country," in speech after speech, but when he
used it in his inaugural the pro-Kennedy media seized upon it as
something new. While the media may not treat Reagan that kindly,
bear in mind that the great majority of the television audience
will not have heard Reagan use these lines and will not have seen
them even on the television news (or if they have, they will have
forgotten). Dust off the best lines he has used over the past few
weeks and urge him to find opportunities to use those lines again
in answering questions.

In conclusion, I emphasize again: Don't let Reagan get bogged
down in detail with regard to the nitpicking questions the media
will be asking. Don't let him or his overeager staffers worry
about slips that may occur. Remember that what matters most is
overall tone, which solidifies the impression people already have
of a confident leader they can trust. On the issue front, all
that matters is to leave the impression that people are better-off
now than they were under Carter-Mondale and that they will be
better-off in the future under a Reagan Administration than under
a Mondale Administration.

Another idea that has just occurred to me as I dictate this
is that you might have somebody cost out Mondale's votes in the
Senate as far as domestic spending are concerned. I used this

-- 4 --

very effectively against Humphrey in 1968, incidentally, and came
up with the conclusion that he was the biggest spender in the
Senate. The point here that I would try to get across, if the
figures bear it out, is this: "If Mondale had had his way, the
deficit today would be $300 billion a year more than it presently
is." I picked a number out of the air, but I am sure that Mondale
has voted for so many big domestic spending programs that were
either vetoed or did not pass the Senate that the overall figure
will be astronomical.

APPENDIX 10

RICHARD NIXON

October 15, 1984

26 FEDERAL PLAZA
NEW YORK CITY

PERSONAL AND CONFIDENTIAL

Dear Ken —

Here are some random thoughts that you may or may not find useful in the briefing material for the foreign policy debate.

Mondale will probably make his usual point that Reagan has made no agreements with the Russians and then list other agreements that have been made, including SALT I. If he does so Reagan might well say, "I have noted that you have spoken with approval of SALT I, an agreement limiting defensive anti-ballastic missiles. But I note also that in the Senate you voted against the ABM program. If you and others who voted against that program had had their way, there would have been no SALT I treaty. The Soviet Union already had an ABM system. We didn't have one. We would never have gotten them to limit their system unless we had one on the way that they wanted to limit. The Russian leaders are not philanthropists and they're not fools. You can't get something from them in a negotiation unless you have something to give.

"The same analysis applies to the MX. The greatest destabilizing threat to peace is not the MX, which has not yet been built, but 300 Soviet SS-18s, the most powerful nuclear weapons in the world with the capability of taking out every one of our 1,000 ground-based Minuteman missiles in a first strike. There is no

KEN KHACHIGIAN

way we are going to be able to get them to negotiate a
limitation on those weapons unless we have something on
our side of the table that they want to limit.
Abandoning the MX program would destroy any chance for
an arms control agreement that would reduce the number
of nuclear weapons and contribute to the cause of
peace.

"With regard to arms control generally, we must
remember that the only kind of arms control that
contributes to peace is one that is based on equality.
A freeze at present levels, before our new programs are
completed, would leave the Soviet Union -- an admittedly
and avowedly offensive power -- in a position of
superiority in land-based missiles and therefore a
threat to peace. That is why the only kind of a freeze
we should agree to must be one based on equality and
moving toward reduction." (I think it is important for
the President not to come out flatly against the freeze
in view of the fact that all polls indicate that an
overwhelming majority of people support a freeze -- even
though for the wrong reasons. I think therefore it
would be good to have a formulation where he was opposed
to Mondale's freeze, which does not have the word
"equality" in it, and favors a Reagan freeze, which
would insist upon equality.)

If a question comes up on verification, he might
well observe, "An arms control agreement which controls
us and not them increases the danger of aggression and
of war, since the Soviets are an avowedly offensive
power. We know if we make an agreement that we're going
to keep it. But based on their record, we can't be sure
that they will keep it. That is why verification is
absolutely indispensable."

In terms of getting a possible lead, if the
question of Grenada comes up I think he might well say
that he faced a situation where the communists already
had two beachheads in the Western Hemisphere -- one in
Cuba, another in Nicaragua. They are trying to get
another one in El Salvador and were in the process of
consolidating one in Grenada. If we hadn't stopped
them, we faced the danger that the Caribbean would

Mr. Kenneth Khachigian
October 15, 1984
Page 3

become a Red Sea.

As I have already indicated to you, I feel that he
should, if at all possible, work in a statement on his
economic policy even though the subject is foreign
policy. The way he can do so, either in expanding an
answer to a question or in his closing statement, is to
say that the most important and indispensable program we
can undertake if we want to build a more peaceful world
is to continue policies which will assure that we have a
strong, free, and productive American economy. "Without
a strong economy we cannot afford the defense expendi-
tures that we need to deter aggression. Without a
strong economy we cannot afford the programs of
assistance for allies and friends abroad who are
threatened by Soviet subversion. If the American
economy becomes weak, the economies of our friends and
allies abroad will become weak, and inevitably the
leaders of a nation turn inward and isolationist when
they have severe economic problems. To sum it up, a
strong economy is an indispensable foundation for a
strong foreign policy."

I have no information as to the general tone which the
President intends to convey during the debate. I would
strongly urge that he reject the advice of those who say
that his primary and only purpose is to convince people
that he is dedicated to peace. While he must reassure
people on that score, he must remember that he must show
the difference between himself and Mondale, who is a
peace-at-any-price man. That is why the President must
not back away from a spirited defense of his policies in
Central America and his defense buildup. Remember that
George Bush's most devastating attack on Ferraro was on
the Central America issue.

Sincerely,

Mr. Kenneth Khachigian

*As soon as I get your specific question
I will try to send some further thought.*

429

APPENDIX 11

RICHARD NIXON

October 16, 1984

28 FEDERAL PLAZA
NEW YORK CITY

PERSONAL AND CONFIDENTIAL

Dear Ken,

    This letter supplements the one I sent you yesterday before I received your specific questions.

    With regard to arms control, I would strongly recommend that you read the attached editorial from the Economist of October 13th. The discussion is probably too complex to include in the debate format, but it does set forth some fundamental points that you should have in mind in preparing the brief for the President on this subject.

    "Let us understand at the outset that a bad arms control agreement is worse than none. It increases the danger of war. Only one based on equality reduces the danger of war. When we came here four years ago, we would have been fools to negotiate an arms control agreement with the Soviet Union. The Soviet Union at that time had superiority in the most powerful and accurate nuclear weapons: land-based strategic missiles. They had 300 SS-18s, by far the most powerful missiles in the world. They were targetted on all of our 1,000 Minuteman land-based missiles and could take them out in a first strike. In Europe, the Soviet Union had 300 SS-20s, which had the capacity to take out every military target in Europe. The U.S. four years ago had no land-based missiles in the United States which could counter the Soviet Union's SS-18s and no missiles in Europe which could counter the Soviet Union's SS-20s. If we had entered arms control negotiations at that time, we would have had nothing whatever

Mr. Kenneth Khachigian
October 16, 1984
Page 2

to bargain with. They would have been looking down our
throats. That is why we are producing the MX missiles as a
counter to the Soviet's SS-18s and are putting Pershing II
and cruise missiles in Europe to counter their SS-20s. As a
result of the Congress having approved those programs, we now
have something to bargain with. The table is set for
negotiating the only kind of arms control agreement which can
contribute to peace: one that is based on equality and
preferably one which will lead to a reduction of nuclear
weapons and not just limiting them at their present levels.
In a nutshell, what we have to bear in mind in negotiating
with the Soviets -- or, for that matter, with anyone else --
is that you can't get something from them unless you have
something to give."

If the question is raised as to why Reagan is the first
President in 40 years not to meet with his Soviet
counterpart, the answer might be along these lines: "We did
not have a meeting for a very good reason. There was no one
well enough or strong enough in Moscow to make a deal. If
Chernenko demonstrates that he has the political support and
the strength to make an agreement, we are ready to talk. Let
us understand once and for all that meeting the Soviet
leaders simply for the sake of meeting does not further the
cause of peace. On the contrary, it can create a false sense
of euphoria which might lead the Congress to reducing support
for the defense programs we need in order to establish a
position of equality in land-based missiles with the Soviet
Union. We have an advantage in sea-based missiles and in
air-launched missiles, but they are not an adequate counter
to the Soviets' far more powerful land-based missiles."

If the question is raised as to whether Reagan's harsh
rhetoric has been responsible for the deterioration of
U.S.-Soviet relations, he might respond along these lines:
"Let us understand at the outset that the Soviets are the
world's champions when it comes to using harsh rhetoric. Our
policies are not influenced by their rhetoric, and I am sure
their policies will not be influenced by ours. What we have
to recognize is that we have profound differences with the
Soviet Union. Some of them will never be settled. We have
one common interest, and that is to avoid a nuclear war which
could lead to mutual suicide. In serving that interest it
doesn't help to gloss over differences. We should put our
differences on the table and then devote our efforts to
developing a relationship in which we learn to live with our

431

differences rather than dying over them."

With regard to El Salvador and Nicaragua, I would
strongly urge that the President not go overboard and create
euphoria with regard to the meeting Duarte has had with the
rebel leaders. Having dealt with the North Vietnamese, I
know that communists are masters of the talk-fight strategy.
We also have to have in mind that whatever agreements they
may make at this meeting may not hold and that the guerrillas
might engage in some violent actions deliberately just before
the election in order to embarrass Reagan. Consequently, I
think his answer might well be along these lines: "This is a
positive development. President Duarte deserves great credit
for his courage. We support him in his effort to negotiate
with the guerrillas and if possible to stop the killing. But
we must continue to provide military and economic aid to the
government of El Salvador so that it will be able to contain
the situation in the event that negotiations break down. And
we should continue to do what we can to deter Nicaragua and
Cuba in their attempts to export more violence to the area.
As far as Nicaragua is concerned, our purpose in supporting
the contras is not to overthrow the government of Nicaragua,
but to prevent Nicaragua from continuing to try to overthrow
the government of El Salvador. Our purpose is to prevent
them from exporting the misery of totalitarian rule they have
imposed on their own people to other countries in the area.
One way to keep them from making trouble abroad is to cause
them trouble at home. As far as elections in Nicaragua are
concerned, we are for them -- but only if they are free and
if they are fair. An election which is stacked in advance
and which does not allow those who oppose the totalitarian
Sandinistas from participating on a fair basis is a procedure
we cannot and should not condone."

If the question is raised with regard to sending
American combat forces into El Salvador, the answer might go
along these lines: "I see no possibility whatever that
American combat forces would be sent to El Salvador, for the
very good reason that they are not needed. This situation is
totally different from the situation in Vietnam. When
President Kennedy sent the first 15,000 combat troops into
Vietnam in 1963, he said that he was taking that action
because North Vietnam was sending its troops into South
Vietnam. This is not the case in El Salvador. The
guerrillas are receiving arms, but there are no foreign

Mr. Kenneth Khachigian
October 16, 1984
Page 4

troops in El Salvador. As long as we meet our responsibility for seeing that the El Salvador armed forces receive adequate military aid, there is no question but that they will be able to handle the fighting by themselves. In that connection, it should be noted that Mr. Mondale originally opposed the action we took to remove the communist beachhead in Grenada, and that he has also been critical of our program of military aid to El Salvador. <u>If he had had his way, the Caribbean would have inevitably become a Red Sea</u>. By the action we took in Grenada and by our support of the government of El Salvador, <u>we have not only given peace a chance</u> in that area, but just as important <u>we have given democracy and freedom a chance to survive</u>."

With regard to Star Wars, an approach along these lines might be considered: "<u>The purpose of our developing space defense weapons is not to wage nuclear war in the heavens but to prevent nuclear weapons from destroying the earth</u>. We would threaten no one with a defensive system. We do not want a space defense system as a shield so that we can use the sword of our offensive weapons. I have made this clear by suggesting that we would be willing to share on a mutual basis our research in this area with the Soviet Union. We have a common interest in developing the capacity to protect ourselves against a nuclear attack that might come from a third nation. Who knows what some madman like Qaddafi might do if he had such weapons? It should also be noted that the main reason we need a defense against nuclear weapons is because of the enormous threat of the Soviet Union's offensive weapons. Isn't it better to build defensive weapons to meet that threat rather than more offensive weapons? If they will join us in agreeing to limit and reduce offensive weapons, we will join them in limiting defensive weapons."

With regard to government-supported terrorism: "What we need is a united program of action, not just consultation, in which all our major allies participate. In some cases, for example, an economic quarantine of an outlaw country like Libya might be effective, but not if the United States acts along. Unfortunately, our allies have sometimes been reluctant to join us. What all civilized nations must understand is that <u>a terrorist attack against one is an attack on all, and all should respond</u>."

Mr. Kenneth Khachigian
October 16, 1984
Page 5

With regard to the question of first use of nuclear
weapons: "This is, of course, primarily a European problem.
The reason the United States and our NATO allies must not
give up that option is that the Soviet Union has unquestioned
conventional superiority. If we tell them that we will never
resort to first use of nuclear weapons, it invites a
conventional attack, or blackmail, or both. In the event
such a conventional attack came, even though we had renounced
first use, a conventional war between major powers inevitably
would escalate to the nuclear level -- since no great power
would accept defeat without using the ultimate weapon. This,
incidentally, was a point Eisenhower made over and over again
in his White House years. He always insisted that any
conventional war between major powers would eventually
escalate to the use of ultimate weapons to avoid defeat.
Consequently, it can be argued that by retaining the option
of first use of nuclear weapons, the U.S. and our NATO allies
are in fact reducing the danger of nuclear war. Giving up
that option would increase the danger of conventional war and
of nuclear war as well."

On the defense spending questions, the Pentagon should
furnish most of the answers. Generally speaking: "The U.S.
has only one purpose in its defense buildup, and that is to
rectify the balance of power which had shifted to the Soviet
Union during the Carter years. The Soviet Union is an
avowedly aggressive power. History tells us that if an
aggressive power has military superiority, this increases the
threat of war or of blackmail. The United States no
longer seeks superiority. But in the interests of peace we
must make sure the Soviet Union, an admittedly offensive
power, is not superior. By accepting Soviet superiority and
opposing the defense buildup, we would not reduce the danger
of war. We would increase it."

With regard to the Midgetman program, Reagan might well
say that he supports the Scowcroft Commission's
recommendations, but that this is a long-term program and no
substitute in the short run for the MX. "It would be best
for everyone concerned if both the Soviet Union and the
United States would scrap their big land-based missiles and
substitute mobile Midgetmen. Midgetmen do not have
first-strike capability because of their size, and are not
vulnerable to a first strike because of their mobility. If
both sides had only Midgetmen, this would contribute to the

Mr. Kenneth Khachigian
October 16, 1984
Page 6

stability which reduces the chance of nuclear war."

Incidentally, I am attempting to oversimplify these complex questions, and as I dictate these answers I realize that even then it would be difficult for average listeners to comprehend what he is talking about. To the extent possible he should avoid getting into these complexities and reject the advice of those on the White House staff who urged him to cite facts and figures and minute details in order to prove that he was on top of the job. People are not selecting a bricklayer but an architect, not an accountant but a chief executive officer, as their leader.

Reagan's instincts as to his closing statement will be right on target. One possible approach which might be run by him would be that he is proud of the record he has made in his first term in many areas, but particularly proud of the success of his economic policies, which have reduced unemployment, reduced inflation, reduced taxes, and reduced interest rates for millions of people. As a result, the great majority of the American people have regained their confidence about the future and regained their faith in our system of government. In his second term, his top priority will be to lay the foundation for real peace in the world. To do that, he recognizes that there must be a new live-and-let-live relationship between the United States and the Soviet Union, each of which has the capability of destroying the other and the rest of the world as well. This is a goal that is bigger than party, and he hopes to work with Democrats and Republicans in the House and Senate to achieve that goal.

The thoughts that I have dictated are in _very_ rough form, and I am not suggesting that they be run by the President in that way. If you think well of some of the lines I have used, I would suggest that you hone them down and sharpen them up in the same manner in which you have so brilliantly crafted some of the President's major speeches over the years, and particularly those hard-hitting statements he has been making since the first debate.

Incidentally, it may be that I have missed it, but I don't believe I have heard the President use the line: "A great Democrat, Al Smith, once said, 'Let's look at the record.' I suggest we all do that, etc." You can follow

Mr. Kenneth Khachigian
October 16, 1984
Page 7

this with the record on the economy, the record on reducing
crime, the record on restoring respect for the U.S., etc.

One final thought: The President should again make the
point that during his watch not one inch of territory has
come under communist domination or been lost to the West.
This is in stark contrast to what happened during the
previous Administration, when Ethiopia and Nicaragua, to name
two, have come under communist domination and Iran was lost
to the West. That, in the final analysis, is the test of the
success or failure of foreign policy, combined with the fact
that this has been accomplished without the U.S. becoming
engaged in war.

Another thought with regard to the closing statement: He
might note that he has seen polls indicating that a majority
of young people felt that there would be a nuclear war in
their lifetime and that he noted that at a great eastern
university (Brown), had voted for a proposal that would have
the school provide a stockpile of suicide pills, to be
distributed to students in the event that nuclear war were to
come. He then might say, "I understand their concerns. But
I want to assure them and all Americans that I firmly believe
we are not going to have a nuclear war. The very destructive
power of the nuclear weapons we both possess is in itself a
deterrent to war. The Soviet Union and the United States
have profound differences, but for both of us war is an
unacceptable option. I intend to spend the rest of my time
in office and the rest of my life working for the goal of
building a structure of peace in the world, not only reducing
nuclear weapons but removing them from the face of the earth,
and making war obsolete as an intrument of policy by great
nations."

Sincerely,

Mr. Kenneth Khachigian

P.S. Another thought re defense: "Walter Mondale claims he is

Mr. Kenneth Khachigian
October 16, 1984
Page 8

for a strong defense. As a great Democrat, Al Smith, used to
say, 'Let us look at the record.' During his ten years in
the Senate no Senator voted against our defense program more
often that he did. He voted against the Trident II, the
cruise, etc. If he had had his way we not only would have a
dangerously weak defense today but we would have no
bargaining chips on our side of the table when we negotiate
with the Soviets. They would be superior across the board
and would have no incentive to negotiate. The only kind of
arms control agreement which reduces the danger of war is one
based on equality."

The
Economist

OCTOBER 13, 1984

Are they trapped?

The conventional wisdom is starting to say that it is all up with arms control. The hope of reopening negotiations that could set limits to the world's nuclear armouries, it is argued, "is not for today, and only possibly for tomorrow". Conventional wisdoms should always be challenged—by the time they are conventional, they are generally no longer wise—and this gloomy specimen deserves a cold eye. It is true that one rather naive theory about arms control, popular in the days of "detente", has been knocked on the head. It is not true that the practical business of keeping some sort of lid on nuclear weapons has to be abandoned—either because the superpowers have lost interest in trying, or because the intelligence of the nuclear machines has outrun the intelligence of the negotiators.

The dreamy theory which bit the dust was the idea that arms-control negotiations could be, as it were, the tranquilliser of east-west relations. If only America and Russia could sit down and sign some agreements about nuclear weapons, the theory ran, a beneficent glow would spread through the rest of their relationship. They would stop feeling so tense about their differences over Europe, over the Middle East, over Central America: you name it, a dose of Salt would help to relax it. This theory got things upside down.

"Tension", which is the polite word for a clash of interests, leads to the production of armaments, not the other way round. So long as east and west are separated by a political chasm—and the contest between Marxism and pluralism is as deep a difference of interests as the world has seen for a long time—neither side will cheerfully let the other have an advantage in the weapons with which it can pursue its aims. For the past four years, the first Reagan administration has been struggling to stop the Russians getting nuclear dominance over Europe, by way of their SS-20s. It has also been trying to deal with the theoretical first-strike power that the Russians have built up against America's land-based missiles. The Russians have been trying to hold on to their advantages. In those circumstances, the arms negotiators were bound to be talking into a gale.

That period, however, may now be drawing to a close. The arrival of cruise and Pershing-2 has brought western Europe back under the American nuclear umbrella. The Reagan rearmament programme has started to rebuild American strength: pretty wastefully,

to be sure (that's America), but competently enough to make the Russians sit up and take notice. President Chernenko and his colleagues, if they do their sums, must be starting to realise that any attempt to recapture the advantages the Russians thought they enjoyed four years ago would be hideously expensive.

This is why a return to arms control is possible in a second Reagan administration—provided it is understood what "arms control" means. It is not the Valium of east-west relations. It is one factor in the tangle of things to be negotiated about. It can add a bit of stability to the military balance. Above all, it is a way of providing yourself with the military means of protecting your interests at the lowest possible cost.

Why it's not too late

But it may already be too late, say the mourners for arms control, because nuclear technology moves so fast. They exaggerate. A Pershing-2 missile, they point out, can reach Russia from western Europe in eight minutes. Yes, but Russia's old SS-4 and SS-5 missiles back in the early 1970s (not to mention its SS-20s now) could reach western Europe in about the same time; and the 30 minutes' travelling time of an intercontinental missile has not changed much in the past decade. The intercontinental missile now has a fifty-fifty chance of landing within 600 feet of its target; but it could do it within 1,000 feet in the early 1970s. These are relative nuances. The big change happened a generation ago, when the computer-aimed missile first replaced the lumbering bomber. The only really new problem is the fact that some weapons are now confusingly movable and others (such as cruise missiles) can conceal either a nuclear warhead or a non-nuclear one, with nobody to tell the difference.

These things are complications for the arms-control business. They are not a cause to start shovelling earth on its coffin. If anything, they add to the belief that both sides have an incentive to get back to the negotiating table. Russia's incentive may be even stronger than America's. Consider what each side could get from the three negotiations that ought to be taking place, but aren't, and some surprising conclusions emerge.

First, anti-missile defences. The Russians seem to be saying that they want an agreement to ban all weapons from space, including defensive ones; Mr Reagan, with

11

..ars in his eyes, is reluctant to agree. In fact, the Russians must now be wondering whether they need at least a limited anti-missile defence system of their own. They keep two thirds of their attacking warheads in land-based missiles (the Americans have two thirds of theirs safely hidden out at sea). By the end of the 1980s, the accurate new D-5 warhead on America's submarine missiles will make this land-based Russian force at least theoretically vulnerable to an American first strike. Meanwhile, President Reagan is being told that his original Star Wars idea of building a leakproof anti-missile roof over the whole United States is a budget-buster, and probably won't work anyway. One possible compromise: an agreement to let both sides put up a smaller screen that would provide some protection for their land-based missiles—and thereby make them both less nervous about a surprise attack?

Second, the Start long-range missile talks. So far, the Russians have rejected all Mr Reagan's proposals in this field, partly because he wants to cut warhead numbers more than they do, but mainly because Mr Reagan's cuts would fall most heavily on the land-based missiles Russia prefers. But the advent of the American D-5 warhead means that, unless the Russians go in for a new anti-missile defence screen, they will have to move more of their weapons out to sea—which could cost them a fortune. Result: the Russians may show increasing interest in a low-numbers deal which would cut both sides' armouries sharply, and so cut the cost of moving Russia's out to sea.

Third, the Euromissile talks on medium-range missiles. The Russians say they will not return to these negotiations unless Nato agrees to withdraw the cruise and Pershing-2 missiles it has deployed over the past year. But that is not going to happen. The extra missiles Russia is now putting into East Germany and Czechoslovakia by way of retaliation have very little military effect (they are mostly pointing at targets already covered by the SS-20s). They seem to be frightening the Czechs and the East Germans more than they frighten the west. So the Russians have to decide whether they want to watch Nato go on deploying all its planned 572 missiles—give or take Holland's 48—or sign an agreement that holds down the Nato deployment in return for cutting back their own SS-20s. If they go for compromise in the other negotiations, they will probably go for compromise here too.

The money, and the glory

Arms control is not dead. The Russians are pulled back towards it by the thought of what four more years of the arms race would do to a Soviet economy that is only about half the size of America's (and even less than that, per Russian). The Americans have to worry about money, too; and, for Mr Reagan himself, if he gets re-elected, there is the lure of going down in the history books as the man who first restored America's strength and then used that restored strength to strike a deal with the Russians. The negotiating will be horribly complicated; it always was. It will not "bring peace"; it never could. But, with a spell in the intensive-care unit, the patient can be revived.

Thatcher's police

Throwing the police into the breach against Scargill's men raises problems, but had to be done

Should Britain's police forces be in the front line of the government's battle to defeat the miners' strike? The answer, unfortunately, is yes.

After the orgy of police-bashing at last week's Labour party conference, it was inevitable that the leader of the National Union of Mineworkers' militant faction, Mr Arthur Scargill, should be arch-villain of this week's Conservative conference. It was equally inevitable that no amount of praise was too much for the police, now the poor bloody infantry of the government's long overdue campaign to restructure the coal industry.

No alternative

The government has a guilty conscience about the police and miners. Its trade-union legislation, formulated in the aftermath of the secondary picketing of 1972-74 and introduced in the last parliament, had been presented as ending the outrage of the flying picket. But the outrage has continued, the new legislation has not been used and public-sector employers have been discouraged by ministers from using it. Instead, the government has relied on the common law enforced by large quantities of police. Injuries have been mercifully few and magistrates' courts in mining areas have handled prosecutions cautiously.

This has been wise. The use of the common law has done something to isolate Mr Scargill and assist the cause of working miners in his union. It is not the government's caution that has forced the police into the front line. Indeed, it is possible that invocation of the secondary picketing laws would have involved an even greater confrontation with the police, by drawing other unions—and conceivably more miners—into the dispute and into jail to contest what many trade-unionists still see as political legislation. As it is, if a group of citizens is determined systematically to breach the peace to stop other citizens going about their lawful business, as Mr Scargill's pickets unquestionably are, then no government has any alternative but to resort to the police.

However, the cost has been high and the government's picketing legislation has been mocked by disuse. Public opinion, as reflected in opinion polls more than

12

APPENDIX 12

RICHARD NIXON

October 17, 1984

26 FEDERAL PLAZA
NEW YORK CITY

Dear Dick,

    Before leaving for the Bahamas for a short
vacation I wanted to pass on to you some brief
comments with regard to your upcoming bout with
Mondale on Sunday.

    You have every reason to be confident as to
the outcome. Even though you felt that you were
not in top form for the first debate, your
performance on substance could not be faulted. In
fact, right after it ended Pat turned to me and
said, "Mondale lost." Only because he did better
than expected and you did not knock him out of the
ring did the media seize on the opportunity to made
it appear as if he had won. The polls at the
conclusion of the debate showed it very close.
Only after a week of the media hammering home their
prejudices on TV and in print did the public
perception shift decisively in Mondale's favor.

    This, however, is now an advantage to you.
You go into the debate Sunday as an underdog. And
in addition, while most of the liberal pundits
believe that foreign policy is a weak issue for you
and a strong issue for Mondale, I totally disagree.
I believe a Mondale Administration would be a disaster for the nation economically. But the American economy is so strong that it could recover from
the damage he would inflict upon it. On the other
hand, Mondale's foreign and defense policies are so

440

The Honorable Ronald Reagan
October 17, 1984
Page Two

fatally flawed that the damage he would do in four
years would probably be irreparable. That is why I
am confident that when people see the choice they
will be making on Election Day they will come down
solidly on your side.

While the polls seem to be getting somewhat
closer, it is not because of the first debate. Its
effect was minimal and temporary. What we are
seeing is the predictable pattern of registered
Democrats returning to their party as the election
draws closer. But your almost unanimous support
among Republicans, overwhelming support among
Independents and young voters, and a solid base
among conservative Democrats who left their party
permanently as you did thirty years ago can mean
only one thing: You will win an overwhelming
victory in the popular vote on Election Day and a
decisive victory in the electoral vote approaching
the one you achieved in 1980.

Pat joins me in sending our warmest regards to
Nancy and to you.

Sincerely,

The Honorable Ronald Reagan
The White House

APPENDIX 13

May 1985

"Off Stride" trumpets the headline of the New York _Times_ "Week In Review" on Sunday, April 28th. The _Times_ reporter observes, "Less than six months after his landslide, Ronald Reagan seems, quite suddenly, politically vulnerable. His decision to proceed with the visit to a Germany military cemetery, the rebuke that the House of Representatives handed out in rejecting aid to the rebels in Nicaragua, the uncertainty that dominated the end of the week's Senate debate on the President's compromise budget proposal, the resistance in Congress to a possible tax overhaul," are cited as examples of the President's decline in popularity and influence.

The Washington _Post_, the weekly newsmagazines and the network TV anchors parrot the same line. Dr. Austin Ranney, a former President of the American Political Science Association, chimes in by declaring, "Mr. Reagan has finally become a lame duck." And the usual anonymous White House officials speaking on "condition their names not be used," acknowledged that the decision to visit the German cemetery was a "political disaster." Gallup reports that the President's approval rating has dropped 12 points since the Inauguration.

Before everyone pushes the panic button, it is time to put some of these recent developments in perspective. First, consider the source as far as most of the criticism writing Reagan off is concerned. The New York _Times_ and Washington _Post_ both endorsed Mondale. The columnists who take the same line, like Tom Wicker, Anthony Lewis and James Reston, were all for Mondale. The same is true of television anchormen like Dan Rather. They did not want Reagan to win in 1984 and they predictably gloat over any "failures" he experiences as proof that they were right.

We have witnessed the same syndrome in the media's revolting "celebration" of America's defeat in Vietnam ten year ago. The TV networks competed with each other in showing how happy the Vietnamese people are now that the U.S. has left the scene and in outrageously blaming U.S. troops who were trying to _prevent_ a communist takeover for the communist

442

- 2 -

massacre of two million Cambodians. Communist
Vietnam leaders have been paraded before the
cameras in the best-possible light, and those who
opposed them have been viciously attacked. Why
this obscene gloating over a defeat for American
forces? Because after Tet in 1968 the great
majority of the media heavyweights turned anti-war
and predicted the U.S. would lose. Now they never
miss a chance to prove to their audience that they
were right and their government was wrong.

A bit of political history will help to put
Reagan's present troubles in perspective. Early in
1983, the title of the New York Times lead
editorial was, "The Stench of Failure." In strident
and apocalyptic terms, the Times ponderously
proclaimed that he had failed on all fronts: the
economy was in the doldrums; no progress was being
made on arms control or other issues with the
Russians; various Reagan officials had come under
attack or investigation because of questionable
personal and financial activities. Eighteen months
later, Reagan was re-elected in one of the greatest
landslides in history.

The purpose of recounting history is not to
prove that the Administration is not going through
a difficult time. The second terms of Presidents
in this century, particularly after landslide
victories, have without exception run into
difficulties. But what we must always keep in mind
is that things are never as bad or as good as they
seem in the short term and that what matters is
whether the long-term policies of the President and
his Administration are fundamentally sound.

The German cemetery visit, without question,
is harmful to the President in the short term. The
heat he is taking, particularly from Republicans in
the House and Senate, must seem at times almost
unbearable to him. Someone asked me a few days ago
whether I would have made the same decision with
regard to visiting the cemetery. My answer was,
"No, and neither would President Reagan if he had
known then what he found out later about who was
buried there." But having accepted Kohl's
invitation to go, it would have been a major
mistake for him to have changed his mind and

refused to go because of domestic political
pressure. The image of being a weak leader would
have encouraged opponents at home and abroad to
apply pressure on him in the future whenever he
made a decision they didn't like.

Despite the unfortunate publicity, we must
remember that the President's visit to Bitburg
commemorates two profoundly important, watershed
events: the end of one of the most tragic episodes
in human history, Hitler's Holocaust; and the birth
of a new German nation opposed to all Hitler stood
for. The supreme irony is that the new Germany is
one of the indispensable building blocks of the
strategy which can prevent another holocaust in the
future. We must never forget that without the
Federal Republic of Germany, NATO would be a hollow
shell which would collapse under Soviet pressure.
Only the loyal participation of German troops makes
it possible to prevent the Soviet Union, the most
anti-semitic nation in the world, from overruning
Western Europe.

Anthony Lewis's snide suggestion that Reagan's
decision showed "insensitivity" to the horrors of
the Holocaust is both viciously unfair and untrue.
No President in the postwar era has been a stronger
supporter of Israel. Truman, for example, was
pro-Israel for political reasons. Reagan is
pro-Israel because he has deep personal affection
and respect for the Jewish people and heartfelt
concern over the tragedy they have had to endure.
I am convinced that the speech he will make in
Bitbury will enable him to set the record straight
and repair most of the damage which has been done
up to this point. It is unfortunate that so many
who claim to be friends of Israel -- and I think I
have earned that distinction -- have gone overboard
in castigating a President who has been and will
remain one of their strongest supporters.

His media critics are gleefully congratulating
each other over the House vote rejecting his
request for $14 million in non-military aid for the
Contras in Nicaragua. I predict that their cheers
will turn to tears by Election Day 1986. I would
not like to be a Democratic candidate who had voted

- 4 -

against aid to the anti-communist Contras running
against an opponent who would remind the voters
that the Nicaraguan communist government had
praised his vote and that the communist President
Ortega ended up the next day exchanging kisses on
the cheek with his Soviet sponsors in Moscow.

The opponents of aid to the Contras now must
take the responsibility for what happens in
Nicaragua. My prediction is that within a few
months, the President will be able to go to the
Congress again and get a request for military aid
approved by both the House and the Senate. It is
ironic that those who oppose aid to the Contras
have as their slogan, "No more Vietnams." What
they fail to recognize is that the way to avoid
another Vietnam in Nicaragua is to provide aid now
to anti-communist Nicaraguans who are willing to
risk their lives to fight against the communist
government rather than to have to send in Americans
later to neutralize a Soviet base which, just like
Cuba, will be built if the Contra effort
collapses.

The program offered by the President's
opposition is ludicrous. They say: Use diplomacy,
not military power, to persuade the Nicaraguan
communists to change their position. Diplomacy
without military power to back it up is impotent.
In the 40 years since the UN has been in existence,
can anyone name one example where a UN resolution
prevented Soviet aggression or repression? In his
Notre Dame speech in 1977, Jimmy Carter said, "We
do not want to be the world's policemen, but we do
want to be the world's peacemakers." The media
were ecstatic and praised his eloquence and wisdom.
But when you have a murderer running amok in your
neighborhood, you have to call on armed policemen
to arrest him. That is why they call them peace
officers.

I am enclosing an article from Time Magazine
of April 22nd which accurately reflects my views on
Soviet/American relations. I hope that in view of
some of the hard-line statements being made by
Gorbachev and the Soviet Union's reversing their
position and now insisting they have a right to

- 5 -

shoot first and ask questions later as they did in
the case of Major Nicholson, the Administration may
cool the idea of a "get-acquainted" session with
Gorbachev when he comes to the UN in October and
take a posture of being <u>willing but not anxious</u> to
have a properly-prepared meeting next year which
would provide time for preparing an agenda with
real substance. I can hear the self-proclaimed
Soviet experts in the media and the political
opposition sharpening their knives now to cut the
President to pieces if he holds a summit which
produces headlines and handshakes but no real
progress on reducing tensions between the two
superpowers. A quickie, get-acquainted summit will
be immensely popular and will raise the President's
approval rating spectactularly in the short term,
but in the long term it will do far more harm than
good by raising hopes and then dashing them.

These foreign policy issues are, of course,
the most newsworthy. But all of them pale into
insignificance compared with the importance of the
economic issue. The President can get military aid
for the Contras and have a highly successful
substantive meeting with the Soviets and still fail
in his second term if the economy goes to hell.
That is why the battle on the budget is one that
the President is very properly mustering all of his
forces to win. If he can get a substantial
percentage of his budget cuts approved and a tax
simplification bill passed by the end of 1986, the
groundwork will have been laid for a strong economy
in 1987 and 1988. If he loses the battle on the
budget, however, and a recession occurs, it will be
a very sad second term. Again, I turn to history
to prove this point. In 1958, Eisenhower had an
enormously successful foreign policy initiative in
Lebanon where, by sending in 15,000 Marines, he
quieted down a potentially dangerous situation,
bluffed the Russians out, and did so without losing
a single American life. Yet, the deep recession
later that year drove his popularity for the first
and only time below 50%. The President's advisors
should bear this historical evidence in mind as
they try to determine where to commit their major
forces for the legislative battles of the second
term.

- 6 -

There is one fallout from the Bitburg controversy which could do permanent damage if not dealt with quickly. The backbiting and leaks to President Reagan's critics in the media from inside the White House staff cannot be tolerated. Blaming Don Regan for the foulup is ridiculous. The President accepted Kohl's invitation to go to Bitburg long before Regan took over as chief of staff. If Kohl would not withdraw the invitation, Reagan had no choice but to go through with the visit or risk doing irreperable damage to the NATO alliance and lending credence to the view that he is only interested in being popular and will succumb to political pressure. By the same token, by going through the fire of criticism the President has immeasurably strengthened his image as a strong leader who will do what he thinks is right regardless of political pressure. This will help him in the balance of the second term as he deals with the Soviets, other foreign governments, and his political opposition at home.

What we must never forget about Don Regan and Pat Buchanan is that, whatever their alleged faults, they are first, last, and always Reagan loyalists. That is one reason the anti-Reagan media heavyweights are attacking them so unmercifully. I am reminded of what President Eisenhower told me shortly after the Inauguration in 1953. I asked what was the most important single quality a staff member should have. He thought a long time before answering, and then he said, "Selflessness." Not high IQ or willingness to work hard or any of the other attributes one might think of, but "selflessness." That is what Regan and Buchanan have in spades. Neither is in business for himself. Both are dedicated to only one goal: the success of Ronald Reagan in his second term. Unfortunately, that cannot be said for some of their critics on the White House staff who have been leaking their complaints to Reagan's critics in the press. The going is going to get even rougher in the days ahead, and it is time for all hands to shape up or get out.

APPENDIX 14

SENT BY:Xerox Telecopier 7020 ; 2- 9-88 ; 3:30PM ;   2024552883→   CCITT G3:# 1

1988 Overview

General Theme: Preparing for the Challenges of Tomorrow

--this focuses on the future;

--provides the framework for legislative actions;

--describes specific goals for the President but also sets out a course for his successor;

--states what must be done to meet these goals;

--provides the opportunity to look back and then look forward.

Objective:

To provide a forum to advance and institutionalize the Reagan agenda; to lay down the framework for a political victory by the Republican Party in 1988.

Leading Issues:

--war/ peace (arms control; East/West relations)

--quality education

--combating illicit drugs

--government spending (budget/deficits/process)

All of these issues are consistent with the Reagan agenda and can be a major part of the 1988 agenda. While there is the opportunity to score legislative victories in 1988, there is also the opportunity to sketch what the future should be and where it might go. An extremely important point: this agenda is relevant, consistent, optimistic.

BEHIND CLOSED DOORS

SENT BY:Xerox Telecopier 7020 ; 2- 9-88 ; 3:31PM ;   2024582883→   CCITT G3:# 2

1988 Monthly Agenda

January:

Theme: looking ahead/ setting the agenda

--State of the Union Address
--quality education/jobs
--dealing with illicit drugs
--INF/arms control/growth of democracy
--economy/process reform

February:

Theme: legislative action/ a winner

--Contras
--budget/ two-year agreement/ process
--Supreme Court confirmation
--North American Accord scene-setter (mexico)

March:

Theme: working with the Alliance/ national security

--NATO
--national defense/ national security
--conventional weapons
--arms control/arms reduction

April:

Theme: North American relations/ world relations

--Canada Free Trade Agreement
--North American Accord (Canada/US/Mexico)
--Central America (possible)
--INF ratification

SENT BY:Xerox Telecopier 7020 ; 2- 9-88 ; 3:31PM ;   2024562883→   CCITT G3:# 3

May:

Theme: the role of the Peacemaker

--Moscow summit
--arms control/arms reduction
--human rights/ regional issues/ bilateral issues

June:

Theme: forging domestic/international economic policy

--Economic summit in Canada
--debt strategy
--budget/ deficit reduction/ process reform
--monetary policy

July:

Theme: developing new economic markets

--Pacific Rim to support market-oriented growth
--Democratic National Convention occurs

August:

Theme: recognizing our American institutions/ setting political agenda

--culmination of bicentennial of Constitution
--citing 100th Congress/ role/ changes/ improvements
--Republican National Convention occurs

September/October/November/December:

Theme: role of the presidency/ political debate

--American values
--the future (education/technology)
--managing foreign policy
--the institution of government/relationships
--economic and budget policies

--Farewell Address: Vision of America (late December-early January)

BEHIND CLOSED DOORS

May:

Theme: the role of the Peacemaker

--Moscow summit
--arms control/arms reduction
--human rights/ regional issues/ bilateral issues

June:

Theme: forging domestic/international economic policy

--Economic summit in Canada
--debt strategy
--budget/ deficit reduction/ process reform
--monetary policy

July:

Theme: developing new economic markets

--Pacific Rim to support market-oriented growth
--Democratic National Convention occurs

August:

Theme: recognizing our American institutions/ setting political agenda

--culmination of bicentennial of Constitution
--citing 100th Congress/ role/ changes/ improvements
--Republican National Convention occurs

September/October/November/December:

Theme: role of the presidency/ political debate

--American values
--the future (education/technology)
--managing foreign policy
--the institution of government/relationships
--economic and budget policies

--Farewell Address: Vision of America (late December-early January)

451

Endnotes

Chapter 1

1   *New York Times* Staff, *The End of a Presidency* (New York: Bantam, 1974), 272.

2   Ibid., 272–273.

Chapter 3

3   David Frost, *I Gave Them a Sword: Behind the Scenes of the Nixon Interviews* (New York: William Morrow & Company, Inc., 1978), 200.

4   Ibid., 44.

5   Ibid., 199.

6   Ibid., 200.

7   Ibid., 266–276, drawing from Frost's extracts of the interview's transcripts.

Chapter 4

8   Richard Reeves, "Why Reagan Won't Make It," *Esquire*, May 8, 1979, 6.

Chapter 5

9   Robert Lindsey, "Reagan Remark—A Bump on Campaign Trail," *Los Angeles Herald Examiner*, January 15, 1980.

10   Richard Bergholz, "Reagan Modifies His Stance on Cuban Blockade—Says It Was Only Hypothetical," *LA Times*, January 31, 1980.

11   Bill Stall and William Endicott, "Record Doesn't Always Support Reagan's Claims," *LA Times*, April 12, 1980.

12   James M. Perry, "As Nomination Nears, Reagan Isn't Quite Set with Staff and Policies," *Wall Street Journal*, July 7, 1980.

13   Craig Shirley, *Rendezvous with Destiny* (New York: ISI Books, 2009), 452, quoting Jack W. Germond, "Reagan Labels Carter Cause of 'Depression,'" *Washington Star*, August 27, 1980.

14   Lou Cannon, *Reagan* (New York: G.P. Putnam's Sons, 1982), 271.

15   Ibid. 274.

16   Conversation with Stuart Spencer, June 15, 2015.

17   Conversations with Stuart Spencer, November 2, 2012, and June 15, 2015.

18   Ibid., December 2, 2015.

19   Ibid., July 1, 2019.

Chapter 6

20 David Halberstam, *The Teammates: A Portrait of a Friendship*, (New York: Hachette Books, 2003).

21 Interview with Stuart Spencer, Miller Center of Public Affairs, Ronald Reagan Oral History Project, Charlottesville, Virginia, November 15, 2001, tape 4 of 13, final edited transcript, 39.

22 Paul Recer, *U.S. News & World Report*, October 13, 1980, 36.

23 Morton Kondracke, "Politics—Stalled Out," *The New Republic*, October 18, 1980, 8.

24 William Endicott, "Reagan Inspires Yawns as He Tries to Avoid Gaffes," *Los Angeles Times*, October 3, 1980, 8.

25 Lou Cannon, *Reagan* (New York: G.P. Putnam's Sons, 1982), 285.

26 Press Pool Report of October 7, 1980, Pat Sloyan/Jack Nelson—partial transcript of Reagan's comments to a group of 150 representatives of local industry in Steubenville, Ohio. From author's personal files—I retained copies of almost all press pool reports from the time I joined the campaign through election day, a valuable supplement to my own diary.

27 Press Pool Report, October 9, 1980, Bruce Drake, *New York Daily News*, Doug Brew, *Time Magazine*.

28 Ibid.

29 John Osborne, "White House Watch—Preferring Jimmy (II)," *The New Republic*, October 25, 1980, 6.

30 Marlene Cimons, "Campaign 80 a Traveling Road Show," *Los Angeles Times*, October 11, 1980, 1.

Chapter 7

31 Eleanor Randolph, "Reagan Rally in Northridge Draws Backers, Hecklers," *Los Angeles Times*, October 11, 1980.

32 Stuart Spencer in telephone conversation with author, December 2, 2015.

33 Ibid.

34 "Battle for the Bigger Half," *Time Magazine*, October 27, 1980, 25.

Chapter 8

35 Gallup Poll recorded in author's diary.

36 Transcript, Ronald Reagan press conference, October 14, 1980, Los Angeles, California, Travelodge Los Angeles International Airport.

37 Martin Schram and Lou Cannon, "Key is Voters League Decision on Anderson," *Washington Post*, October 16, 1980, A-1, as cited in Craig Shirley, *Rendezvous with Destiny—Ronald Reagan and the Campaign That Changed America* (New York: ISI Books, 2009), 507.

38 "A Showdown, One-on-One," *Newsweek* magazine, October 27, 1980, 34.

39 James A. Baker, III, with Steve Fiffer, *Work Hard, Study and Keep Out of Politics!* (Evanston, Illinois: Northwestern University Press, 2006), 115–116.

40 Lyn Nofziger, oral history. Miller Center of Public Affairs, Presidential Oral History Program, Ronald Reagan Oral History Project, March 6, 2003, Washington, D.C., tape 5 of 6, transcript 34–35.

41 Lou Cannon, *Reagan* (New York: G.P. Putnam's Sons, 1982), 292.

42 Lyn Nofziger, oral history, 34.

43 Stu Spencer, oral history. Miller Center of Public Affairs, Presidential Oral History Program, Ronald Reagan Oral History Project, November 16, 2001, Charlottesville, Virginia, tape 5 of 13, final edited transcript, 53.

44 Stuart Spencer in discussion with author, April 15, 2021.

45 Transcript, Ronald Reagan press conference, October 14, 1980.

46 Peter Baker and Susan Glasser, *The Man Who Ran Washington: The Life and Times of James A. Baker, III*, (New York: Doubleday, 2020), 125–126.

Chapter 9

47 Press Pool Report, October 20, 1980, Larry Barrett, *Time Magazine*, Lisa Myers, *Washington Star*, Lou Cannon, *Washington Post*.

48 Press Pool Report, October 22, 1980, Rachelle Patterson, *Boston Globe* and Jerry Lubenow, *Newsweek* magazine.

Chapter 10

49 "Highest Rated Presidential Debates 1960 to Present," Nielsen, October 6, 2008.

50 Lou Cannon, *Reagan* (New York: G.P. Putnam's Sons, 1982), 297.

51 Craig Shirley, *Rendezvous with Destiny* (New York: ISI Books, 2009), 548.

52 "Now, a Few Words in Closing," *Time Magazine,* November 10, 1980, 18.

53 Ibid.

54 "The Great Homestretch Debate," *Newsweek* magazine, November 10, 1980, 34–35.

55 Spencer quoted in Peter Baker and Susan Glasser, *The Man Who Ran Washington—The Life and Times of James A. Baker, III*, (New York: Doubleday, 2020), 131.

56 Peter Baker, "A Four-Decade Secret: One Man's Story of Sabotaging Carter's Re-Election," *New York Times*, March, 18, 2023.

57 Interviews with Richard Allen, Stuart Spencer, and Office of Edwin Meese, March 27 and 28, 2023.

58 Press Pool Report, November 2, 1980, Joe Rice, *Cleveland Plain Dealer*, George Embrey, *Columbus Dispatch*, David Hoffman, *Washington Post*.

59 Lee Fremstad, "Reagan Jolted on Hostages," *Fresno Bee*, November 3, 1980, A-1.

Chapter 11

60 Rowland Evans and Robert Novak, "It Could Have Been a Landslide," *Washington Post*, November 3, 1980, A21.

Chapter 12

61 Richard E. Meyer and Roger Smith, "Media Supplied Clues to Race's Outcome," *Los Angeles Times*, November 6, 1980, 22.

62 Louis Harris, "Post-Election Poll Gives President Some Low Ratings," *Los Angeles Herald Examiner*, November 17, 1980.

63 Adam Clymer, "Poll: Last-Minute Switches Hurt Carter Campaign," *Los Angeles Herald Examiner*, November 16, 1980.

64 Lisa Myers, "Reagan Readies Transition Team—Plans to Revamp Role of Cabinet," *Washington Star*, November 5, 1980.

65 Lee Fremstad, "California Aides Likely to Receive Top Reagan Jobs," *Fresno Bee*, November 6, 1980, A8.

66 Steven R. Weisman, "Reagan Takes Oath as 40th President; Promises an 'Era of National Renewal.' Minutes Later, 52 Hostages in Iran Fly to Freedom After 444-Day Ordeal," *New York Times*, January 21, 1981.

Chapter 13

67 Martin Anderson, *Revolution* (Harcourt Brace Jovanovich, 1988), 222 et seq.

68 Kenneth T. Walsh, *Reagan—A Biography* (New York: Random House Value Publishing, 1997), 94.

69 Lou Cannon, *President Reagan, The Role of a Lifetime* (New York: Simon & Schuster, 1991), 238–239.

70 Ronald Reagan, Public Papers of the President, Ronald Reagan, 1981, United States Government Printing Office, Office of the Federal Register, National Archives and Records Service, General Services Administration, 45.

71 Ibid., 62.

72 William Greider, "The Education of David Stockman," *The Atlantic*, December, 1981, 33.

73 Andrew Glass, "Reagan Outlines Plan for Economic Recovery," Politico, February 18, 1981.

74 Ronald Reagan, *The Reagan Diaries* (New York: Harper Perennial, 2009), 20.

75 Robert A. Kittle, "White House Notes," U.S. News and World Report, April 30, 1981, quoting David Gergen, "Selling the Cuts," Sara Fritz Papers, Ronald Reagan Presidential Library and Museum, 3.

76 Chris Matthews, *Tip and the Gipper: When Politics Worked* (New York: Simon & Schuster, 2013), 53–54.

Chapter 14

77 Del Quentin Wilber, *Rawhide Down: The Near Assassination of Ronald Reagan* (New York: Henry Holt and Company, 2011), 91.

78 George Bush with Victor Gold, *Looking Forward: An Autobiography* (Doubleday, 1987), 224–25.

79 Mollie Dickenson, *Thumbs Up: The Life and Courageous Comeback of White House Press Secretary Jim Brady* (William Morrow and Company, 1987), 102.

80 Public Papers of the President, Ronald Reagan, 1981, Office of the Federal Register, National Archives and Records Service, 358–359.

81 Robert Pear, "President Reagan Pardons 2 Ex-F.B.I. Officials in 1970's Break-Ins," *New York Times*, April 16, 1981, A1.

82 Chris Matthews, *Tip and the Gipper: When Politics Worked* (New York: Simon & Schuster, 2013), 124.

83 Ronald Reagan, *The Reagan Diaries* (New York: Harper Perennial, 2009), 35.

84 Peter Goldman with Eleanor Clift, Henry W. Hubbard, and John J. Lindsay, *Newsweek* magazine, May 1, 1981, 22–23.

85 William Greider, "The Education of David Stockman," *The Atlantic Monthly*, December, 1981, 43.

Chapter 15

86 Louis Harris, "Special to the Herald Examiner," *Los Angeles Herald Examiner*, June 8, 1981, A7.

87 "Rest In Peace, New Deal," *Newsweek* magazine, August 10, 1981, 16–17.

88 Sara Fritz memorandum to colleagues, July 29, 1981, Sara Fritz background session with David Gergen, Sara Fritz Papers, Ronald Reagan Presidential Library and Museum.

89 Ronald Reagan, *The Reagan Diaries, Volume I, January 1981-October 1985*, Douglas Brinkley, ed. (New York: HarperCollins, 2009), 60.

90 Sara Fritz, memorandum to colleagues, December 29, 1981, Sara Fritz background session with Rich Williamson, Sara Fritz Papers, Ronald Reagan Presidential Library and Museum.

91 Howell Raines, "Supply-Side Battle Rages on 2 Fronts," *New York Times*, December 21, 1981.

92 Interview and correspondence with Edward J. Rollins, March 22, 2022, in author's files.

93 Raines, "GOP to Focus Campaign on 'Give Him a Chance,'" *New York Times*, September 3, 1982, 1.

94 Robert A. Kittle, "White House Notes," August 9, 1982, background session with Larry Speakes, Sara Fritz Papers, Ronald Reagan Presidential Library and Museum.

95 Reagan, *Public Papers of the Presidents of the United States, Ronald Reagan, 1982, Book II* (Washington, D.C.: United States Government Printing Office, 1983), 1233–1236.

96 Jeremiah O'Leary, "Reagan Pins Fiscal Woes on Liberals, *Washington Times*, September 30, 1982.

97 Francis X. Clines, "President Scorns Democrats' Rule," *New York Times*, September 30, 1982.

98 Rich Jaroslovsky, "Reagan Campaign Effort Is Meandering, Becoming Too Partisan, Advisers Assert," *Wall Street Journal*, October 7, 1982, 6.

99 Correspondence with Edward J. Rollins, March 24, 2022, in author's files.

100 Rowland Evans and Robert Novak, "President Just Drifts—to Election Disaster?" *Evans and Novak*, October 10, 1982.

101 Richard Darman, *Who's in Control: Polar Politics and Sensible Center* (Simon & Schuster, 1996), 75.

102 Robert A. Kittle, "Reagan Economic Policy," August 11, 1982, background interview with Craig Fuller, Sara Fritz Papers, Ronald Reagan Presidential Library and Museum.

103 James A. Baker, III, with Steve Fiffer, *Work Hard, Study and Keep Out of Politics!* (Evanston, Illinois: Northwestern University Press, 2006), 187–188.

104 Interview with James A. Baker, III, Miller Center of Public Affairs, Ronald Reagan Oral History Project, Houston, Texas, June 15, 2004, file 2 of 5, final edited transcript 22–23.

105 Public Papers of the Presidents of the United States, Ronald Reagan, 1983, Book I," p14, United States Government Printing Office, Washington, 1984.

106 Ronald Reagan, from Transcript for "A Time for Choosing," delivered on national television on October 27, 1964.

Chapter 16

107 James A. Baker, III, with Steve Fiffer, *Work Hard, Study and Keep Out of Politics!* (Evanston, Illinois: Northwestern University Press, 2006), 38.

108 Richard Darman, *Who's in Control: Polar Politics and Sensible Center* (Simon & Schuster, 1996), 37.

109 Ibid., 29.

110 Ibid., 33.

111 Marjorie Williams, "The Long and the Short of Richard G. Darman," *Washington Post*, July 29, 1990.

112 Ibid.

113 Darman, 136.

114 Sara J. Fritz, August 19, 1981, deep background, not-for-quotation interview with Richard Darman, Sara Fritz Papers, Ronald Reagan Presidential Library and Museum, 1 and 4.

115 Ibid., 2–3.

116 Larry Speakes with Robert Pack, *Speaking Out: The Reagan Presidency from Inside the White House* (New York: Charles Scribner's Sons, 1988), 154.

117 Ibid.

118 Darman, 131.

119 Williams, "The Long and the Short."

120 David Gergen, *Eyewitness to Power: The Essence of Leadership, Nixon to Clinton* (Simon & Schuster, 2000) 168.

121 Memorandum, Dave Gergen to James A. Baker, February 9, 1981, [Correspondence and Memos, 1981] B (3), Box 10531, Gergen, David, Ronald Reagan Library.

122 Ibid.

123 Lou Cannon, "White House Reorganizes Its Communications Staff," *Washington Post*, June 18, 1981.

124 Robert A. Kittle, background interview with Larry Speakes, June 18, 1981, Sara Fritz Papers, Ronald Reagan Presidential Library and Museum, 3.

125 Speakes with Pack, 244.

126 Peter Baker and Susan Glasser, *The Man Who Ran Washington: The Life and Times of James A. Baker, III*, (New York: Doubleday, 2020), 137.

127 Kittle, "White House Odds and Ends," June 8, 1981, interview with David Gergen, Sara Fritz Papers, Ronald Reagan Presidential Library and Museum, 3.

128 Fritz, background interview with Richard Williamson, assistant to the president for intergovernmental affairs, August 26, 1981, Sara Fritz Papers, Ronald Reagan Presidential Library and Museum, 1–3.

129 Peter Baker and Susan Glasser, *The Man Who Ran Washington: The Life and Times of James A. Baker, III*, (New York: Doubleday, 2020), 160-161.

130 Sara J. Fritz, U.S. News and World Report, "Report from Santa Barbara, California," August 28, 1981, Sara Fritz Papers, Ronald Reagan Presidential Library and Museum.

131 Sara J. Fritz, U.S. News and World Report, "Interview with Craig Fuller, Cabinet Director at the White House," July 23, 1981, Sara Fritz Papers, Ronald Reagan Presidential Library and Museum.

132 Sara J. Fritz, background interview with White House chief of staff James A. Baker, September 1, 1981, Sara Fritz Papers, Ronald Reagan Presidential Library and Museum.

133 Sara J. Fritz and Robert A. Kittle, U.S. News and World Report, "Interviews with the Big Three about the Big Three," September 14, 1981, Sara Fritz Papers, Ronald Reagan Presidential Library and Museum.

134 Ibid.

Chapter 17

135 Sara J. Fritz, background session with James Baker, III, White House chief of staff, July 30, 1981, Sara Fritz Papers, Ronald Reagan Presidential Library and Museum, 3.

136 Ronald Reagan, *The Reagan Diaries, Volume I, January 1981-October 1985*, Douglas Brinkley, ed. (New York: HarperCollins, 2009), 314.

137 Ibid., 305.

138 Ibid., 306.

139 Ibid., 310.

140 Ibid., 312.

141 Ibid., 325–326.

142 Ibid., 282 and 310.

143 Memoranda for James A. Baker, III, through Edward J. Rollins, from Lee Atwater, in author's files.

144 Memorandum, Darman to McFarlane, May 15, 1984, Baker, James A. III, Files Box 7, "Dick Darman File," Ronald Reagan Presidential Library.

145 Ronald Reagan, *Public Papers of the Presidents of the United States, Ronald Reagan, 1984, Book I—January 1 to June 29, 1984*, (Washington, D.C.: United States Government Printing Office, 1986), 727.

146 Conversation with Edward Rollins, March 25, 2022, in author's files.

147 Memorandum from Richard B. Wirthlin, June 25, 1984, in author's files.

148 Reagan, *The Reagan Diaries*, 368.

149 Memorandum to James A. Baker, III, from Richard B. Wirthlin, June 11, 1984, "RE: Reagan-Bush '84—Campaign Decisions," copy in author's files.

150 Memorandum from Richard B. Wirthlin, August 3, 1984, in author's files.

151 Richard Cohen, "The Audience That Wouldn't Listen," *Washington Post*, August 26, 1984, C8.

152 David S. Broder, "A Partisan Reagan Gives No Ground," *Washington Post*, August 24, 1984, A-1.

153 Peter Goldman et al., *The Quest for the Presidency 1984* (Bantam Books, 1985), 246.

154 Martin Schram, "GOP Polls Reflect Minimal Boost from Made-for-TV Convention," *Washington Post*, August 26, 1984, A13.

155 Gary Holmes, *Fortunate One: From Nantucket to The White House: A Memoir*, (Academy Press, 2021), 293.

Chapter 18

156 Thomas M. DeFrank with Gerald C. Lubenow, "The Feature Film," *Newsweek* magazine, September 3, 1984, 38.

157 Edwin Diamond and Stephen Bates, "The Ads," *Public Opinion*, December/January, 1985, 57.

158 Sidney Blumenthal, "The Reagan Millenium," *New Republic*, November 19, 1984, 12–13.

159 Private letter and memorandum from President Richard Nixon to author, October 2, 1984.

160 Peter Baker and Susan Glasser, *The Man Who Ran Washington: The Life and Times of James A. Baker, III*, (New York: Doubleday, 2020), 241.

161 Beth Bogart, "Politicians Campaign for Pretested Ads," *Advertising Age*, February 13, 1986, 21.

162 Diamond and Bates, 64.

Chapter 19

163 Ronald Reagan, *Public Papers of the Presidents of the United States, Ronald Reagan, 1984, Book II* (Washington, D.C.: United States Government Printing Office, 1987), 1296–1297.

164 Peter Goldman et al., *The Quest for the Presidency 1984* (Bantam Books, 1985), 303.

165 Ira R. Allen, "Walter Mondale Warned the American Voters Today Not to Trust the New Reagan," UPI Archives, September 25, 1984.

166 The White House News Summary, Tuesday, October 2, 1984—6:00 a.m. edition, A-2

167 Ibid., B-4–B-5.

168 Reagan, *The Reagan Diaries, Volume I, January 1981-October 1985*, Douglas Brinkley, ed. (New York: HarperCollins, 2009), 387.

169 Ibid.

170 Stuart Spencer, oral history, Miller Center of Public Affairs, Presidential Oral History Program, Ronald Reagan Oral History Project, tape 5 of 13, Charlottesville, Virginia, November 16, 2001, final edited transcript, 54.

171 Reagan, *The Reagan Diaries*, 388.

172 James A. Baker, III, oral history, Miller Center of Public Affairs, Presidential Oral History Program, Ronald Reagan Oral History Project, file 1 of 5, Baker Institute, Houston, Texas, June 15, 2004, final edited transcript, 8.

173 Paul Laxalt, *Nevada's Paul Laxalt: A Memoir* (Jack Bacon & Company, 2000), 344.

174 Richard Darman, *Who's in Control: Polar Politics and Sensible Center* (Simon & Schuster, 1996), 134.

175 Darman, 135–136.

176 Rowland Evans and Robert Novak, "A President Unleashed, *Washington Post*, October 15, 1984.

177 Goldman et al., 323.

178 Reagan, *Public Papers*, 1596.

179 Peggy Noonan, *What I Saw at the Revolution: A Political Life in the Reagan Era*, (New York: Random House, 1990), 128.

180 Ibid., 121.

181 Goldman et al., 250.

182 Ibid..

183 Reagan, *Public Papers*, 1765.

Chapter 20

184 Nancy Reagan with William Novak, *My Turn—The Memoirs of Nancy Reagan* (Random House, 1989), 63.

185 Michael Deaver with Mickey Herskowitz, *Behind the Scenes* (William Morrow and Company, 1987),183–184.

186 Edvins Beitiks, "Embattled Author Braves Enemy Turf," *San Francisco Examiner*, October 17, 1999.

187 Lou Cannon, *President Reagan: The Role of a Lifetime* (New York: Simon & Schuster, 1991).

188 Ronald Reagan, *The Reagan Diaries, Volume I, January 1981-October 1985*, Douglas Brinkley, ed. (New York: HarperCollins, 2009), 444.

189 Ibid., 445.

190 Ronald Reagan, *Public Papers of the Presidents of the United States, Ronald Reagan, 1984, Book I—January 1 to June 29, 1984*, (Washington, D.C.: United States Government Printing Office, 1986), 457.

191 Ronald Reagan, *The Reagan Diaries*, 446–447.

192 Ronald Reagan, *Public Papers*, 462.

193 "The Wounds of War: Furor Over the Reagan Trip," *Newsweek* magazine, April 29, 1985, 14.

194 Ronald Reagan, *The Reagan Diaries*, 447.

195 Edmund Morris, *Dutch—A Memoir of Ronald Reagan* (Random House, 1999), 527.

196 Patrick J. Buchanan, *Nixon's White House Wars* (Crown Forum, 2017), 396.

197 Telephone interview with Patrick J. Buchanan, June 5, 2019.

198 Ibid. Former president Nixon moved to Saddle River, New Jersey, in 1981 and became known as the "Sage of Saddle River."

199 Richard Nixon memorandum in author's personal files.

200 Ronald Reagan, *The Reagan Diaries*, 450.

201 Ibid.

202 Ibid.

203 Aris Kalfaian, *Chomaklou—The History of an Armenian Village* (Chomaklou Compatriotic Society, 1982), 185.
204 Ibid., 188–190.
205 Ronald Reagan, *The Reagan Diaries*, 454.
206 "Paying Homage to History," William R. Doerner, reported by Laurence I. Barrett and William McWirter, *Time Magazine*, May 13, 1985, 16.
207 "Journey to Bitburg," *Newsweek* magazine, David M. Alpern with Eleanor Clift, Andrew Nagorski, Rich Thomas, Scott Sullivan, Thomas M. DeFrank and John Walcott, May 13, 1985, 26.
208 Lou Cannon, "Reagan Speaks to Allay Uproar," *Washington Post*, May 6, 1985, A-14.
209 Jack Nelson, "President Places Wreath at Bitburg," *Los Angeles Times*, May 6, 1985, 16.
210 Ronald Reagan, *The Reagan Diaries*, 458.

Chapter 21

211 Ronald Reagan, "Remarks at the Annual Convention of the National Association of Evangelicals in Orlando, Florida," March 8, 1983, https://www.reaganfoundation.org/media/50919/remarks_annual_convention_national_association_evangelicals_030883.pdf.
212 Ronald Reagan, "A Time for Choosing" speech, October 27, 1964, https://www.reaganlibrary.gov/reagans/ronald-reagan/time-choosing-speech-october-27-1964.
213 Reagan, "A Strategy for Peace in the '80s," televised address, October 29, 1980, https://www.presidency.ucsb.edu/documents/televised-address-governor-ronald-reagan-strategy-for-peace-the-80s.
214 Ronald Reagan, First Inaugural Address, January 20, 2981, https://www.presidency.ucsb.edu/documents/inaugural-address-11.
215 Letter to Brezhnev, author's personal files and Ronald Reagan, *An American Life* (Simon & Schuster, 1990), 273.
216 Ronald Reagan, *An American Life* (Simon & Schuster, 1990), 626.
217 Ronald Reagan, *The Reagan Diaries, Volume I, January 1981-October 1985*, Douglas Brinkley, ed. (New York: HarperCollins, 2009), 503.
218 Ibid, 507.
219 Presidential Address to the United Nations General Assembly, New York, NY, October 24, 1985, Speechwriter's Files (Elliott/White) 3 of 7, Ronald Reagan Library.
220 "What the President Left Out," *New York Times*, October, 25, 1985.
221 "On to the Summit," *Wall Street Journal*, October 25, 1985.
222 Robert Timberg, "Reagan Offers Plan to Defuse Global Tension," *Baltimore Sun*, October 25, 1985.
223 Ronald Reagan, *The Reagan Diaries*, 509.
224 Memorandum of Conversation, Thatcher-Reagan Meeting at Camp David, "Thatcher Visit—December 1984," December 22, 1984, (2 of 7), RAC Box 15, European and Soviet Affairs Directorate, NSC, Ronald Reagan Library.
225 Telephone interview with Bud McFarlane, February 9, 2019.
226 Nancy Reagan with William Novak, *My Turn—The Memoirs of Nancy Reagan* (Random House, 1989), 63–64.

227 Karen Tumulty, *The Triumph of Nancy Reagan* (New York: Simon & Schuster, 2021), 440.

228 Ibid.

229 Ibid., 445–446.

230 Donald T. Regan, *For the Record: From Wall Street to Washington* (Harcourt Brace Jovanovich, 1988), 3.

231 Nancy Reagan, *My Turn*, 47.

232 Ibid., 53.

233 Lou Cannon, *President Reagan, The Role of a Lifetime* (New York: Simon & Schuster, 1991), 585.

234 Ibid. 586.

235 Tumulty, *The Triumph of Nancy Reagan*, 350–351.

236 Joan Quigley, *What Does Joan Say?: My Seven Years as White House Astrologer to Nancy and Ronald Reagan* (Carol Publishing Group, 1990), 138–139.

237 Zero Option was the American proposal to withdraw all Soviet and US intermediate range nuclear missiles from Europe.

238 Richard Nixon, *Seize the Moment: America's Challenge in a One-Superpower World* (Simon & Schuster, 1992) 110–111.

Chapter 22

239 Donnie Radcliffe, "The Great Communicatrix," *Washington Post*, September 9, 1986, C2.

240 Editorial, "The Reagans Lead on Drugs," *Christian Science Monitor*, September 16, 1986.

241 Peter Bunzel, "The Ron and Nancy Show Comes to Town," *Los Angeles Herald Examiner*, September 21, 1986, F-1.

Chapter 23

242 Gallup, "Presidential Job Approval Center," President Ronald Reagan, https://news.gallup.com/interactives/185273/presidential-job-approval-center.aspx.

243 Robert S. Greenberger and Jane Mayer, "Shultz's Top Aide Blasts Reagan Staff on Iran Sales, Escalating Public Feud," *Wall Street Journal*, November 25, 1986, 3.

244 Donald T. Regan, *For the Record: From Wall Street to Washington* (Harcourt Brace Jovanovich, 1988), 70.

245 Peggy Noonan, *What I Saw at the Revolution—A Political Life in the Reagan Era*, (New York: Random House, 1990), 204.

246 Note, Dennis Thomas to Ken, January 13, 1987, Folder "1987 State of the Union Background Materials [and final version] (3)," Box 15, Thomas, Dennis Files (Office of the Chief of Staff).

247 Memorandum, "DT to DTR," January 18, 1987, Folder "1987 State of the Union [Draft] (Thomas) (8)," Box 16, Thomas, Dennis Files, (Office of the Chief of Staff).

248 "State of the Union Comparison," Folder "1987 State of the Union—Memorandum/Meetings (3)," Box 17, Thomas, Dennis Files (Office of the Chief of Staff).

249 Ronald Reagan, *The Reagan Diaries, Volume II: November 1985–January, 1989*, ed. Douglas Brinkley (HarperCollins, 2009), 680.

250 Memorandum in author's files.

251 Ronald Reagan, *The Reagan Diaries*, 680.

252 Regan, *For the Record*, 77.

253 Phil Gailey, "'Seminal' Message by Reagan Seen," *New York Times*, January 23, 1987.

254 Mayer and Doyle McManus, *Landslide: The Unmaking of the President 1984–1988* (Houghton Mifflin, 1988), 44–45.

255 Lou Cannon, "Reagan Turns to His Savior," *Washington Post*, January 26, 1987.

256 David Hoffman and Cannon, "Reagan's Iran Plan Focus Was Hostages, North Said— President Prepares for Pivotal Speech," *Washington Post*, January 25, 1987, 1.

257 Ibid.

258 Ibid.

259 "For Reagan, It Will Be a State of the Presidency Address," Stephen Wildstrom, ed., *Business Week*, January 26, 1987, 47.

260 David Hoffman, "A State of the Union Short on Substance," *Washington Post*, January 29, 1987.

261 David S. Broder, "Gloom Gathers at Signs of a Hapless Presidency," *Los Angeles Times*, January 30, 1987.

262 Mayer and McManus, *Landslide*, 42.

Chapter 24

263 Ronald Reagan, *The Reagan Diaries, Volume II: November 1985–January, 1989*, ed. Douglas Brinkley (HarperCollins, 2009), 821.

264 Ibid., 867.

265 Ibid., 899.

266 Michael Dukakis, "Address Accepting the Presidential Nomination at the Democratic National Convention in Atlanta, July 21, 1988. Excerpted from text provided by the American Presidency Project, UC Santa Barbara

267 David Broder, "GOP Pays Reagan Homage," *Washington Post*, August 16, 1988, A-1.

268 Ibid.

269 Thomas B. Rosenstiel, with John Balzar contributing, "Oversize Hall, Bad Acoustics: Production Trouble Plagues Convention," *Los Angeles Times*, August 17, 1988.

270 Ibid.

271 Ibid.

272 Michael Oreskes, "In Middle of the Action and Missing It," *New York Times*, August 17, 1988, A-13.

273 Ibid.

274 "Let Bush Be Bush," *Wall Street Journal*, August 17, 1988, 20.

275 "National Politics: Reagan Job Approval," ed. Kevin Phillips, *The American Political Report* XVII, no. 26 (American Political Research Corporation), September 2, 1988, 4.

276 Ronald Reagan, *Public Papers of the Presidents of the United States, Ronald Reagan, 1984, Book I—January 1 to June 29, 1984*, (Washington, D.C.: United States Government Printing Office, 1986), 439.

277 Peggy Noonan, *What I Saw at the Revolution—A Political Life in the Reagan Era*, (New York: Random House, 1990), 312–313.

278 Interview with Mari Maseng Will, April 6, 2023.
279 Paul A. Gigot, "Duberstein's Loyalty," *Wall Street Journal*, November 5, 2008.

Chapter 25

280 Richard Nixon, *In the Arena: A Memoir of Victory, Defeat and Renewal* (Simon and Schuster, 1990).
281 Ronald Reagan, *An American Life* (Simon & Schuster, 1990).

Index

Page numbers in *italics* indicate illustrations; n indicates a footnote

Acknowledgments

Conventional memoirs span life stories, but when I began writing, I decided it was more important to confine the narrative to my participation in America's political history. I initially intended to record only my unique view alongside Ronald Reagan in two presidential campaigns, and the eight extraordinary years I treasured in his years in office at the pinnacle of US government. While that adventure dominates my story, it could not have been written without the background of my political stewardship in the '60s and '70s in Richard Nixon's White House and, subsequently, as one of his handful of trusted aides and advisers in the last quarter of the twentieth century.

I did not have a ghostwriter, so bear full responsibility for the contents, including most of the core research—a great deal of it new and original to the history of those two presidents. But I had much help along the way in the form of advice, encouragement, assistance, oversight, critiques, and editing. No one who writes a book will admit to these words—but "hand holding" is not an overstatement when it comes to those who provide counsel over the weeks, months, and years of disruption that go into the final product.

I owe enormous gratitude to longtime friend and former White House colleague Dwight Chapin, who has been a relentless cheerleader throughout the entire editorial process. Pat Buchanan's valued friendship and counsel continues to this day and inside my journey, and he is responsible for my entire career for having taken faith in a Columbia Law student for Richard Nixon's 1968 campaign and subsequently taking me on as White House sidekick. I would have never made it onto the Reagan election staff in 1980 if Stuart Spencer hadn't rolled the dice on a "former Nixon speechwriter" and brought me aboard to fill out his traveling campaign operation. Stu offered memories and filled in critical blanks to enrich the political chapters in the book.

To color the flavor of our days in Reagan White House and the 1984 presidential campaign, I received additional insights from Ed Rollins, day-to-day operational manager for our landslide victory. My good friend Larry Kudlow enriched the background of Reagan's economic and tax revolution, and Hugh Hewitt provided valuable depth and insight to both the Nixon and Reagan presidencies. I'm grateful to White House colleagues Ben Stein, Richard Allen, Bud McFarlane, Peter Robinson, Sheila Dixon, and Mari Maseng Will—all generous with their time when I reached out for information, review of chapters, or critical insights. Pathways in politics and the White House include many who never fail to pick up the phone when I reached out, and I include among those K. T. McFarland, Geoff Shepard, Mary Matalin, Noel Koch, and Monica Crowley.

As I sought to refresh slivers of events that were part of the history of the Reagan presidency and campaigns, many were ready to chip in: Nancy [formerly Nance Roberts] Hise, Gary Holmes, Mona Charen, Tom Messner, Doug Watts, and Dennis Cuddy. Thanks go to Ryan Wah and Kevan Blanche for their periodic research assistance and Rebecca Tucker, Jim Bieber and Randy Salisbury and the Angent Group for important help as I shaped the book's outline. The diaries that form the core of my 1980 campaign chapter were laboriously typed from mini-cassette tapes by Gina Linder. The diaries wouldn't have existed if Buck Johns didn't insist that I record these critical episodes of history. Without Buck's role, I would not have had the contemporary background material that enriched the six chapters of the 1980 presidential campaign.

Many informed historians offered guidance as I probed heretofore untouched chronicles of that era. They include respected Reagan biographers Lou Cannon and Karen Tumulty and the former CEO of the Ronald Reagan Foundation John Heubusch. Three former law firm colleagues, Peter Ajemian, Mitch Langberg, and Ellen Schulhofer, have been very generous with their time. Peter is my wise legal counsel, while Ellen and Mitch looked at chapters and outlines to help move the project along.

A fine editor, Susan Shelley, reviewed several chapters and contributed excellent guidance and suggestions along the way. Susan's spirited view of the manuscript offered a push at important crossroads of production. A shout-out goes to the devoted archivists at the Reagan Library and especially to Jennifer Mandel who tirelessly guided me through the labyrinth of documents that complemented my own files. Jenny was a consequential resource throughout, along with Steve Branch, who never failed to take the time for a search in the audiovisual files when I needed documentation. Aimee Muller, Jenny's colleague, filled in when I had to look for presidential news summaries. Deep gratitude to all.

Words have no effect until they see the light of day, and for that I extend my thanks to Reagan biographer Craig Shirley and his assistant Kevin McVicker for their efforts in introducing my memoir to Alex Novak at Post Hill Press. Alex has been a partner and advocate in wanting to share with readers important new details of the history that was created by these presidential giants. His editorial team at Post Hill led by Caitlin Burdette has been persistent in meeting schedules. Hearty thanks to Kate Post, my copy editor and proofreader for the painstaking work of wading through tens of thousands of words in search of names and spellchecks, commas, semicolons and style and minutiae only an editor could love—and fix.

When the long slog of creativity seems to lag, family and personal friendships provide support and impetus. My brother Luther had a lifelong passion for politics and was tireless in pressing his encouragement throughout the long years of my research and writing. I wish to single out a trio of backers: Jim Byron—President and CEO—and his professional team at the Richard Nixon Foundation who have been generous with their support, as have my longtime friends at the Orange County Lincoln Club, and Bobby McDonald, the Executive Director of the Orange County Black Chamber of Commerce. Their combined decades-long embrace of the two legendary American leaders in this book's title is critical to promoting their place in history.

Norm Brownstein and my colleagues at Brownstein Hyatt Farber Schreck were generous with offering flexibility as I combined work with writing, and I am indebted to Todd Suntrapak for his loyalty and goodwill throughout. Joe Termini, my close friend and longtime pal, offered support or prods as needed, as did Rob Saroyan. Greg Kahwajian has been especially unflagging in his determination to help ensure the progress and the realization of the time I committed to my account. His time and relentless energy have been tonics when the moments dragged.

My personal assistant, Joni Johnson, has been an indispensable partner for nearly four decades. Her nonstop help in organizing files, producing records, typing manuscripts, proofreading, and managing my office was critical throughout. She has been remarkable in juggling the demands of my law practice and maintaining order in the chaos of documents in addition to the demands of my personal schedule.

And at home, Meredith has survived nearly five years of my immersion in a "second marriage" as I worked to fulfill the commitment to this book. She has been patient while I have poured so much energy and time outside of the home, while at the same time she has supported and encouraged me to tell a full and honest account of the years about which I write. Like other political "widows," she was an equal eyewitness to the turmoil as well as the triumph.

Finally, I cannot imagine any achievement in my life without the guidance that began at my roots. From my father, a survivor of the Armenian Genocide who gave a guiding principle for success: "Whatever you do, you must be resourceful." In another era, Mom would have been a US senator from California. She provided books, took us to concerts, made sure we went to see presidential candidates when they arrived in the San Joaquin Valley, and oversaw every activity from 4-H club to schoolwork. Their legacy hovered over every day on the campaign trail, every late night in the office, each message I managed to create. They share my achievements and have no responsibility for my failures.